Anonymous

Report of the Testimony and Proceedings taken before the Senate Committee on Constitutional Amendments, etc.

Anonymous

Report of the Testimony and Proceedings taken before the Senate Committee on Constitutional Amendments, etc.

ISBN/EAN: 9783337154356

Printed in Europe, USA, Canada, Australia, Japan

Cover: Foto ©ninafisch / pixelio.de

More available books at **www.hansebooks.com**

REPORT

OF THE

TESTIMONY AND PROCEEDINGS

TAKEN BEFORE THE

Senate Committee on Constitutional Amendments, relative to Senate Constitutional Amendment No. 8, abrogating provisions of Constitution as to Railroad Commission, and placing Distance Tariff in Constitution.

SENATE COMMITTEE ON CONSTITUTIONAL AMENDMENTS:

SENATORS EARL, CHAIRMAN; HART, CARPENTER, SEAWELL, BURKE.

FRED. J. MARTIN, Clerk.

LUKE KAVANAGH, Official Stenographer.

INDEX.

A.

B.

C.

Page

J.

K.

L.

M.

Page

N.

O.

Page

P.

R.

S.

T.

Senate Constitutional Amendment No. 8.

INTRODUCED BY MR. GESFORD, JANUARY 11, 1893.

REFERRED TO COMMITTEE ON CONSTITUTIONAL AMENDMENTS.

A RESOLUTION

Proposing to the people of the State of California an Amendment to the Constitution, repealing Sections 22 and 23 of Article XII of said Constitution, relating to the Railroad Commission, and adding to Article IV of said Constitution a new section, to be known and numbered as Section 36, relating to railroad freights and fares.

Resolved by the Senate, the Assembly concurring, That the Legislature of the State of California, at its thirtieth session, commencing on the second day of January, A. D. eighteen hundred and ninety-three, two thirds of all the members elected to each house of said Legislature voting in favor thereof, hereby proposes that sections twenty-two and twenty-three of article twelve of the Constitution of the State of California be repealed, and that said Constitution be amended by the addition thereto, and to article four thereof, of a new section, to be known and numbered as section thirty-six; said proposed new section to read as follows:

Section 36. It shall be the duty of the Legislature, at the first regular session thereof after the adoption of this amendment, to prescribe the rates of fares to passengers, and to provide a classification of property, and to fix and determine the rates of freight to be charged for the transportation on all railroads in the State of California; and until such legislation shall be enacted and go into effect, or whenever no such enactment shall be in operation, the charges of transportation by such railroads shall be: For the transportation of passengers, not more than two cents per mile; and the charges for freight and merchandise shall not be more than the charges specified in the distance tariff in this section hereinafter mentioned and set forth, the same being hereby designated as "The California Distance Tariff." The classification referred to in said California Distance Tariff is that adopted and issued by the Western Classification Committee (of which J. T. Ripley was Chairman), and which took effect January first, eighteen hundred and ninety-three. Said California Distance Tariff, including the rules forming a part thereof, and governing the same, is as follows, to wit:

CALIFORNIA DISTANCE TARIFF.

Applicable to local traffic between all stations in the State of California, subject to the Western Classification and the rules govering the same, which took effect January 1, 1893:

*

Distances.	Merchandise—Rate per 100 Pounds, in Cents.				Carloads of Not Less than Minimum Named in Classification, nor More than Marked Capacity of Car—Rate per 100 Pounds, in Cents.												Live Stock in Carloads—Rate per 100 Pounds, in Cents.		
	First Class	Second Class	Third Class	Fourth Class	Fifth Class	Class A	Class B	Class C	Class D	Class E	Lumber, Lath, and Shingles	Salt, Lime, Cement, and Stucco	Coal	Wheat, Flour, Flaxseed, Castor Beans, Broomcorn Seed, and Beans	Barley, Rye, Oats, Corn, Mill Stuffs, and Chops	Stone and Brick (common or pressed), Sand, Clay (common)	Horses and Mules	Cattle and Hogs (Single Deck Cars, as to Hogs)	Sheep (Single Deck Cars)
5 miles and under	3¾	3¾	3¾	3¾	3	3	3	3	3	3	3	3	2½	2½	2½	2½	3	3	5
10 miles and over 5 miles	4½	4	4	4	3½	4	3½	3	3	3	3	3	2½	2½	2½	2½	4	4	5
15 miles and over 10 miles	8	7	6	5	4	5	4	3½	3	3	3	3	3	3	2½	2½	4	4	6
20 miles and over 15 miles	12	10	9	7	5	6	5	4	3	3	3	4	3	3	2½	2½	5	5	6
25 miles and over 20 miles	15	12	11	8	6	7	6	5	4	3	4	5	3½	4	3	3	6	6	7
30 miles and over 25 miles	18	14	13	9	7	8	6½	5½	4½	3½	4	5½	3½	4	3	3	6	6	7
35 miles and over 30 miles	20	16	14	11	8	9	7	6	5	3½	4½	6	3½	5	4	3½	7	7	8
40 miles and over 35 miles	22	18	16	13	8	9	7	6	5	3½	4½	6	3½	5	4	3½	7	7	8
45 miles and over 40 miles	24	19	17	14	9	10	8	7	6	4	5	6	4	5	4	3½	8	8	9
50 miles and over 45 miles	25	20	18	15	10	11	8	7	6	4	5	7	4	6	5	4	8	8	9
55 miles and over 50 miles	27	22	19	16	11	12	9	8	6	4	5	7	4	6	5	4	9	9	10
60 miles and over 55 miles	28	23	20	17	12	13	9	8	6	5	6	7	4	6	5	4	9	9	10
65 miles and over 60 miles	30	24	21	18	13	14	10	8	7	5	6	8	5	7	6	5	10	9	11
70 miles and over 65 miles	32	25	22	18	13	14	10	9	7	5	6	8	5	7	6	5	10	10	11
75 miles and over 70 miles	33	26	23	19	14	15	11	9	7	5½	7	8½	5	7½	6½	5½	11	10	12
80 miles and over 75 miles	35	28	24	19	14	15	11	9	7	5½	7	8½	5	7½	6½	5½	11	10	12
85 miles and over 80 miles	37	29	25	20	15	16	12	10	8	6	7	9	5	7½	6½	5½	12	11	13
90 miles and over 85 miles	38	30	26	21	16	18	13	10	8	6	8	9	6	8	7	6	12	11	13
95 miles and over 90 miles	39	31	27	21	16	18	13	11	8	6	8	9	6	8	7	6	13	11	14
100 miles and over 95 miles	40	32	28	22	17	19	14	11	8	7	9	10	6	9	8	6½	14	12	15
105 miles and over 100 miles	41	33	29	23	18	20	14	11	9	7	9	10	6	9	8	6½	14	12	15
110 miles and over 105 miles	42	34	30	24	19	21	15	12	9	7	10	11	6	9	8	6½	14	12	15
115 miles and over 110 miles	43	35	31	25	20	22	16	12	9	7	10	11	7	10	8	7	15	13	16
120 miles and over 115 miles	44	36	32	26	21	23	16	13	10	8	10	11	7	10	8	7	15	13	16
125 miles and over 120 miles	45	36	32	26	21	23	17	13	10	8	11	12	7	10	9	7	16	14	17
130 miles and over 125 miles	46	37	33	27	22	24	17	13	10	8	11	12	7	10	9	7	16	14	17
135 miles and over 130 miles	47	38	33	27	22	24	18	14	10	8	11	12	7	10	9	7	16	14	17

140 miles and over 135 miles	48	39	34	28	23	25	18	14	11	8	11	12	8	10	9	7½	16	14	18
145 miles and over 140 miles	49	39	34	28	23	25	19	14	11	9	12	13	8	10	9	7½	17	15	18
150 miles and over 145 miles	50	40	35	29	24	26	19	15	11	9	12	13	8	10	9	7½	17	15	19
155 miles and over 150 miles	51	40	35	29	24	26	19	15	11	9	12	13	8	11	10	7½	17	15	19
160 miles and over 155 miles	52	41	36	30	25	27	20	15	11	9	12	13	8	11	10	7½	18	16	20
165 miles and over 160 miles	53	42	37	30	25	27	20	16	11	9	12	13	8	11	10	7½	18	16	20
170 miles and over 165 miles	54	43	38	31	26	28	21	16	12	10	13	14	8½	11	10	8	18	16	20
175 miles and over 170 miles	55	44	39	32	27	29	22	17	12	10	13	14	8½	11	10	8	19	17	21
180 miles and over 175 miles	56	44	39	32	27	29	22	17	12	10	13	14	8½	11	10	8	19	17	21
185 miles and over 180 miles	57	45	40	33	28	30	22	17	12	10	13	14	8½	12	11	8	19	17	21
190 miles and over 185 miles	58	46	40	33	28	30	23	18	12	10	13	14	8½	12	11	8	19	17	21
195 miles and over 190 miles	59	47	41	34	29	31	23	18	13	11	14	15	9	12	11	9	20	18	22
200 miles and over 195 miles	60	48	42	35	30	32	24	19	13	11	14	15	9	12	11	9	20	18	22
210 miles and over 200 miles	62	50	43	36	31	33	25	20	14	12	15	16	9½	12½	11½	9½	21	19	23
220 miles and over 210 miles	64	51	44	37	32	34	26	21	14	12	15	16	9½	12½	11½	9½	21	19	23
230 miles and over 220 miles	65	52	45	38	33	35	27	21	15	12	16	16	10	13	11½	9½	21	19	23
240 miles and over 230 miles	66	53	46	39	34	36	28	22	15	13	16	17	10	13	12	10	22	20	24
250 miles and over 240 miles	68	54	47	40	35	37	29	23	16	13	17	17	10½	13½	12	10	22	20	24
260 miles and over 250 miles	69	55	48	41	36	38	30	24	16	13	17	17	10½	13½	12	10	22	20	25
270 miles and over 260 miles	70	56	49	42	37	39	31	24	16	14	17	18	11	14	12½	10	23	21	25
280 miles and over 270 miles	72	58	50	43	38	40	31	25	17	14	18	18	11	14	12½	10½	23	21	25
290 miles and over 280 miles	73	59	51	44	39	41	32	25	17	14	18	18	11½	14½	12½	11	23	21	26
300 miles and over 290 miles	75	60	52	45	40	43	33	26	18	15	19	19	12	15	13	11	24	22	26
310 miles and over 300 miles	76	61	53	46	41	44	33	26	18	15	19	19	12	15	13	11	24	22	26
320 miles and over 310 miles	78	62	54	47	42	45	34	27	18½	15½	20	19½	12½	15	13	11	25	22	27
330 miles and over 320 miles	80	64	55	48	43	46	34	27	19	16	21	20	13	15½	13½	11½	25	22	27
340 miles and over 330 miles	81	65	56	49	44	47	35	28	19	16	21	20	13	15½	13½	11½	26	23	27
350 miles and over 340 miles	83	66	57	50	45	48	36	28	19½	16½	21	21	13½	16	14	12	27	23	28
360 miles and over 350 miles	84	67	58	51	46	49	36	29	19½	16½	21	21	13½	16	14	12	27	23	28
370 miles and over 360 miles	85	68	59	52	47	50	37	29	20	17	22	21½	14	16	14	12	27	23	28
380 miles and over 370 miles	87	70	60	53	48	51	38	30	20½	17½	22	22	14½	16½	14½	12½	28	24	29
390 miles and over 380 miles	89	71	60	53	48	51	38	30	21	18	23	22	15	16½	14½	12½	28	24	29
400 miles and over 390 miles	90	72	61	54	49	52	39	31	21	18	23	23	15	17	15	13	29	24	30
410 miles and over 400 miles	91	73	61	54	49	52	39	31	21	18	23	23	15	17	15	13	29	24	30
420 miles and over 410 miles	92	74	62	55	50	53	40	31	21½	18½	23½	23	15½	17½	15½	13	30	25	31
430 miles and over 420 miles	94	75	63	56	51	54	41	32	22	19	24	24	15½	18	16	13½	31	25	32
440 miles and over 430 miles	95	76	64	57	52	55	41	32	22	19	24	24	15½	18	16	13½	31	25	32
450 miles and over 440 miles	97	77	65	58	53	56	42	33	22½	19½	24½	25	16	18½	16½	14	32	26	33
460 miles and over 450 miles	98	78	66	59	54	57	42	33	22½	19½	24½	25	16	18½	16½	14	32	26	33
470 miles and over 460 miles	100	79	67	59	54	57	43	34	23	20	25	26	16	19	17	14	33	27	34
480 miles and over 470 miles	101	80	68	60	55	58	43	34	23	20	25	26	16½	19	17	14½	33	27	34
490 miles and over 480 miles	102	81	68	60	55	58	43	34	23½	20½	25½	26½	16½	19½	17½	14½	33	27	34
500 miles and over 490 miles	103	82	69	61	56	59	44	35	24	21	26	27	17	20	18	15	34	28	35
510 miles and over 500 miles	104	83	70	62	57	60	44	35	24	21	26	27	17	20	18	15	34	28	35
520 miles and over 510 miles	106	84	71	63	58	61	45	36	24½	21½	26½	27½	17½	20½	18½	15½	34	28	36

Distances.	Merchandise—Rate per 100 Pounds, in Cents.				Carloads of Not Less than Minimum Named in Classification, nor More than Marked Capacity of Car. Rate per 100 Pounds, in Cents.												Live Stock in Carloads. Rate per 100 Pounds, in Cents.		
	First Class	Second Class	Third Class	Fourth Class	Fifth Class	Class A	Class B	Class C	Class D	Class E	Lumber, Lath, and Shingles	Salt, Lime, Cement, and Stucco	Coal	Wheat, Flour, Flaxseed, Castor Beans, Broom-corn Seed, and Beans	Barley, Rye, Oats, Corn, Mill Stuffs, and Chops	Stone and Brick (common or pressed), Sand, Clay (common)	Horses and Mules	Cattle and Hogs (Single Deck Cars, as to Hogs)	Sheep (Single Deck Cars)
530 miles and over 520 miles	107	85	71	63	58	61	45	36	25	22	27	28	17½	20½	18½	15½	35	29	37
540 miles and over 530 miles	108	86	72	64	59	62	46	37	25	22	27	28	18	21	19	16	35	29	37
550 miles and over 540 miles	109	87	73	65	60	63	47	37½	25½	22½	27½	29	18	21½	19½	16	36	30	38
560 miles and over 550 miles	110	88	73	65	60	63	47	38	25½	22½	27½	29	18	21½	19½	16	36	30	38
570 miles and over 560 miles	112	89	74	66	61	64	48	38½	26	23	28	29½	18½	22	20	16½	36	30	39
580 miles and over 570 miles	113	90	75	67	62	65	49	39	26	23	28	30	18½	22	20	16½	37	30	39
590 miles and over 580 miles	114	91	76	68	63	66	49	39½	26½	23½	28½	30½	18½	22½	20½	16½	37	31	39
600 miles and over 590 miles	115	92	77	69	64	67	50	40	27	24	29	31	19	23	21	17	38	31	40
610 miles and over 600 miles	116	93	78	70	65	68	50	40	27	24	29	31	19	23	21	17	38	31	40
620 miles and over 610 miles	117	94	79	71	66	69	51	40½	27	24	29½	31	19½	23½	21½	17	38	32	41
630 miles and over 620 miles	119	95	80	72	67	70	52	41	27½	24½	29½	31½	20	24	22	17½	39	32	42
640 miles and over 630 miles	120	96	80	72	67	70	52	41½	27½	24½	30	31½	20	24	22	17½	39	32	42
650 miles and over 640 miles	121	97	81	73	68	71	53	42	28	25	30½	32	20½	24½	22½	18	40	33	43
660 miles and over 650 miles	122	98	81	73	68	71	53	42	28	25	30½	32	20½	24½	22½	18	40	33	43
670 miles and over 660 miles	123	99	82	74	69	72	54	42½	28	25	31	32	21	25	23	18	40	33	43
680 miles and over 670 miles	124	100	83	75	70	73	55	43	28½	25½	31	32½	21	25	23	18½	40	33	44
690 miles and over 680 miles	125	100	83	75	70	73	55	43½	28½	25½	31	32½	21	25½	23½	18½	41	34	44
700 miles and over 690 miles	126	101	84	76	71	74	56	44	29	26	31½	33	21½	26	24	19	41	34	45
710 miles and over 700 miles	127	101	84	76	71	74	56	44	29	26	31½	33	21½	26	24	19	41	34	45
720 miles and over 710 miles	128	102	85	77	72	75	56	44½	29½	26	32	33½	22	26½	24½	19	42	35	46
730 miles and over 720 miles	129	103	85	77	72	75	57	45	29½	26½	32	34	22	27	25	19½	42	35	47
740 miles and over 730 miles	130	104	86	78	73	76	57	45½	30	26½	32½	34	22½	27	25	19½	42	35	47
750 miles and over 740 miles	131	105	87	79	74	77	58	46	30	27	33	34½	23	27½	25½	20	43	36	48
760 miles and over 750 miles	132	106	87	79	74	77	58	46	30	27	33	34½	23	27½	25½	20	43	36	48
770 miles and over 760 miles	132	106	88	80	75	78	58	46½	30½	27	33	35	23	28	26	20	43	36	49
780 miles and over 770 miles	133	107	88	80	75	78	59	47	30½	27½	33½	35	23½	28	26	20½	43	36	49
790 miles and over 780 miles	134	108	89	81	76	79	59	47½	31	27½	33½	35½	23½	28½	26½	20½	44	37	49

800 miles and over 790 miles	135	108	90	81	76	80	60	48	31	28	34	36	24	29	27	21	44	37	50
810 miles and over 800 miles	135	109	90	82	77	81	60	48	31	28	34	36	24	29	27	21	44	37	50
820 miles and over 810 miles	136	110	91	82	77	81	61	48½	31½	28	34	36	24	29½	27½	21	45	38	51
830 miles and over 820 miles	137	110	92	83	78	82	61	49	31½	28½	34½	36½	24½	30	28	21½	45	38	51
840 miles and over 830 miles	138	111	92	83	78	82	61	49½	31½	28½	34½	36½	24½	30	28	21½	45	38	52
850 miles and over 840 miles	139	111	93	84	79	83	62	50	32	29	35	37	25	30½	28½	22	46	39	53
860 miles and over 850 miles	139	112	93	84	79	83	62	50	32	29	35	37	25	30½	28½	22	46	39	53
870 miles and over 860 miles	140	112	94	85	80	84	62	50½	32	29	35	37	25	31	29	22	46	39	53
880 miles and over 870 miles	141	113	95	85	80	84	63	50½	32½	29½	35½	37½	25½	31	29	22½	46	39	54
890 miles and over 880 miles	142	114	95	86	81	85	63	51	32½	29½	35½	37½	25½	31½	29½	22½	47	40	54
900 miles and over 890 miles	143	114	96	86	81	85	64	51	33	30	36	38	26	32	30	23	47	40	55
910 miles and over 900 miles	144	115	97	87	82	86	64	51	33	30	36	38	26	32	30	23	47	40	55
920 miles and over 910 miles	145	115	98	87	82	86	64	51½	33	30	36	38	26	32½	30½	23	48	41	56
930 miles and over 920 miles	145	116	99	87	82	86	64	51½	33½	30½	36½	38½	26½	33	31	23½	48	41	57
940 miles and over 930 miles	146	116	100	88	83	87	65	52	33½	30½	36½	38½	26½	33	31	23½	48	41	57
950 miles and over 940 miles	147	117	101	88	83	87	65	52	34	31	37	39	27	33½	31½	24	49	41	58
960 miles and over 950 miles	148	117	102	89	84	88	65	52	34	31	37	39	27	33½	31½	24	49	42	58
970 miles and over 960 miles	148	118	103	89	84	88	65	52½	34½	31½	37½	39½	27½	34	32	24	49	42	59
980 miles and over 970 miles	149	119	104	89	84	88	66	52½	34½	31½	37½	39½	27½	34	32	24½	50	42	59
990 miles and over 980 miles	150	120	105	90	85	89	66	53	35	32	38	40	28	34½	32½	25	50	42	60
1,000 miles and over 990 miles	150	120	105	90	85	89	66	53	35	32	38	40	28	35	33	25	60	42	60

1. This tariff shall apply to individual railroads, in this State, and they shall be considered independently in computing distances, except that a system of railroads consisting of leased, operated, or independent roads, operated under a common management, although working under different charters, shall be considered as one road, and the distance shall be computed over the shortest operated line composed of two or more of such roads.

2. When the rates herein named and the Western Classification heretofore referred to conflict, the rates named in this tariff shall govern.

3. Minimum Charges.—Single shipments of one or more classes will be charged for at the actual weight at tariff rates, subject to a minimum charge of twenty-five cents for the entire consignment for distances of five hundred miles or less, and fifty cents for greater distances.

RULES GOVERNING SHIPMENTS OF LIVE STOCK IN CARLOADS.

Minimum Weights.—Horses and mules, cattle, hogs, and sheep shall be way-billed at the minimum weights named below, subject to correction at destination to actual weight, but in no case less than the following minimums:

	Horses and Mules.	Cattle and Hogs (S. D.)	Sheep (S. D.)
Cars 27 feet 6 inches long, inside measurement	17,700	16,800	10,000
Cars 28 feet long, inside measurement	18,000	17,100	10,200
Cars 28 feet 6 inches long, inside measurement	18,400	17,500	10,400
Cars 29 feet long, inside measurement	18,800	17,900	10,600
Cars 29 feet 6 inches long, inside measurement	19,000	18,000	10,800
Cars 30 feet long, inside measurement	19,400	18,400	11,000
Cars 30 feet 6 inches long, inside measurement	19,700	18,700	11,200
Cars 31 feet long, inside measurement	20,000	19,000	11,400
Cars 31 feet 6 inches long, inside measurement	20,300	19,300	11,500
Cars 32 feet long, inside measurement	20,600	19,600	11,700
Cars 32 feet 6 inches long, inside measurement	20,900	19,900	11,800
Cars 33 feet long, inside measurement	21,200	20,100	12,000
Cars 33 feet 6 inches long, inside measurement	21,600	20,500	12,200
Cars 34 feet long, inside measurement	21,800	20,700	12,300
Cars 34 feet 6 inches long, inside measurement	22,200	21,100	12,400
Cars 35 feet long, inside measurement	22,600	21,500	12,600
Cars 35 feet 6 inches long, inside measurement	22,900	21,800	12,800
Cars 36 feet long, inside measurement	23,200	22,000	13,000

Committee Substitute for Senate Constitutional Amendment No. 8.

INTRODUCED BY MR. GESFORD, JANUARY 11, 1893.

REFERRED TO COMMITTEE ON CONSTITUTIONAL AMENDMENTS.

A RESOLUTION

Proposing an Amendment to the Constitution of the State of California, repealing Sections 22 and 23 of Article XII of said Constitution, relating to the Railroad Commission, its powers and duties, and adding a new section to Article IV of said Constitution, to be numbered Section 36, relating to railroad freights and fares.

Resolved by the Senate, the Assembly concurring, That the Legislature of the State of California, at its thirtieth session, commencing on the second day of January, A. D. eighteen hundred and ninety-three, two thirds of all the members elected to each house of said Legislature voting in favor thereof, hereby proposes that sections twenty-two and twenty-three of article twelve of the Constitution of the State of California be repealed, and that article four of said Constitution be amended by adding to said article a new section, to be numbered section thirty-six.

SECTION 1. Section twenty-two of article twelve of the Constitution of the State of California is hereby repealed.

SEC. 2. Section twenty-three of article twelve of the Constitution of the State of California is hereby repealed.

SEC. 3. Article four of the Constitution of the State of California is hereby amended by adding to said article a new section, to be numbered section thirty-six, said new section to read as follows:

Section 36. The Legislature shall have the power, and it shall be its duty, to establish rates of charges for the transportation of passengers and freight by all railroads operated in this State, and to enact such laws as may be necessary for the enforcement and carrying into effect of such rates; *provided, however,* that the Legislature shall have no power to prescribe rates of charges for the transportation of passengers on any railroad or system of railroads whose gross annual earnings are more than four thousand dollars a mile, to exceed three cents per mile; *and provided further*, that the Legislature shall have no power to prescribe the rates of charges for the transportation of freight on any railroad or system of railroads whose gross annual earnings are more than four thousand dollars a mile, to exceed the rates specified by the "California Distance Tariff," as in this section hereinafter set forth. Until the Legislature shall prescribe such rates as aforesaid, or in the event that any such prescribed rates shall from any cause become inoperative, the rates of charges for the transportation of passengers on all railroads in this State whose gross annual earnings are more than four thousand dollars a mile, shall be three cents per mile; and the charges for the transportation of freight by any such railroad, shall be the rates specified in the following distance tariff, hereby designated as the "California Distance Tariff," to wit:

CALIFORNIA DISTANCE TARIFF.

This distance tariff shall be applicable to local traffic between all stations in the State of California now established or that may hereafter be established. The classifications of property provided for in this distance tariff are based upon the "Western Classification," and the rules governing the same adopted and issued by the Western Classification Committee, of which J. T. Ripley was Chairman, and which took effect January first, eighteen hundred and ninety-three, to which said classification reference is hereby made; *provided, however*, that no rule or rules governing said Western Classification providing for any change, modifications, or additions to the classifications mentioned in this distance tariff, shall have any application hereto.

[Here follows table, same as in original Amendment No. 8.]

RULES GOVERNING SHIPMENT OF LIVE STOCK BY THE CARLOAD.

MINIMUM WEIGHTS.—Horses and mules, cattle, hogs, and sheep shall be way-billed at the following minimum weights per car, subject to correction to actual weight at destination, but in no case less than the following minimum weights:

[Here follows table, same as in original Amendment No. 8.]

ADDITIONAL RULES.

1. Railroads shall be considered independently in computing distances; *except, however*, that a system of railroads consisting of leased, operated, or independent roads controlled under a common management, although working under different charters, shall be considered and treated as one road, and the distances shall be computed over the shortest operated line composed of two or more of said roads.

2. When any rate herein named conflicts with the Western Classification aforesaid, this tariff shall govern as to such rate.

3. MINIMUM CHARGES.—Single shipments of one or more classes will be charged for at actual weight at tariff rates, subject to a minimum charge of twenty-five cents for the entire consignment, or shipment, for a distance of five hundred miles or less, and fifty cents for all distances over five hundred miles.

PROCEEDINGS.

SACRAMENTO, January 23, 1893.

Proceedings before the Senate Committee on Constitutional Amendments (Senators Earl, Chairman; Carpenter, Hart, Seawell, and Burke), on Constitutional Amendment No. 8, and Senator Gesford's substitute therefor, providing for an amendment to the Constitution, fixing the rates of fares and freights to be charged by railroads of the State of California.

SENATOR GESFORD: Mr. Chairman, and Gentlemen of the Committee: Constitutional Amendment No. 8, which has been printed and which is before you, I will state to the committee, was introduced by myself in the Senate. Since its introduction a substitute has been prepared to that proposed amendment, which I would like to present to the committee and ask the committee to propose it as a substitute for Amendment No. 8—the committee substitute I have here.

CHAIRMAN EARL: Does it vary very materially from the one printed and under consideration? A. Yes, sir. It varies in two or three very material aspects from the one printed and before you.

EARL: If there is no objection on the part of the members of the committee, we will consider the two together to save time, if you will state the material variations in the one you suggest as a substitute.

GESFORD: There is no variation with reference to the repeal of the provisions of the Constitution relating to the Railroad Commission in this printed bill and the committee substitute that I now propose. Sections 1 and 2 of the original bill provide for the repeal of the Railroad Commission, or words to that effect. Section 3 of the proposed substitute provides for the addition of Section 36 to Article IV of the Constitution, reading as follows:

"Section 36. The Legislature shall have the power, and it shall be its duty, to establish rates of charges for the transportation of passengers and freight by all railroads operated in this State, and to enact such laws as may be necessary for the enforcement and carrying into effect of such rates; *provided, however*, that the Legislature shall have no power to prescribe rates of charges for the transportation of passengers to exceed 3 cents per mile; *and provided further*, that the Legislature shall have no power to prescribe rates of charges for the transportation of freight to exceed the rates specified by the 'California Distance Tariff,' as in this section hereinafter set forth. Until the Legislature shall prescribe such rates as aforesaid, or in the event that any such prescribed rates shall from any cause become inoperative, the rates of charges for the transportation of passengers on all railroads in this State shall be not to exceed 2 cents per mile, and the rates of charges for the transportation of freight by any such railroads shall be not to exceed the rates specified in the following distance tariff, hereby designated as the 'California Distance Tariff.'"

The California Distance Tariff, as embodied in this proposed committee substitute, is the same as the one in the original proposed amendment. I will state to the committee that Mr. Godchaux, in the Assembly, has introduced a bill which is a counterpart of this one, and now proposed as a committee substitute. I think that bill is printed, and probably we had better get some copies of that, if your clerk will do it. [The clerk was here directed to procure some copies of Assembly Constitutional Amendment No. 14, but was unable to obtain them.]

GESFORD: The California Distance Tariffs, as embodied in both of these amendments—the original and the one I now propose as a substitute—are identical, excepting the phraseology at the head of each table has been changed somewhat, making it a little plainer. That is all. There is no material change in the schedule at all. Then, in addition to that, in this proposed committee substitute there is embodied an article providing for the submission of the amendment to the people for ratification, provided that it shall be submitted on the 18th day of April, 1893.

EARL: That is in addition to what is embodied in the original amendment? A. Yes, sir. But the only question that arises in reference to it is whether or not it can be placed in the same amendment as the provision for submission to the people—whether that should not be done by a separate Act. I think we had better leave that matter until after discussion of the other provisions of the amendment.

EARL: We will be pleased to hear now, on the point of facts upon which this proposed amendment is based. I understand it is based on substantially the same grounds as the other.

GESFORD: Mr. Leeds is here, and I think he also represents the Traffic Association.

EARL: Mr. Leeds, we will be pleased to hear from you.

MR. LEEDS: The first proviso of the bill in reference is for the amendment of the Constitution by the abrogation of Sections 22 and 23 of Article XII, removing the present Board of Railroad Commissioners, and abolishing that portion of the Constitution which provides for them. I do not know as it is necessary to discuss that proposition, as I believe the State is generally conceded to be in favor of that portion of the proposition. With reference to the figures of the tariff, I will say that they are made upon the usual basis, as far as rating by distances is concerned, as in effect in other parts of the country where a distance tariff is in use. I have before me Wisconsin, Nebraska, and Kansas, all of which are made up by graduations of five miles for the shorter distances and upwards. I have examined pretty carefully the situation in California, and this tariff here is based upon what, in my judgment, would yield a reasonable revenue to the principal roads of California. The shorter distances in this tariff are based according to the present figures charged by the roads in the State, recognizing no distance, however, less than five miles; carrying the rate then, at 15 cents per ton per mile, for twenty miles; after that, basing it as nearly as practicable on what are the earnings to-day upon roads in Kansas. It differs somewhat from the distance tariff of roads in that State, from the fact that, after three hundred miles is reached there, the advance, after three hundred, four hundred, or five hundred miles, is greater than it is for a shorter distance, but the tariff would give, in my judgment, on all the tonnage, about what a like tonnage would yield under the tariff at present in effect in that State. As near as I can estimate, the reduction from the Southern Pacific tariff in the State of California will amount to from 25 to 30 per cent. Considering the earnings of that company—from what I can determine they are from their own figures—within the State of California, it seems to me that would not be an unreasonable proposition.

Q. Have you examined the earnings of the San Francisco and North Pacific Railway? A. I have not examined the earnings of any road in California but the Southern Pacific Company; in fact, I have not the data from which to obtain the information.

Q. The data you base this on, then, is derived from the Southern Pacific Company alone. It is what you estimate the cost of transportation, cost of the road, etc.? A. So far as the data is concerned, it is what I obtained in reference to the Southern Pacific Company's business.

Q. Mr. Leeds, now, you said this would yield, you thought, a fair revenue to the roads affected by the figures, or all the roads in the State. How do you arrive at your calculations? What percentages have you taken and what percentage would it yield to the Southern Pacific road? What earning to the Southern Pacific? A. I say that I believe it will reduce their earnings on local traffic 25 to 30 per cent. Their local traffic, according to their own figures, amounts to something like 80 per cent. Taking 80 per cent as a basis, and take 30 per cent of that, the reduction would be 24 per cent of the gross earnings.

Q. Have you attempted to ascertain what the net revenue would be to the roads affected, the Southern Pacific Company for instance? Have you taken what would be netted to them by the proposed California Distance Tariff under the operation of this amendment, taking the present tonnage and traffic into consideration? A. I do not know as I get the drift of your question.

Q. What I say is this: Say the existing rates of the Southern Pacific are reduced 25 to 30 per cent, approximately. Well, now, what profit is left them in the operating of their road; have you ascertained that point? A. According to their own figures, their operating expenses for the Pacific System is 59 per cent of their gross earnings.

Q. What is meant by the Pacific System lines? A. The Pacific System of that road comprises the lines, I believe, this side of El Paso, Texas, and thence to Ogden, Utah, and Portland, Oregon.

Q. That percentage does not include all expenses; that does not include bonded indebtedness—interest and bonded indebtedness?. A. No, sir.

Q. Do you know what the interest account is annually—the interest charge? A. On the Pacific System? Yes, sir; I have the memoranda here, somewhere, if you will wait a minute.

Q. I would like to have you elaborate on that matter as much as you can. A. The interest on their bonded indebtedness, as reported for the Pacific System, is $8,675,587 42. I will say for your information that the figures which I have with reference to the Southern Pacific Company are one year old. This indebtedness represents a capital, at 6 per cent interest, of $144,593,124.

Q. What do you mean by capitalization? A. The mortgaged indebtedness. This is on the mileage of the Pacific System, some four thousand odd miles. I will give you the mileage in a minute. It is four thousand seven hundred and eleven miles.

Q. Have you figures there to show the gross earnings? A. The gross earnings of the Pacific System were $37,010,078 16. I separated from that as far as I could the mileage outside of California, being obliged to consider entire the mileage of the Central Pacific system, making a mileage of three thousand four hundred and ninety-eight miles in the State of California, and, including the Central Pacific outside of California. I find the earnings on that would have been $31,555,716 05, or $9,021 07 per mile per annum; while, for the portion of the system outside of the State, the amount was $4,496 50.

Q. Aggregating about $6,000,000 of the total of $37,000,000? A. $5,454,362 11. The gross earnings per mile on the entire Pacific System were $8,002 and some cents.

Q. In your computations, did you consider the interest on the cost of operating the road, in addition to the cost of the road? A. Other roads pay their interest and fixed charges with a less net earning. I have some comparisons, if you please, with one or two other lines. I happen to have the reports, and find that the earnings of the Missouri Pacific system for the same period were $4,965 81 per mile—a little over one half—and that they consumed 70.96 per cent, or nearly 71 per cent, of their gross earnings in the operation of the road. I also find that the Atchison, Topeka and Santa Fe consume 69.19 per cent of their operating expenses, and their gross earnings per mile are $5,142 57. I also find that, in connection with the operation of their road, they run 26.12 miles to the ton of coal, while, on the Southern Pacific, in California, or the Southern Pacific System lines, run 29¾ miles to the ton. I also find that the Southern Pacific consume, per mile run for locomotives, 56 pounds of coal, while the Atchison consume 108; that this 56 pounds of coal carried 6 tons per train more than the 108 tons of the other road.

Q. What is the cost of this coal? A. It is set down here for the Southern Pacific at $5 79 per ton, and for the Atchison at $2 11. I think there is a difference in the matter of transportation helping to make this, but I am not sure about that. I think there is. I also find that the percentage of empty to loaded cars carried by the Southern Pacific Company was 24.79 per cent and the Atchison 28.32 per cent. Taking the price of coal on other roads, I find that the Southern Pacific Company's coal costs them 8.9 per cent of their operating expenses; the Atchison, 7.8 per cent, or 1.1 per cent difference. I find that the average haul on through freight is 906 miles, and the rate received $10 79 a ton; on local business 101 miles, and the rate per ton $2 74; the aggregate haul, 206 miles, and the aggregate receipts $3 78. The rate per ton per mile on through was 1.119 cents; on local, 2.699 cents—practically 2.7 cents; on all freight, 1.835 cents; that the local rate was 226.6 per cent of the through.

Q. I do not understand your statement. A. Two and one fourth times as much per ton per mile as the through traffic over the same lines. The tons of freight per train for the Southern Pacific were 124.63; on the Atchison, Topeka, and Santa Fe, 118.84—a difference of 5.79, or 6 tons.

Q. What is the proportion of passengers per mile of road? A. Judging from the earnings here, I should say there is more traffic per mile of road than there is on the lines of which I have spoken.

Q. Than the Atchison? A. Yes.

Q. The Missouri Pacific? A. I think there is more.

Q. This table set forth here, called a distance tariff, like the one in Kansas, is based on the Atchison system you have given figures for, is it not? A. It is based on their tariff. They make tariffs over there which are really less than shown in the distance table. There is a series of distance tariffs. In fact, each State or Territory has, as a general thing, east of the Rocky Mountains, a distance tariff which is peculiar to that particular State. It forms a basis for the local tariff generally, in the State or Territory, and differs somewhat. There is one in Illinois, one in Wisconsin, Iowa, Minnesota, the Dakotas, Nebraska, Kansas; and, in fact, as far as my knowledge extends, there is a distance tariff in effect in each of the States and territories.

Q. What basis would you take to arrive at this tariff. Do you consider that the carrier is entitled to interest on the cost of carriage—of operating expenses, and also interest on the cost of the road. Do you take those two elements into consideration? A. Yes, and you are paying a good deal more than that in California. You are considering rates which, as I understand them, are within the limits of California alone. I am endeavoring to show by these figures that the earnings are $9,020 per mile of road—and, in fact, taking out that portion of the Central Pacific in Nevada, you are paying at least $10,000 a mile annually to the Southern Pacific Company for transportation over every mile of road they have in the State; for operating expenses, at 59 per cent, they would pay $5,900, leaving at least $4,100 to pay fixed charges on the road in this State.

Q. The total capitalization you state is $144,000,000 for the Pacific System, so called. What portion of this is in California? A. I have not the material to segregate it.

Q. I understand this proposed amendment is put forth largely under the auspices of the Traffic Association, in San Francisco? A. Yes, sir.

Q. We would like a statement as explicit as you are able to give us of all the facts taken into consideration in making up this California Distance Tariff—just as full as you can. A. The operations, earnings per mile of road, the comparison of operating expenses, the information that California is paying to this road about twice or more than twice as much per mile as is earned by roads in other portions of this country; also, the proposition that it is no more expensive here to operate a road, or should not be, than in that territory, should be quite sufficient, it strikes me, and demonstrates the necessity for some reduction. It has been insisted upon that this system shall be considered as a whole, including Oregon, Arizona, New Mexico, and Texas; but I claim, and the Supreme Court of the United States has held, I believe, that in the matter of local commerce, each State is an integral part by itself, and such State has a power to fix the rates on all State business. Interstate commerce is a subject over which the States have no jurisdiction; that belongs exclusively to the Federal Government. You must not call upon California to support a business in another State or Territory. As soon as the road passes over the line of your State, you have nothing more to say with reference to the traffic which they carry, and all responsibility as to their earnings or losses, so far as you are concerned, ceases. Whenever a system of this kind is set up, it seems to me that is contrary to the principles of justice and equity. I will say for your information that such claims were set up in Kansas and Iowa, and they were thrust aside by the Commission, and they were sustained.

Q. By the Courts? A. No, sir; sustained by the people, and the rates prescribed by the Commission were put into effect. Yes; I think they were sustained by the Courts.

Q. They were? A. By the Courts.

Q. Have you the citations here? A. No, sir; I believe I can get them, though. They claim that the operating expenses are higher here than in the East, owing to the high price of coal. I believe I have shown that one half the amount of coal here provides the same service as in Kansas.

Q. How can that be; are not the grades here heavier? A. I think, perhaps, there is not more than 10 per cent of the local traffic of this State that moves over the heavy grades. Furthermore, the equeable climate here, I should say, would enable the performance of more service with a ton of coal than in the colder countries East. In the warm weather here an engine should do nearly double the service that it would East over the same kind of track. In fact, that seems to be borne out by the fact that only about one half the amount of coal is used here for the movement of a train of 5.79 more tons than in that territory. There is another fact that is worthy of consideration. You have very little stone ballast here in your roads, and very little is required. Your soil is better adapted to making a roadway, I should think, than that East, and besides there are nine months you have no elements to contend against, and in the other three there is very little storm and interruption. Where they are obliged to have stone ballast in the road it requires the service of a section man, I believe, per day, to take out and put in three ties in a rock-ballasted road. Besides, you have here a tie that lasts two or three times as long as ties east of the Rocky Mountains, and less ties are to be taken out and put in. When your ties are worn out for track purposes it makes a good fence post, while over there when worn out in the track it is rotten and gone.

Q. Some of the committee would like to hear further from you on this subject; whether the California Distance Tariff here will pay the operating expenses, say for the Southern Pacific road, and interest on bonded indebtedness, and leave a reasonable profit for the operation of the line. Are you able to give us an answer to that? A. I think it would be a pretty good plan, perhaps, to determine what the fixed charges are; whether the bonds are not largely in excess of any original cost of the property; whether the capital stock of the road cost anything or not; whether or not you are being called upon to-day to pay a large amount of money on something that never had any tangible existence. My calculations are based upon a comparison of what has been done, and found more than sufficient, in other and less favored portions of the country, to accomplish the same thing. I do not admit that the cost of operation in the State of California will be 59 per cent. In fact, I have a little comparison here which may shed some light on that subject, which I have overlooked. I will mention it. The Southern Pacific Railroad of California earns in gross $9,279,822 50, or $6,611 54 per mile, and the operating expenses were 58.50 per cent. The South Pacific Coast earned $1,107,772 87, or $10,651 66 per mile, and 64.46 per cent for operating expenses. This was probably to largely rebuild the road during that time, which should have been obviated by building it properly in the first place. The California Pacific earned $1,528,047, or $13,242 79 a mile, and the operating expenses were 50.31 per cent. This road runs from Vallejo to Sacramento.

Q. That was during the year 1891? A. Yes, sir.

Q. Then the interest and bonded indebtedness is not included in the operating expenses, Mr. Leeds? A. No, sir.

Q. Do you know whether or not the bonds passed into the hands of interested parties? Do you know anything about the disposal of those bonds? A. No, sir.

Q. Do you know what the roads are bonded for in California? A. No; but it would not take a great while to find it out.

Q. Your suggestion is, that the bonded indebtedness of this road is very much in excess of the cost of construction? A. Yes, sir; I believe it is.

Q. What would be the effect, Mr. Leeds, if you could answer, of the adoption of this statutory amendment upon the independent lines of road in this State, other than the Southern Pacific? A. I think some of those roads are earning to-day $6,000 and more per mile, and they should stand it as well as the other road can. I believe they could stand it, and believe the tariff would be its own compensation; believe it would operate to increase the business.

Q. Do you think that the independent lines of road you refer to would be able to operate at a profit—at a reasonable, fair profit? A. As far as my experience has extended in the application of uniform tariffs in other portions of our country, the roads have continued to operate. They do not all operate at a profit in any State. People make bad investments in railroads as well as other things. I do not think there is a State in the Union where every road operates at a profit.

Q. As a general proposition, rates fixed by the State must be reasonable with reference to the cost of construction and the cost of operating the road; such a rate as would yield over operating expenses, etc., a reasonable interest on the cost of construction? A. As a general proposition, I believe they should make a profit over operating expenses and interest on bonds.

Q. We understand you to say that you do not know the cost of these roads in the State of California? A. No; but I have seen some estimates made by competent engineers with reference to the building of roads in California.

Q. At the time these were built? A. No, sir; at the present time. On the basis of present prices for material and labor—the expense of reproducing these roads at the present time.

Q. You have no idea what the original investment was? A. I know nothing of that.

Q. We understand you to say that you made estimates from which you come to the conclusion that the Southern Pacific had been bonded for about all of its original cost? A. The estimates are for the construction of a road at the present time. For what they could be reproduced at the present time.

Q. Do you know how many roads there are, independently of the Southern Pacific, in this State? A. I do not know as I do; I do not believe I could recall them, although I have seen the names.

EARL: At this rate of 2 cents a mile for passengers, prescribed in this proposed amendment—2 cents a mile, I understand, until the Legislature should act, when 3 cents is the maximum. Is that a reasonable rate?

LEEDS: Until the Legislature acts, the passenger rates shall be 2 cents; the maximum fixed by the Legislature is 3 cents.

Q. How did you arrive at that figure? A. That figure is more of a proviso than anything else; to induce the making of a rate on passenger business by the Legislature.

Q. You say that is a just and reasonable rate for the carriage of passengers? A. It is a lower rate than is made on some other roads in the country and in other territories. The usual rate is 3 cents a mile; that is the usual rate.

Q. That is the usual rate, say on the Atchison road? A. Yes, sir.

Q. And on the Missouri Pacific? A. Yes, sir.

Q. Is that the general rate, 3 cents? A. Yes sir; 2 and 3 cents are the pretty general rates in the East. There are more places where the rate is 3 cents than any other. The almost universal rate is 3 cents.

Q. Three cents is the almost universal rate? A. Yes, sir.

Q. Then, you mean to say that 2 cents is a just and reasonable rate for the carriage of passengers in this State, from your investigations? Is that so? A. I told you what my investigation was.

LEEDS: Counting the entire business of the Southern Pacific Company, I find they report their passenger business as being done at 2.16 per mile; segregating their ferry and suburban business and through business, I find 2.73, or say 2¾ cents per mile. Taking the business, excluding suburban and ferry business, it is 2.499 cents. The Atchison, Topeka, and Santa Fe business, covering the same class, would be 2.388, or .111 cents less. I do not know as I care very much what the passenger rate is. It amounts to very little of the burden, anyhow, whether it is 2 or 3 cents. Three cents is enough, and may be too little; I don't know.

EARL: What do you mean by saying that the passenger rates is very little of the burden? A. It only amounts, outside of the suburban business, to less than 30 per cent of the gross earnings.

Q. Not one third of the profit—that is, you mean suburban and other business excepted. How much would that amount to? A. Something like a third; whatever rates are made would not disturb them, because they carry their ferry and suburban business at about 1 cent per mile. This amounted in 1891, as near as I can figure it, to $1,121,754 25; they carried 11,845,443 suburban and ferry passengers; the average distance was 9.6 miles, about. The average rate per passenger, 9.47 cents. The intention of reducing the passenger rates is to increase the business.

Q. The bill provides here that a rate of 2 cents shall be imposed until the Legislature shall make a higher rate, and whenever the Legislature has made a rate, which from any cause becomes inoperative, 3 cents per mile will apply. According to the statement, Mr. Leeds, the rate of 2 cents per mile seems to be at least 16 per cent less than the average rate now charged? A. The proviso to make that 3 cents per mile was put in, perhaps, on account of some doubt, and it might be found reasonable to make that rate—to advance the rate to 3 cents.

Q. You think that the rates fixed in this proposed amendment here will encourage, or do you think it will discourage the building of roads, that is, competing roads? A. I don't believe it would discourage the building of competing lines in this State. That has not been the history of other States where such legislation has taken place. The best equipped States of the country to-day are those where the largest amount of mileage has been added in the last two or three years, or in years during which the legislation took place. Take for example the States of Illinois, Wisconsin, Minnesota, Iowa, Nebraska, and Kansas. In all of those States there has been what railroads term "adverse legislation." They are all of them to-day pretty well equipped with railroad facilities.

Q. Do you know whether these roads are operated with a profit or not? A. Many of them are, yes.

Q. This California Distance Tariff, "Western Classification."

[The Chairman then read from the proposed amendment, wherein it is stated that the distance tariff applies to all roads built now or to be built hereafter in the State of California; shall be subject to the "Western Classification" and the "rates" governing the same.]

Leeds (interposing): It should read "rules" instead of "rates."

[Chairman instructed Senator Gesford accordingly.]

The Chairman (continuing): The "Western Classification," issued January 1, 1893, said classification being made part of this distance tariff, and to all intents and purposes as if same were actually incorporated herein. What is that Western Classification, Mr. Leeds? A. The "Western Classification" is a classification of goods for shipment which is in effect in all territory east of California and west of Chicago and the Mississippi River.

Q. Is it in effect in any portion of the State of Nevada? A. I believe it is. I know it is in effect with reference to interchange of business with connecting lines; with reference to local traffic between points in that State, I am not positive. It is also in effect in Southern California. I don't know where the dividing point is, but I think it is at Mojave. It is also in effect in this part of California, and business which is consigned through to a point beyond what is known as the terminal, when coming from points east of the connecting points with a connecting line. I don't know exactly the definition put on the tariff, but I believe that is the application of it; anyway, it is interchange business, and applies on shipments which might come to Sacramento, and then going to outlying points.

Q. What is this "committee;" who are they, and how are they made up? A. That committee is composed of representatives of each road named under the classification; they are seventy-four in number.

Q. Is the Southern Pacific one? A. The Southern Pacific is one. They got two members on the committee for their Atlantic System and the Pacific System.

Q. How many are there in the committee? A. The Southern Pacific count two in the committee, but there are seventy-four members on the committee. Their business is largely done by the sub-committee, which meets one or two days before the full committee come together, and passes on many articles which come up for consideration, and its recommendations are acted upon by the full committee.

Q. How many are there in the sub-committee? A. I don't know to-day how many. There used to be seven, I believe. I was a member at one time.

Q. This classification, is it in book form; is it published? A. Yes, sir.

[The Chairman, on inquiring for a copy, was informed by Mr. Gesford and also by Mr. Leeds that a copy had been submitted, and they would furnish others.]

Q. Are the rules governing the same in this book? A. Yes; it is complete in itself.

Q. In a general way, Mr. Leeds, is it a classification of all commodities shipped—all commodities of trade? A. Yes, sir; it is a very full classification. It has been the work of ten years in preparation. The committee first organized in 1883, and it has been revised and added to and carefully compiled—I should say by as good talent as there is in the country anywhere—and after very full consideration of most of the items of the classification as between the members of the committee and the shipping public.

Q. Now, are these classifications rigid or are they fixed. Suppose some new commodity comes in the market—something new, unlisted in the classification? A. That would naturally come up at the next meeting of the Classification Committee, and in the meantime would be passed upon by the Chairman of the Classification Committee.

Q. And would he list it? A. He would send out notices, I believe, with his ruling on it, whatever it might be.

Q. Does he exercise this power in the rules referred to, the rules regulating and governing the Western Classification? A. There is a rule which gives him that authority; yes, sir.

Q. Then the classifications contained in this Western Classification would not be a fixed and rigid thing, but would change, possibly? A. Quite likely.

Q. Taking new commodities that arise? A. (Interrupting.) You can't provide the new commodities in advance in any event.

Q. That is exactly what I thought. You can't provide in advance for them, and if they should come into existence, the Western Classification as it exists to-day, or when it went into effect, January 1, 1893, would not determine what class it would go in, but it would be classified by the committee that might sit at the next session, and in the meantime the Chairman might make a ruling, you say, classifying it? A. Yes, sir.

Q. That would be changing the classification? A. Oh, no; the classification is specific within itself to-day.

Q. But take a new commodity, something like telephones, or some new things introduced, some new matter, how would they be listed, say in the Western Classification, so called? A. They would naturally be listed as they would be if no such proviso that we were talking here about were in existence.

Q. Do I understand you to say by that, that we do not adopt the rules of the Western Classification? A. You may adopt that rule, as far as I can see, and yet be consistent.

Q. But if the Chairman was to rule on this new commodity, or commodities, my point is this: If he were to rule, or make a rule as he is empowered under this Western Classification here, he would be doing something that is now new in this Western Classification, which is complete in itself. Suppose this amendment was adopted and inserted in the Constitution, that would be a final and complete classification, and the Constitution would have to be changed whenever the Chairman made a ruling, as he is empowered to do from time to time? A. Drop that rule. Then you want to know what you would do if you were making a tariff to-day, making a constitutional proviso. I only answer the question by asking another one, to show you that you can't provide for something that don't exist to-day.

Q. But it is attempted here. Is it not the thought of the drafter of this that rulings of the Chairman of the Western Classification Committee, for instance, and his committee should be a part of our Constitution from time to time? A. You provide there that you shall do with this committee precisely what he will do with it anyhow, and precisely what the parties affected by this tariff would do if that rule were entirely left out from this constitutional proviso.

Q. If this rule, that we have been speaking about, becomes part of our Constitution, was adopted April 18th, as I understand it here; if the proposition was adopted, then the Constitution would be changed from time to time as these rules? A. No, because it is not part of the Constitution. That which he does afterward is not a part of the Constitution—would not be a part of any Constitution.

Q. How would the new commodities be classified? Supposing one came into existence, how would they be classified by this particular classification covering, say three thousand commodities? There is a development, and in the course of time new commodities spring into existence. How are they to be classified? Who would classify them? Suppose you adopt a tariff and classification. You do it as a specific proposition? Well, how would you classify the new commodities? A. Why, classify as you do with the others, as they come up. It need not be a part of your Constitution, so far as I can see.

Q. This Western Classification would be a part and portion of our Constitution, fixed and rigid. A. Does it become a part of the Constitution?

Q. Yes, sir. A. It becomes a part of the tariff.

Q. The tariff becomes part of the Constitution, because it is all set forth; and we are all impressed here that this classification, being made part of this distance tariff, as if the same were actually incorporated in it, is a part of the amendment, as proposed. A. I am not a constitutional lawyer, but I should say that you can refer to that tariff, or that classification in the tariff, as you might refer to Webster's dictionary, or any other standard publication, and yet not make it a part of the Constitution.

[The Chairman then read portions of the proposed amendment, wherein it was stated that the distance tariff and classification, as he understood it, was to be made part of said amendment.]

[Mr. Leeds, however, could not agree with him on this point.]

Earl: I understood the table set forth, together with all the figures, became a part of our organic law, together with the Western Classification.

Leeds: That is not my theory. It is a specific publication, readily referred to and understood, and it is not necessary it should become part of the Constitution any more than any other publication referred to should become a part of it.

Earl: It is not only my impression, but the impression of every member of the committee, that the classification, together with the rules and also the tariff and tables set forth herein, were to become part of our Constitution, to all intents and purposes.

LEEDS: They were put in for the purpose of saving time. It is not my idea that they were to become a part of the Constitution.

EARL: What is your idea as to how much should be inserted as a part of the Constitution?

LEEDS: Only the table of figures in reference to the classification. The classification is a publication, easily set forth and referred to, as any standard publication.

[In conferring with the other members of the committee, their impression was the same as that of the Chairman (Mr. Earl), viz.: That the classification would become part of the amendment to the Constitution; and, instead of being the rigid and fixed thing, would shift from time to time, according to the rules laid down by the Chairman.]

GESFORD: The words "after January 1, 1893," should be stricken out, and also an exception made as to the rules giving the Chairman power to classify new commodities.

EARL: Under those rules of the classification, does the Chairman, Mr. Leeds, of that committee have the right to reclassify articles in there already? A. No, sir; not to make changes without the vote of all the members of the committee. As I understand it, they meet about once a year.

Q. Why are these powers given to the committee, to reclassify articles from time to time in case of emergency, or as the trade demands? A. There have been such things recognized in connection with the classification, and many changes have been made. There was an effort made some three years ago to make a uniform classification of the United States, but it fell through. It was impossible to reconcile the differences between the trunk lines east of Chicago and the Mississippi River, and the lines west thereof. But there was a disposition, however, to make as many articles as were consistent, uniform with the trunk line, or what is known as the "Official Classification," and thereby facilitate the interchange of business between the roads which use the two classifications, "Official" and "Western." Uniformity is a very desirable thing to have in the interchange of traffic between roads, and in that way there was some last year. I think in 1891 a good many changes were made. Very frequently the trades people come before this committee with propositions to be made in classification, to assist in furthering their interests on certain articles, when it is determined, if desirable to do so, to make the change.

Q. Then your idea is that the same necessity would apply on the lines here in California, would it not? A. Yes, sir.

EARL: I think the classification would become part of our Constitution. Now, suppose it is necessary to the demands of trade that these matters which are controlled under the Western Classification come into play here, and this amendment were adopted. There being no committee, would not the vote of the people of the State of California upon their proposed amendment be necessary to make the change in the classification? In other words, the only way I can see is for the adoption of the resolution to pass both houses of the Legislature by a two-thirds vote, and the submission of the proposition to the people, when, if it receives a majority vote, the proposition is accepted and becomes part of our organic law; while according t› the scheme modified by yourself and Senator Gesford, the scheme would become a fixed and rigid one. The power of a classification committee and the Chairman thereof to classify articles as they are now or may be to-day under the rules governing this committee would be eliminated from this constitutional amendment here. The constitutional amendment would be fixed and rigid, and the classification would never be changed or modified. There would be no power to change it as the demands of trade would require. There would be no power excepting the Legislature and submission to the people.

LEEDS: The first paragraph of Section 36, making it the duty of the Legislature at the first regular session after the adoption of the amendment to prescribe rates of fares for passengers, and provide classification of property, and to fix and determine the rates of freight that were charged on all railroads in the State of California, covers the point.

EARL: I do not think it is just or fair to have to wait the convening of the Legislature before the classification could be changed, in order to meet the exigencies of trade and commerce.

LEEDS: It will be a vast improvement on what we have at present if we only had the classification changed once in two years. I do not think the classification has been changed in ten years; that rates and fares could not very well be provided without a governing classification, which need not necessarily be the Western Classification. It is not the intention of the bill, so far as my idea is concerned, to make the classification part of the Constitution.

CARPENTER: I see very little use sitting here with a bill that can only be read by one member of the committee at a time, and discussing this question. I don't think it is parliamentary or right to send the bill here in that shape. I move this bill be referred to the Assembly, with the request to have it printed and recommitted.

LEEDS (interrupting): I don't think it is necessary to waste time about that. This tariff and classification are only calculated to afford relief in the interim, until the Legislature can act upon that question. There is certainly no such idea connected with the bill there, as to fix the rigid classification in the Constitution of this State, or even a rigid schedule of rates.

CARPENTER: It may be a waste of time, according to the idea of Mr. Leeds. I don't propose to go into argument of the question with Mr. Leeds, or anybody else, and want to know what we are doing on a question delivered to us in that form. The Chairman don't agree with Mr. Leeds, and it seems the distinguished Senator who introduced the bill don't agree with him, and I want a printed bill.

EARL: Mr. Gesford asked the indulgence of the committee for having the bill in this form, which was granted.

CARPENTER: Well, I insist that the bill should be reported back to the Assembly, to be printed and recommitted.

EARL: The bill should be printed, and will be sent back, and the committee will proceed with its other business. I understand there are a number of representatives of railroads present, some of whom were anxious to get away to-night and wish to be heard.

JUDGE MARTIN: I would suggest that the same difficulty which has confronted the committee as to a proper understanding of the amendment would confront the gentlemen representing the railroads also, and therefore if we could have this reported back, the gentlemen representing the railroads would take this subject up with the committee at some future time. The matter is one of vast importance to the railroads, and I do not see how any gentleman could properly understand the details proposed in the amendments until we get copies of it. It would only be a waste of time to consider it further at present.

[Some of the gentlemen present had to go away immediately, and it was understood the bill would not be reported back before at least Wednesday.]

EARL: The meeting will stand adjourned to Wednesday evening, at 7:30 o'clock.

JANUARY 25, 1893.

Meeting called to order at 7:30 P. M.

MR. EARL: All the committee are present except Senator Carpenter. The matter that the committee will take up and consider this evening will be the Committee Substitute for Senate Constitutional Amendment No. 8, so entitled; the same proposition that was being considered last Monday evening. The oral amendments are now incorporated in this printed resolution. We will be glad to hear from Senator Gesford.

SENATOR GESFORD: Mr. Chairman and Gentlemen of the Committee—You have before you the proposed Committee Substitute for Senate Constitutional Amendment No. 8, which embodies the one that I proposed at the last sitting of the committee, together with some amendments that were suggested at that time, and one or two additional. You will notice that the resolution, after providing for the repeal of Section 22 of Article XII of the Constitution, provides for an additional section, 36, to Article IV, and that I may be understood in what little I have to say, I will read the section:

"The Legislature shall have the power, and it shall be its duty, to establish rates of charges for the transportation of passengers and freight by all railroads operated in this State, and to enact such laws as may be necessary for the enforcement and carrying into effect of such rates."

As to this clause in the section, the committee will observe the Legislature have the power, it is their duty, to establish rates on all roads in the State; that is, the general proposition that, in lieu of the Railroad Commission having this power, in lieu of the establishment of freights and fares by a Railroad Commission, that power is given to the Legislature.

(Continuing to read):

"*Provided, however*, that the Legislature shall have no power to prescribe rates of charges for the transportation of passengers on any railroad, or system of railroads, whose gross annual earnings are more than $4,000 a mile, to exceed 3 cents per mile."

It was suggested at the last sitting of the committee, and upon further investigation and more deliberate examination, it has been ascertained that there are a number of roads in this State, small roads, that could not be operated with the same tariff, to net a profit, as the larger roads; and in order to provide a clause it has been thought advisable to classify the roads into two classes: Those whose annual gross earnings are less than $4,000 per mile, and those whose gross annual earnings are more than $4,000 per mile; so that, so far as this clause of the amendment is concerned, these small roads will not be burdened, or injured, or prejudiced by the rate that the larger roads can operate under.

(Continuing to read):

"*And provided further*, that the Legislature shall have no power to prescribe the rates of charges for the transportation of freight on any railroad or system of railroads whose gross annual earnings are more than $4,000 a mile, to exceed the rates specified in the 'California Distance Tariff,' as in this section hereinafter set forth. Until the Legislature shall prescribe such rates as aforesaid, or in the event that any such prescribed rates shall, from any cause, become inoperative, the rates of charges for the transportation of passengers on all railroads in this State whose gross annual earnings are more than $4,000 a mile, shall be 3 cents per mile, and the charges for the transportation of freight by any such railroads shall be the rates specified in the following distance tariff, hereby designated as the 'California Distance Tariff,' to wit."

The same classification being made with reference to freight schedule as to passenger. And you will also notice the 2 cent proposition has been eliminated. Upon further investigation, and after considering the matter more fully and carefully, it has been deemed advisable to incorporate 3 cents instead of 2 cents; the 3 cent rate being an almost universal rate, it being the opinion of the gentleman who investigated this that a 3 cent rate is a fair and reasonable rate.

(Continuing to read):

"Until the Legislature shall prescribe such rates as aforesaid, or in the event that any such prescribed rates shall from any cause become inoperative, the rates of charges for the transportation of passengers on all railroads in this State whose gross annual earnings are more than $4,000 per mile, shall be 3 cents per mile, and the charges for transportation of freight by any such railroads shall be the rates specified in the following distance tariff, hereby designated as the 'California Distance Tariff.'"

Now, gentlemen, there is one amendment that I desire to make to this bill, and to present to the committee and ask them if they pass upon the bill favorably: That after the word "mile" on line seventeen, in order to have some fixed manner to determine what the "gross earnings" of a railroad are, these words be incorporated, namely: "As shown by the Thirteenth Annual Report of the Board of Railroad Commissioners of the State of California," making that provision read then as follows:

"Until the Legislature shall prescribe such rates as aforesaid, or in the event that any such prescribed rates shall from any cause become inoperative, the rates of charges for the transportation of passengers on all railroads in this State, whose gross annual earnings are more than $4,000 per mile, as shown by the Thirteenth Annual Report of the Board of Railroad Commissioners, shall be 3 cents per mile, and the charges for the transportation of freight by any such railroads shall be the rates specified in the following distance tariff, hereby designated as the 'California Distance Tariff.'"

Now, the committee should bear in mind this proposition: This Legislature can fix no schedule of freights and fares, that power being delegated alone to the Railroad Commission, and until the Railroad Commission is abolished, until those provisions of the Constitution are abrogated, the Legislature will have no control over the establishment of freights and fares, so that this bill proposes now: *First*—To abolish the Railroad Commission, to wipe it out, and provide, in the interim, a schedule of freights and fares; in other words, if this amendment to the Constitution should go into effect, say on the first day of July, 1893, then from that time until the Legislature shall have fixed a schedule of freights and fares, the rates provided in this amendment would govern until that time; in other words, it is intended only as a provision to bridge over the interim between the time the amendment shall have gone into effect and until the time the Legislature shall have established the rates of freights and fares.

(Continuing to read):

"CALIFORNIA DISTANCE TARIFF.—This distance tariff shall be applicable to local traffic between all stations in the State of California now established, or that may hereafter be established. The classifications of property provided for in this distance tariff are based upon the 'Western Classifications' and the rules governing the same adopted and issued by the Western Classification Committee, of which J. T. Ripley was Chairman, and which took effect January 1, 1893, to which said classification reference is hereby made."

The objection was made that that classification, in the manner in which it was incorporated in the bill, would become a variable classification—that is, it would be subject to change by the Chairman of the railroads composing that Classification Committee, and therefore it would not be a fixed and determined classification. Now, the idea is not to incorporate that classification into this amendment, but simply to refer to it as a basis upon which this California Distance Tariff is based.

(Continuing to read):

"*Provided, however*, that no rule or rules governing such classification providing for any change, modifications, or additions to the classifications mentioned in this distance tariff shall have any application hereto."

In other words, that this Western Classification is fixed, determined, invariable; and if adopted—if this distance tariff is adopted by us—I think there will be a provision of the Constitution subject to no change. Of course it will be argued—and I do not claim to be a railroad expert; don't claim to be an expert on freights and fares; claim to know very little about them—I don't pretend to be an expert, as I say, but I have undertaken to assist in this bill to the best of my ability, and I have presented it here on behalf of the Traffic Association. If there are defects in it, it is for this committee to remedy those defects. I contend the people are looking for some relief in this matter. I am not one of those so-called "anti-railroad" fellows; I am not one of those fellows who believe that in order to gain notoriety it is necessary to burn railroad bridges and destroy railroad property; I am not made out of that kind of material. I believe in a fair and honest adjustment of this question. I don't believe in this demagogy. I don't believe in this howling about corporations and railroads for the purpose of creating sentiment against any class of people or property rights. The whole State of California expects the Legislature to do something—they are looking to it to do something. I don't believe the State of California wants to confiscate any property or deprive anybody of their rights. But they simply want us to do that which is for the interests of all parties concerned, and therefore this bill is submitted by me in that spirit, and in that spirit alone.

SEAWELL: Is there any other Constitution that you know of where this maximum rate is embodied in the organic law?

GESFORD: There is no such a provision in any Constitution that I have examined. I know of nothing of this kind having been embodied; it is an innovation; entirely so. We are in this position in this State: if the people will vote for this amendment that we propose to them, abolishing the Railroad Commission, we leave the railroad companies from the time of ratification of that amendment until the time the Legislature is clothed with power to fix rates, to manage and control rates of fares and freights by themselves. This is simply a temporary affair. The Legislatures of other States have done it, and I believe California can do what other States do, and that we can arrive at a proper and a just solution of this question of freights and fares which has troubled us so long, and for all the years we have had railroads in this State. This distance tariff, gentlemen, denominated in this amendment as the "California Distance Tariff," is based on the Western Classification, a classification for property made for the purpose of fixing rates by representatives of seventy-four railroads. This classification is one that has been changed from time to time, and the one referred to here is the one that went into effect January 1, 1893. There are very few changes on staple articles. I imagine, and I believe that no one would suffer by the adoption of the schedule of rates for a short period, until the next Legislature should have provided a different system or different rate. Now as to the question as to whether these rates are equitable or not, Mr. Leeds has told you, and it has not yet been disputed, that this was a reasonable schedule of rates; it was some twenty-two per cent lower than the freight rates established.

LEEDS (correcting): It was 25 or 30 per cent lower than the present tariff of the Southern Pacific; that it applied to probably, within the limits of the State of California, to something like 70 per cent of their business; I should judge, as near as I can calculate, their through business, which would not be disturbed by this tariff, and applying 25 or 30 per cent to 70 per cent, would be 21 or 22 per cent.

GESFORD: It is a material reduction of freight charges now, being a matter of 22, 25, or 30 per cent; it is a material reduction, and a reduction that the railroads can stand; that they can operate at a profit under. this reduction. Now, then, if these rates are not equitable and just, with the statement of Mr. Leeds—and I believe it will not be contradicted, he is well posted on the subject of rates of freights—with this proposition before us, if these rates are not fair, it seems to me it is for those who controvert the proposition, to show wherein it will be ruinous or injurious to the freight traffic of the State.

(Continuing to read:)

"Rules governing shipment of live stock by the carload," etc.

Then there are some additional rules had to be made for the protection of shipments.

(Continuing to read):

"Railroads shall be considered independently in computing distances; except, however, that a system of railroads consisting of leased, operated, or independent roads controlled under a common management, although working under different charters, shall be considered and treated as one road."

So that there would not be two or three different rates on a system of roads; the rates would follow right along through to the end of the system.

(Continuing to read):

"And the distances shall be computed over the shortest operated line composed of two or more of said roads. Whenever the rate herein named conflicts with the Western Classification aforesaid, this tariff shall govern as to such rate. Single shipments of one or more classes will be charged for at actual weight at tariff rates, subject to a minimum charge of 25 cents for the entire consignment or shipment for a distance of five hundred miles or less, and 50 cents for all distances over five hundred miles."

In other words, the railroads will not be compelled to charge anything less than 25 cents for five hundred miles or less, and 50 cents for over five hundred miles. It seems to me, gentlemen, it is a simple proposition, and the question it seems to me for this Constitutional Amendment Committee to consider is, first, whether or not this plan is feasible; second, whether it is constitutional. If there is any provision that would prohibit the incorporation of a distance tariff of this kind, or system of rates of freight and fares of this kind, it is a question that it seems to me ought to be determined. I know of nothing, and think the people of this State have set their minds on this subject, and think they would incorporate this in, so to speak, the "belly" of the Constitution. There may be questions of a serious nature that will arise that we have not thought or provided for. There never was a Constitution framed yet, or statute or law made, but astute lawyers could find some flaw; but I will state to the committee that I have devoted, off and on, a week or ten days to the subject, new to me. I have been prosecuting criminals, etc., and this is about all the railroad I have had in mine, though I expect I shall have a good many questions to answer before I get through with this proposition; but I submit it to this committee, and I ask their kindly consideration of this bill. It seems to me it covers every phase of the question. It seems to me it is what we want. I don't see how any one can object to it, unless the rates are ruinous and would confiscate the roads; but I believe there are only four or five in the State to which they apply.

If that bill will result in ruin, we want to know it. Mr. Leeds says no. Now, then, if the railroad people say and can demonstrate that these rates will ruin their property and confiscate it—so to speak, wipe it off the face of the earth—let us hear from them, and if that be the case, I will not vote for the bill or resolution, because I do not believe we can get along without the railroads. The only question is: Shall the people be the creatures of the railroad, or the railroads the creatures of the people; that is all there is to it. We have to have railroads, but let us control them, keep them in proper bounds; let us make them our servants and not our masters. We know they have not been our servants but our masters in this State, what we are trying to do is to put them in the niche where they belong.

EARL: The committee, unfortunately, since the adjournment on Monday night, have not had very much time to examine into this matter. The committee, I will state, of course is in no way informed on the important matters that are involved in this amendment, and we desire to say to Senator Gesford, and to all here that are interested in this matter, that we wish to investigate it very carefully, and fairly, and sincerely, simply for the truth; and I speak, I think, for all the committee—certainly do for myself—and any of our inquiries that are made here from the gentlemen that propose this resolution, this constitutional amendment, and from the gentlemen who may be opposed to the adoption of this amendment, will be prompted by an earnest and sincere desire to arrive at the truth—the wisdom of the passage of this amendment. There will be, I am sure, no prejudice on the part of the committee. I for one will say my mind is open, and I want to make a thorough investigation of the merits of the matter before me, after hearing, as far as we can consistently with the time we have, what may be said, pro and con, in regard to this matter; the committee will then review the evidence, considering all, and determine on a report.

This afternoon, since printing of this measure, I was looking through it, and I would like to ask Senator Gesford or Mr. Leeds some further questions. The point I wish first to inquire about is, is it intended in section thirty-six, on page two, in the paragraph reading:

"Until the Legislature shall prescribe such rates as aforesaid, or in the event that any such prescribed rates shall from any cause become inoperative, the rates of charges for the transportation of passengers on all railroads in this State whose gross annual earnings are more than $4,000 a mile, shall be 3 cents per mile, and the charges for the transportation of freight by any such railroads shall be the rates specified in the following tariff, hereby designated as the 'California Distance Tariff.'"

Is it the intention of the proponents of this resolution to fix a limit below which a road could not go in case of emergency for the encouragement of traffic? How would you consider that, Mr. Gesford? You say these rates shall be the rates for passenger traffic—3 cents—the rates prescribed; I apprehend that it is the purpose of the drafter of this to fix a maximum limit. Is that also the minimum?

Gesford: No, sir; that was not the intention.

Earl: But, observe the language; does it not fix it?

Gesford: Yes, but the words "shall be not to exceed" should be entered.

Earl: It seems to be a minimum as well as a maximum.

Leeds: The old bill reads "not to exceed;" that is included in the old bill (looking at a copy).

Gesford: That was left out. It should read "not to exceed." It is "not to exceed" on the old bill, and you will observe, where mentioned above it also reads "not to exceed." The words "not to exceed" were omitted unintentionally. You will observe, Mr. Chairman, the words "not to exceed" are used in the first provision, relating to the power of the Legislature, and those same words should be used below, also.

Earl: Another matter. It seems to me obscure. I followed the argument very closely, but it seems to me on bottom of page two, after the words "California Distance Tariff" (reading from the bill):

"The classifications of property provided for in this distance tariff are based upon the 'Western Classification,' and the rules governing the same adopted and issued by the Western Classification Committee, of which J. T. Ripley was Chairman, and which took effect January 1, 1893, to which said classification reference is hereby made; *provided, however*, that no rule or rules governing said Western Classification providing for any change, modifications, or additions to the classifications mentioned in this distance tariff, shall have any application hereto."

I understand from your explanation of this matter, Senator Gesford—I understand you draw a distinction between the language used in this paragraph and the language used in the original amendment, as proposed in the original amendment, and the substitute offered at the last meeting, referring to this Western Classification and tariff, and used language to the effect that it shall be considered as set forth here to all intents and purposes as if it were a part of the Constitution; perhaps I did not apprehend you correctly just now——

GESFORD: That is explanatory of the classification made in the California Distance Tariff; you will notice the first, second, third, fourth, fifth, A, B, C, D.

EARL: You mean to imply that the Western Classification is not to be considered as set forth in the Constitution?

GESFORD: It is not part of the Constitution; simply referred to as explanatory of that classification referred to.

SEAWELL: Then it must be part of the Constitution, this distance tariff; certainly the California Distance Tariff is part of the Constitution, and the idea of Mr. Earl is this Western Classification is also made part of the Constitution.

EARL: You will observe, Senator, that (reading):

"No rule or rules governing said Western Classification providing for any change, modifications, or additions to the classifications mentioned in this distance tariff shall have any application hereto."

Is it not to be implied that the other rules shall have application, and those rules and the application shall be ascertained from the Western Classification?

GESFORD: I think all other rules, except that rule two—I refer to page one of the Western Classification (reading):

"When articles are not classified, or not clearly analogous to articles which are, a special ruling must be asked for."

Making it a shifting classification. Instead of being a shifting classification, or a classification subject to change, it is a classification subject to no change.

EARL: I follow you close, Senator, but is it not to be implied in line twenty-six (reading):

"That no rule or rules governing said Western Classification providing for any change, modifications, or additions to the classifications mentioned in this distance tariff shall have any application hereto;" is it not by implication provided that the other rules shall govern?

GESFORD: The rules govern the classification; there is no question about that; but it seems to me the correct construction—the opposite construction would be the proper construction—that while those rules govern as rules of the Western Classification, they do not govern to such an extent as to make that Western Classification a shifting and unsettled classification. (Reading):

"No rule or rules governing said Western Classification providing for any change, modifications, or additions to the classifications mentioned in this distance tariff shall have any application hereto." The other rules do have application under this distance tariff.

EARL: Then your idea is to make the Western Classification a part of this amendment, save and except the rules referred to on lines twenty-six to twenty-nine, making it a rigid classification?

GESFORD: If I understand you, simply referring to the Western Classification as to fixed rates specified—rates provided for in the California Distance Tariff. Now, you don't have to make, as I understand it, the Western Classification part of the Constitution; you simply refer to it as explanatory of your classification. The distance tariff, instead of enumerating under Classification One, certain articles embodied in it, simply refers to Classification One as the class mentioned in the Western Classification, for brevity sake.

EARL: That is what I understand; for the sake of brevity; it is as if every commodity in the Class One, to which you refer, was set forth in the classification as Class One.

GESFORD: Yes; if you please. I do not think it is any more a part of the Constitution than the Bible would be if you refer to a passage—than the whole Bible would be.

EARL: But the portion you refer to would become part——

GESFORD: It would be for the sole purpose of explaining and stating this portion. Class One, for instance, simply explains the articles in the Western Classification, taking that class. I wish we could get them all there; I don't care how it would look, I wish we could get them there; but the State Printing Office now is an extravagant concern; that is what they say.

EARL: Then, Senator, in that same idea, the proviso which you put in there, saving the adopting of rules in the classification regarding any change, modifications, additions, etc., it is intended, is it not, that the other rules and conditions of the Western Classification set out in this Western Classification back here should have effect——

GESFORD: Should have the effect to govern the distance tariff; yes, sir.

EARL: The committee would like to hear from you on the main proposition, if we may go back to sections one and two of this proposed amendment. If you would like to be heard on the proposition as to the abrogation of the Railroad Commission—as to the necessity for it; as to the wisdom of it.

GESFORD: Mr. Chairman, and Gentlemen of the Committee—That, it seems to me, that is a conclusion that nearly every one not directly interested, has arrived at—in favor of abrogating that Railroad Commission. It is a notorious fact that the Railroad Commission of this State, as organized and existing under the Constitution, has been a failure; that is notorious. The present Railroad Commission—and I do not know one gentleman, and I am only speaking of them now as Railroad Commissioners, am not acquainted with any one of them—but if it is true what is said of them in the public press, and among reputable people of this State, if it is true what is said of them, I do not want to be acquainted with them. The Railroad Commission of this State has done nothing to lighten the burdens of the producers and people; there is a crying demand for the abrogation of that Railroad Commission. Great political parties have taken hold of the matter; county political conventions have taken hold of the matter. There has been a crying demand for the abrogation of that Commission because it has been proven a failure. Railroad Commissions in other States seem to have proven a success. I understand that in most States, where Railroad Commissions are in operation, they have proven successful, but for some reason or other best known to the Railroad Commission itself, it is a failure to-day in California. And while it is true that there is some objection on the part of many citizens to relegating again to the Legislature the power to fix freights and fares, I believe, with the limitation provided by this amendment, that we will have an improvement on the administration of this power, and get a better system, a better schedule of freights and fares. Now, of course, I do not suppose this committee wants to go into the question as to whether the Railroad Commission, as at present organized and existing, performs its duty.

SEAWELL: The scope of this constitutional amendment is, the people shall fix the maximum—the representatives of the people shall fix the freights and fares.

GESFORD: That is the purpose exactly. That is the proposition in a nutshell; in other words, taking it out of the hands of three men to control this matter, and let the Legislature control it, within these limitations.

EARL: And it is the wisdom of the move—dispensing with the question of what the Railroad Commission is or may have been in California—it is this question I would like to hear in regard to, and I think I voice the sentiment of most of the committee; is it wise to cast back into the Legislature the regulation of the transportation companies?

GESFORD: Mr. Chairman, and Gentlemen of the Committee—That, I think—I think providing a maximum rate as we do in this, it is perfectly safe to do, to place it back into the hands of the Legislature. I do not believe that the difficulties will arise that are arising in the present method of the business of freights and fares. I would not be in favor of relegating this matter to the Legislature without provision as to maximum rates. I believe there ought to be some limitation; that is about all there is to be said on the proposition, unless you want to go into the question as to whether the Railroad Commission shall be abolished because the three Railroad Commissioners do not do their duty.

EARL: The idea I have in mind is this, making it more specific and particular: Is the comparative wisdom between the scheme as herein proposed, the abrogation of the Railroad Commission and fixing maximum rates, etc., between that and the service of a Commission to regulate the transportation companies; and my thought lies along the line, that theoretically, the subject is one so intricate, the subject of rate making for transportation companies, that theoretically, at least, the service of several men sitting for a term of years could more intelligently act than one hundred and twenty men sitting for any length of time. It is along that line of discussion that I, for one, as a member of this committee, would like to hear arguments on the comparative wisdom of the Commission fixing and regulating rates, etc., and the method that is proposed in this amendment of placing the matter back into the hands of the Legislature, that is generally composed of new members, not sitting continuously, and therefore uninformed in any of the technical matters; for instance, if there was a Commission of three men of experience and wisdom—not being personal, say Mr. Leeds—three such men—would it not be more successful in this matter than the Legislature of one hundred and twenty men? That is the thought I have in mind.

GESFORD: I would say, Mr. Chairman, that if you could find three men possessing the information necessary, not to be controlled by any outside influence, they might be able to fix a schedule of freights and passenger rates that would be just and equitable, and give satisfaction to the people even under the existing law. That fixes a maximum beyond which the Legislature cannot go. Heretofore, of course, the Legislature has been charged with having been corrupted by use of money in fixing of rates. Now the rates will be fixed by the Constitution; they are fixed by the Constitution until the Legislature fixes some other rates. If the railroad people want any different rates, the burden is on them; it will be a good deal harder for the railroad companies, if they are so disposed, to corrupt the Legislature, where the burden is on them to obtain legislation. Under this maximum rate, they must obtain legislation. In other words, if the rates fixed under the Constitution are not satisfactory, the burden is on them to ask for a higher rate.

EARL: Could they ask—they could not, of course, ask for any higher rate than 3 cents per mile?

GESFORD: Supposing the Legislature fixed the rate at 2½ cents per mile, then the railroad wanting a change would have to ask for relief.

SEAWELL: But it is fixed now; they must change it. If we incorporate this in the Constitution, they are authorized to change it under the provisions of this constitutional amendment—the rates enacted in this schedule; now, to change those rates, it will require affirmative legislation on the part of the Legislature, and if they are too low—if the Legislature goes too low, then the railroad company, if an injustice were done them, would be required to come in and say to the Legislature: "You are limited by the Constitution to a certain amount, but we ask you to increase the rates on this classification."

EARL: That would be seeking relief, provided the Legislature cut the rate down. I would like to ask further—passing the matter as to the wisdom of the acts of the Legislature—now, speaking specifically, the Southern Pacific, a corporation, as it is generally understood to be, is the lessee of lines operating several roads in this State—how many I do not know, but suppose five, six, seven, eight, ten—the Central Pacific, Southern Pacific, Western Pacific, Northern Railway, running to Berkeley, and others. Now, that system of roads is operated as a system, as it is designated, and will come under the sweep of the proposition as suggested here:

(Reading:)

"Railroads shall be considered independently in computing distances; except, however, that a system of railroads consisting of leased, operated, or independent roads, controlled under a common management, although working under different charters, shall be considered and treated as one road, and the distance shall be computed over the shortest operated line composed of two or more of said roads."

Now, suppose for a moment, that the Southern Pacific should disincorporate and cease to operate these roads under its management, and diverse corporations, which are lessors under this system now—suppose they should operate independently and go in and lease to some other and smaller roads, or the gross earnings of these different roads making up the general system should be less than $4,000 per mile; if they should operate independently, on a smaller system, your idea is they would not go under this regulation of Section 36; the maximum rates herein prescribed would not apply to them if they acted independently, and their rates fall under $4,000 per mile, gross earnings?

GESFORD: Of course not.

EARL: Suppose that on operating those lines, I presume some of them are now earning less than $4,000 per mile, yet under this proposition here prescribed, they come within the maximum rates fixed here, because they belong to a system. I do not know as to the stockholders, but suppose that the stock is controlled by a number of individuals, who control most of the stock in the several corporations; would not this operate in a measure on the stockholders of these individual corporations? A road not obtaining $4,000 per mile, yet coming under this rate, whereas, roads which are not paying four thousand per mile, and are not part of the Southern Pacific system, would be able to charge a larger rate. Is it not injustice to the stockholders in the combined system, for their road to come within the sweep of this amendment; is it not an injustice; does it not deter them leasing the road, for instance?

Gesford: I do not think so. If I understand you correctly, there is a system of roads, and that system earns less than $4,000 per mile; of course the Legislature fixes a different rate.

Earl: The stockholders in a particular corporation that might be leased to a common management, would not receive as much on their investment as a corporation which does not lease and operates independently, and does not come under the maximum rate.

Gesford: Yes.

Earl: And yet some roads might be built and operated—running, say through fertile districts, and having, for instance, say like the Yreka road—being complete practically in itself, might be able to operate independently, and gain larger returns from an investment, than a road running, for instance, in the San Joaquin Valley, costing as much per mile, and which, in order to operate at all, must lease itself to some other and larger company, and by this provision being put in here, the rate of profit for this investment to the San Joaquin Valley road would be less than that for the Yreka road.

Gesford: Yes, it might; but I don't see that we can help that.

Earl: Mr. Leeds, will you give the committee a resumé of the figures you gave the other night? Senator Seawell is here to-night.

Leeds: I don't know whether I can give them in the exact order as I gave them the other evening. One statement which I made the other night was that the earnings of the roads within the State of California, including the entire system of the Southern Pacific Company, were $9,021 per mile; that covers three thousand four hundred and ninety-eight miles of road; that the interest on bonded debt paid by the Pacific System upon some of that was $8,675,587 42. I have since learned that the capitalization on that three thousand four hundred and ninety-eight miles of road—their funded debt—is $144,494,500, or $41,305 per mile; the capital stock of same would be $165,311,300, or $47,-255 50 per mile, and an aggregate capitalization for the two, funded debt and bonded issues, of $88,560 50 per mile. Taking the entire Pacific System, if you please, now, the rate per ton per mile—giving this backwards, however——

Earl: Meaning by the entire Pacific System, from El Paso and Portland to San Francisco, and from Ogden, also——

Leeds: Yes; the rate per ton per mile on through freight was 1.119 cents; on local freight, 2.699 cents, and on all freight, 1.835 cents; that the local freight is two and a half times more than, or 226.6 per cent of the rate charged on the through. The average haul on through freight was 906 miles on each ton, and on local, 101½; the aggregate on all, 206 miles. The rate per ton per mile on the Atchison, Topeka, and Santa Fe road, on all its tonnage, is 1.219 cents. The difference between them is .616 of a cent, or a little over .6 of a cent per ton per mile, between the two. The average train on the Pacific System of the Southern Pacific Company is 124.63 tons; the Atchison, Topeka, and Santa Fe. 118.84. The difference is 5.79 in favor of the Southern Pacific. They consume fifty-six pounds of coal to haul this one hundred and twenty-four and a fraction tons, as against the Atchison's one hundred and eight pounds in carrying 118.84 tons. The cost to the Southern Pacific, as reported, is $5 79 per ton; the Atchison, $2 41—per mile run by their locomotives per ton of coal. I will say in explanation that this amount of coal per mile run for locomotives includes, I believe, all coal consumed by both companies. The miles of run per ton of coal on the Atchison is 26.12, and by the Southern Pacific, 29.74, indicating that notwithstanding they use less coal, they make better mileage with a ton of coal than roads east of the Rocky Mountains.

The percentage of gross earnings to operating expenses on the Southern Pacific is 59 per cent.

Earl: The what? I don't exactly understand. A. The percentage of gross earnings used in operation on the Southern Pacific is 59 per cent; on the Atchison 69.19 per cent. Following are some of the gross earnings on different parts of the Southern Pacific on traffic in California: Southern Pacific of California, gross earnings, $9,279,822 50, or $6,611 54 per mile; they use 58½ per cent in operations. South Pacific Coast earn $1,107,772 87, or $10,631 56 per mile; they use 64.55 per cent in operation. California Pacific earned $1,528,047 72, or $13,242 79 per mile; they use 50.31 per cent in operation. The earnings of the Pacific system, 4,625 miles, is $8,002 18 per mile, of which they use 59 per cent. The Atchison earnings, $5,114 57 per mile, of which they use 69.19 per cent. The percentage of empty cars and loaded on the Southern Pacific (Pacific System) was 24.79; the Atchison, 28.32. The coal on the Southern Pacific, according to their report, cost them 8.9 per cent of their gross earnings; on the Atchison, 7.8 per cent. I think that is about all the figures I gave the other night. Now, I want to say a word in reference to a question you asked Mr. Gesford a few minutes ago. I am not an attorney, but I have made some observation of your law here in regard to the Railroad Commission. It has been a notable fact, at least so far as I am connected with it, ever since the Railroad Commission has been in existence, that all rulings they made, whether favorable or unfavorable to the railroad company, were put in effect under written protest, claiming that this Commission had no authority to regulate the rates and fares, indicating, I should think, that if anything were done that was considered undesirable the constitutionality of the proposition would be tested, and, judging from what has taken place in Texas, it would appear that you have relegated all the power you have in the State to fix rates and fares, to three men who are supposed to have the power, or rather the authority, but not the power to enforce what they may propose. And whether this proposition were put in effect or not. if the law, as it stands to-day, is effective, it strikes me it should be tested and something put in effect, if it is not, which will reach the case.

Earl: You refer to the fact that by the terms of the present Constitution, regarding the powers of the Railroad Commission, that the rates which they fix are not prima facie, but presumed to be just and reasonable? A. It would be necessary to go into the Courts to enforce that.

EARL: The Courts have the power, whether coming through the Legislature or Commission, or any other governmental agency, to fix rates, with this proviso and limitation, that the rates fixed must be reasonable. I believe that was the statement you gave at the last session of the committee, was it not? A. Yes; but the Commission do not act, and seem to be powerless.

EARL: I was referring to the Constitution. What they fix is presumed to be reasonable and just; their acts—the reasonableness of their acts—is not reviewable in the Courts. It seems to me the intent of the framers of that organic law was to give absolute power to the Commission. That was the theory under which the organic law was framed. By judicial interpretation since then the power to fix rates has a limitation placed on it, the limitation being that the rates are and must be reasonable and just to the carrier. Now, so far as our Constitution is concerned, that feature of the Constitution giving power to the Commission, undoubtedly its form, so far as the absolute conveying of the power is concerned, I think is recognized; and I understand you stated the other evening that the rates fixed must be just and reasonable, otherwise they could be annulled by the Courts.

LEEDS: That is very true. In a decision recently I think the Court made use of this language, that: "Whether the rates prescribed were reasonable or not they were still subject to the sanction of the Court."

EARL: This is a question of reasonableness. The Railroad Commission, under the organic law of this State, can get out a writ of mandamus, or a writ of injunction, as they have a mind to, enforcing the application—or compliance, rather—to the schedule of rates they may prescribe, and if they fix the rates at given figures, say two cents per mile, and the carriers decline to conform, they would get out a writ of mandamus against the carrier; and, in order to prevent the rates becoming effective or operative, the railroad would have to go into Court and show its injustice, otherwise the rates would apply. They have that power, Mr. Leeds. A. They may have the power, but do not seem to exercise it.

EARL: Yes, the power is lodged there. I was trying to ascertain your thoughts, so far as the power is concerned; you say they have the power, but no way of putting it into effect. A. It must go through the Court whether reasonable or not; they must secure the enforcement of what they do whether reasonable or not. Regarding the practicability and use of the Western Classification, which may be brought up if it is put in effect, say for two years, without any fluctuations, I will only say that, on staples, changes in the classification are seldom made. Articles, say taking fifth class, or Class A, which carry a great amount of tonnage, are not very frequently changed. And the changes which are made, are made more frequently to facilitate the interchange of business between lines which cover more largely less than carload shipments than carload business, and would have less effect, so far as the changes that may occur through the instrumentality of the Classification Committee, than might be expected from the number of them. And there is also this, that a large number of those changes are made on manufactured articles, the factors of which you have not here, and hence they would not very seriously interrupt the business of the State; the application of it would only be on business picked up at one point and laid down at another point in the State. Furthermore, this classification covers a very large territory. It has got a very large number of articles in it, perhaps, that seldom move in any one locality; there are something like fifty-two or fifty-three hundred articles in the classification. Perhaps 5 per cent of those articles would be 75 per cent of the tonnage that moves from one station in California to another, so that whatever changes might be made in that classification, would not likely materially disturb the situation in California if an inflexible application be made. It would not disturb the situation even if it were put in effect for two years without any changes. Besides, the hardships that might occur by reason of such changes, would be more likely to occur by reason of a reduction than by an advance. There is no proviso in the resolution that I know of that prevents a rate being made which would take care of any exigency that might arise. You have but seldom changed the classification here for many years past. The Board of Railroad Commissioners are given the full power to regulate this matter of rates of freight, and I don't believe any one can point to a time within the past two years that the Railroad Commission have made any revision of the classification, or, in fact, that they ever made any. Furthermore, the Western Classification is in effect in Southern California; it is also in effect in this portion of the State on interchange business by the Southern Pacific Company, and I do not see just exactly why it became necessary for them to put the Western Classification in Southern California, and when the road applies it on through business, or interchange business, in this part of the State, why it becomes necessary to hold in effect two separate local classifications in this part of the State, and why they have made no changes in them by reason of changes which may have been made in the Western Classification, provided the business might require it.

Earl: I would suggest, Mr. Leeds, that there is a competitive road down there that uses the Western Classification? A. But the Commission have the power, and they must have put it in effect down there; it certainly would not have gone into effect without their doing so; there is no power to make a rate in the State without that; they must have done it.

Earl: You understand from the language of the proposed section that the Legislature can change this classification? A. Certainly.

Earl (reading):

"The Legislature shall have the power and it shall be its duty to establish rates of charges for the transportation of passengers and freight by all railroads operated in this State."

Q. You would give them full power to fix the rates? A. I understand that gives full power to change in any way that was most expedient.

Seawell: You will notice there is a proviso.

Earl: The question is whether the Western Classification can be changed by the Legislature. If that power is given to the Legislature by this language of Section 36, can they fix the rates or revise the classification? There is a difference between this bill and the bill first proposed. The language is very obscure.

Gesford: They have the power. Providing they do not fix a higher rate than is reasonable, they may fix any rate they see fit.

EARL: They would have to change the classes in the Distance Tariff, as that is where the rate is ascertained.

LEEDS: Suppose they want to make a higher rate than on Class Third —a lower rate, rather—and that it shall be Class B.

EARL: Can they do it? A. Yes; why not?

EARL: Well, what roads, Mr. Leeds, in this State now would be affected by this amendment; in other words, those whose earnings are $4.000 a mile or over?

LEEDS: The Southern Pacific Company, California Southern, North Pacific Coast, and the San Francisco and North Pacific.

EARL: North Pacific Coast; the so-called Donahue road? A. Yes, sir; and also the Arcata and Mad River.

Q. That is a narrow gauge; and the Santa Cruz Road, that is part of the Southern Pacific system? A. Yes; I believe those are all.

Q. The Southern California is the Atchison branch? A. Yes; the Atlantic and Pacific is not in, but the Southern California would be. I also say further, that what is proposed is no experiment; that such a tariff is in effect in almost all States east of the Rocky Mountains, and there is nothing in this proposed here different than the basis applying to other Territories and States.

EARL: What, Mr. Leeds—referring to some information you afforded us last Monday evening—what basis is to be considered in fixing a rate which is just and reasonable; what elements?

LEEDS: I should say that the operating expenses, and a reasonable return on the investment of the property.

Q. Would bonded indebtedness—the interest on bonded indebtedness—be an element? A. If it were reasonable. I do not believe that the people ought to be called upon to stand between a purchaser of bonds and a dishonest capitalization of property.

Q. How can we arrive at cost, and the honesty or dishonesty of capitalization? A. There are plenty of men competent to tell what a road will be built for; that can be very closely demonstrated.

Q. What it has been built for, but not duplicated or can be duplicated for? A. I know of no good reason why a piece of property is worth more than it can be rebuilt for to-day.

Q. But it is the investment that should be considered? A. But should there be any discriminations between investments one for one and another for another; should you direct everybody in their investments, whether good or bad?

Q. It is different, however, with investments in which the public are interested. The State having the power, has laid down in the so-called Green cases—having the power to fix a rate, and by judicial determination held that this rate must be just and reasonable—that limitation being on the State to fix rates in any business like a carrier's business, or elevator, water companies, gas companies, etc., is it not inevitable that the cost of the investment itself must be considered; not, what in the course of time, by cheapening of material and labor, and perhaps other items, a duplicate would cost? A. Perhaps; we have been told in California, here, within a few months past, that the owners of this road have never received any return on the investment, and some were barely able to meet their funded debt obligation. I would like to ask if it is reasonable here—that there is any road in California—in the valleys especially—that ought to represent a capitalization of $163,073 per mile; that ought to represent a capitalization of—a bonded indebtedness of $59,126, and another $54,349, making an aggregate of $103,475; another one aggregating $58,434; another $110,576; another $41,435; and still another, $76,301 97? I do not know whether it would be reasonable to expect the public to put up for earnings on that kind of a proposition. I should think not. That represents three thousand, four hundred and ninety-eight miles of railroad, which you are expected to put up the necessary money to pay the interest on a capitalization amounting to $309,805,800, or $88,560 average per mile.

EARL: Bonded indebtedness? A. No, sir; that is the aggregate of it; the bonds amounts to $41,305. The aggregate of the capital stock is $47,255.

Q. In turning over some Interstate Commerce reports this afternoon, I find it laid down that the matters to be considered in fixing rates were the operating expenses, bonded debt, fixed charges, and dividend on the capital stock. A. Well, let us see if you are being fairly treated on that basis. The earnings per mile of road on this portion I have talked about is $9,021; taking the entire Pacific System it is $3.002. The earnings of the road in Oregon is $3,502 37; the earnings of the road in New Mexico and Arizona is $5,506 16; the earnings of the Central Pacific, for the entire system, is $12,224 76 per mile; the earnings of the South Pacific Coast (narrow gauge) road is $10.651 66; the California Pacific is $13,247 79 on 115.44 miles, indicating at least $10,000 a mile for all the roads inside the limits of the State of California.

Q. Leaving the Southern Pacific road out of consideration, Mr. Leeds, are those the elements that make up the basis upon which a rate is to be calculated? A. Do you want to know how I made up this tariff?

Q. I will arrive at that presently. Are those the elements entering into the calculation upon which a fair rate is ascertained; that is to say, the operating expenses, the interest on bonded debt, the fixed charges, and the dividend on capital stock? A. Well, I don't believe you ought to put in the dividend on capital stock here unless it costs something.

Q. Taking the matter theoretically, are those the elements? A. Theoretically, you would want to find out how much it costs to do business, and if you have anything left for a dividend on capital stock, make a dividend on that.

Q. The elements of debt—the interest on debt comes in? A. Well, the bonds are supposed to cover that, unless you have a floating debt, which you have to pay, of course.

Q. You were about to make some observation when I discussed the matter? A. I was. I made a good many comparisons of rates, charged in California, with those charged in other portions of our country east of the Rocky Mountains. I discovered that, on general merchandise, you were paying considerably more than 30 per cent higher rates, on actual tests as to the business done. On wheat, about 23 or 24 per cent; on other grain, 45 per cent. The tonnage here, taking the earnings of the roads and the rates, was greater on the roads in California per mile, than it was on the roads for which I made the comparison, from the fact that their gross earnings are a greater percentage over the road I made the comparison with, than 30 per cent, or any other per cent in the difference in the price charged. I then undertook to make a tariff which I believed would make an aggregate yield on the tonnage moved, as large as that accruing to the roads for which I made the comparison. These comparisons were made mostly with Kansas and Nebraska roads.

Q. Those roads were built since the Central Pacific and Southern Pacific railroads? A. Well, there was a good deal of the Southern Pacific road built about the same time as these roads were.

Q. The Atchison road you were speaking about was built more recently, was it not? A. Well, it was begun pretty early, and considerable of it built within four or five years of the time of the building of the Central Pacific.

Q. Have you any data that would give us a comparison between the cost? A. No, sir; I have not.

Q. If you have any further information to offer the committee, we would be very glad to have it. A. I believe I have not.

Statement of Mr. A. Burrows.

(Representing the Nevada County Narrow Gauge Railroad.)

Chairman Earl: The other evening there were some gentlemen here that wished to be heard, representing some short lines, saying that Thursday would be an improper time for them, or at least an inconvenient time. The committee is not desirous of holding a late session to-night, but will afford a few moments to any gentleman that desires to be heard and cannot be here at subsequent sittings of the committee.

Mr. Burrows: I believe I am the party referred to. I am here in the interest of the Nevada County Narrow Gauge Railroad. I don't want to impose on the committee by having the session taken up. If I could understand that this committee could meet at any convenient time subsequent to Thursday night—say Friday night, or some night after to-morrow—I would try to be here.

Senator Seawell: I belong to six or eight committees, and cannot meet with all of them. I will meet here to-morrow night. Cannot you come before the committee to-morrow night?

Burrows: No, sir. I have a motion before one of the Courts in San Francisco at that time, and must be there. I cannot get back here in time; but if the committee can tell me how much time they can afford me——

Seawell: About how long do you desire; about half an hour? A. Oh, about twenty minutes. I do not think I will be more than twenty or thirty minutes.

Seawell: Oh, well, if that is all, we will hear you to-night.

Mr. Burrows: Gentlemen of the Committee—As I stated, I represent a little line way up in the mountains, known as the Nevada County Narrow Gauge Railroad. It runs from the station at Colfax, on the Central Pacific Railroad, to the town of Nevada City, a distance of twenty-two and one half miles. The proposed amendment to the Constitution that is here before you, though from their report technically we are not included, as a matter of fact I will show you that we are included with those longer lines; the receipts of the road being not exactly $4,000 per mile, but thirty-nine hundred and a fraction, leaving us no margin whatever for an increase which we have a right to hope and expect in the future; so that we are placed in the predicament, that if our traffic should increase our receipts would diminish. That is the position we are placed in, and that is one proof of the fact that there is something very clumsy about this proposed amendment to the Constitution, when such an extraordinary result will take place under those circumstances. The distance, as I have stated, is twenty-two and a half miles. It is a narrow gauge railroad, winding around the mountains, in and out, here and there, with very little local traffic, except what comes from the two towns of Grass Valley, with six thousand inhabitants, and Nevada City, with five thousand inhabitants; being originally built more for a wood road than for anything else, yet being a matter of vast accommodation to that portion of the country, which in the winter months, if it were not for that road, you might say would be almost shut out from civilization, because the ordinary wagon roads are almost impassable. The cost of that road was $625,000; it has a bonded indebtedness of $260,000, paying interest at the rate of 8 per cent per month.

EARL: You mean per year. A. Oh, yes, per year; that is what I meant. In reaching those points it crosses five trestles from thirty to one hundred feet high, one of which is seven hundred feet long. Wooden trestles require a vast amount of yearly repair to keep them in condition so that they will be sufficiently safe for travel. The average cost for repairing bridges, etc., for the past year, and several years past, is $3,000. The average cost of keeping up the road for several years past has been $15,000. The average receipts for the years 1890, 1891, and 1892, averages about $88,000, in round numbers. Those receipts for 1880, Mr. Chairman, amounted to $115,000. The shrinkage that has occurred between 1880 and the present time amounts to $38,500, or thereabouts, yearly, caused by the stoppage of hydraulic mining, which has decreased both the freight traffic, and also the passenger traffic. This shrinkage in the past ten or twelve years is about 20 per cent. This road has paid dividends up to 1880, which have paid the stockholders $21,000. Since then it has paid no dividends whatever, except an amount to which I will refer in a few moments, but it is not worth while to take into consideration. It is very nominal. The decrease in population in Nevada County during that period was 20 per cent, which, of course, has had the effect upon the road of decreasing the revenue from $21,000 to $17,000. The interest on those bonds is $21,000 per year, and taxes $3,000. The operating expenses amount to $63,000. It expends annually in construction, improvement, etc., the sum of $3,000, so that for the past year or two the profits of the road, that is to say after taking out all the expenses, amount to less than $500 per annum. Its net income has been less than $500 for several years.

EARL: That is, per annum? A. Yes, sir; per annum.

Now, as I said before, this road is placed, not in the same class with the longer roads, yet the margin is so small that any increase whatever will cause it to be placed in that category, and subject to the provisions as herein set forth. We feel we are like the man who has a cord around his neck, who, when asked if it is pretty tight, says: "I can stand that." "Do you think you can stand another knot?" "No, I am afraid it will choke." The effect of the existence of that amendment to the Constitution will necessarily be—I don't think I need dwell particularly upon that fact to you—would necessarily be to pull that rope. Our present rate for both freights and fares is high, as compared with other roads, but not high as compared with the income of the road and the expenses of running the same. A franchise granted in 1874 called for this:

"It shall be lawful for the parties aforesaid, and their assigns, to charge and receive a sum not to exceed 10 cents per mile for each passenger, and 20 cents per mile for each ton of freight per mile, transported on said road."

It also contains:

"If it shall appear upon the annual statements made by the road that the net revenue arising from the earnings exceeds 12 per cent per annum, it shall be proper for the Board of Supervisors to adjust the fares and freights, and fix such rates as will realize a net revenue equal to but not to exceed 12 per cent per annum."

In order to exist it has got to charge the maximum rates, and a decrease in any of those rates would render the road bankrupt; because, running as it exists to-day, why it is just barely able to live, and the effect of this proposed amendment to the Constitution would be to practically bankrupt the road—wipe it out of existence. As I said before, it seems to be a very strange state of affairs, that an amendment to the Constitution should have the effect that a small increase of traffic to the road would place it under the influence of such an iron rule as would practically destroy its existence. Now, I don't know much about railroads or about the minutiæ concerning the running of this road or any other road. The President of the road is here; also the Secretary, with all the official papers and all the data, who will explain to the committee, if necessary, under oath, to bear out the statements I have thus given to you in brief. I have here a little bit fuller report of the road and its income for the year 1890. The gross earnings for that year were $87,259; operating expenses, $74,049; construction expenses for that year, $1,494; interest on bonded debt, $20,601 47; interest on floating debt, $311; total, $96,455 47.

The par value of the stock is $100 per share, and it is at present quoted in the market, where you can get anybody to buy it, at $10 per share; so the road, as it exists to-day, is not a source of profit to its stockholders, but it is a source of vast convenience to us, living way out in the backwoods, and its destruction or bankruptcy would be regarded as a calamity in many a home. I want to say, with your permission, a few words in relation to the general principles of that proposed amendment to the Constitution. From what the Chairman has already said, I know that you, Mr. Chairman, and no doubt the rest of the committee, are entirely familiar with the more recent decisions of the Supreme Court of the United States in relation to matters of this kind, notably that one which is contained in the 134th U. S., wherein Justice Lamar—who has just died—filed a dissenting opinion, claiming that the Supreme Court, or a majority of that body, had almost entirely destroyed the effect of the Granger cases, as well as that of other similar cases. I do not know but that Justice Lamar, who was a most profound constitutional lawer, was about right, that effect of the so-called Granger cases, and other cases of the same character, in which it was held and maintained that a State had almost absolute right and control of corporations, and to fix fares and freights, was so modified that the force of those decisions had been knocked out of them.

I will read a little bit from some portions of it:

In 134th United States, in the case of *Chicago, Milwaukee, and St. Paul Railway Company* vs. *Minnesota:*

In fixing fares and freights, the Legislature declared in the organization of the Railroad Commission that they should have absolute right, and that the fairness of those fares and freights fixed by the Commission should be conclusively presumed, was not to be attacked or capable of being attacked in any Court; in other words, they wanted to shut out the Commission from any judicial investigation, and the Court says, in reviewing a number of cases, page 455:

"In *Stone* vs. *Farmers' Loan and Trust Company*, 116 U. S. 307, 325, the whole subject is fully considered. The authorities are cited and the conclusion is arrived at, that the right of a State reasonably to limit the amount of charges by a railroad company for the transportation of persons and property within its jurisdiction cannot be granted away by its Legislature, unless by words of positive grant or words equivalent in law; and that a statute which grants to a railroad company the right 'from time to time to fix, regulate, and receive, and tolls and charges by them to be received for transportation,' does not deprive the State of its power, within the limits of its general authority as controlled by the Constitution of the United States, to act upon the reasonableness of the tolls and charges so fixed and regulated. But after reaching this conclusion, the Court said (page 331): 'From what has thus far been said, it is not to be inferred that this power of limitation or regulation is itself without limit. This power to regulate is not a power to destroy, and limitation is not the equivalent of confiscation. Under pretense of regulating fares and freights, the State cannot require a railroad corporation to carry persons or property without reward; neither can it do that which in law amounts to a taking of private property for public use without just compensation, or without due process of law.' There being, therefore, no contract or chartered right in the railroad company which can prevent the Legislature from regulating in some form the charges of the company for transportation, the question is whether the form adopted in the present case is valid."

It says, "This power to regulate is not a power to destroy," and it would amount to destruction to this little road.

Gesford: If I understood you, your road does not pay $4,000 per mile, does it? A. I say it is on the margin; it is so close to the margin that the effect of any improvement—if there was any improvement—the effect of it would be to place it in that class.

Gesford: Do you charge 10 cents per mile? A. Yes, sir.

Seawell: Well, you could not get along then at three and haul the traffic? A. Not for a great distance, sir.

Earl: You were quoting from Justice Lamar's opinion there; you were, were you not, and concurred in by the Court? A. Yes, sir. I will now read from the "American Encyclopædia of Law," page 914:

"*Charter Provisions Relating to Freight as Contracts.*

"Where a carrier's charter contains a provision that the company may establish such rates of fare and freight, or such rates as do not exceed a certain maximum, the question arises: 'Does the grant of such a privilege constitute a contract, leaving to the carrier the adjustment of charges unrestrained by other limitations than that they shall be either reasonable or within the maximum?' Although there has been some conflict of opinion, the question must be answered in the negative. The common law rule that the carrier's charges shall be reasonable, would in any event be read into a charter. The grant of a right to fix reasonable charges does not carry with it the power to declare what shall be deemed reasonable; such a privilege belongs to that class of powers the grant of which can only be made in express terms, every presumption being against it. (Case of *Ruggles* vs. *Illinois*, 108 U. S., page 526.)

Ruggles vs. *Illinois*, 108 U. S. 526: "An amendment was made to the charter of a railroad company in Illinois, 'providing that the said company shall have power to make, ordain, and establish all such by-laws, rules, and regulations as may be deemed expedient and necessary to fulfill the purposes, and carry into effect the provisions of this Act, and for the well ordering, regulating, and securing the affairs, business, and interest of the company; *provided*, that the same be not repugnant to the Constitution and laws of the United States, or repugnant to this Act, the Board of Directors shall have power to establish such rates of toll for the conveyance of persons or property upon the same, as they shall from time to time by their by-laws determine, and to levy and collect the same for the use of the same company.' *Held*, That inasmuch as the power to establish rates was to be exercised through by-laws, and the power to make by-laws was restricted to such as should not be repugnant (among other things) to the laws of the State, the amendment did not release the company from restrictions for the amount of rates contained in general and special statutes of the State.

"The Court observes that there is nothing which even in the remotest degree indicates that a by-law fixing rates is to be of a different character from those regulating the other business of the company. When, therefore, in a section of the charter which expressly declares that no by-law shall be made that is in conflict with the laws of the State, we find that the rates of charge to be levied and collected for the conveyance of persons and property are to be regulated by by-laws, the conclusion is irresistible that only such charges can be collected as are allowed by the laws of the State. This implies that in the absence of direct legislation on the subject, the power of the Directors over the rates is subject only to the common law limitation of reasonableness; or, in the absence of the statute or other appropriate indications of the legislative will, the common law forms part of the laws of the State, to which the corporate by-laws must conform. But since, in the absence of some restraining contract, the State may establish a maximum of rates to be charged by railroad companies for the transportation of persons and property, it follows that when the maximum is so established, the rates fixed by the Directors must conform to its requirements; otherwise, by-laws would be repugnant to the laws."

Chief Justice Waite, in deciding one of the cases, has stated:

"Under pretense of regulating fares and freights, the State cannot require a railroad corporation to carry persons or property without reward; neither can it do that which, in law, amounts to the taking of private property for public use without just compensation, or without due process of law. What effect this would have we need not now say."

If it was evident from the franchise that the State "did not desire, or decline, or was unwilling," from which it could be clearly inferred that the State did not desire, or had surrendered its right to control the fares and freights of corporations, then, as a matter of fact, such result can be obtained, I take it for granted, from reading the franchise in this case, Mr. Chairman—the franchise granted to the Nevada County Narrow Gauge Railroad. There is a fixed maximum stated in all the Granger cases, and language of this character was used:

"The Board of Trustees, etc., of the corporation shall have full right to fix such charges which to them may seem reasonable," using that word.

Under that provision, and similar language, it was held that the State could not be said, by the exercise of that franchise, to have abandoned their right to interpose and fix what those reasonable rates were.

Under the charter granted to this little road, the language occurs which, I think, complies with what Chief Justice Waite has said, and must be fair. The State, in granting this franchise, had surrendered the right to control fares and freight by the language of the franchise of this little road.

This road is allowed to charge 20 cents per ton per mile. I claim that is a contract. I know it is regarded as a chestnut to say that a franchise can bind the State. I say it is regarded as a chestnut to say that there can be anything like a contract between the State and a corporation by their franchise. I claim any one who will carefully read the recent decisions of the Supreme Court of the United States, in connection with the Granger cases, and other similar cases, will see that it has been held fairly that, where the language of a franchise is such as shows that the State intended thereby to abandon its right to fix fares and freights, it amounts to a contract; that in this sense, in the case here at bar, in the case of the franchise of the Nevada County Narrow Gauge Railroad, our franchise is set above the amendment of the State by its Legislature or Constitution. See the effect of putting into a Constitution an amendment of the character proposed here. Here you have a Constitution which attempts to fix the fares and freights; somebody objects to it; it finds its way into the Court. Well, the Court decides that they are unfair, unreasonable; and the people of the State, the authorities, and the Constitution must succumb to that decision, and there is one hole knocked in the Constitution. Another railroad company takes up the question at a subsequent time, and the Court declares in this case the rates are unreasonable and unfair. It gets into Court and gets a judicial determination. There is another hole knocked in the Constitution. And so on, one railroad company after another makes successful attacks upon that provision of the Constitution until you have a State Constitution, or at least a provision in it, as full of holes as a milk strainer. And the result of it is that you do not know where you are standing. I claim such a Constitution of that kind would be a disgrace to the State, and I stand upon that assertion.

I refer you to case of *Munn* vs. *Illinois*, 94 U. S., page 113, and to other cases.

Railroad companies are carriers for hire. They are incorporated as such and given extraordinary powers in order that they may the better serve the people in that capacity. They are, therefore, engaged in a public employment affecting the public interest. And in the decision of *Munn* vs. *Illinois*, page 113, subject to legislative control as to their rates of fare and freight, unless protected by their charters.

So far as the Nevada County Narrow Gauge Railroad is concerned, the State has absolutely stated that they may fix the charge at 20 cents per ton per mile, whether reasonable or not. No such provision is in the Granger cases which permits the State afterwards to intervene and take a hand. If there had been any intention of that kind in our case, it would have been easy to have said so. I can say conclusively that there was no such intention. Now, there is a number of authorities here I intended to quote, but which the lateness of the hour prevents my doing. I claim, so far as this railroad is concerned, under its franchise, no one can say what rates it shall charge, or what it should receive. I say it is unfair to have the people of this State, either by Legislature or any provision in this Constitution, interfere with the fares and freights of that railroad. I will say that we insist as a rule, which applies to all railroads, which I suppose will go without saying, or at least among lawyers, as the reason the State has no right to impose any unreasonable fares and freights, if any commission or State undertakes to do so, that the remedy may be obtained by judicial proceedings.

SEAWELL: Don't you think the corporate State provision of the Constitution would affect all franchises hereafter granted; would it not? Would it affect railroads the language of whose franchises do not fix maximum rates? A. It would affect railroads where similar language is used as passed upon in the Court in the case of *Munn* vs. *Chicago*, where reasonable rates were left to be fixed subsequently.

SEAWELL: Well, you say the State has no right to interfere with you; that your franchise is above the State? A. Well, a party may set up as many defenses as he wants, whether he has any or not.

Q. I do not see that even if it was incorporated in the Constitution, according to your idea, this would affect you. I do not see that you are interested in any way, are you? A. I contend we should not be. The Attorney-General may not think so by and by. The Attorney-General of the State may see fit to put us to a vast amount of expense. We may have to go to the Supreme Court of the United States. We may have to go through the Supreme Court of the United States to have our rights sustained; we cannot afford to let the matter rest.

In relation to the general question, the gentleman here who supported this proposed amendment, from Napa, has asked whether or not this bill is constitutional. As I have already stated, and I think he will agree with me in stating, this bill is a clumsy affair, to say the least. It is a very clumsy thing to incorporate into a Constitution. It is very clumsy to incorporate some matter which has to be explained by referring to private records; to the records of a traffic association, which are only private records. It would appear to be a very absurd matter to place in the Constitution—to place in the Constitution a thing which must be explained by referring to the private books of some banker or some mercantile corporation. I say it has no precedent to put a matter into the Constitution of that kind, the force and effect of which must be discovered by rummaging into the private books of some association. Now, as to the effect—as to whether it is constitutional, or not. As I have already stated, it is constitutional, and it is not constitutional. It affects to give control by this bill to fix the matter of fares and freights without any regard to the reasonableness of the same. It provides for no records whatever, and any judicial tribunal will discover it to be arbitrary—for the people can be arbitrary, too, just as well as the Commission can be arbitrary. The history of the world shows that from the earliest times up to the present, the people frequently, not only in moments of frenzy, as was illustrated in the events of the French Revolution, but also in their calmer moments can be unjust.

I claim where provision is inserted in the Constitution, which provides for bad judicial methods, upon which the fairness or unfairness of the plan therein set forth can be determined by test, it seems to be otherwise than feasible.

One word more I will say in conclusion. There is a decision, Mr. Chairman, you will find here in this volume of American and English Encyclopædia, wherein it is held that it is no excuse for unfairness for a schedule compelling a railroad to carry freight and passengers over a certain point at a loss, to say that they can make it up because the balance of the road would pay. There is a decision here, from the Supreme Court of the United States, in reference to that, the substance of which is, that in order that fares and freights should be reasonable, the amount fixed for charges between any two points should be reasonable, regarding those two points as a link between two other portions of the road.

Now, there is a portion of the road which we have to travel over to get up to the mountains; we have to pass from Rocklin to Colfax, and from Colfax still further to Truckee and the State line, over a portion of the Central Pacific road. I am not here as the attorney of the Central Pacific road, at the same time it is important to us as a connection between that portion of the mountains and the valley. I claim and know well enough from the traffic that goes over that portion of the road, and the running expenses of it, there must be a very small amount of profit in that portion of the road—for that portion of the Central Pacific. The profits of that portion of the road must be exceedingly small, as I know well enough from the traffic, which is very small. I claim, so far as those mountain portions of the road are concerned, that it is inequitable and unfair, under the Supreme Court decisions of the United States, to compel them to carry freight and passengers over that portion of the road at the same rates as over the valley portion, because it is a very expensive portion of the road, the operating expense being much larger than the balance of the road. I think that is an important matter and a matter that cannot be overlooked.

Earl: Do you think this State regulates a rate on any through freight? Would it be within the powers of the State to do that? A. No, sir; I claim that it would not. My idea is, this applies to rates of freight between any two stations within the State; that the rates must be fair and reasonable as between those two stations, regardless of the fact that the balance of the road pays; therefore, I do not think that you can start right in, and provide fares and freights by the constitutional amendment proposed here, or by anything of the kind. I will say, as a citizen, that the only trouble I can see with the present Railroad Commission is, they are too lazy; they do not earn their salary, sometimes. In some States, there is a Commission appointed by the Governor, which is removable at the pleasure of the Executive. Perhaps the best thing that could be done with the present Commission would be to provide for a Commission of that kind.

In New York, Delaware, and elsewhere, they have found the safest method for the people is to have a strong Executive, and to allow the Executive of the State or the Mayor of the city to have a large exercise of power in appointments. I do not know whether the people of California are ready for such an idea as that or not; but I, for one, believe in that doctrine, though it may seem to be undemocratic and unrepublican, but the history of each of the States, and the history of political government of this country, goes to show a prompt and better administration is frequently obtained by extending the power of the Executive in the matter of appointments, etc., giving him unreserved power of appointment.

Earl: The receipts of your road have fallen off the past years, have they not? A. In 1880, the receipts were $115,000. Those were boom times of hydraulic mining. Now they are $88,000.

Q. Then there is hardly any probability of striking the limit named in the amendment? A. It may, sir; it is now $3,900.

Seawell: It would strike the 10 cent rate pretty hard, then.

Burrows: The indications are business will revive, and it will strike the $4,000 limit.

Earl: If there is any scheme revived? A. If hydraulic mining is revived, within five years thereafter the receipts would run up from $88,000 to within $100,000, and be then above the $4,000 limit. We do not want to have this shadow resting on us all the time. It is not fair to start right in under a shadow such as this one. When you attempt to increase the business, if you attempt to develop your trade or improve, the effect will be hari-kari suicide. We have great hopes of our industries; there are thousands of fruit trees which have been planted out on the hillsides which are not yet in bearing, but from which the road expects great results by and by. Within two or three years we expect a large product from those trees. I will say then, further, we have very strong hopes that within a few years our income will be increased to such an extent, perhaps, that we may be able to pay a dividend, which we cannot do now.

Thursday Evening, January 26, 1893.

Mr. Earl: At the point of adjournment last evening, the Nevada County Narrow Gauge road had concluded its argument. I don't know whether Mr. Kidder has anything further to add to that or not.

Kidder: Mr. Chairman, I have something further to add to the remarks of my attorney, but there are several representatives here at this meeting this evening who wish to get away. Mr. Martin has a list of the roads in order in which they will appear, and I am willing to stand aside for the roads anxious to get away.

Earl: The Yreka road; is that represented?

Mr. H. P. Gillis.

Representing the Yreka road, addressed the committee as follows:

Mr. Chairman, and Gentlemen of the Committee—I have been selected by Mr. Churchill and the other members of our Board of Directors to present what little we have to say to-night. I am here to represent in part one of the smallest roads in this State, one of the shortest roads; in the way of wealth a poor one, probably the weakest road in the State of California. We did not particularly desire to build this road, Mr. Chairman; it was rather built under protest than otherwise. We were so situated that on coming up there the Southern Pacific Railroad would pass about eight miles to the east of us. Surveys were made, but after several conferences with the Southern Pacific officials it was not thought practicable to pass through our town, and that leaves us about eight miles off the line of the main road. The place where the Southern Pacific proposed to build a depot was not pleasant, so the people of Yreka got together (Yreka being a town of between 1,500 and 1,800 people) and concluded to make an effort to build a road themselves, calling on the best of the community to devote their business capacity to further the enterprise, not for the purpose of money speculation, but to save the homes of those villagers from coming down about their ears, to prevent the enterprising members of the village from moving away to other places for homes. With that end in view, they selected as one of the Board of Directors one of the attorneys of Yreka, and the others were the best business men of the town. The company was organized and right of way secured, and the road built, with the assistance of the townspeople, who contributed about $50,000 in cash, and going in debt about $50,000 more. The Board of Directors has served from the organization of the corporation to the present time, and notwithstanding we have had some complications, we have never paid $250 for attorney's fees from that date to this. The Board of Directors has contributed its services, and from the commencement it has been a great expense to them. Those are the circumstances under which the road was built. None of my people have ever appeared before the Legislature before, but this bill compelled them to come here; that if it was passed it would cause our engine and car houses to become empty and deserted barracks; it would destroy the property, and to a large extent destroy the homes that the property was built to save, for by the bill it was found that for passenger rates they were allowed but 2 cents per mile, and with the consent of the Legislature, 3 cents, while at the present time they are charging 8 cents. For freight rates the bill would allow but 3½, 4, and 4½ cents, while at present they were charging 7½ cents. And with these rates of charges, and this service on the part of the Directors and managers, the road never paid a dollar, and they never expected it would; it was only with the utmost effort they could pay expenses.

Notwithstanding my road was not included in the class earning $4,000 gross earnings per annum, we still object to the bill as it stands at present. If the bill should become a law, giving the Legislature power to fix rates of freights and fares, bills would be constantly coming requiring the presence of some of our Directors here all the time to look out for their interests; there would necessarily be many complaints from both railroads and others in regard to rates; changes, alterations, and modifications would constantly be requested. We are not able to send a representative here, and keep watching the affair all the time, to see that our interests are not sacrificed. I also object to the bill because I consider that the bill, if it should become part of the fundamental law, would deal with a subject of this character as it should not be dealt with. The honorable Senator who introduced the bill, and whose name is appended to it, in speaking to the committee said he would hesitate before he would chance a bill of this character, without placing in that bill a limit beyond which the Legislature could not go. I ask that the matter be most carefully considered; that the members were not here as representatives of the railroad companies, but of the people of the State of California, whose sworn duty it was to look out for their interests. And if the author of the bill is unwilling to chance the bill without fixing in the constitutional amendment a clause beyond which they cannot go, I ask a most careful consideration of the proposition. While they cannot make them go beyond 3 cents for hauling passengers, they may make them haul for 1 cent. In other words, there should be a saving clause for the railroad companies, as well as for the people of the State. I consider the cost of construction should be taken into account in basing the rates for freights and fares, but the bill merely classifies into two classes, those earning gross over $4,000 per annum, and those earning less, making no provision for the costly operations of roads having streams to cross which overflow in winter, others having heavy mountain grades, but classifying all alike, whether valley or mountain roads, taking only the gross earnings into consideration. I submit for the consideration of the committee, whether or not this Act becomes a law, I desire to say for my own railroad company, that in my humble judgment it would be unfortunate for the railroads of the State, and also for the Legislature of the State, which latter for years has professedly been trying to keep the railroads out of politics, and now they not only invite but absolutely command the railroad companies within the State to come forward and hold sessions biennially. It would inject the unhappy state of affairs in regard to our political machinery of bringing back with all the unfortunate circumstances surrounding it not only one railroad, but all the fertile railroads within the State, and necessarily forcing and keeping them there. The matter would be better conducted by a Commission who would fairly and conscientiously perform their duties; better by a Commission of three, five, or smaller number. who have a special knowledge of the subject, much better than by one hundred and twenty men coming together biennially and only having sixty days to perform the duties. I consider, with all the complications thrown around the business of freights and fares, it is a good deal more than it could do in sixty days so as to stand the test of two years following. With my own road, while the smallest in the State, and least complicated interested of all roads in the State, the Board of Directors meet every month. In their monthly meetings they take into consideration, certainly every few months, the rates and fares, and there was no time yet they did not make some alterations, modifications, or changes of the rates of freights and fares; they were absolutely required to make changes every few months. How would it be possible for the Legislature, with all the complicated ramifications of all these vast roads, to enter into the duties and perform them as well as they should be done? The above I respectfully submit to the consideration of the committee.

BURKE: What is the length of your road?

GILLIS: A little short of eight miles.

Q. What is the gross earnings? A. Gross receipts per mile, $1,600.

STATEMENT OF D. A. BENDER.

(Representing the Carson and Colorado Railroad.)

MR. CHAIRMAN: I ask the indulgence of the committee in this: that the brief statement I will make was prepared before the present amendment eliminating the short roads was offered, and that I have not had the time to revise my statement accordingly.

The Carson and Colorado Railway Company, an incorporation of the State of California, operates a line of narrow gauge railroad starting from its connecting point on the Virginia and Truckee Railroad, in the State of Nevada, to the town of Keeler, on Owens Lake, in Inyo County, California, a distance of two hundred and ninety-three miles, to which point it was built in 1883—one hundred and eighty-five miles of the line being in Nevada, and one hundred and eight miles in California.

This railroad property was bonded at the rate of $15,000 for each mile of road constructed, equal to $4,380,000 in bonds for the two hundred and ninety-three miles, same bearing 6 per cent per annum interest, making an interest charge to be earned in addition to the earnings required for operating and taxes, of $262,800 per year.

The company during the past ten years has been able to earn a small surplus above the amount required for expenses of operation and taxes, but not enough to make much of an impression on the amount necessary to meet the annual interest charge of $262,800, for it found itself on July 1st last behind in unpaid interest coupons due to the bondholders, something in the neighborhood of a million and a half of dollars.

The steadily increasing sum of unpaid and unearned interest finally became such a "specter" as to call for relief, and in August last the property was deeded to a new incorporation, under an arrangement with the stockholders and bondholders whereby they surrendered their bonds and shares of stock in amount $4,380,000 each for $2,000,000 in bonds bearing but 4 per cent per annum interest, and running for a period of fifty years—thus reducing the annual interest from $262,800 to $80,000, a difference of $182,800. When this action was taken it was confidently expected that the new company would be able to earn annually this low interest charge of $80,000 per year; less, by the way, than 2 per cent per annum on the actual cost of the property; but its expectations have proved to be—from the decreased traffic enjoyed—again most disappointing, as its earnings for the past twelve months, ending December 31st last, have been but $45,000 in excess of the amount required and paid for operating expenses and taxes—but little more than 1 per cent per annum interest on the original cost of construction and equipment.

Let us now see what this company does for the State and county governments to which it is compelled to contribute support in the shape of taxes. Last year—1892—its gross earnings were about $210,000—but about $700 per mile of road operated. Operating expenses, $137,000, about 65 per cent. Taxes, $28,028, or about 83 per cent, altogether, of the earnings for operating and taxes. Here we find 13⅓ per cent of the gross earnings of this railroad paid to the State and county governments of Nevada and California for taxes.

A passenger rate of 2 cents per mile is proposed by the bill before this committee, which, if enacted, would be a reduction of about 4 cents per mile, our rate now being an average of about 6 cents per mile. The reduced freight rates also proposed by this measure would give us in some of the principal commodities we now carry a rate of 6 cents per hundred pounds, where we now charge and receive 25 cents per hundred pounds. Now, it can be readily understood that we could not, under such ridiculously low rates, carry passengers and freight except at a positive loss.

It is proposed to place all roads in the State under the exactions of this law, regardless of the cost of construction and operating of the different roads.

This is manifestly unjust, and discriminates with great severity against such lines, which, by reason of their distance from tidewater, and their great cost of construction, cannot be operated as cheaply as roads running mainly through the level and populous valleys of the State.

As an illustration: The Carson and Colorado Railroad paid to the Southern Pacific Railroad Company, and the Virginia and Truckee Railroad Company, its connection roads, in the neighborhood of $200,000, freight charges on the material, rails, ties, locomotives, etc., used in its construction. Is it not apparent that this and other additional cost items of construction of its railroad, over other railroads affected by this bill, should be considered in the application of lower freights and passenger rates, and that failure to consider such items, forming part of the cost of construction, is discrimination of the most pronounced type?

Who calls for the rates proposed to be put in force on this railroad line? Has any citizen or taxpayer in Mono and Inyo Counties, through which the road runs, appeared before this Legislature, and complained that the rates of fare and freight we charge and collect are greater than what is reasonable? Has any patron of the company made known anywhere the fact that he is not satisfied with its prevailing rates? None.

It may be said that the bill before us affects only the local traffic in the State of California. To this we say that such local traffic is an important factor in our revenue, as the line in California through the fertile Owens Valley gives us the best local business we have on the entire line.

Note.—Average freight rate on through and local freight business for year ending June 31, 1892, .0520 per ton per mile. Average cost, not including taxes, per ton per mile, .0360.

Passenger Traffic.—Average rate per mile per passenger, .0546; average cost per mile per passenger is more than what was received.

Since preparing the above matter, I find that the amendment now before this committee does not affect the Carson and Colorado Railway Company in its present condition. Notwithstanding, it does affect its future prospects.

The builders of this property, all of whom are either residents or heavy taxpayers of the State of California, certainly anticipated, when they invested their own personal funds in its construction, that its earnings would reach $4,000 or more per mile. The Virginia and Truckee Railroad, with which it connects (and whose owners control in a measure the Carson and Colorado), for the year ending June 30th last, earned in the neighborhood of $10,000 per mile, hence it could have been no stretch of the imagination to have anticipated that the per mile earnings of the Carson and Colorado would reach, say 50 per cent of the per mile earnings of the Virginia and Truckee. And further, we do not now believe that it will be possible for the Carson and Colorado Company ever to earn the sum per mile which will place it within the restrictions of this proposed amendment.

I have already shown you that the operating expenses of our company for the past twelve months reached 83 per cent of its gross earnings, and it is probable that this percentage would not go much below 75 per cent (the bulk of our freight being mineral products, handled at minimum rates), in the event of our per mile earnings reaching $4,000 per annum, which would give us say $1,000 per mile net earnings. Now I claim, Mr. Chairman, that this sum would not compensate the owners of the property for their investment, as the property has been operated long enough to require a considerable portion of said net earnings for depreciation—arising from the wearing out of its rails and equipment—no charge having ever been made against such depreciation since commencing operations in 1883.

Hoping, and ever anticipating, as we do, that the future will yet bring us reasonable returns for our investment, we object to the amendment before the committee as "handicapping," if I may use the word, our efforts to secure and create greater traffic, knowing that if we should succeed, our apparent success really would result in disaster.

Our people have in contemplation the extension of its line to a connection with the trunk lines of railroad now running and to be run to Southern California, whenever it appears to them that such extension would be a good business proposition; but I can assure this committee that they will not, in my judgment, entertain the matter of additional investment for such extension, should the amendment proposed be accomplished.

Thanking you for your attention, I will be glad to answer any questions the committee desires to ask.

Mr. Earl: Is there any one present representing the Colusa and Lake Railroad?

Statement of Mr. E. W. Jones.

Mr. Jones: We have here this evening the Superintendent of our railroad, and I rather expected he would address the committee. It is the first instance on record where his modesty overpowered him. I certainly thought he would open the ball at any rate. Not being an attorney, and our company not being able to afford the luxury of one, we shall not attempt to make any great argument, but leave that entirely to the gentlemen on the committee. We believe they are better able to judge as to matters of that sort, having several prominent attorneys on the committee.

I will proceed in as concise and few words as I can to give you a business-like statement of the conditions of our road, and leave you to judge whether or not we can operate under the provisions of this constitutional amendment, as proposed. Like the gentleman who preceded me, or opened the argument this evening, I might say our road was also built more from necessity than choice, and at least one of the members of your committee is probably aware of that fact—I refer to Senator Hart. He probably is familiar with the organization and construction of our road.

In 1885, the general line of the Northern Railroad having been surveyed, the road, if built, would pass our place, leaving us some ten miles off the line of the road, and it became necessary that we should have railroad communication with the outside world. For this reason we organized a company of business men and farmers along the line of our road, each taking stock to the extent of his ability. Many of our stockholders are men of limited means—not capitalists—and not men who want to operate the road at a loss, even if they were able to do so. We constructed our road at a time when the materials which enter into the construction of a road were very cheap. We bought our rails at a low price; I believe we paid $35 per ton in New York. We paid $10 freight from New York to San Francisco by way of the Isthmus, and $15 over the Sunset route—about as cheap freight as any railroad ever had the advantage of. We contracted for grading, and trestle, and other work at the lowest possible prices; I believe the highest price we paid for any grading on our road was 12½ cents per cubic foot, which was certainly very low, taking into consideration that on some portions of the road there was considerable rock work and blasting to be done. Our road cost us in the neighborhood of $200,000. It extends a distance of twenty-three miles. The Board of Directors of that railroad have served up to this time without one cent compensation; no officer has a salary, with the exception of the Superintendent, who receives $1,200, and the Secretary, who receives $180 per annum. We pay our engineers from $60 to $90 per month. Conductors receive $60, and all of our train men in the same proportion. I do not think there is a railroad in the State that is run as economically as the Colusa and Lake Railroad.

And yet, with all these things in our favor, and our road costing us less than $10,000 per mile, and with its bonded indebtedness of about $3,000 per mile, we have never yet been able to pay a cent in dividends. The stock of the railroad to-day, if sold at all, would not bring 20 cents on the dollar. In fact, that was about the price the last stock was sold at. At the present time, and from the time the road has been in operation, we have been charging 8 cents per mile for passengers, and from 5 to 10 cents per mile for merchandise, according to the classification, on the different classes of merchandise hauled over the road.

Now, gentlemen, if with that sort of showing and that cost of road we cannot pay a dividend, and but little more than our operating expenses, I would like to have the committee tell me what we are going to do if you reduce fares to 2 cents and freight to the basis proposed in this constitutional amendment. We would simply have to lock up our railroad and stop running, or turn the road over to the bondholders for the $70,000 that we owe. The net income from the road, after paying interest on bonds, was $6,500, and that was the best year we have had since the road was running. This would amount to a little less than 3½ per cent interest on the capital invested. Certainly the committee will bear me out in the assertion that this is as reasonable a rate of profit as any rate. It has been said that this amendment which is proposed—the provision being 2 or 3 cents per mile to railroads earning more than $4,000 per mile—would not affect a road of our standing; but as I understand, the original bill is still before this committee; it never has been withdrawn. We are not aware and do not know what bill this committee will report, and it is proper and in order for us to argue on that basis. It is liable to fix rates at 2 cents per mile.

GESFORD: With the permission of the gentleman—the idea was, if it was not stated in specific terms, to consider the other bill as withdrawn; this was proposed as a substitute for that bill, or that resolution. The proposed substitute would provide for 3 cents instead of 2 cents; this bill is proposed in lieu of that bill. That is the idea, that the other bill is withdrawn.

EARL: I understand the Senate has referred to this committee the consideration of original Bill No. 8, called "Constitutional Amendment Bill No. 8;" that at the hearing Monday night, you also, at that time, prepared what you designated as "Committee Substitute." In case we desire to act favorably on a bill that we can refer that one back, if we see fit to adopt. It may be the desire of the committee to report back the original.

GESFORD: Yes, but I understand the committee have reported back the substitute to the Senate; so it was passed to print and referred to the committee.*

EARL: Yes, but the original.

GESFORD: But the proponents of this bill, do not insist on the original bill, but of course the committee have that within their discretion. The proponents, however, do not insist on the original bill as proposed at all.

JONES: Even with that understanding of the bill, the railroad at the present time might possibly be enumerated under the 2 or 3 cent provision. But it is not the intention of the incorporators and the gentlemen who are operating our railroad to let it stand where it now is. There is a large amount of business we are reaching out for in the valleys and timber lands, and we hope to bring in settlers. Add to this, the fact that our own town of Colusa, has planted something like five thousand acres of orchard—those trees are just beginning to bear, and of course we expect to receive a large amount of traffic from that.

EARL: Your gross earnings are how much?

JONES: $1,200 per mile. Add to this the extension of our road, which we are liable to make at any time, and the constant development of the country along our line, and you can very readily see we might before very long come in that class, and probably be in that same situation that the Nevada County Narrow Gauge is; in other words, if we increase our traffic, we get less revenue. I believe that the Constitution of the United States guarantees to every citizen life, liberty, and the pursuit of happiness. Now so far as life and liberty are concerned, it might be that a corporation, after a constitutional amendment like that under consideration became a law, might still live; but if any one thinks he will have any happiness in running a railroad at 2 or 3 cents a mile, he had just better get in and try it; I think he will find he is sadly mistaken. I presume our road may be one that Mr. Leeds characterizes as a "bad investment." We might have made a bad investment; but if we made a bad investment we don't want it all taken away from us. We are fighting for our lives.

If there are any questions your committee would like to ask and wish answered, I shall be pleased to do so.

Statement of J. M. Fulton.

(Representing the Nevada-California-Oregon Railway.)

Mr. Fulton: I represent the Nevada-California-Oregon road, an association of individuals of which Mr. E. Gest is Custodian and Manager. We hear a good deal about the "dear people," and people working for the "dear people," but I think I can give the committee a little illustration of what this is, in fact. In 1884, the proposition was looked over by the firm that now own the Nevada-California-Oregon Railway, as to building into Lassen County, and Modoc County, and Lake County, Oregon. They were without means or any way to market anything that could be produced in a good agricultural and stock-raising country. The laws of the State of California were looked into as regards the maximum rates permitted to be charged for freights and fares. The situation was taken in as any good business man would naturally look it over, and our people outside of the State, doing business in the State of New York, concluded to make an investment and build a railroad in the State of California, starting from Reno, Nevada, and traveling in a northwesterly direction to the Nevada State line; going thence about four miles to the summit of the Sierra Nevada Mountains at Beckwith Pass, and northerly fifty-two miles in the State of California into Honey Lake Valley, to a point known as Amadee. The actual amount of investment in the construction of the road to this stage exceeds $1,000,000. There is no stock or bonds. The road does not owe a dollar. It is not incorporated. The expenditure to this date, as I said before, exceeds $1,000,000. The road has never paid its owners a penny. Our expenditures for the calendar year 1892, were $110,423 10. Our income from all sources was $74,463 82. For betterments there was used $10,590, showing a loss in operating the road of $25,369 28. We have experimented on the proposition of giving the people a very low rate, trying to develop the country, and see if we could not get returns in that way instead of charging a higher rate. The maximum rate, as allowed by law, as we found in 1884, is 10 cents a mile for passengers, and 15 cents a ton a mile for freight in the State of California, upon which we based the making of the investment, but this rate has never been used.

Our passenger rates have never been 7 cents a mile, and our freight rates have never been 10 cents a mile, on any article. Our passengers between all stations for the calendar year 1892 were seven thousand seven hundred and ninety-five; average number per train, twelve. If Mr. Leeds were here he would bear me out in the proposition, that it would not have cost any more to haul fifty than it does twelve. The average distance each passenger was carried was sixty-one miles.

The receipts from each passenger were $2 67. The receipts per mile from each passenger were 4 cents. The total number of tons of freight of all classes was fourteen thousand five hundred and eighty-eight; the average tons in each train, twenty-three—a very light load for an engine, but you have got to go. The average distance hauled one ton was sixty miles. The receipts from each ton of freight were $3 16; per ton per mile, 5 cents. We find that the portion of the road that was constructed in 1884, 1885, and 1886 shows signs of decay; our bridges are costing a great deal of expense, and our ties are about gone. In maintaining this year we have met with the heaviest expense we have in any previous years. The ties rot. Mr. Leeds seems to doubt that. He thought, with the climate we have here—he thought we did not have snow or any of the elements to contend with, which they did in Kansas —that it was very much cheaper to operate a road here. We get five or six or seven feet of snow on the level in parts of Lassen County, near the summit of the Sierra Nevada Mountains. We spent, in the hard winter of three years ago, $8,000 to haul $500 worth of hay to the starving cattle of Lassen County, in trying to open the road from the snows. We did not do this for the cattle. I am not making any such assertion as that; but in trying to operate the road and haul business that might be offered; but we have had no winter business to speak of in the past years. It would have been a business proposition for us to have closed the road in the month of November, and let all engines stand in the roundhouse until the month of April; but as people had settled on the line of the road because the railroad was there, we felt if the road was worth having at all, it was worth operating through the entire year. I spoke of the decay that constantly takes place on the road. Our fences rot just as fast, and go just as fast if we run one train each way a day, or one train a week, as the road that runs one hundred. The storms come and do us the same damage. Our banks wash away and our ties rot, and in many other respects these expenses connected with a railroad are the same, whether the trains are many or few.

You have the right of way to take care of, which is the same whether trains are many or few. We might cheapen our service. We might hire cheap men—incompetent men to run the trains, as they did in Wisconsin and Minnesota. I was there at the time there was a pressure of economy brought about by adverse legislation, that caused the property of the Milwaukee and St. Paul Railroad to run down, to the detriment not alone of the stockholders of the different lines, but the people as well. We had a survey made and estimates carefully prepared, ascertaining the price of steel rails, which the entire line is laid of, as we thought of extending the road into Modoc County, California, which I believe is the best undeveloped country in the United States. I believe it is the best undeveloped country. Our folks did not build the road for charitable purposes, but with the hope, and they have been running it with the hope that, with the proper development of the country, it would be a splendid piece of property. Our income last year, for the thirty miles, was $74,000. If we were to build into Modoc County and extend the line one hundred miles, that county would develop and make homes for so many people that our earnings would very soon be $4,000 a mile.

It would not be profitable for us to make it $4,000 a mile, and if we did make it $4,000 a mile, and if we were so disposed, we could cover it up from getting out, as Mr. Leeds might do it. We are brought up in the face and eyes of the fact that this proposed amendment, which Mr. Leeds has found a gentleman, representing the State of California, to introduce, will take from us the little we have now got, by bringing our good money from another State and investing it in California. Mr. Leeds said here Monday evening he could not get the data necessary to state what was right in regard to the smaller roads in the State of California. Mr. Chairman, and the gentleman who introduced this bill, you well know, and Mr. Leeds knows, that each and every one of us has a sworn statement on file with the Railroad Commissioners of the State of California, which is open for inspection by any one. His assertion that he could not get the data from which to find what would be just, is not sound. A bill or amendment to the Constitution, taking away the right to make a reasonable interest on an investment, after paying ordinary expenses, is dangerous; it is discouraging to capital; it will not bring capital to the State; it will make the capital get out of it as soon as possible. I will say right here for our road, and it can be distinctly and absolutely and plainly understood, that it is a fact that we would not extend the road one mile, nor spend one dollar, while this class of legislation continues, under no circumstances. On the contrary, we will part at a great loss with what we have and gladly withdraw. I never saw Mr. Leeds; I never met the gentleman. I had read of him a great deal, and he was great in the newspapers, but when I came here and heard him talk and make his assertions in regard to railroads, claiming to be an expert, I was much disappointed. The statement he made in regard to the consumption of fuel in the State of California, being very much less than it is in the Eastern States, is not at all sound. I do not understand it, but I would be pleased to argue the subject with him. He said, as a matter of economy that could be exercised by the Southern Pacific Company—a bright idea advanced by him was, that they could lessen their operating expenses by taking the old ties, after they were rotted and worn out, and use them for fence posts. We are a narrow gauge road; the ties are only five feet long, and I want the gentlemen now assembled in the Legislature to know, when the time comes to canvass this bill under consideration, that the ties are surely not long enough for fence posts. We cannot take rotten ties and make any particular use of them. I do not know anything else that I need detain the committee with; if there are any questions, I am ready.

Mr. Fulton: I want to speak of the expense of constructing railroads in California. Steel rail, free on board cars in the East, cost $29. The last rails we purchased for the construction of our road, in San Francisco, cost $55. We have found that the Pacific Rolling Mills people, or the people we buy from in San Francisco—many of them members of the Traffic Association, and becoming well posted on the proposition of freight rates—quote us the Eastern price with freight added from Eastern countries to San Francisco. When it is necessary for us to buy materials for the construction of our roads, we find the prices prevailing in San Francisco are the Eastern prices with freight added, or "all the commodity will bear." By the amendment to the Constitution proposed—we do not like to take the medicine; but taking lumber, shingles, laths, etc., for a distance of fifty miles, the present tariff is 12½ cents per one hundred; by the amendment, 5 cents. Flour, wheat, etc., 24 cents at present; by the tariff in the amendment, 6 cents. That is the justice of the amendment. It was intended that Mr. Leeds, with his $10,000 a year, intended to do justice to the railroads of California. Barley, rye, oats, etc., present 20 cents; by the amendment, 5 cents. Bricks, sand, etc., present, 10 cents; by the amendment, 4 cents. Our first-class rate for one hundred pounds for fifty miles is 40 cents; by the amendment, 27 cents.

Mr. Dolbere here arose and asked: "Does this bill include all roads using rails and locomotives?"

Chairman Earl: I cannot say; you must judge.

Mr. Dolbere: There are forty or fifty roads that have steel rails and haul goods. Some unincorporated, and some are common carriers.

Mr. Earl: Do you mean the logging roads?

Mr. Dolbere: Yes, sir; our firm is the half owner of one. Can't the author of the bill tell us if we are taken in?

[Mr. Dolbere was told that he must judge of that. The committee was not there to reply, but to hear.]

Mr. Kidder: Yes, sir; and there is the Towle Bros'. road, twenty miles long. It carries freight. Bring it in and cinch it too.

Mr. Earl: Mr. Dolbere, do you refer to the Mad River road?

Mr. Dolbere: No, sir; to a Eureka road, and to others, two of which I am interested in.

The Committee here adjourned until Tuesday evening.

Statement of K. H. Wade.

(Representing Southern California Railway.)

To the honorable Chairman and Gentlemen of Senate Committee on Corporations:

Gentlemen: Representing the interests of the Southern California Railway—Santa Fe route—I respectfully ask your consideration of the following points bearing on the proposed constitutional amendment relating to "freights and fares:"

We believe the construction and operation of railway lines is a matter of mutual benefit for the owners as well as the general public, and that persons who have invested in such property are entitled to the same consideration and protection as if their capital was invested in other enterprises; we therefore trust your honorable body will decline to entertain the proposed amendment, and respectfully call your attention to some of the important facts herewith stated.

The owners of this Southern California Railway Company have invested over ten millions of money in its construction and operation, and have just begun to receive a portion of the interest on fixed expense in return; they have received no benefits from subsidies or land grants, which could be utilized for the benefit of this company; the rates of interest, State, county, school, and irrigation taxes, have been higher than in the Eastern States.

The population in the six southern counties is not over six persons per square mile; in Kansas it is thirty-eight, while in Illinois it is sixty-seven. The proportion of this territory available for cultivation in Southern California is not over one third of the total area, while in Kansas and Illinois at least 90 per cent of the entire country can be tilled to advantage.

The construction of these lines of railway was undertaken under many difficulties, and the promotors are certainly entitled to protection. The roads were difficult to build and costly to maintain; the percentage of heavy grades and sharp curves are double that of any line in Illinois or Kansas. The future requirements for additional facilities and equipment will require large expenditures, the same as any other industry, and this expense must be met by increased earnings.

The maintenance of railways in this territory is much more expensive than in Illinois or Kansas. Repairs on account of floods and washouts will average $100,000 per year, and will continue to be a great expense for many years. Most of our line requires ballasting, the soil being of such a nature that in wet seasons the road becomes almost impassable; some fifty miles have already been treated in this manner at an average expense of $1,500 per mile, and the entire road must be ballasted before the track can be maintained economically. Modern equipment must be added at heavy expense from time to time as business interests require; this is specially the case as regards the fruit and vegetable traffic to the East. The operation of our railway shows largely increased cost over those in Kansas or Illinois. Fuel is one of the largest items.

The Wabash road in Illinois shows cost of fuel, 4 cents per ton per mile; Atchison, Topeka, and Santa Fe road, as a system, most of their lines being in Kansas, cost 7 cents; Atlantic and Pacific, 8 cents; Southern California Railway, 24 cents. As compared with Illinois roads, increased expense on Southern California Railway equals 20 per cent of gross receipts, or, in round numbers, amounts to $1,000 per day; general labor expense is, at least, 30 per cent greater than in Illinois. The comparisons with Kansas would show about 25 per cent, or $750 per day, increased cost for fuel in Southern California, and 25 per cent more for labor. In the matter of traffic, our records show: In Kansas, average distance freight hauled was two hundred and thirty-seven miles; on Southern California Railway, ninety-one miles. Distance passengers hauled: Kansas, sixty-eight and eight tenths miles; Southern California Railway, thirty-five and six tenths miles. The Wabash Railroad, in Illinois, loads each day an average of one car per mile of road; Southern California Railway averages one car to each five miles of road.

The rates proposed, as we understand them, would in many cases bring the rates below actual cost for performing the service. Our result for the past year shows as follows: Average revenue, all freight traffic, 2.71 per ton per mile; average cost, all freight traffic, 1.67 per ton per mile. Cost does not include extraordinary expense of improvements, additional facilities, new equipment, handling company freight, such as coal, ties, timber, etc., which would amount on an average to 50 cents per ton on the year's business, leaving only .0054 per ton per mile to apply on interest and other fixed charges. Average revenue, all passenger traffic, .02672 per mile; average cost, all passenger traffic, .02615 per mile, showing apparent net of .0057 per mile. The same conditions exist regarding extraordinary expenses, in the freight traffic

The proposed rate is 23½ per cent less than Kansas rate for our average haul of ninety miles, and also averages less than Illinois.

Expense for protection against fires and claims to be settled on this account is no small item. Expense in holding trains down the heavy grades should be considered, as well as the extra power required to haul trains up the grades. The average train load in freight service in Southern California is not over three hundred tons, while in Illinois or Kansas the same power would haul at least six hundred tons. I speak of the Wabash road from the fact that I was engaged with that company for twenty-five years in various capacities, from operator to General Superintendent, and only state what I know to be facts. We have no complaints regarding rates in Southern California, to my knowledge, and believe existing conditions are satisfactory. I attach copies of comparative statement as between existing tariffs and the amendment proposed, and trust you may realize the equity of our claims for largely increased rates over those enjoyed by the thickly settled States in the East.

As the volume of business increases, and competing lines develop new country, we must expect to reduce rates. The Santa Fe system has carried the Atlantic and Pacific line for years at an annual loss of over $1,000,000 per year, trusting in the future development of this country, and believe they have a legitimate claim upon the kind consideration of your honorable body—and in view of the satisfactory relations existing between our company and its patrons in Southern California, we trust no action will be taken which would lessen our revenues, or prevent us from providing desirable facilities, and advancing the development of this territory. The Railway Commission in the State of Illinois, under which I operated for years, was put in effect under a law adopted in 1871, and has, I think, given the most general satisfaction, both to the public and to the railways, of any system which has come under my notice. All of which is respectfully submitted.

I will submit the following statements:

Comparison of Freight Rates as between Southern California Railway, Kansas and Illinois Distance Tariffs, and Proposed California Amendment.

Miles		Maximum	First	Second	Third	Fourth	Fifth	A.	B.	C.	D.	E.
5	So. Cal. Ry.	......	3	3	3	3	3	3	3	3	3	3
	Kansas	3¾	13	11	9	7	6	6	5	4	4	3
	Illinois	......	13.16	11.28	9.40	7.52	6.01	4.70	4.23	3.76	3.29	2.96
	Amendment	......	3¾	3¾	3¾	3¾	3	3	3	3	3	3
10	So. Cal. Ry.	......	7	7	7	7	7	7	7	7	7	5
	Kansas	7½	15	13	11	9	7	7	6	5	4	3
	Illinois	......	15.04	13.16	11.28	8.46	6.76	5.64	5.17	4.23	3.76	3.46
	Amendment	......	4½	4	4	4	3½	4	3½	3	3	3
15	So. Cal. Ry.	......	11	11	11	11	11	11	10	9	9	7
	Kansas	11¼	18	15	13	11	8	8	7	6	5	4
	Illinois	......	16.92	15.04	13.16	9.40	7.52	6.58	6.11	4.70	4.20	3.59
	Amendment	......	8	7	6	5	4	5	4	3½	3	3

Comparison of Freight Rates—Continued.

Miles		Maximum	First	Second	Third	Fourth	Fifth	A.	B.	C.	D.	E.
20	So. Cal. Ry.		15	15	15	15	15	15	12	11	11	8
	Kansas	15	20	17	15	13	9	9	8	7	5	4
	Illinois		18.80	16.92	14.10	10.34	8.27	7.05	6.58	5.17	4.23	3.81
	Amendment		12	10	9	7	5	6	5	4	3	3
30	So. Cal. Ry.		23	23	23	23	20	20	16	15	15	9
	Kansas	22½	24	21	19	15	11	11	9	8	6	4½
	Illinois		22.56	19.74	15.98	11.98	9.58	7.99	7.52	6.02	4.70	4.23
	Amendment		18	14	13	9	7	8	6½	5½	4½	3½
40	So. Cal. Ry.		30	30	30	30	26	26	20	18	18	12
	Kansas	30	28	25	21	19	13	18	10	8	6	5
	Illinois		26.32	21.62	17.86	13.16	10.52	8.93	8.46	6.58	5.08	4.57
	Amendment		22	18	16	13	8	9	7	6	5	3½
50	So. Cal. Ry.		38	38	36	35	35	35	26	23	23	15
	Kansas	37½	32	29	25	21	15	15	11	9	7	4.91
	Illinois		29.14	23.50	19.74	14.10	11.28	9.64	9.40	6.96	5.45	5½
	Amendment		25	20	18	15	10	11	8	7	6	4
60	So. Cal. Ry.		45	44	42	41	40	40	30	27	27	16
	Kansas	45	36	32	28	23	17	17	12	10	8	6
	Illinois		31.52	25.38	21.62	15.04	12.03	10.58	9.87	7.33	5.83	5.24
	Amendment		28	23	20	17	12	13	9	8	6	5
70	So. Cal. Ry.		53	51	49	47	46	46	34	31	31	17
	Kansas	52½	40	36	31	25	19	19	13	11	8	6½
	Illinois		32.90	27.26	23.03	15.98	12.78	11.05	10.34	7.71	6.16	5.55
	Amendment		32	25	22	18	13	14	10	9	7	5
90	So. Cal. Ry.		68	65	63	61	58	58	42	38	38	20
	Kansas	67½	48	42	36	29	25	23	15	13	9	7
	Illinois		36.66	30.08	24.34	17.86	14.28	11.98	11.09	8.46	6.77	6.09
	Amendment		38	30	26	21	16	18	13	10	8	6
100	So. Cal. Ry.		75	73	70	70	63	63	46	41	41	22
	Kansas	75	52	44	38	31	27	24	16	14	10	7½
	Illinois		38.54	31.02	24.90	18.80	15.04	12.45	11.47	8.84	7.05	6.34
	Amendment		40	32	28	22	17	19	14	11	8	7
120	So. Cal. Ry.		90	87	84	81	71	71	53	48	48	25
	Kansas	90	57	48	43	35	31	26	18	16	12	9
	Illinois		42.30	32.90	26.03	20.30	16.24	13.35	12.22	9.59	7.66	6.89
	Amendment		44	36	32	26	21	23	16	13	10	8
140	So. Cal. Ry.		105	102	98	90	78	78	58	52	52	30
	Kansas	105	61	52	47	39	34	28	20	18	12	10
	Illinois		44.18	34.78	27.16	21.80	17.44	14.10	12.88	10.34	8.22	7.41
	Amendment		48	39	34	28	23	25	18	14	11	8

ATCHISON, TOPEKA, AND SANTA FE RAILROAD COMPANY.

Locomotive Performance Statistics.

September, 1892.

Total miles run		2,309,909
Total miles run, exclusive of switch and work train		1,875,190
Total engines owned		834
Average number of engines on line (owned and rented)		738
Average miles run per engine		3,130
Average number of engines (owned and rented), less switch and work		531
Average miles run per engine		3,531
Average number engines (owned and rented), less switch, work, and No. in shop		465
Average miles run per engine		4,033
Cost per mile run—		
For stores	(cts.) 0.14	
For oil and waste	0.28	
For fuel—coal and wood	6.50	
For engineers and firemen	6.59	
For other attendants and help	1.40	
For repairs	4.73	
		19.64
Miles run to one ton of coal		24.63
Miles run to one pint of engine oil		30.88
Miles run to one pint of valve oil		50.01
Miles run to one pint of illuminating oil		48.84
Miles run to one pint of lubricating oil		19.09
Miles run to one pint of all kinds of oil		13.73
Miles run to one pound of waste		95.42
Tons of coal used, 93,802.600; rated at		$1 54
Cords of wood used, 2,221.14; rated at		$2 16
Total mileage of road		4,706.77

October, 1892.

Total miles run		2,391,942
Total miles run, exclusive of switch and work train		1,974,671
Total engines owned		834
Average number engines on line (owned and rented)		737
Average miles run per engine		3,246
Average number engines (owned and rented), less switch and work		593
Average miles run per engine		3,330
Average number engines (owned and rented), less switch, work, and No. in shop		481
Average miles run per engine		4,105
Cost per mile run—		
For stores	(cts.) 0.14	
For oil and waste	0.28	
For fuel—coal and wood	7.36	
For engineers and firemen	6.96	
For other attendants and help	1.49	
For repairs	4.19	
		21.02
Miles run to one ton of coal		22.83
Miles run to one pint of engine oil		32.84
Miles run to one pint of valve oil		53.05
Miles run to one pint of illuminating oil		44.69
Miles run to one pint of lubricating oil		20.28
Miles run to one pint of all kinds of oil		13.95
Miles run to one pound of waste		100.44
Tons of coal used, 104,784.800, rated at		$1 58
Cords of wood used, 3,334.12, rated at		$2 12
Total mileage of road		4,706.77

November, 1892.

Total miles run		2,312,940
Total miles run, exclusive of switch and work train		1,911,239
Total engines owned		834
Average number of engines on lines (owned and rented)		739
Average miles run per engine		3.130
Average number engines (owned and rented), less switch and work		603
Average miles run per engine		3,169
Average number engines (owned and rented), less switch, work, and No. in shop		498
Average miles run per engine		3,838
Cost per mile run—		
For stores	(cts.) 0.14	
For oil and waste	0.27	
For fuel—coal and wood	6.73	
For engineers and firemen	6.79	
For other attendants and help	1.50	
For repairs	4.91	
		20.34
Miles run to one ton of coal		22.92
Miles run to one pint of engine oil		35.22
Miles run to one pint of valve oil		54.52
Miles run to one pint of illuminating oil		38.74
Miles run to one pint of lubricating oil		21.40
Miles run to one pint of all kinds of oil		13.78
Miles run to one pound of waste		92.89
Tons of coal used, 100,921.1100, rated at		$1 48
Cords of wood used, 2,540.1, rated at		$2 07
Total mileage of road		4,706.77

ATLANTIC AND PACIFIC RAILROAD COMPANY

Locomotive Performance Statistics.

November, 1892.

Total miles run		337,418
Total miles run, exclusive of switch and work train		299,974
Total engines owned		95
Average number engines on line (owned and rented)		110
Average miles run per engine		3,067
Average number engines (owned and rented), less switch and work		100
Average miles run per engine		2,999
Average number engines (owned and rented), less switch, work, and No. in shops		68
Average miles run per engine		4,411
Cost per mile run—		
For stores	(cts.) 0.07	
For oil and waste	0.40	
For fuel—coal and wood	8.04	
For engineers and firemen	7.02	
For other attendants and help	1.78	
For repairs	7.42	
		24.73
Miles run to one ton of coal		18.54
Miles run to one pint of engine oil		23.74
Miles run to one pint of valve oil		43.54
Miles run to one pint of illuminating oil		39.03
Miles run to one pint of lubricating oil		15.59
Miles run to one pint of all kinds of oil		11.15
Miles run to one pound of waste		92.47
Tons of coal used, 18,200, rated at		$1 50
Cords of wood used, 152½, rated at		$1 38$\frac{3}{10}$
Total mileage of road		834

December, 1892.

Total miles run		297,700
Total miles run, exclusive of switch and work train		262,626
Total engines owned		95
Average number engines on line (owned and rented)		113
Average miles run per engine		2,633
Average number engines (owned and rented), less switch and work		103
Average miles run per engine		2,549
Average number engines (owned and rented), less switch, work, and No. in shops		69
Average miles run per engine		4,314
Cost per mile run—		
For stores	(cts.) 0.06	
For oil and waste	0.43	
For fuel—coal and wood	9.31	
For engineers and firemen	7.37	
For other attendants and help	1.94	
For repairs	8.65	
		27.76
Miles run to one ton of coal		16.27
Miles run to one pint of engine oil		20.81
Miles run to one pint of valve oil		42.29
Miles run to one pint of illuminating oil		31.38
Miles run to one pint of lubricating oil		13.95
Miles run to one pint of all kinds of oil		9.65
Miles run to one pound of waste		76.16
Tons of coal used, 18,298, rated at		$1 50
Cords of wood used, 397½, rated at		$0 66⅔
Total mileage of road		834

THE WABASH RAILROAD COMPANY.

PERFORMANCE OF ENGINES, MONTH OF SEPTEMBER, 1892, MIDDLE DIVISION.

Miles of road operated	159
Total number engines	715
Number making mileage	141 1/10
Average miles per engine	4,204.08

Engine Mileage.

Passenger	153,399
Freight	334,876
Switching	100,883
Working	4,038
Total miles run	593,196

Miles Run to—

One ton of coal	24.48
One pint lubricating oil	20.94
One pound waste	195.19

Cost per Engine per Mile, in Cents.

Repairs	2.99
Stores	.27
Fuel	3.80
Engineers' and firemen's wages	6.50
Dispatchers and cleaners	.87
Total cost per mile	14.43

Car Mileage.

Passenger	768.132
Freight—loaded	4,698,880
Freight—empty	2,265,678
Average passenger cars per mile	5.01
Average loaded freight cars per mile	18.18
Cost of one passenger car per mile	2.57
Cost of one loaded freight car per mile	0.88
Pounds of coal per car mile—passenger	12.53
Pounds of coal per car mile—freight	5.46
Cost of coal per ton	93.058
Average number of freight cars per mile (loaded and empty; five empty cars equal to three loaded)	20.80
Miles run to one ton of coal { Passenger	31.88
Miles run to one ton of coal { Freight	20.25
Miles run to one ton of coal { Switch work and other service	36.37

Performance of Engines, Month of October, 1892, Middle Division.

Miles of road operated	715
Total number of engines	161
Number making mileage	144.5
Average miles per engine	4,219.07

Engine Mileage.

Passenger	158,790
Freight	335,931
Switching	109,161
Working	5,774
Total miles run	609,656

Miles Run to—

One ton of coal	22.95
One pint of lubricating oil	20.22
One pound of waste	183.74

Cost per Engine per Mile, in Cents.

Repairs	3.23
Stores	.29
Fuel	3.99
Engineers' and firemen's wages	6.71
Dispatchers and cleaners	.89
Total cost per mile	15.11

Car Mileage.

Passenger	799,656
Freight—loaded	4,570,798
Freight—empty	2,188,258
Average passenger cars per mile	5.04
Average loaded freight cars per mile	17.51
Cost of one passenger car per mile	2.52
Cost of one loaded freight car per mile	1.00
Pounds of coal per car mile—passenger	13.76
Pounds of coal per car mile—freight	6.11
Cost of coal per ton	0.91.65
Average number of freight cars per mile (loaded and empty; five empty cars equal to three loaded)	20.12
Miles run to one ton of coal { Passenger	28.86
Miles run to one ton of coal { Freight	18.72
Miles run to one ton of coal { Switch work and other service	37.19

November, 1892—Middle Division.

Miles of road operated	715
Total number of engines	165
Number making mileage	142.7
Average miles per engine	3,896

Engine Mileage.

Passenger	150,218
Freight	296,887
Switching	102,337
Working	6,517
Total miles run	555,959

Miles Run to—

One ton of coal	21.52
One pint of lubricating oil	20.74
One pound of waste	160.68

Cost per Engine per Mile, in Cents.

Repairs	3.50
Stores	.30
Fuel	4.29
Engineers and firemen—wages	6.64
Dispatchers and cleaners	.96
Total cost per mile	15.69

Car Mileage.

Passenger		753,864
Freight	Loaded	3,927,574
	Empty	1,967,329
Average passenger cars per mile		5.02
Average loaded freight cars per mile		17.21
Cost	One passenger car per mile	2.79
	One loaded freight car per mile	1.04
Pounds of coal per car mile	Passenger	14.75
	Freight	6.73
Cost of coal per ton		0.92.4
Average number of freight cars per mile (loaded and empty; five empty cars equal to three loaded)		19.86
Miles run to one ton of coal	Passenger	27.02
	Freight	17.26
	Switch work and other service	35.40

SOUTHERN CALIFORNIA RAILWAY COMPANY.

Locomotive Performance Statistics.

October, 1892.

Total miles run		145.263
Total miles run exclusive of switch and work train		124,038
Total engines owned		20
Average number of engines on line (owned and rented)		44
Average miles run per engine		3,304
Average number engines (owned and rented), less switch and work		37
Average miles run per engine		3,352
Average number engines (owned and rented), less switch, work, and No. in shop		35
Average miles run per engine		3,544
Cost per mile run—		
For stores	(cts.) 0.04	
For oil and waste	0.37	
For fuel—coal and wood	24.53	
For engineers and firemen	6.69	
For other attendants and help	1.75	
For repairs	4.38	
		37.76
Miles run to one ton of coal		31.8
Miles run to one pint of engine oil		23.3
Miles run to one pint of valve oil		35.5
Miles run to one pint of illuminating oil		69.5
Miles run to one pint of lubricating oil		14.1
Miles run to one pint of all kinds of oil		11.7
Miles run to one pound of waste		116.6
Tons of coal used, 4,564½; rated at		$7 75
Cords of wood used, 67½; rated at		$1 00
Total mileage of road		492.4

Testimony of Mr. F. T. Perris.

(Chief Engineer, Southern California Railway.)

Mr. Wade: Our Chief Engineer, Mr. Perris, is here, and is more familiar with the construction of the road, the difficulties and obstacles to be overcome, than myself. He will be pleased to show you profiles, showing the mountain ranges we cross, and information of that character.

Chairman Earl: We will be glad to hear Mr. Perris.

Mr. Perris: Mr. Chairman, and Gentlemen of the Committee—I have been associated with the California Southern Railway since its inception, a period of about twelve years. I am, consequently, more or less acquainted with the general characteristics of the road, as well as the history of its building; and, referring to the former, I may say that there is hardly any comparison between our system, composed as it is of a number of little branch lines, and the roads of Iowa or Illinois. We have a variety of topographical features blended over our entire system, from mountains at an elevation of about 4,000 feet to sea level. We have mountains, gorges, and other physical varieties of engineering to encounter which are not common to the roads of Iowa or Illinois. For instance, from San Bernardino to the Summit, a distance of only 26 miles, we have to overcome an elevation of about 2800 feet. On that piece of the line we have in the neighborhood of 18 miles of grade of 116 feet to the mile, and some 6 miles of grade of 158.04 feet to the mile. We have in the neighborhood, I suppose, of 10 or 12 per cent, or, in mileage, 490 miles of grades of 116 feet, and perhaps 40 per cent of our mileage is composed of grades of from 1 per cent to 1.02 per cent, and the balance is largely made up of lighter grades. There is comparatively little level country in all of it.

In regard to the history of the building of the road, as I said before, it was commenced about twelve years ago, not over, and the first extension was from San Diego to San Bernardino. The first one hundred and sixteen miles were built, I think, in the year 1882; following that up was a little extension made to San Bernardino, and later, Barstow. This made the first portion of the California Southern road, with its extension, known as the California Southern extension, a total distance of two hundred and ten miles. The California Central Railway was then formed, building a number of branches in various directions to serve the country in the future, and help in the work of bringing the three counties together.

At the time of the completion of the California Southern Railway, the business was all handled by a locomotive and about one car. There was no settlement to speak of from San Diego to Oceanside, and from Oceanside to Colton. I presume, a half a dozen houses would have covered the entire number of houses along the line of the road at that time. Subsequently, when the California Central Railway was inaugurated, the boom of 1887 followed, and with that boom came the development of Southern California from that time forward, resulting in the wonderful growth that is witnessed on every hand, and especially following the lines of our road. This development, of course, was not made without a very large expenditure of money, some ten million dollars making up part of the cost.

Among the disasters that have followed the building of this road, I may mention that of 1884, which devastated the Temecula Cañon, sweeping out the entire line from the head of the cañon nearly to the ocean, a distance of over twenty-five or twenty-six miles, carrying with it about fifteen miles of steel rail, five of which were never found, and are unfound to this day, and some twenty or thirty bridges, resulting in a pecuniary loss of about $250,000. In other words, it cost about $250,000 to reinstate that which had been washed away during this particular flood. There was a period of some eight or nine months during which it was exceedingly doubtful whether the people who owned the road would ever put the money back again in order to reinstate it, but finally they did so, with the result that again, a few years ago—two years ago, I think, it is now—another flood came, resulting not quite so disastrously as the first, still, devastating the country to the extent of requiring $150,000 to now rebuild the cañon with a proper road. However, the line is not absolutely necessary to the traffic, because of the construction by the California Central of a line of road following the coast by the way of San Juan Capistrano, Santa Ana, and Orange, and around up the Santa Ana Cañon back to San Bernardino, making the line a little over seventeen miles longer than it was originally by the direct line through the Temecula and San Jacinto Cañons.

Within the past few years, notwithstanding the growth of the country, we have endeavored from time to time to increase our mileage by desirable little additions to our system. They have been made and resulted in development of the country, by reason of the showing we were enabled to make of their necessity to our system in order to reap the growth and development of the country.

I feel that if this bill—the one proposed—takes effect, that it will result in a total annihilation of the free and rapid development of the southern country, about which we promise so much. Mr. Wade has already given you the figures in relation to the business of the road, or at least he stated that they are at hand so that they can be had, and from those you will doubtless see that the stockholders as yet have had but poor return from their ten millions invested, except for the fact that they have developed the southern country to a very large extent; in fact, to an extent hardly appreciated by the people who live in the northern portion of the State.

I do not know that I can add anything more to what I have already said in regard to the physicial characteristics of the road or to its operating as a feature in the development of the country.

Testimony of William Collier.

(Attorney for the Southern California Railway.)

Mr. Wade: Mr. Chairman, I will be pleased if you would listen to Mr. Collier, who would like to make some statements in regard to his experience in the State of Illinois and Iowa, on the effect of laws on the regulation of rates in those States.

Chairman Earl: We will be pleased to hear from you, Mr. Collier.

Mr. Collier: Mr. Chairman, and Gentlemen of the Committee—I will only occupy a few moments of your time, in order to briefly call your attention to something you may be already familiar with, but having been myself a resident of the State of Iowa, in a time something like this, the matter occurred to me at once upon my attention being called to these matters. In 1874, in the laws of the Fifteenth General Assembly, on page 1,861, you will find the result of an excitement something similar to this. The Legislature for that year adopted in that State a distance tariff and classification, and put it into the Statute Book, not in the Constitution. This matter was suggested to me by a question asked by one of the committee as to whether or not there was any precedent. I believe that the question, however, was confined to the matter as to whether or not there was any precedent for adopting into a State Constitution such a provision as has been proposed here.

This, of course, does not apply, as it was not in their State Constitution. It was simply a State statute of the State of Iowa. It was adopted in 1874. There had been a very exciting election preceding the adoption of this tariff, and both houses were enthusiastic for such legislation. It is complete here; it covers forty or fifty pages of this statute book. I presume there are others of this kind in other States, but this is the only one experiment of which I have any knowledge resulting from such legislation. It continued in force just four years. In 1878 they repealed this law so far as it applied to freights; they left, however, the passenger tariff stand, as it stands to-day, at 3, 3½, and 4 cents per mile. Being a resident, I might further say that, on the repeal of this statute, they adopted a Commissioners' law, providing for the appointment of three Commissioners by the Executive Council of the Governor and the heads of the other departments. That continued in force for some considerable length of time, and, since my removal to the State of California, some ten years ago, they provided for the election of these Commissioners by the people, as is done in the State of California. I remember very distinctly the result of this legislation in that State. It resulted in a complete cessation of railroad building in the State of Iowa, and other results that statistics will probably furnish to your committee. It was repealed without objection. The people of the State of Iowa were so well satisfied with it that it was done without a ripple on the public surface. I will endeavor to ascertain in the State Library here the mileage of railroads built some four or five years preceding the passage of this law, and the railroad building in that State during the pendency of this statute and the repeal of it. While I have not yet had an opportunity to get it, I will endeavor to furnish it to the committee before the close of your session.

Mr. Earl: Have you compared the schedules there with the proposed schedule, Mr. Collier? A. I have not. I am not capable of making such a comparison. It is outside of my profession. It is here, all in detail, and complete, in this statute, which you can examine, or have comparisons made. I could not make such a comparison, because it is not within my experience. I stated this matter here because I believe it to be one of the best and most satisfactory arguments, especially to gentlemen accustomed to basing their conduct on occasions upon precedents. I believe it speaks louder in regard to the question of the expediency and propriety of legislation of this kind than anything we can suggest, to show an instance of this kind where it was tried and where it failed, and where they have returned again to the Commissioner system. And if you will examine the statutes of the State of Iowa since that time, and especially the laws of the Twenty-second General Assembly, you will find the most recent legislation in that State upon this subject, where they have gone on amending, changing, and modifying, sometimes in the interests of the companies and sometimes in the interests of the people, these provisions regulating the action of the Railroad Commissioners, until they have made very decided advances in that particular direction, and so corrected the matter that the people and the railroad companies seem to be in entire harmony. I say this from my knowledge of the condition of things there, being a native of that State and still keeping up very friendly interests there.

Mr. Earl: Has competition there not allayed this irritation more than anything else? A. I am glad you suggested that question. At the time of the adoption of this law, in 1874, as I now recollect, the Chicago, Burlington, and Quincy road extended clear across the State of Iowa in one tier of counties; the Chicago, Burlington, and Northern extended clear across the State in another tier of counties; the Chicago and Northwestern extended clear across in another tier; the Illinois extended nearly across in another tier of counties; and the Chicago, Milwaukee, and St. Paul road clear across in another tier of counties. I think all of these lines of roads reached from the easterly to the westerly line of the State, unless the Illinois Central, which was afterwards built. There was competition there. At the same time the Cedar Rapids road reached to the north of the State, running into Minnesota; the Central Railroad of Iowa reached from Ottumwa to the north line of the State; and the Keokuk, Fort Des Moines, and Minnesota reached from the Mississippi River to Fort Dodge; and other branch lines of road radiated out from these lines in every direction as feeders. Therefore, you will see there was active competition at the time of the adoption of this statute. Still, after an experience of four years, finally, to sum up, finding the unyielding condition of things under an arbitrary fixed statute made it impossible to adapt themselves to any conditions that arise between the meetings of the Legislature, the people and the railroads consented, because there was no objection to it—I remember very distinctly at the time—consented to wipe out that fixed tariff.

Mr. D. Freeman,

Of Los Angeles, spoke for the Southern California Railroad as follows:

Mr. Chairman and Gentlemen: I appear before you not only as a representative of the Southern California Railway Company, of which I am a Director, but as a shipper and payer of freight to a large extent. To show you that I am interested in cheap freights, I will state that the freight I will have to pay during 1893 on the fruit, grain, and bricks from my rancho near Los Angeles will amount to about $37,000. I contributed largely to the building of a railway from Los Angeles to the Pacific Ocean, which now forms part of the Southern California Railway system, and I have been for years doing all in my power to get a road built from the present terminus of either the Rio Grande and Western or the Union Pacific in southern Utah to Los Angeles. I should also be glad to see the Santa Fe system extended to San Francisco. I tell you these things so that you may know that I do not speak as one having no experience and no interest in legislation pertaining to railways and freights.

I came to Los Angeles twenty years ago, when she had no railway connections with San Francisco or the East. I have seen that country grow from a barren plain covered by sheep and cattle to one of the most fertile, favored, and prosperous parts of the United States. And this prosperity and growth have been largely brought about by the building of railways connecting us by two great lines with the Eastern and Central States, and giving us four shipping points on the ocean, instead of but one, as in former days. Before the advent of the railways, I paid nearly $5 per ton to put barley on board ship at San Pedro. I can put grain on board ship now for $1 10 per ton. Therefore it is, that looking at all the benefits the railways have conferred upon California, and seeing that we need other competing lines, I think it unwise to pass any law that will cripple the railroads now in operation in this State, or prevent the building of the other lines we so badly need. In my attempts to get the road from Los Angeles to Utah under way, I have had to consult capitalists who might be induced to buy the bonds of the road; and there has been received from all of these men one universal answer, "The danger of unfriendly legislation and disastrous interference with freights and fares, render railway bonds an unsafe investment."

A gentleman came from Salt Lake City last week to aid us in our scheme for the Utah road, but it was agreed on all hands that if this proposed bill became a law, we must abandon the project; not only that, but it will prevent the building of a railway from Mojave to San Francisco. Similar legislation to this proposed, was tried in Iowa five years ago, and it resulted disastrously to the public and the railroad people.

During the time this law was in force, railway building was practically suspended all over the State. Now, it is proposed to apply to the railways in California a tariff considerably lower than the tariffs now in force in Kansas, Illinois, and Iowa. But the railway conditions are totally different in California to what they are in those States. Look at the profiles of the Atlantic and Pacific, the Southern California, and the Southern Pacific Railways in California, and compare them with the profiles of the roads through Illinois, Iowa, and Kansas. Illinois and Iowa are practically level countries. You will see that from Chicago to Kansas City the line is practically level, while from Kansas City to the western border of the State of Kansas the elevation is but slight, and is gradual and the grades are easily overcome; and you will notice that as soon as the railway leaves the State of Kansas expensive mountain climbing commences, and from there to the Pacific Ocean it is but one interrupted climb, first up a mountain on one side and then down it on the other. It goes up at the Continental Divide to a height of nearly a mile and a half above sea-level, then down nearly a half mile to Springer, and so on up half a mile and down half a mile five times, till you come to Flagstaff, and from Flagstaff to the Needles down again six thousand four hundred feet, and then up again four thousand feet to the Cajon Pass, then down to the San Bernardino Valley. This climbing up and down, as you know, is only done by long and circuitous routes, and the building of a railway over a mountain range is very expensive. It frequently happens that to overcome a distance of one mile more money has to be expended than on twenty miles in the plain below.

Then, again, the railways in Illinois, Iowa, and Kansas run directly over the coal fields, and coal in these States can be bought at less than one quarter what it costs in California.

Again, the soil of Illinois, Iowa, and Kansas is universally fertile, and these States are well settled. But on the Atlantic and Pacific Railway from Alburquerque to San Bernardino, a distance of nearly one thousand miles, the country is but sparsely settled, and for nearly half that distance the road passes over a desert, or partially desert, country, affording no local freight or passengers to add to the revenue of the railway.

In Illinois 85 per cent of all the land lies within five miles of a railway, and there is but 1 per cent of all the land in that State that is between fifteen and twenty miles of a railway. Wages paid to railway employés in all States east of the Rocky Mountains are much less than those paid on this coast. Confining ourselves to the State of California, we find that of the three hundred and ten miles, between the Needles and Los Angeles, two hundred and fifty of these miles, between the Needles and the foot of the Cajon Pass, run over a desert country.

The Eastern States above referred to have all the railways they need; they are gridironed with them; coal is cheap and wages are low. But we in California have not one quarter of the railways we need, and the only way we can get them is to encourage railroad companies and not hamper them. People talk sometimes as if the railway companies were coining money out of the needs of the people. But few of the Western roads are paying dividends. Take three of the roads forming the Santa Fe System. The Atchison, Topeka, and Santa Fe Railway Company have $102,000,000 capital stock, upon which but three small dividends have been paid within the past eight years. The Atlantic and Pacific have $80,000,000 tied up in their road upon which no dividends have been paid. The Southern California has invested $13,000,000 in Southern California, on which no dividends have been paid. Is it fair to the men who have built these roads, at this enormous and unremunerative outlay, and have added so largely to the prosperity of California, to ask them to accept rates of freight and fares for their expensive roads similar to those in force in the old, well-settled, and level countries, where cheap coal exists and lower wages prevail, and no obstructions to cheap railway construction appear, and where all supplies for railway construction and maintenance are cheap?

California is badly cut up by mountain ranges, and with the exception of Colorado, it presents more obstacles to railway construction and operation than any other State in the Union. Then again, it is sparsely settled. In that part of the State in which the Southern California Railway operates, there are but five people to the square mile, while in Kansas there are eighteen, and in Illinois nearly seventy to the square mile. Only about one quarter of the land in the State is subject to cultivation. The rest is desert or mountains. Illinois and Iowa, on the other hand, have less than 5 per cent of untillable land, and Kansas less than 9 per cent.

And now in conclusion, what would be the condition of California to-day without her railroads? The railroads have done more than any other factor in bringing about our present prosperity. We are too much inclined to overlook the benefits we have derived and are deriving from our railways. We need more of them. Let us encourage the building of new roads. Plenty of roads and plenty of competition will regulate freights and fares much better and more equitably than legislation will. This continued agitation and legislation on this question has a tendency to unsettle values and prevent the building of new roads, and is bad for the State.

I am satisfied that if the proposed tariff becomes a law, it will have the effect of not only putting a stop to all railroad building in California, but many of the short roads, now used principally as "feeders" to some of the larger systems, will cease to be operated. The whole effect will be bad for the railroads, and worse for the people.

Committee met January 31st, at 7:30 P. M.

Statement of C. O. Johnson.

(Representing the Pacific Coast Railway.)

Mr. Chairman and Gentlemen: It will not take much time for me to make my statement, and I would like to be heard to-night. I represent the Pacific Coast Railway. While our earnings are something under the $4,000 limit, yet, we are advertising our section and productions of the soil along our line, having great hopes of its future growth and a corresponding increase in earnings. We also have in mind now, a prospective extension into the easterly interior valleys; and when these are accomplished we may expect to increase our gross earnings to or beyond $4,000 per mile. The adoption of the proposed amendment now under discussion would work an injustice to our owners, preventing a fair remuneration and the further investment of capital necessary for such extensions, and it would result in our sitting down and quietly closing up, as soon as we have worked up $3,999 per mile, and studying to prevent our earnings going beyond that figure, so that our owners may at least enjoy a small net earning that now accrues to them, and not decrease these net earnings by further extensions or increase in business. I have been in the railroad business for the past twenty-one years, thirteen years of which time as freight agent and at the heads of the various departments in the service. My experience commenced prior to the inauguration of the Interstate Commerce Act, and prior to the adoption by the various States of supervision by Commissions of railroad rates and fares. Naturally I am opposed to any supervision except those whose money is invested in the plant or the owners themselves; but if you can and must supervise these matters, then in all justice to the capitalists do so reasonably, and then you will improve your transportation facilities, thereby bringing about regulation in rates and service. I say, in justice to these people, give them a fair and just supervision by an honest, fair-minded Board of Railroad Commissioners, made up of men with some experience in the business. This supervision cannot, in my judgment, be just as well made by a temporary Act of your Assembly, as a clear study of the peculiar conditions of the details of railroading in this State must be made; the cost of fuel and the heavy grades limiting the number of cars each engine can pull; the cost of labor, also figures. When you pull a loaded car over the line you must bring it back empty. It requires much study and personal inspection, which a temporary Act cannot give. The just remedy then, in my judgment, is a Board of Commissioners composed of fair-minded, experienced men, whose supervision shall be such that no objection can be made on the part of the State, the people, or the railroad.

In our particular case the facts are: Our road was incorporated in September, 1882, under the laws of the State of California, and was built in sections. The actual cost of the road, the full amount, was $972,827; interest on this amount at a rate of 4 per cent would be $118,913. The net earnings of the road have never reached anything near these figures. Our average gross earnings per annum for the last four years were $174,949, while the net for 1892 was only $61,727. The average gross earnings per mile for the past four years was $2,636; the gross for 1892 was $2,397. The average net earnings per mile for the past four years was $989; net for 1892, $812. The average compensation to all employés, including general officers, was $2 03 per day; the average in Kansas, Nebraska, and Missouri was about $1 60 per day, as shown by statistics. Fuel for locomotives cost us: coal, $10 per ton; wood, $5 50 per cord, which on the basis of one and one half cords per ton of coal, makes the value of wood $7 75 per ton; this is against $1 40 to $1 50 per ton for Kansas and Nebraska. I know this is a fact, because I operated in Missouri and Kansas. Maintenance of way and bridges cost $32,578 for 1892. Our line crosses three divides at about equal distances. The grades are heavy going north or south; these grades vary from one hundred and five to one hundred and eighty feet to the mile. In three cases these are over two miles long, in one case three miles, and in another four miles long. There is a difference between short grades and a rapid ascent and ascending the same distance in long distances. You will find it is a greater strain upon your engines. Our two heaviest engines, and they are as heavy as our forty-five pound steel will bear, cannot pull over eight loaded cars to a train; the lighter engines pull only six loads. Our conditions are such that we are obliged, for economic reasons, to haul grain on flat cars, running the risk of storms. The bulk of our business is grain and beans, and is done in three months of the year. This necessitates hauling empty cars one way over long distances, and empty mileage in the other direction, which is very costly. Another element we have to contend with which does not exist in Kansas, in Nebraska, or in any other State, is the factor of grass on the track; with the constant work of section men with this element alone, it requires four months so the road can be operated. During this period it is necessary to have larger gangs of section men, and two thirds of the maintenance of way expense for three or four months is for fighting grass, which is not so in Kansas, Missouri, or Iowa. It is claimed ties last much longer in this country than east of the Rocky Mountains. This is not proven by our experience. Eight or nine months of the year it is very dry, and we have known ties, even of redwood, to be affected by dry-rot, making renewals frequent. And the Southern Pacific Company's line is now under construction to Santa Barbara and will parallel our line for a long distance, running between us and the ocean; this will make our entire line strongly competitive. Their expense of operating is less on the long lines than ours on the shorter, on account of our general officers. And we could not operate under the proposed figure with competition of the Southern Pacific. We would have to make a reduction of 71 per cent on the principal commodities. Our average revenue on passengers in 1891 was 4 cents, while the average cost of carrying a passenger one mile was 3 cents. We have tried the experiment of reduced rates, but with no success, and I respectfully submit that this would bankrupt the road and prevent future extensions of the line.

Statement of J. F. Kidder.

(Representing Nevada County Narrow Gauge Railroad.)

Mr. Chairman and Members of the Committee on Constitutional Amendments of the Senate of the State of California:

Gentlemen: As President, Manager, and Chief Engineer of the Nevada County Narrow Gauge Railroad, I desire to present to you some of the characteristics of that road, and to give my reasons why the bills now before your committee, in my humble opinion, should be reported back to the Senate, with the recommendation that they do not pass.

The road extends from Colfax, a station on the line of the Central Pacific, through Grass Valley to Nevada City, total distance twenty-two and one half miles, over a broken and rugged country, situated among the foothills of the Sierra Nevadas.

The distance from Colfax to Grass Valley in an air line is nine miles, whilst by rail it is seventeen miles; from Grass Valley to Nevada City, by an air line, three and one half miles, by rail five and one half miles. It being impossible to construct the road on a shorter line without increasing the gradients above one hundred and twenty-one feet to the mile, which is the maximum used on our line.

Our curvature is very sharp, the minimum radius being about two hundred and eighty feet, total curvature being over 7,600 degrees, or over twenty-one full circles; total length of curve line is 12.26 miles, and tangent or straight line, 10.24 miles.

The sum of ascending grades from Colfax to Nevada City is 1,158 feet, the aggregate length of same 12.16 miles, an average of over 95 feet per mile; the sum of descending grades between the same points is 1,049 feet, the aggregate length of same 9.66 miles, an average of over 108 feet per mile, whilst the total length of level grade is .68 of a mile.

The elevation above sea-level of various points on the line, located in the order as placed in the list, is as follows:

Colfax, 2,414 feet; Bear River, 2,076 feet; Green Horn, 2,152 feet; Kress Summit, 2,851 feet; Grass Valley, 2,448 feet; Town Talk Summit, 2,771 feet; Nevada City, 2,525 feet.

The following comparative table, showing the gross earnings and the expenses of operating, including taxes, interest on bonded indebtedness, and amount expended in construction from 1880 to 1891, inclusive, will be found of interest, as showing the fluctuation of business and the decrease of same by the stoppage of hydraulic mining:

Year.	Gross Receipts.	Expenses.	Profit.	Loss.
1880	$115,655 55	$94,800 72	$20,854 83	
1881	116,465 91	98,667 21	17,798 70	
1882	105,273 20	106,924 71		$1.651 51
1883	100,978 07	101,571 76		593 69
1884	84,861 66	82,139 04	2,722 62	
1885	89,133 21	91,319 98		2,186 77
1886	98,247 63	102,752 50		4,504 87
1887	94,411 49	88,973 70	5,437 79	
1888	89,211 89	80,783 90	8,427 99	
1889	84,978 69	94,472 50		9,493 91
1890	87,259 49	96,655 47		9,395 98
1891	89,196 18	88,893 21	302 97	

Our statement for 1892 has not yet been completed, as our annual meeting does not take place until April. Of the expenses incurred in 1882, renewal of bridges amounting to over $11,000 were included; in 1883, renewal of bridges, over $16,000; in 1889, repairs of passenger coaches, over $3,000, and new buildings and works, over $3,000 more, and in 1890 the expenses of snow blockade were nearly $9,000.

In regard to the economy of the management, I would simply state that the salaries of the general officers are low, each one filling two or three offices, and there is not even a clerk in any one of these departments.

The amount of wood used in the service of the road is about two thousand cords annually, costing $3 50 per cord. The supply is becoming short, and I will soon have to build a branch of three or four miles to obtain a supply.

Regarding the increase of travel by reducing rates, I would offer the following pertinent example: Our regular passenger rate between Grass Valley and Nevada City is 50 cents, and the public were very anxious that I should try the experiment of a local at half rates. So, in order to satisfy them, I established a double daily service in 1884 between those points, running at such hours as would best satisfy the traveling public, and placing the fare at 25 cents, with the result that at the end of four months our receipts had averaged $3 90 a day, and our expenses had been over $11 a day.

The gentleman representing the Traffic Association of San Francisco has gravely informed you that railroads should be operated in California cheaper than in other portions of the United States, for the following reasons: On account of the equable climate, on account of our roads not being ballasted with rock ballast, and on account of the durability of our timber, permitting our worn-out ties to be used for fence posts. Permit me to state, for his benefit, that in Nevada County we have as high as one hundred and fifteen inches of rain in six months, our average rainfall per annum being about sixty inches.

And it strikes me very forcibly that if the one hundred and fifteen inches of rain should fall in his States of Iowa and Kansas, that he would not be obliged to apply to the Legislatures of those States to wreck the railroads, but would rather have to search the Gulf of Mexico for the remains. On January 12, 1890, a storm commenced and snow fell to a depth of five feet, blocking the road till the 25th of the same month; and on February 18th, another storm deposited snow to about the same depth, causing a blockade till the 26th. The cost to the road of attempting to raise these blockades was nearly $9,000. Of course it is apparent to any one that it is cheaper to operate roads in California than anywhere else. To his second reason, I would answer that our road is ballasted with rock ballast taken from one thousand five hundred to two thousand feet below the surface of the earth, and still it does not take one of our section hands a whole day to remove and replace three ties, as the gentleman thought, and so expressed himself, it did on some of the roads in the East, with which he was familiar; a remark which I am afraid would subject him to the ridicule of all the trainmen in the United States.

Answering his statements about the durability of timber, let me give you an example: In 1875 we completed two spans of Howe truss bridges, one hundred and sixty feet each in length, and in 1882 and 1883 we were compelled to rebuild the same entirely, as the timber was so rotten as to be unsafe. These bridges were kept well painted. I have put redwood planks four inches thick under the subsills of our trestle bridges, and in three years have had to replace the same, as they were so rotten as to be nothing but punk. The acid in the red soil of the foothills decays timber faster than in any other section with which I am familiar; and instead of being able to sell our removed ties for fence posts or fuel, we collect and burn them as we would brush to get rid of them.

Does it not, to say the least, seem presumptuous in the Manager of the Traffic Association, after a residence of one short year on this coast, to formulate a bill for the government of thirty roads of this State, when he coolly informed you that he has not inquired into the characteristics, or applied for any information in reference to any line save and excepting the Southern Pacific Company? In other words, if he can only cinch that company he cares not how the other roads, representing millions of capital, may be affected. It was a very easy matter to find out all about the outside roads, from the sworn statements on file with the Railroad Commissioners of this State; and if he could only find time in one year to formulate a bill to regulate the Southern Pacific Company, and incidentally, without examination, the other twenty-nine roads of California, how can it be expected that the Legislature of California, in a session of sixty days, and with some other little business before it, can give this matter such attention as to do justice to all concerned?

In conclusion, I would state, as you have already been informed by our attorney, that we stand upon our special charter, and certainly will submit to no interference with the same until the question has been decided by the highest tribunal in the land. But I would ask, is it fair or just for the Legislature of the State of California, after entering into a special contract with the promoters of this enterprise, guaranteeing to them rates of freights and fares, without which they would not have invested their money, to now force us to the expense and annoyance of defending our charter before the Courts?

I thank you, Mr. Chairman, and gentlemen of the committee, for your courtesy.

Statement of J. F. Burgin.

(Representing San Francisco and North Pacific Railway.)

Gentlemen: In the open session of the California Senate, bills are introduced right and left on all subjects. Some are inspired by good motives, some inspired by selfish motives, and many from mistaken and ill-considered ideas.

Little time can be given to the discussion of the subject there; but the people of the State of California, as a body, cannot take evidence and decide these questions; the Senate is expected to do this in their sphere. The Senate here stands between the temper of certain classes on the one hand, and the property rights of her citizens and corporations on the other; and the quintessence of this responsibility is put upon you gentlemen of this committee, as far as the railroad legislation is concerned.

On behalf of the San Francisco and North Pacific Railway Company, better known as the "Donahue line," I wish to claim only a few minutes of your time to lay before you certain facts and certain evidences which, independent of all public clamor, must bear their ligitimate weight when you come to conclude the open controversies this proposed bill has brought up.

In the first place, I represent a railroad of a total mileage of one hundred and sixty-five miles. It runs from Point Tiburon, in Marin County, to Ukiah, in Mendocino County, and by branches to other points, and is a standard gauge railroad. This railroad would be severely affected by the proposed bill. The North Pacific Coast Railway, with a mileage of eighty-seven miles, will be similarly affected; so will the Eureka and Eel River Railroad, of thirty miles, and all the other railroads.

The public agitation which has been waged against the Southern Pacific Company in this State entirely ignored all consideration of these smaller railroads, pro or con.

It aimed its political javelin at the Southern Pacific Company, with its grand aggregate of total mileage, which is greater than the mileage of all the smaller railroads put together.

A law designed for a number of railroads operated in one system, such as the Southern Pacific Company, cannot possibly be justly applied to the short distance roads, or to the roads operated singly. A bill that would regulate the large road would injuriously discriminate against the short roads, and a bill that would discriminate against the large road would annihilate and close up the short roads altogether.

Now I will state a few facts to show this from a strictly business standpoint. I do not propose to plead poverty on behalf of the Donahue properties, but simply to compare the result of our present operations with what the result would be in case we operated our road under the present proposed bill.

The building of our road cost $7,090,059; its bonded indebtedness is $4,188,000. The necessities of the case compel us to pay interest each year on our mortgage in the sum of about $230,000; all this, with payments to our sinking fund, must come from our net profits. If we did not pay it out of our net profits we would have to close up the railroad altogether.

Now, if our company should be reduced immediately to an established rate of 3 cents or less per mile in passenger, and to a freight rate as proposed in the schedule, what would the consequence be to us?

Mr. Leeds has stated that this reduction would affect the Southern Pacific Company to the extent of 25 per cent of their gross earnings. We will show that the reduction to our company would be near 50 per cent. It is a well known fact that the comparative expenses of a small railroad are greater than those of a larger one, over a corresponding distance. But, Mr. Leeds has stated that a 25 to 30 per cent reduction on the gross earnings of the Southern Pacific Company would be the result if this bill should become a law. Apply this reduction instead of the 50 per cent reduction, to our company, and what would be the result?

Under the favorable auspices of the past, our road's earnings for the last fiscal year show a surplus of $106,007, after paying interest and betterments. If the road had been run under the regulations of the proposed bill, the same road, with the same economy, and the same prosperity, would have run behind that year $130,125 67, and would have plunged the stockholders in debt to that extent. If I may use an old expression, "figures do not lie." For the fiscal year ending June 30, 1892, our company's gross earnings were $886,471; less Mr. Leeds' 25 per cent reduction, $221,619 75; making our gross earnings only $664,978 92. Now, our operating expenses and interest amount to $794,978 92; making us run behind, in one year alone, $130,125 67.

Would you, gentlemen, as business men, like to make an investment in the stock of our road if you were compelled to run it on a basis of three cents a mile, and with the proposed freight tariff, knowing that, no matter how the traffic was kept up, and no matter how smoothly things ran, your final balance sheet, which formerly showed a small profit, would then alarm you with a great annual loss?

Now, as far as the people of the State of California, represented in the Senate and in your committee, are concerned, they do not ask you to regulate the freight and fares of the Donahue road; the people do not complain of our rates; the people do not want our rates cut; the people do not want this proposed bill, as far as our road is concerned.

Why, even the shippers on our line of road are not complaining, nor will you hear from our passenger traffic. And what is the reason of this? Simply because the people in the districts our road penetrates, want our train service; not only that, they want more; they come to us from the north, from the northeast, and from the northwest, and beg us to extend our road and come to their relief. They all realize that we are not able to reduce our rates and live; they pay our rates cheerfully and willingly. They would rather do that than suffer a reduction of train service, and a partial loss of the facilities of transportation, which, of course, would be the result of the passage of this bill.

In these days of anti-railroad agitation it may seem strange to you that the people are thoroughly satisfied with our rates. I may as well confide in you a portion of the secret history of the road. We have had only two complaints filed against us with the Railroad Commissioners during the last eight or nine years of the road's operation; the charges were dismissed; it was found that the same individual had filed both charges, and it was further found that he had only shipped during the whole period one or two tons of freight, and he himself had only traveled over the road twice, and on one of those occasions he traveled on a free pass.

You, gentlemen, have already heard the opinion of Mr. Leeds on the subject. I cannot call it testimony, for he knows no facts; he simply gives his opinion; it is entitled to no greater weight than the opinion of any of you gentlemen in the absence of facts to support it. Some of his assertions are not universally admitted; for instance, in the case of maintenance I do not agree with Mr. Leeds' assertion that the cost is less in this State than in the State Mr. Leeds uses as an example for establishing the rates of fare and freight which you have before you in the printed bill.

In this State much greater are the hire of labor, the cost of rails, the cost of cars, the cost of locomotives, the cost of fixtures, and greater than all the cost of coal. The cost of this commodity in particular, to us has been on an average $7 25 per ton (placed upon our locomotive tenders), and in some years has run as high as $14, according to the condition of the coal market, reaching this figure in 1886, the cost to the Eastern roads being from 75 cents to $1 50.

Mr. Leeds has stated in answer to a question from your honorable committee, that the effect of the reduction of these rates upon the independent roads would be an increase in travel. M. Leeds in his answer did not state his reason for this increase of business to the roads except the reduction of rates. I would like to call the committee's attention to the fact that it took eighteen years for the Illinois Central, the Pennsylvania Central, and the Lake Shore and Michigan Southern, to come down from an average 3 cent to an average 2 cent earning per mile, with a population ten times as great as that of this State. Yet this bill calls for an immediate reduction and allows for a reduction of even less than 2 cents per mile.

Let us compare the population of the State of California, also that of the counties through which we run, with the several Eastern States which operate their lines upon the passenger rates and freight tariff like unto the one Mr. Leeds has brought forward to be a basis for the operation of the roads of this State. Below I give you a table taken from the "Statistician" of 1892:

	Population per Square Mile.	Square Miles.	Inhabitants.
Marin County	10	590	13,072
Mendocino County		3,694	17,612
Sonoma County		1,548	32,721
Lake County		1,125	7,101
	10	6,957	70,506
California	8	158,360	1,208,130
Connecticut	150	4,990	746,258
Illinois	60	56,650	3,826,351
Indiana	65	36,350	2,192,404
Massachusetts	250	8,315	2,238,943
New York	150	49,170	5,997,853
Pennsylvania	175	45,215	5,258,014
Ohio	90	41,060	3,672,316

One glance at these figures will show you why roads can operate with passenger rates in the States enumerated above, with the exception of this State, at a 3 or 2 cent rate, and even less.

It is my opinion that if this bill should pass and become a law, this State, instead of progressing, would retrograde. It is the ambition of the people of the State of California to have additional railroad communications with the East. Do you think that in the face of adverse legislation capitalists will expend their money, when they see that they will not get a fair return of interest for their investment; but, instead, that the chances are greatly that it will be a losing investment? Mr. Leeds has said before you that people sometimes make bad investments.

The people of Humboldt County have been in a manner isolated from the balance of the State. The only approach to their county is by water, over one of the most dangerous bars on the coast, or by stage line overland for a distance of one hundred and fifty miles. They have been clamoring for a railroad communication. It will take several millions of dollars to make this desired extension from the terminus of our road. This county has only a population of twenty-five thousand people. Do you think, gentlemen, that a railroad could be built into this new county, and be operated upon a passenger rate of 2 cents per mile, or even 3? Do you think that this railroad could be operated upon a freight basis such as has been brought forward by Mr. Leeds, and pay the interest upon the investment?

It can be conclusively shown you that with skillful and fostering care, the San Francisco and North Pacific Railway the Donahue railroad, has penetrated the fertile valleys of Marin, of Sonoma, and of Mendocino, and if the Legislature does not kill railroad enterprise in these counties by mistaken or hurriedly considered legislation, this railroad will pierce the neglected forests and valleys of upper Mendocino and Humboldt but I assure you they will never get there on 2 cents a mile basis, or on the proposed freight tariff.

I think, gentlemen, that, as far as our road is concerned, I can leave this matter safely in your hands, for if I quote Mr. Leeds' answer when your honorable committee asked him what effect this tariff would have upon the independent roads, he stated he had never examined into the costs of operation, the prospects of freight and of travel, or the condition of the country, or even into the cost of the construction of the various railroads. I think Mr. Leeds, himself, has already given a negative answer to the proposed bill, as far as our road is concerned.

Statement of Thos. Mellersh.

(Of the San Francisco and North Pacific Railway Company).

Mr. Chairman and Gentlemen: No measure has ever come before the Legislature of California of as great importance to the road I am here to represent as the present amended bill, or present bill before the Legislature.

It would be fallacious at this time to predict how far-reaching it may be, but the measure that has been introduced here has already preceded us and has gone as far as Chicago. In order, gentlemen, that we may fully make you conversant with our road, and what we have to give you in the way of statistical details, I would like, with your permission, to present you each with a copy of our Annual Report, in order that you may more clearly follow me.

[Each member of the committee was here presented with a copy of the Annual Report of the San Francisco and North Pacific Railway Company for the year ending June 30, 1892.]

Our road, gentlemen, if you will turn to the first page, you will notice commences, you will find by the map, at San Francisco, and we run to Point Tiburon, employing in the operation of ferriage, three steamers, one of which was burned January 1st, leaving but two. From Tiburon we run to Ukiah, north, a distance of one hundred and six miles, and at Ignacio we run to Glen Ellen, a distance of thirty miles, east. At Santa Rosa we have a branch to Sebastopol, and from Fulton we run to Guerneville.

The total mileage, if you will kindly turn to the first page in the printed matter you will find, is one hundred sixty-four miles and sixty-five hundredths. The first feature that we would like to ask you gentlemen to consider, is one of the factors in our operating expenses, and will be found on page forty-five, table F, and you will there find that we spend, this little company of ours, the amount of $19,810 23 per year—the third line—for advertising. Of course, you will say this advertising is for our benefit. We grant it, but in order that we may bring people to California, we spend a good deal of that advertising money in New York. We even go so far as to put articles in New York papers. We even go so far as to print books and circulars, and send them East and distribute them, and we do not stop at New York; we cross the Atlantic Ocean and put those folders and papers in Germany. Now, gentlemen, if people come here from such remote parts, and pay us the fare for traveling over our road, which they consider reasonable, I do not think the people of this State should be dissatisfied. I think the State, gentlemen, gets infinitely more benefit than we do. The next feature I will ask you to turn to now is on same page, and below you will find that the cost of operating our steamers, consisting of steamer repairs, steamer expenses, wages of crews, and dock repairs, and fuel for steamers, amounts to $91,835 21. But, gentlemen, the expenses do not stop there. Whilst we show that as being the cost of operating our steamers, with your permission, Mr. Chairman, I would like to now give you a further statement.

In addition to the actual running expenses, $91,835 21, as shown in that statement, you will find that we pay for rent of slips to the Harbor Commissioners $1,400 per month, amounting to $16,800 per annum. Further, we pay also to the Harbor Commissioners for switching cars, 75 cents for each car, amounting to $5,505 per year. This latter figure is approximate. Making a total for operating our steamers of $114,140 21. The percentage of operating the steamers to gross receipts, or in other words, out of every $100 that we take in for gross receipts, we pay out $12 87, or 12.87 per cent; the percentage of cost for operating our steamers to gross expenses is 19.85 per cent. Now, if you will consider the fact, that outside the Southern Pacific Company, the North Pacific Coast, and ourselves, that we are the only one that is taxed with this most extraordinary expense, it does seem to me that therein lies a fact why we, above all other companies, should have at least some special consideration.

Then, gentlemen, while the steamers, as I have outlined here, show so much cost to operate them, it does not altogether rest there, because they are constantly being disabled. For instance, the steamer

"Tiburon" over a year ago broke her shaft—cost about $5,000 to replace it, besides we lost the use of the steamer for two months. Only last month she broke her crank-pin—cost $300 or $400 and laid her up two or three weeks. Then, in order that she might begin the year auspiciously, on the 1st day of January, she went and burned up; true, she was insured, but the cost to put that steamer into service again, over and above the amount that we shall recover for insurance, will be a considerable amount—in fact, quite an item. These are points, gentlemen, that we particularly wish you to take into consideration this evening. Now, our little road is not by any means a cheap road to operate in the matter of grades. Our grades are particularly heavy.

We will take, if you like, Colonel Morgan's report; it is good enough for us, and I suppose you will be satisfied to take his figures—but I have had them verified by our engineer, and he shows that after leaving Tiburon, just above San Rafael, we have a grade of one hundred and forty feet to climb; further on, one hundred and fifty-one feet; then it drops down to ninety-nine, and finally near Ukiah, it is six hundred and ten feet above sea-level. In connection with that matter—all of our heavy traffic has necessarily to pass over the worst grade—the worst grade is just above San Rafael—so that all of our north bound and all of our south bound traffic has necessarily to pass over that heavy grade.

To show you the additional cost it is to operate over heavy grades on our road, I will read from the engineer's report:

The aggregate length of tunnels on this road is eight thousand eight hundred and ninety-nine feet, or one and seven tenths miles. He says the maximum grade going north is one and three hundredths per mile. Passenger locomotives will haul seven cars north, and ten cars south; an extra locomotive being used in trains exceeding these numbers. Freight locomotives haul twelve cars north, and eighteen cars south. When trains exceed these numbers, extra locomotives are used, or two or more trips made. Maximum grades in both directions are near San Rafael, only ten miles from the southern terminus, and nearly all passenger and freight traffic to and from San Francisco must be hauled over that. In tunneling, I show you that on our road it is greater than what it is on the Pennsylvania Railroad. I don't think you gentlemen would have thought of that; that we, a little road running from San Francisco to Ukiah, one hundred and sixty-five miles, have more tunneling on our road than the Pennsylvania Railroad Company; in other words, one and seven tenths miles of tunnels. How expensive these are to keep up, to carefully and constantly watch, no one but a railroad man knows.

The next thing I would like to call the attention of you gentlemen to, is the rough country. We run over a very rough country, and a very sparsely populated one; from Ignacio to Glen Ellen is a valley, and we run through a marsh. The Southern Pacific parallels us through the valley; the valley itself is only one and one half miles wide, and the population is so slim that it is hard to find them, and you can imagine how much two roads can earn in that mile of territory. You can imagine how little there will be for us.

Now we come to Cloverdale and the new extension to Ukiah. From Cloverdale to Ukiah, thirty miles, with the exception of Hopland, where there are a few houses and a small number of people, there is absolutely nothing but high bluffs and rough country, sheep ranges. We don't transport the sheep, and we hardly transport the ranges.

The next feature, and the one of very great importance, is the question of fuel; you have heard that discussed before. Our friend Leeds, of the Traffic Association, made the assertion here—in fact he made several—that in the matter of fuel, we can do relatively so much more than Eastern roads. In connection with that, I have prepared some more figures, and I would like to submit some statements to your committee. [Handing each of the committee a statement.]

This statement—if you will please follow me—the first column I show the average number of cars in passenger trains; the average number of tons per engine mile; the miles run per ton of coal; the average cost per engine mile for fuel; pounds of coal used per engine mile; average cost of fuel per ton. So as to make a favorable comparison with our company, I have chosen the Queen and Crescent system. The Queen and Crescent system runs in an air line from the city of Cincinnati, Ohio, through Kentucky, Tennessee, Alabama, Mississippi, into New Orleans, Louisiana.

Again, it runs from Meridian, in Mississippi, to Vicksburg, Mississippi; there crosses the Mississippi River and runs to Shreveport. Those States that it runs through, excepting Ohio—for instance, Kentucky, Tennessee, Louisiana, Alabama, and Mississippi—are all more or less of an equable climate. The lower States compare not unfavorably with the climate of our own climate here. As Mr. Leeds has seen fit to lay so much stress on equable climate, it is just as well to give him a little climate. Now, gentlemen, if you will then follow me, having explained the different features of our road:

You will find the San Francisco and North Pacific Railway haul an average number of cars in passenger trains, 4.1; the Cincinnati Southern—that is, their division running from Cincinnati to Chattanooga, Tennessee, three hundred and thirty-six miles—4.3; the Alabama and Great Southern, two hundred and ninety-five miles, running from Chattanooga to Meridian, 4.9; the New Orleans and Northeastern, one hundred and ninety-six miles, 4.5; the Alabama and Vicksburg, one hundred and forty miles, 5.1; Vicksburg, Shreveport, and Pacific, one hundred and seventy miles, running from Vicksburg to Shreveport, across the Mississippi River, 4.6.

The next, the average number of tons per engine mile, is 63.60 on our road; the average number of tons per engine mile on the Cincinnati Southern Railroad is 201.09, or, you will see, three times as much as ours; on the Alabama Great Southern Railway, 178.98, or three times nearly; on the New Orleans and Northeastern, 204; the Alabama and Vicksburg Railway, 213; and on the Vicksburg, Shreveport and Pacific, 126.

Now, gentlemen, the miles run per ton of coal: we make nearly double the mileage. Our road is 45.86; on the Cincinnati Southern Railway it is 23.70; on the Alabama Great Southern Railway, 30; the New Orleans and Northeastern, 27.90; the Alabama and Vicksburg, 32.50; the Vicksburg, Shreveport, and Pacific, 37.20. It is very easy, I think, for you to see, gentlemen, why we can make nearly double the miles per ton of coal, when we haul sixty-three tons as against their two hundred. In fact, to make the figures relative, we should run three times the number of miles if we only haul one third the tonnage.

Now, again, the next figures, the average cost per engine mile for fuel: Our road, you will notice, is 16.1 cents; the Cincinnati Southern Railway, 5.72 cents, or about one third; Alabama and Great Southern Railway, 4.52 cents; New Orleans and Northeastern, 7.31 cents; Alabama and Vicksburg Railway, 5.80 cents; Vicksburg, Shreveport, and Pacific, 7.51 cents.

Now, gentlemen, the next feature that Mr. Leeds made, and which I remember distinctly, is that we here ran a mile on fifty-five pounds of coal, as against any Eastern road running on one hundred and ten; I believe that was right.

Now, if you will refer to our column, you will find that the pounds of coal used per engine mile with us is fifty pounds; with the Cincinnati Southern, ninety-five pounds; Alabama and Great Southern Railway, seventy-four pounds; New Orleans and Northeastern, eighty pounds; Alabama and Vicksburg, sixty-nine pounds; Vicksburg, Shreveport, and Pacific, sixty pounds. But they, in order to cost more to run the mile, haul over three times the same amount of freight that we do.

Now, then, the next column is the average cost of coal per ton. And right here, I would like to interpolate the fact, gentlemen, that these figures—in fact, I will substantiate them, with your permission, as I proceed; and you, gentlemen, can see for yourselves that these figures are not gathered up for the purpose of making an argument, but they are actual facts, and you, gentlemen, can follow them just as readily as I can.

The average cost of coal per ton on the San Francisco and North Pacific Railway is $7 25.47; Cincinnati Southern is $1 37; Alabama and Great Southern is $1 36; the New Orleans and Northeastern is $2 03; the Alabama and Vicksburg Railway is $1 88; the Vicksburg, Shreveport, and Pacific Railway is $2 79.

I am exceedingly sorry that Mr. Leeds is not here to-night, for I would have liked him to have heard the figures.

Now, gentlemen, we will refer, if you please, to the climatic conditions. Again, Mr. Leeds has seen fit to allege that on account of climatic conditions we can do all kinds of impossible things that Eastern roads cannot do. Now, let us see how that comes out. In the matter of snow on our road, we are not troubled with it; our friends, the Southern Pacific and other roads are. The slides and washouts we are troubled with, because we never have a heavy rain that we do not have slides and washouts; in fact, up above Cloverdale, where the bluffs run high and the hills slip back for three or four hundred feet high, just as soon as we remove anything from the base, the water comes down and carries the hill with it, and we find our track, instead of being over it, is out in the river. This is not an infrequent occurrence.

Now, in the matter of cross-ties: Mr. Leeds distinctly made the statement the other night that the Eastern roads replaced their cross-ties two or three times as often as we do. Now, let us see how that comes out. I call your attention, Mr. Chairman, to a comparative statement of replacement of cross-ties. [Mr. Mellersh here handed each member of the committee a statement in regard to cross-ties]. You will notice it gives the names of railroads, and the rate per one hundred thousand ties replaced per year in 1891 and 1892, and the cost per tie. I again use these same roads, because, as I stated, they run through States whose climate is about as equable, as a general thing, as our own. I have lived down there, and I know whereof I am speaking:

On the San Francisco and North Pacific Railway we replace, per one hundred thousand cross-ties, fourteen thousand five hundred, or one seventh, and the cost per tie was 35 cents.

The Cincinnati, New Orleans, and Texas and Pacific Railway replaced twenty thousand per hundred thousand cross-ties, or one fifth the first year, or one quarter the second year, costing 30 cents per tie.

The Alabama and Great Southern Railway replaced twenty thousand in 1891, or one fifth, and in 1892 one quarter, at 30 cents per tie.

The New Orleans and Northeastern Railway replaced only ten thousand, you will notice, or less than ourselves by forty-five hundred per hundred thousand; one tenth, as against our one seventh in 1891, and one ninth the next year against our one seventh, and they paid for their ties 25 cents each.

The Vicksburg and Meridian replaced twenty thousand, or one fifth in 1891, and one quarter in 1892, at 30 cents per tie.

The Vicksburg, Shreveport and Pacific replaced twenty thousand cross-ties, or one quarter the first year, and one fifth the second year, at a price of 30 cents per tie.

Now, the whole of the question does not rest there, Mr. Chairman; for the fact is that we, in California, use generally redwood for our ties; East, they use mainly pine. Our engineer, who has studied this question, says:

"From the above, it will be seen that the average life of ties, principally of pine, referring now to Eastern ties on the Queen and Crescent road, with the exception of the New Orleans and Northeastern, is from four to five years.

"On this road, our run is seven years. While the redwood is an excellent wood to resist decay, from the fact that it is very soft; a majority of the ties on this coast are renewed on account of being worn out, or cut out under the beds of the rail. The fact also remains, Mr. Chairman, that inasmuch as those Eastern roads run so much heavier engines than we do, haul so much heavier loads, longer trains, that they, as compared with ourselves, would naturally use ties a little oftener; but we claim that our one seventh, as against their one tenth or one fifth, is not an unequal comparison; and hence, that Mr. Leeds, in having made the assertion that we can use our ties two or three times as long as they can East, is not, according to records that we have obtained—and we contend our records are reliable—is not strictly correct.

Now, gentlemen, he made another assertion—it is becoming a hackneyed assertion—but I went to the pains of asking our General Manager and our Engineer to figure out the assertion made by Mr. Leeds in regard to the use of cross-ties, and I would like him to know that it is a fact that we do use some of our cross-ties after they have been taken out of the track for fence posts, and so far as we can find out, during the last three or four years we have used a sufficient quantity to result in the saving to our company of something like, all told, an aggregation of $159.

Now, gentlemen, it is also a fact—and with so many railroad men present, if I do not make figures that are absolutely reliable, there are plenty here that would catch me up—that a railroad company does duplicate its road practically in every ten or fifteen years, so far as its roadbed is concerned; that is the ties, and rails, and wooden bridges, and equipment, but iron bridges not so often; they might run to twenty or twenty-five years, or perhaps longer. But, you say, we have an engine that we have been using for twenty years. Yes, we have; but during that time that engine has had new driving wheels, new trucks, cylinders, new jacket, and perhaps so much has been renewed of the engine to what it originally was, that you can say it is not the same engine. Now, if you will take that fact into consideration, that the railroad has practically to duplicate itself in every ten or fifteen years, you can see what resources railroad men are put to in order to maintain at all times a standard, not only required for the safety of the people, but for the safety of the road.

Now, another feature we have to contend with lies in the fact that our traffic, if you will kindly refer to page 58, table M, you will find that products of the forest are 25.96 per cent of our total freight traffic; therefore, on such conditions we are relying on timber, lumber, shakes, shingles, tan bark and such forest products for that much of our revenue. By reason of the country contiguous to our railroad at Guerneville, Ukiah and other sections having been cleared, the haul of such timber, lumber, etc., is so much, that hardly any of those men can now ship the same quantity as heretofore, by reason of the expense of hauling; therefore, our revenue by that reason is mulcted to that extent. Then again, we haul rock, and in hauling rock we get something between half a cent and three quarters of a cent per ton per mile; or, if you figure out the cost of hauling it, an actual loss to the company. Then again, we have no mineral traffic to haul, with the exception of blocks or something like that; we have no coal, so that our road is purely dependent on agricultural and forest products.

Then again, the next feature, and which I particularly wish you to bear in mind, lies in the fact that we are subject to the severest competition. At San Rafael and as high as Petaluma we have water competition. The sloughs run up as high as Petaluma, so that steamers and schooners run at all times, and they haul freight so exceedingly low because their cost of transportation is so low, that no railroad company can compete with water transportation. That harasses us more than you can imagine, and hurts our revenue not a little.

Now again, in regard to the measure that you speak about, of making rates 3 cents per mile. The State has given us the permission to charge 15 cents per mile.

Earl: Wherein?

Mellersh: The laws of the State, I believe; the Commission. To show you that we, as a corporation, are always willing to conform to the laws, and do better than the law requires, our average rate per passenger per mile, if you will kindly refer to another table, table J, on page 53, for last year, is two and two hundredths cents per mile. The reason why that figure is so low, I explain to you, lies in the fact that a good deal of our traffic is suburban traffic. That traffic consists of three or four hundred, or may be less, people, who pay us $5 per month for carrying them sixty trips, each trip being sixteen and a half miles, or less than half a cent per passenger per mile. Then again, to hunters and excursionists, to all those who come in parties, we are always ready to meet them half way on any proposition they may have to offer; so that I contend that our passenger rate, two cents per mile, compares very favorably, when you consider the expense of operation, with any railroad fare in the world; not only America, but the world.

Now, gentlemen, a word as to the cost of our property. Mr. Burgin in his report, and I confirm all that the President has said, made the statement that our road cost us $7,059,026. Mr. Leeds has contended—I don't exactly remember where, but I think that such can be borne out as the fact—that a railroad company cannot, he says, expect to earn dividends upon its present cost, because railroads can be built now cheaper than when they were originally constructed, and he gets out of it by saying that if you make a bad investment that is your affair. That is all right. Now, then, for the argument. We are willing to concede the fact that our road cost $7,090,000. We are willing to put it on the basis of 75 cents per dollar upon its cost in order that we may to-day make a fair return to the investors in the property. Three-quarters of the value of the figures I gave you would amount to $5,317,544 44. The mortgage bonds of the road are $4,188,000, leaving therefore $1,129,544 44. Now, then, on Mr. Leeds' basis, we should earn a dividend on that, and I think 5 per cent you will concede is a fair dividend. Five per cent on that would result in giving us $56,477, or less than 1 per cent upon the capital stock of the company at present. But on that basis we could pay on $1,000,000, $1,129,500 44—5 per cent, equal to $56,477. Before, however, we can pay $1 out in dividends we have to pay for interest on the mortgage bonds, per year $209,400, in addition to which a sinking fund of $25,000, making a total of $234,400, which must be provided—otherwise it means foreclosure.

Therefore, gentlemen, I contend that last year, page number ten, if you care to refer to it, you will find that we succeeded in obtaining a net result of $81,017 19, which, under ordinary circumstances, would have been available as dividends, but—and there always seems to be a but in these dividend questions—the money has never been paid to the stockholders; in fact, since the inception of this company, the 19th day of March, 1889, up to now, not one dollar has been paid to the men that put their money in the property, in the way of dividends. Therefore is it not fair, is it not right to ask you, gentlemen, to pass no measure that shall disturb our present basis. Now, Mr. Leeds seeks to introduce —or the Traffic Association, or by some means, I don't exactly know how—a bill here on what he calls a California Distance Tariff.

By way of explanation, Mr. Chairman, I would like to say that you will see under the class rates—the first column is our rates at present in effect, the blank column the rates that would be in effect under this distance tariff—you will there find that five miles and under, where we now get per hundred pounds, 5 cents, this new schedule would give us but 3¾ cents; then if you like to jump down to, say fifty miles, you will find where we are getting 37 cents, this new measure would give us 25 cents; now if you like to jump down again further, say eighty miles, you will find that where we are now getting 43 cents, we will get 35 under the new tariff.

Now these rates, Mr. Chairman, and we have figured them out carefully, simply mean that it is an absolute reduction in our present freight tariff of between 35 and 50 per cent on our class rates, and on our carload business—and most of our traffic is carloads, consisting of lumber, shingles, and stuff like that—the reduction would be, and I will read them out to you: 52 per cent, 54 per cent, 51½ per cent, 50 per cent, 51 per cent, and so on, plainly showing to you, gentlemen, that the reduction would mean to this company a cutting down of our freight revenue, by the introduction of such an amendment, of over 50 per cent in our revenue. Colonel Morgan in his report has given a statement showing the population of the country, which Mr. Burgin made to you—but he makes another statement here that I think gives a good deal of information, and I think will illustrate how much of certain commodities we have to draw from. We consider that wine, grapes, and such commodities are quite large factors in our business.

If you will look at this report, you will find that Mendocino County contains an acreage in grapes of about two hundred and four acres; in Marin County, about five hundred and two acres, and in Sonoma County, twenty-two thousand six hundred and eighty-three acres; so that our railroad has about twenty-three thousand acres to draw from to get the wine shipments and grape shipments, which are, as I said, quite a large factor.

Then again, the entire population of the three counties is only sixty thousand, about, and out of that sixty thousand there is the San Francisco and North Pacific Railway, the North Pacific Coast Railway, the Southern Pacific Company, and those schooners and steamers that go up there to draw from; when we all cut up that sixty thousand we don't get many each.

In buying our material in California, there is quite an element. Cast iron, per pound, in Kansas is $1\frac{7}{8}$ cents, here it is 4 cents; wheels—and we are bound to have wheels for cars—cost in St. Louis $8 50, in New York they cost $8 75, and here they cost us $14.

Now, gentlemen, that high rate—not the high rate, but the difference in price—does not rest in the fact that the railroad companies are charging too much to get them here, but it is all attributable to the fact that America is too big; the country ought to be condensed, and we could get our supplies. In starting out, Mr. Chairman, I stated to you that already what we were doing in California was making itself felt East; I don't know whether or not this committee would care to know the opinion that the railroad papers have of the situation in California. If you do not wish to hear it, I will not read it.

EARL: Proceed, Mr. Mellersh.

MELLERSH: The "Railway Age," under date of January 20, 1893, reads as follows:

"The bitter and vindictive warfare which is being waged by many of the newspapers and people of Northern California, more especially those of San Francisco, against the railway companies of that State, furnishes an extraordinary example of ingratitude and injustice. Because California is cut off by thousands of miles of desert and mountains from the great markets of the world, and because within its limits the construction and operation of railways is attended with great expense, owing to the character of the country, the lack of diversified industries, the high cost of fuel, and the maintenance of large land holdings, railway rates naturally have to be higher than they are in the thickly settled and productive East. And yet, it is against this result of natural causes that the popular clamor is so unreasonably raised. The demand is, in effect, that the railways shall literally annihilate distance and ignore nature so far as their charges are concerned, and give the people of the mountains and plains of California as low rates for transportation as are offered in Illinois or New York. It is in vain that the railway companies set forth the cost of constructing their pioneer roads across the continent, point to their load of debt and show that the expenses of operation absorb the earnings so that bankruptcy has overtaken some and threatens all the lines. San Francisco merchants, fruit and grain growers, and the politicians and papers that follow after popularity repeat the cry 'rates must come down,' and demand that all the power of the State government shall be employed to this end, oblivious of reason and justice.

"Accordingly, the session of the Legislature just convened promises to be memorable for the passage of laws intended to crush the railways, particularly the Southern Pacific Company, which, having developed the State into independence, is now inconsistently denounced as its enemy. Already three hostile measures are under consideration: First, Shanahan's concurrent resolution, providing for a constitutional amendment abolishing the Railroad Commission; second, Schlesinger's resolution, providing for the appointment of a special committee to investigate the Railroad Commission, and to prepare articles for the impeachment of one or more members of the Commission, if the special committee deem impeachment justifiable; third, the Traffic Association resolution, providing for a constitutional amendment abolishing the Railroad Commission, authorizing the Legislature to fix rates for freight and fares, and providing in the Constitution a tariff to be operative in case the Legislature should not fix rates.

"The last proposed measure, upon which Mr. E. S. Leeds, as Manager of the Merchants' Traffic Association, has concentrated his ability and long experience in the railway service, is an extraordinary embodiment of reckless enmity to the railways. It proposes not only to abolish the Railroad Commission, which has shown some disposition to be fair to the roads, but to insert in the State Constitution a schedule of maximum rates for fare and freight far lower than those now obtained, which rates shall be charged if for any reason the Legislature fails to fix a tariff. Such matter has never been embodied in the Constitution of any State, and the proposition to make it part of the organic law shows the desperate animosity of its authors towards the railways, and their determination to prevent the sober and reasonable regulation of the rate question by the representatives of the people, from time to time, as the facts and conditions shall seem to warrant. The proposed amendment contains a complete table of freight rates fixed to suit the fancy of the shippers, and very much lower than those which the railways consider it possible to operate their roads upon; while the matter of passenger rates is easily settled by declaring that they 'shall not be more than 2 cents per mile,' a rate to which none of the old and populous States in the country (excepting the case of a small portion of the New York Central Railway) has ever had the heart to restrict its railways. In view of the extraordinary conditions surrounding railway operations in California—some of which were shown in the extract which we recently published from the testimony of an impartial expert employed by the Railroad Commission—it is not creditable to the intelligence or sense of fairness of the people of California to believe that they will ratify such a monstrous enactment against one of the interests of the State as is thus threatened—an enactment in comparison with which the anti-railway legislation of the Granger demagogues of Texas appears mild and tender hearted."

EARL: Where is that published?

MELLERSH: In Chicago and St. Paul. I will file it with the committee, if they wish to have it.

Railroads, Mr. Chairman, are quasi-public in character. When people get an idea that railroads must reduce rates they don't exactly find out the cause, but they make up their mind it must be so. To convince them to the contrary is very much like the man, you will remember, who refused to wear clothing. When they asked him why he refused to wear clothing, "Well, when you can bring a man to me who will convince me why it is a sheep raises wool out of eating grass, I will wear clothing." That man went naked, and so he ought to. And so it is with us. We meet the people on any reasonable request. If they want special rates, we give them; and it does seem to me, that inasmuch as our company practically have pleased all of our patrons—because there is nothing on file, except two little citations, to amount to anything—it does seem hard, where we are struggling along for the purpose of trying to make a living—for the purpose of trying to give to the people some little return for the money they put in—it seems hard that the Traffic Association shall get up in their might and ask the Legislature to enact a law that will simply shut us out of existence.

It would not be very difficult, Mr. Chairman, to define two pictures. One shall be ten years hence, if you like. The sun is climbing, gilding the mountain tops, and as it climbs up the horizon, warms up our beautiful and fertile valleys; on each side you see trees in their blossom; later on, the golden fruit and the grain, undulating with the breeze; the people going or gone to their business, traveling in palace cars and palatial steamers; the people happy, and the population increasing.

The other side would be, the Legislature having enacted a law that shall practically crush out all little companies; that where these bright steel rails were, two lines of rust are; the grass overgrown, the cars and engines side-tracked, everything having the appearance of innocuous desuetude, the population decreased, this beautiful State—none better in the Union—instead of being prosperous, simply standing still, or perhaps, retrograding.

Mr. Chairman, I do not want to take any more time of your committee, but it does seem to me that we have given you such facts and figures as will clearly evidence to you why such a law should not be enacted in this State; in fact pleadingly, I might almost say pathetically, we ask you not to pass any law that will not let us make a return to the people who have invested in our property. How can we go East or across the ocean and ask people to come here and buy our bonds? How can we ask people to extend our roads and put their money in them, and have them say at the first legislation, "We get no return; why should we send our money?" This question, Mr. Chairman, will be further reaching than California. It does not stop at California. It will stop almost everything; it will stop our wheels; it will hamper our roads; it will stop our State ten years, in my opinion, if any such bill is passed.

And we now ask, gentlemen of the committee. that you consider this proposition most seriously, and not pass any bill that does not fix bases as high as they are now, so that we shall be enabled thereby to earn as much as we do now.

Mr. Chairman, and gentlemen, I thank you.

GESFORD: I think the line of argument in reference to these short roads will be about the same in each case. The road I would like particularly to hear from is the Southern Pacific Company, and I would like to have a time fixed for them; that is last on our list, and I have some other matters to attend to. Mr. Leeds is unable to be here, but I think I have the trend of the argument of all these short roads.

EARL: During the evening, Mr. Gesford, we will fix the time when the Southern Pacific Company will be heard.

GESFORD: Well, then, I will go before the other committees; most of this argument will be written out, anyhow.

The following statements were filed by Mr. Mellersh:

SAN FRANCISCO AND NORTH PACIFIC RAILWAY COMPANY.

Statement of Cost of Operating Steamers.

Steamer repairs		$14,956 36	
Steamer expenses and wages of crew		36,667 51	
Dock repairs		3,783 37	
Fuel for steamers		36,427 97	
		$91,835 21	
Rent of slip, $1,400 per month	$16,800		
Switching	5,505	22,305 00	
			$114,140 21

Percentage of cost to gross receipts, 12.87 per cent.
Percentage of cost to gross expenses, 19.85 per cent.

Comparative Statement of Replacement of Cross-Ties.

Names of Railroads.	Per 100,000 Ties Per Year.	1891.	1892.	Cost Per Tie.
S. F. & N. P.	$14,500	1/7	1/7	35 cents.
C. N. O. & T. P.	20,000	1/5	1/4	30 cents.
A. G. S.	20,000	1/5	1/4	30 cents.
N. O. & N E.	10,000	1/10	1/6	25 cents.
V. & M.	20,000	1/5	1/4	30 cents.
V. S. & P.	25,000	1/4	1/5	30 cents.

Comparative Statement of Cars per Train, Tonnage per Train, and Cost of Fuel.

NAME OF ROAD.	Average number of cars in passenger train	Average number of tons per engine mile	Miles run p'r ton of coal	Average cost per engine mile for fuel—Cts.	Lbs. of coal used per engine mile	Average cost of coal per ton
San Francisco and North Pacific Railway (162.25 miles)	4.1	63.60	45.86	16.10	50	$7 25.47
Cincinnati Southern Railway (336 miles)	4.3	201.09	23.70	5.77	95	1 37
Alabama Great Southern Railway (295 miles)	4.9	178.98	30.00	4.55	74	1 36
New Orleans and Northeastern Railway (196 miles)	4.5	204.04	27.90	7.31	80	2 03
Alabama and Vicksburg Railway (140 miles)	5.1	213.40	32.50	5.80	69	1 88
Vicksburg, Shreveport, and Pacific Railway (170 miles)	4.6	126.31	37.20	7.51	60	2 79

CALIFORNIA DISTANCE TARIFF,

Applicable to Local Traffic between all Stations in the State of California, subject to the Western Classification, and the rules governing the same, which took effect January 1, 1893.

	Merchandise, in Cents per 100 Pounds.								Carloads of not less than Minimum named in Classification, nor more than Marked Capacity of Car.													
	1st Class.		2d Class.		3d Class.		4th Class.		5th Class.		Class A.		Class B.		Class C.		Class D.		Class E.		Lumber, Lath and Shingles.	
	S. F. & N. P.		S. F. & N. P.		S. F. & N. P.		S. F. & N. P.		S. F. & N. P.		S. F. & N. P.		S. F. & N. P.		S. F. & N. P.		S. F. & N. P.		S. F. & N. P.		S. F. & N. P.	
No. 17—5 miles and under	5	3¼	5	3¾	5	3¾	5	3¾	5	3	5	3	5	3	5	3	5	3	4	3	4	3
No. 18—10 miles and over 5 miles.	10	4½	10	4	10	4	10	4	9	3½	8	4	7	3½	6	3	6	3	5	3	8	3
No. 19—15 " " " 10 "	11	8	11	7	10	6	9	5	8	4	9	5	8	4	7	3½	6	3	6	3	9	3
No. 20—20 " " " 15 "	15	12	15	10	13	9	11	7	10	5	9	6	8	5	7	4	6	3	6	3	9	3
No. 21—25 " " " 20 "	18	15	17	12	15	11	13	8	12	6	12	7	11	6	10	5	9	4	8	3	9	4
No. 22—30 " " " 25 "	22	18	20	14	17	13	15	9	14	7	15	8	14	6½	13	5½	12	4½	11	3½	10	4
No. 23—35 " " " 30 "	25	20	19	16	16	14	14	11	13	8	14	9	13	7	12	6	11	5	10	3½	10	4½
No. 24—40 " " " 35 "	30	22	26	18	22	15	19	13	17	8	16	9	15	7	14	6	13	5	12	3½	11	4½
No. 25—45 " " " 40 "	34	24	27	19	23	17	20	14	17	9	16	10	15	8	14	7	13	6	12	4	11	5
No. 26—50 " " " 45 "	37	25	31	20	27	18	24	15	21	10	20	11	19	8	18	7	17	6	16	4	12	5
No. 27—55 " " " 50 "	39	27	31	22	27	19	24	16	21	11	20	12	19	9	18	8	17	6	16	4	13	5
No. 28—60 " " " 55 "	40	28	32	23	28	20	25	17	22	12	21	13	20	9	19	8	18	6	17	5	13	6
No. 29—65 " " " 60 "	41	30	33	24	29	21	26	18	23	13	22	14	21	10	20	8	19	7	18	5	14	6
No. 30—70 " " " 65 "	42	32	34	25	30	22	27	18	24	13	23	14	22	10	21	9	20	7	19	5	14	6
No. 31—75 " " " 70 "	42	33	34	26	30	23	27	19	24	14	23	15	22	11	21	9	20	7	19	5½	14	7
No. 32—80 " " " 75 "	43	35	35	28	31	24	28	19	25	14	24	15	23	11	22	9	21	7	20	5½	15	7
No. 33—85 " " " 80 "	43	37	35	29	31	25	28	20	25	15	24	16	23	12	22	10	21	8	20	6	16	7
No. 34—90 " " " 85 "	44	38	36	30	32	26	29	21	26	16	25	18	24	13	23	10	22	8	21	6	16	8
No. 35—95 " " " 90 "	47	39	39	31	35	27	32	21	27	16	26	18	25	13	24	11	23	8	22	6	16	8
No. 36—100 " " " 95 "	48	40	40	32	36	28	33	22	30	17	29	19	28	14	27	11	26	8	25	7	16	9
No. 37—105 " " " 100 "	49	41	41	33	37	29	34	23	31	18	30	20	29	14	28	11	27	9	26	7	16	9
No. 38—110 " " " 105 "	49	42	41	34	37	30	34	24	31	19	30	21	29	15	28	12	27	9	26	7	16	10
No. 39—115 " " " 110 "	50	43	42	35	38	31	35	25	32	20	31	22	30	16	29	12	28	9	27	7	20	10

Barley, 4th Class; brick, Class E; broomcorn seed, Class A; beans, 5th Class; cement, Class C; coal, Class D; corn, Class E; clay, Class E; castor beans, 5th Class; flour, 4th Class; flaxseed, 4th Class; lime, Class C; live stock, 3d Class; mill stuffs and chops, 4th Class; oats, Class E; rye, Class E; salt, 4th Class; stucco, Class C; stone, Class E; sand, Class E; wheat, Class E.

Statement of W. F. Russell.

(Representing the North Pacific Coast Railway.)

Representing the North Pacific Coast Railroad, I beg to state that no complaints have been made along the line of our road, either on the rates of fares or freights. From statistics compiled for the last year's business, the passenger rates over the North Pacific Coast Railroad average 1.38 cents per mile, and the freight rates, 3.99 cents per ton per mile. Under this Gesford amendment, it is proposed that roads of our earning capacity shall be limited to a charge for passengers of not to exceed 3 cents per mile, and for freight, according to that mentioned in the "California Distance Tariff," in conjunction with the Western Classification, which would at once reduce our rates on freight from 35 to 45 per cent, and which would compel us to do our freight business at an actual loss. The gross earnings per mile are $4,478.

Being in direct competition with water on one side and a railroad on the other, we are to-day hauling the chief products of Sonoma and Marin Counties at such rates as compel us to carry north-bound freight at our present tariff rates, and the rates on these products are computed at almost first cost. Seventy-five per cent of the earnings derived from freight traffic on this road cover that brought to San Francisco, thereby compelling 50 per cent of our returning freight cars to be hauled back empty; and, owing to the mountainous country through which we travel, the expense of hauling these loaded cars over these steep grades and sharp curves leaves a very small margin of profit.

Again, all the goods that go to or from San Francisco have to be handled or unloaded by us, thereby reducing our freight charge per ton, in some cases, 30 and 40 per cent. Take coal, for instance, where we have to load and haul between San Francisco and San Rafael for $1 per ton. This, coupled with the enormous passenger and freight ferry terminal expense, really reduces our freight charge below that charged by many Eastern roads, because such California Distance Tariff does not calculate on our doing any handling.

Another serious objection to this proposed amendment is the change in classification, which makes an entirely different classification on many articles from that which has been in effect on this road for many years.

One reason for the heavy cost of hauling freight over the North Pacific Coast Railroad, is the cost of fuel. Our coal last year averaged us a cost of $7 81 a ton, and wood $3 a cord, and computing two cords of wood to a ton of coal, our coal, even on the very best proposition, would cost us $6, which is more than double the cost of coal in the East. Labor costs much more here than it does in the East, and we are running through a country composed chiefly of timber land and dairies, giving us very small opportunity to obtain return freight for the cars hauling down the products of the country through which we run. We have got a road that is all grades and curves, and are really without a straight line in it, and to subject us to the same terms and conditions of a road that is perfectly level, running through a thickly populated country, is discriminating against us to the cruelest extent.

We have been in operation now since 1874, and have never yet been able to declare a single dividend to stockholders, and have had to carefully watch every cent of expenditure, and at the same time are compelled to spend vast sums every year maintaining our bridges, all of which are sustained at great expense.

Mr. Earl: How long is your road?

Mr. Russell: Eighty-six and three quarters miles.

Statement of L. T. Garnsey.

(Representing the Redondo Railway.)

To the honorable the Senate Committee on Constitutional Amendments:

Gentlemen: In reference to the pending bill now under discussion before your honorable body, in which there seems to be a disposition on the part of the originators to arbitrarily fix the rates of fare and traffic over the lines of roads in this State, we beg the privilege of submitting our views.

Firstly, in making such rates obligatory and a part of the Constitution, in our judgment is not only ruinous to all the railroad interests now in operation, but to the commercial and agricultural prosperity and development of our entire country. In treating of this question it would seem that the spirit of selfishness should be laid aside, and that we should be actuated by that principle of justice and equity that gives to each and every man a fair and reasonable compensation for his labor and the money invested. In digesting the present bill the solution of the promoters is apparent. To kill the goose that laid the golden egg seems paramount to future prosperity and to all other issues. The argument advanced by these so-called promoters is, that they know it all, and that unsupported statistics have greater value, and should be given more credence and weight, than actual facts. It must certainly be evident to any careful observer that if this bill now before your committee passes, it will work great hardships upon those having money invested in railways, and for the following reasons:

1. It is impossible to compare California with such a State as Kansas, because of the totally dissimilar geographical features. The topography of California is broken up by vast mountain chains and rivers, which, because of these mountains, become raging torrents when fed by melting snows or heavy rainfalls, or both together. These conditions, first of all, compel an immense outlay of money in construction, in order to provide for tunnels, heavy cuts, large fills, long bridges, strong trestles, and an abundance of culverts and water drains. On the other hand, Kansas presents a comparatively flat country, with streams which may overflow their banks, but not with the disastrous consequences following such floods in a country of high mountains and low valleys. The construction of railways in the kind of country as represented by Kansas is, therefore, much cheaper than such a country as California.

2. The cost of maintaining and operating a railroad in California is very much greater than in Kansas or any other country of like character, because of the tunnels, bridges, trestles, grades, etc. The pulling of loads up hill or up grade burns more fuel and is a greater strain upon the rolling stock than through flat countries by quite a large per cent, besides causing more wear and tear upon both rolling stock and track.

3. In California fuel is much more costly than in the Eastern or so-called Western States; wages are very much higher, and material of all kinds is very much more expensive.

4. One other item is of great importance, and one that should receive careful attention in the consideration of this subject, namely, the sparsely settled condition of California as compared with the country east of the Rocky Mountains. This is of prime importance, because the larger the volume of business the cheaper the business can be handled. If in countries thickly settled throughout passengers can be carried for 3 cents a mile at a profit, there is no reason, however, why they should be carried for the same rate in California, even though there were no topographical difficulties, and the wages, fuel, etc., were the same; but they are not, they are higher, much higher. Therefore railroad companies in California should receive much larger compensation for the same amount of work performed than those situated in more populous districts.

5. Another and more important fact should not be forgotten. We require more railroads to develop our country and create new industries. We should not lose sight of the fact that to encourage capital should be one of the incentives in governing our actions. It is a well-known fact that capital will never seek investment when handicapped by constitutional amendments that in effect almost absolutely prohibit a fair return on the money invested. In other words, would it not be in effect the abandonment of all new railroad enterprises for years to come, thereby retarding progress and preventing competition? I am of the opinion that such would be the result, and that the prosperity to which we are all endeavoring to attain would be best subserved by that fostering and encouraging attitude that would enlist new capital, build up the country, and place our noble and illustrious State in the front rank of sisterhood, where she rightfully belongs.

L. T. GARNSEY,
Representing Redondo Railroad Co.

The above is submitted as my views, as representing the Redondo Railway Company. In my individual capacity I will say, I am not biased in favor of railroads, as my private interests in horticulture and agriculture are at least 95 per cent greater than in railroad enterprises. My sole object is to get better results and a larger income from my investments, and a more extended market for my products, thereby I wish to encourage any and all enterprises that will lead to that end.

It appears to me that the nucleus of our future success is more and better railroad facilities, thereby creating competition which will force rates and tariff to seek their proper level, without the aid of ambiguous legislation. By the way of illustrating, permit me to call your attention to the following facts which appear pertinent to the case. For many years I was the largest wholesaler and shipper of foreign and domestic fruits in a number of New York's flourishing interior cities. This is an industry in which we in California are now largely interested, and which bids fair to outrank all other products of the State. By virtue of circumstances, I was forced to give more or less attention to railroad rates, to overcome New York city's competition and protect my trade.

In my investigation of rates in California as compared with classifications and rates East on these goods, I find them scarcely any higher, and in some cases proportionately lower. For instance, the rate on oranges and lemons from Colton and Redlands to San Francisco is but $75 per car of twenty thousand pounds, a haul of five hundred and fifty miles; from Santa Ana, Tustin, and thereabouts, a haul of five hundred and twenty miles, $60 per car. On the same quantity of goods East for a number of years, I considered myself very fortunate in getting them carried the distance of two hundred miles for $50, or a fraction above one third the distance at two thirds the price; you will notice the pro rata rate being largely in favor of California. The tariff on the same class of goods from Colton, Redlands, and thereabouts, to Chicago, a distance of over two thousand seven hundred miles by the Southern Pacific Railroad, is $250 per car of twenty thousand pounds, which is very low, considering that nearly all fruits of this character are shipped in refrigerator cars of twice the weight of ordinary box cars, requiring double the power to make the haul, and as I understand it, the larger portion of these cars return empty for re-loading, adding thereto another large expense. Estimating this with the immense grades, large cost of maintenance, and operating, and the much greater cost of fuel, it would in my judgment, seem that present rates were reasonable, and that shippers were fairly and honorably treated.

Respectfully submitted.

L. T. GARNSEY.

Statement of W. S. Waterman.

(Of the San Diego, Cuyamaca, and Eastern Railway.)

Gentlemen: I do not know that I have anything new to present to this committee. I wish, however, to join with those who have preceded me in objecting to the passage of the proposed amendment. I also wish to object to the passage of any law that will have a tendency to bring the railroad into politics.

I represent the San Diego, Cuyamaca, and Eastern Railway, which runs from San Diego eastward over the mesas, and through Spring Valley and El Cajon Valley. These valleys, and also the mesa lands, are fertile and productive, and are under the waters of the San Diego Flume Company, and the country is improving rapidly. The road was built for the development of the country through which it runs. It was also the intention of the projectors to build the road to a connection with the Southern Pacific Railroad, at or near Salton. This road was built in 1888 and 1889, and was formally opened in March, 1889, to Lakeside, a distance from San Diego of twenty-two miles. Later on 3.37 miles additional was built, to Foster. While the road has always done considerable business, its rates of freight and passenger fares have been comparatively low. The passenger rate is 4 cents per mile, and our freight rates are:

First class	22.4 cents per ton per mile.
Second class	20.0 cents per ton per mile.
Third class	14.2 cents per ton per mile.
Fourth class	12.0 cents per ton per mile.
Fifth class	9.6 cents per ton per mile.
Average	14.2 cents per ton per mile.

Class A	9.6 cents per ton per mile.
Class B	8.8 cents per ton per mile.
Class C	7.2 cents per ton per mile.
Average	8.2 cents per ton per mile.
Raisins	8.3 cents per ton per mile.

The proposed rates are from 25 per cent to 45 per cent lower than these. In spite of low rates the road has always paid its running expenses, has put some money into betterments each year, and has been paying for its rolling stock in payments amounting to about $500 per month. The gross earnings are $1,476 25 per mile, and the cost of operating per mile $890. Of the gross earnings, 47 per cent is from passengers, and the balance is from freight. I run two trains each way a day, all being, when occasion demands it, mixed passenger and freight trains. The freight which we haul out of San Diego is general merchandise, lumber, piping, and building materials. The freight which we haul into San Diego is rock, hay, grain, wood, wool, and fruits of various kinds. The largest one article, excepting rock, is hay, followed by raisins, and then by oranges and lemons. There are several thousand acres of young fruit trees just now coming into bearing, which are beginning to swell our freight receipts. Regarding the rock which we haul, I wish to say that it is used for street paving, building material, and for cemetery work. From this source alone we expect to double our present earnings, possibly more than that. From the prospects before us we have a right to expect to belong to that class of roads that earn $4,000 per mile and upwards, and that in a very few years. For that reason we consider that we have as much interest in this proposed amendment as any road has. This road, though it has done better than many roads in this State, has yet never paid interest on the money invested in it—some $400,000. The interest on this amount for the four years of the road's existence is $100,000. We certainly have a right to consider the accrued interest as an investment, and when this road earns money enough to pay interest on $400,000 and the then accrued interest, I believe we are entitled to it, and also to something more, for the risk we have taken in building a road to develop a country before the country could pay for its own development. Furthermore, I believe the patrons of this road think in the same way. There is a general feeling of satisfaction among our patrons regarding our rates and our service.

Even if this road earned over $4,000 per mile, when the expenses, cost of accidents, cost of replacing worn-out material, etc., are all considered, the profits to the stockholders will be small enough to satisfy anybody.

It is a mistake to think that all the railroad has to do is to sit down and let business come to it. It must look after business, and work up and encourage business, just as one must do in any other line. Many a time a good business is secured simply by hard work. What is the object of hard work, if by it one is to decrease their net income? The absurdity has already been brought to your notice of placing a road in a position where, if it increase its business it diminishes its income. I also wish to ask you if you think such a state of affairs would be beneficial to the country through which any special road runs? I think it would be decidedly detrimental, and I believe you think the same.

We are also contemplating an extension of this road into valleys that are further up in the mountains. The question naturally arises, is it safe to invest more money in an enterprise that is subjected to this kind of adverse legislation? Certainly not. I would not put my own money into such a scheme, and I believe other people would not, either. It seems to me that the result of this kind of agitation will be to make people backward about investing money in this State, and I am equally satisfied that the passage of such a law would effectually and forever stop railroad building in California. We all wish more railroads, and I sincerely hope that this Legislature will not do anything either to hamper those already built, or to have a tendency to keep other railroads out of the country. I might add, in closing, that I consider arbitrary fixed rates, such as those proposed, as entirely wrong. If fares and freights must be regulated in some way, let them be regulated first, on the cost of road, second, on the cost of operating and maintaining.

Statement of Grove L. Johnson.

(Representing the Visalia and Tulare Railroad.)

Mr. Chairman: I appear here to-night in behalf of the Visalia and Tulare Railroad Company, which is what may be denominated a little railroad. It is only eleven and a half miles long. It is owned entirely by residents of Visalia and Tulare. It is owned by the people. There is no question of foreign capital. There is no question of wealthy monopolists, no question of powerful corporations. Simply a question of little railroad, owned by the people, built for the people, and used by the people; and being part of the people, appears before you as representatives of the people to ask that it be not injured by what it deems improper, impolitic, and unwise legislation. This road was built more especially for the benefit of the people of Visalia and vicinity. To the people of Visalia this road and its competitor was an absolute necessity. We have a map here—the map that is published by the Railroad Commissioners—by which is shown location of Visalia and the location of this road, and location of branches of the Southern Pacific. I will explain it by saying that Visalia is situated in the center of a loop, formed by two branches of the Southern Pacific, and deriving no benefit from either branch, standing by itself, isolated, the Southern Pacific a positive injury to it—of absolutely no value—leaving it some miles to the east, and some miles to the west.

The people of Visalia, then, in order to obtain railroad communication, were obliged to build railroads for themselves. One was built from the town of Goshen, on the line of the Southern Pacific, extending to Visalia, which is known as the Visalia Railroad, which is seven miles long. Another was built, commencing at a station known as Tulare, and running to Visalia, which is known as the Visalia and Tulare Railroad, eleven and one half miles long. Those two roads were built, both of them, by the people, and they are absolutely, as I said, a necessity for Visalia, in order that the people of Visalia may obtain advantages of railroad communication; they are a necessity to the people. They are not in any mannner, particularly the railroad that I represent to-night, interested in or connected with the Southern Pacific Company, excepting as being a feeder or being fed by the company. They exchange business with it, the same as other business men exchange business with men of their own character, and men engaged in the same line of business. It has no affiliations; it is not controlled; its stock is not owned by the Southern Pacific Company; it is not managed by it, or controlled by it, or responsible for anything it does.

This road, the Visalia and Tulare Railroad, cost about $115,000, in round numbers. It has a bonded indebtedness of $50,000, carrying 7 per cent interest; it never has paid any dividends; it lives in great expectations; it has hopes for the future. So far, no one has ever complained of it. It does not corrupt any newspapers or members of the Legislature, nor anybody. It does not interfere with anybody, but it lives, as I have said, upon expectations of what the country will become. Within the last few years some 6,000 acres in the immediate vicinity have been set out in fruit trees. The expectations of the owners of this company, and the owners of the other company is that in a few years the country will increase in population by more than double—quadruple—and the business derived from carrying the fruit from this immense orchard will raise their revenues, and enable them to not only pay their interest, but, perhaps, to obtain some little return on their money. They have in contemplation the extension of their line from Visalia into the mountains, for the purpose of holding the local trade. As it is now, a large number of people in that vicinity seek the coast to get rid of the heat of summer. Their proposal is to extend the road into the mountains, to make summer resorts there, where not only the people of Visalia and that vicinity will go, but where people from San Francisco, seeking a summer resort, will also go. They will benefit the people not only of that vicinity, but of the whole State. This they are willing to do and expect to do, if their business is allowed to continue. This road, the Visalia and Tulare Railroad, and the Visalia Railroad, are almost the only instances in this State where roads are directly in competition with each other, and I may say this is the only instance in the State where the competition is such that if this bill becomes a law, one railroad will be ruined, and perhaps the other railroad will be benefited. The competition between the roads is such that although one is seven miles long, and the other eleven and one half miles long, they charge the same rates of fares, and the same rates of freight, and by reason of it they will be amenable to the same rules if this bill becomes a law.

Now, if you will pardon me, before going into detail more, in reference to these two roads, and in reference to the effect upon them of this proposed legislation, I will say a few words of a general character, in reference to this proposed legislation. Now, this resolution is a great and a radical change in the law of California. As you all know, in 1879, the people of this State adopted what is known as the New Constitution, which was a new departure, and which was supposed to be the adoption of a Constitution that would take the railroad question out of politics; that would take the railroad out of legislation, and would place the railroad question with a Commission of three gentlemen, elected by the people of the State, and in that way it would be in the hands of men who would make it a study. In that way it would be in the hands of men who would attend to it, and in that way the people would be freed from the railroad question, and the time of the Legislature would not be consumed, nor the members vexed in considering a question fraught with so much difficulty, and which from the wreck of reputations in the history of this State, is fraught with so much danger to the members of the Legislature.

It was also intended by the Constitution that there should be no more class distinctions, no more arbitrary distinctions in this State—that everything should be put on a level; everything should be put on an equality. There should be no more special legislation; no more legislation directed at one particular thing, one particular company, one particular interest, one particular corporation, or one particular set of men; that everything should be general in its nature—general in its character. So anxious were the framers of this Constitution to have that principle ingrafted in the Constitution, that they took particular pains, in various sections of the Constitution, to enact that, and say that special legislation was prohibited, and to provide in the Constitution for almost everything the people needed, in order that there might be no legislation, and in the articles providing what the Legislature could and could not do in reference to special legislation, it winds up by saying they shall not pass local or special laws in any case where a general law will apply, showing it was the object and aim of the people of the State, at that time, to prevent any more special legislation, any more arbitrary distinctions, any more class distinctions, and leave everything, as I said, on an equality.

Now, for nearly fourteen years we have lived under that Constitution. Some people thought that it was not a good Constitution. Some people thought that it was defective; that it was injurious to the State; but the State has prospered, the State has succeeded, and the forms of special legislation that are growing so powerful and strong in California have, to a great extent, been curbed, and the State to-day is more prosperous than ever before. And while I was one of those who opposed the new Constitution, I am forced by the logic of my convictions to admit that the crusade against special legislation—the laws against special legislation—the constitutional enactment against special legislation—has resulted in good to the State. Now, after living under it for fourteen years, it is sought to change it. It is sought to make a radical change—wonderful change in what for fourteen years, nearly, has been the law in this State. It is sought now to have some more class legislation—some more arbitrary distinctions—some more distinctions not based upon anything, except a desire to have a distinction. Now, when anybody asks for a change to be made, especially such a great and radical change as this, good reasons should be offered. When any one is asked, and the members of the Legislature are asked to impose arbitrary classifications upon the people, good reasons should be given. Is not that true, and is it not true for two reasons—first, when any one asks to make a change, there ought to be a reason for it. If a man buys a new coat, he has a reason for it; if he buys a new horse, he has a reason for it; if he changes his condition in life, and gets married, he has a reason for it.

In everything we do there is a reason for it, and now, when you come to make an arbitrary distinction, a distinction without a reason, a distinction founded simply upon feeling, then reasons ought to be given that will be satisfactory, not only to the persons asking us to make these distinctions, but satisfactory to every person that votes for them, and satisfactory to the people that are to be oppressed or benefited by this arbitrary distinction. Now, Section 3 of this present resolution provides arbitrarily for two classes of railroads in California—arbitrarily sets up two classes of railroads: one, those earning annually over $4,000 per mile, and second, those earning less annually than $4,000 per mile. Now, why is this? It makes by one sweep of the pen two classes in this State. It divides the railroads of this State in twain, exactly as you would cut a piece of bread or cheese with a knife. Now, why is it? Has any reason been given for it? If so, what? Is there any such consensus of opinion among railroad men, amongst people who have given their time, their money, and their labors to the elucidation of railroad questions, as convinces the members of this railroad committee that $4,000 is the necessary legitimate result of the full fruition of labor in railroads?

If so, when, and where, and how? This is an arbitrary distinction, $4,000 per mile. It is asked of you that you make that distinction. It is asked of you that you say by your votes that $4,000 is the limit. That up to $4,000 a mile the Legislature can act in reference to railroads. Over $4,000 a mile it cannot act. Why? Have any facts and figures, any proof, or any evidence been introduced here? Has there been any legislative or congressional committee and their report been presented to you which shows that this limit is a necessary and legitimate limit? Is it true that the railroad which earns more than $4,000 per mile in gross, should be treated any different from the railroads which earn less than that amount? If so, why? It is an arbitrary distinction. It is a distinction not based on anything but the mere arbitrary will of the Legislature. Why not take $5,000, $3,500, or $6,000? Is there any reason given for it? Is there any reason given why this should be put in the Constitution and say that $4,000 per mile is the proper limit for railroads?

We have been told in the past that it was wise to limit the number of acres of land that a man could own. We are told so to-day. But no man yet has agreed upon the number of acres a man should own. I have heard men owning forty thousand and fifty thousand acres argue strenuously in favor of limitation upon the ownership of land, but no man yet was in favor of reducing the number of acres that he held, except by sale. So in this, is there any real reason for taking $4,000? I have listened attentively to the arguments here. I have read everything that has been published by the newspapers in regard to it. I have not seen—I have not heard it. I have heard of people saying—making an argument addressed to the committee in favor of the bill, but what I am speaking of is, where is the evidence, where are the facts, where are the figures?

Some of you gentlemen I know to be lawyers. One Senator I am not acquainted with. I do not know his profession. But you lawyers know that persons seeking a thing, having the affirmative, must introduce proof, because the rule of law is that he who has a complaint must file proof. Has any proof been introduced here, conclusive in this matter? If so, where, and when, and how? Is any rule which makes a railroad earning less than $4,000 better or worse than one earning over—does it make them any more wicked? Is the railroad earning less than $4,000 less liable to be corrupted than the one earning more than $4,000? If so, is that to be the maximum and the limit?

And up to $4,000 per mile you are honest; over $4,000 per mile you are dishonest. Up to $4,000 per mile you can be trusted by the Legislature of this State. Over $4,000 per mile you become a highwayman, with your hand against every one, with the desire to rob, and to get the best of the people. This arbitrary decision of over $4,000 per mile, why is it on that basis? It is such a radical departure, such a tremendous change, and it makes such an arbitrary distinction, that it seems to me that the very best of reasons should be given for it—the very best of reasons, not the mere statement of opinions. I grant you the eminent ability of the gentleman, as well as every gentleman in favor of this bill. I grant you all that may be said by any person in reference to the years that he has spent in railroad study. I grant everything that may be said as to his memory—everything that his friends may say of him. I admit, I grant it all, and yet I say that his opinion ought not to be received by this committee as conclusive.

If there is to be a "bed of Procrustes" in this State upon which all railroads shall be placed, and should they reach over $4,000 per mile they shall be cut in two, as were the guests of Procrustes in ancient times, there ought to be some good reason for it. The only reason adduced here for you gentlemen considering this bill, is that, like Procrustes, you have got the power to do it; that is all; no other reason on earth. You have the power to do it, therefore should do it. Is that a reason to be addressed to members of the Legislature? Should it be a conclusive reason for changing the legislation of the State, for changing the Constitution of this State, for overturning the work of the people, for overturning the way the people have lived for the past fourteen years, and making an arbitrary distinction? This is something which should be justified—something that you gentlemen will be called on to justify on your return to your constituents, because your votes here are simply the expression of your individual ideas.

You represent some persons. You must report to your constituents. Are they interested in this? If so, where is the evidence? Are they believers in these reasons? If so, where and how have they been convinced, and how shall you be convinced? Now, I argue the question, whether before the committee, or before a Court, upon what I believe to be the correct basis and the legal ground. I differ from the learned gentleman who addressed the committee some three nights ago. I grant your power. I admit that the Legislature has the power to grant this constitutional amendment. I admit the people have the right to adopt it. I admit, if the people adopt this Constitution, it becomes a Constitution. Special charters, general charters, special laws, general laws, special privileges and general privileges, the charter of a corporation which forms a little road, the charter of a corporation which forms a large road, the charter of a corporation or a company that is transacting a few thousand dollars a year, or of a company that is transacting hundreds of millions of dollars a year—all become amenable to the Constitution, in my judgment.

If this resolution passes the Legislature, and if the people ratify it, it becomes our Constitution, and all must bow down and obey it; and to take our special charters is, to my mind, somewhat misleading. And inasmuch as you do have that power, inasmuch as the people have the power to adopt this Constitution, and inasmuch as if the people do adopt this Constitution, it strikes so powerfully, it becomes so drastic, it is such a wonderful change, and it does bear with such a heavy hand on all the railroads in this State, that more than ever you should be very careful, it seems to me, and you should ask for the very best reasons in the world. A mere opinion should not always count. No matter how learned the man may be who says this ought to pass, there should be facts, there should be figures, there should be reasons given for it. As for the abolishment of the Railroad Commission, I will speak of that a little later; but first, I want to call your attention to the effect that this will have on the Visalia and Tulare Railroad Company, if it should be adopted. As I said before, the Visalia and Tulare Railroad is in direct competition with the Visalia Railroad. The rates are necessarily the same.

The Visalia Railroad is seven miles long. It charges 50 cents for fare from Goshen to Visalia. The Visalia and Tulare Railroad is eleven and a half miles long, and charges 50 cents for passengers from Tulare to Visalia. The rates on freight are the same on both roads. Now, then, they are in, as I say, direct competition. Each road does just about the same amount of business. The Visalia Railroad being the shorter railroad, has therefore larger apparent gross earnings per mile. The Visalia Railroad mileage being only seven miles, its gross earnings are about $3,000 per mile. The Visalia and Tulare Railroad being longer—its mileage eleven and a half miles—its earnings are less than $2,000 per mile, although it receives about the same amount for freight and passenger traffic as does the Visalia Railroad. The business prospects of both of them are about the same. They both expect an increase in population; they both expect to derive money from the fruit trees that I spoke of; from the people that are expected there; from the subdivision of the large land holdings. And in about two years it is confidently expected by the owners of the Visalia Railroad that its gross earnings will be over $4,000 per mile; but the Visalia and Tulare Railroad will not reach that amount. Being, as I said, eleven miles long, and charging exactly the same rates, it, in all human probability, cannot hope to be more than $3,000 per mile at the same time the Visalia Railroad reaches $4,000 per mile. Just the moment that the Visalia Railroad reaches $4,000 gross earnings per mile, then the rates must be lowered, because this constitutional enactment says so, and its rates of fares will be lowered about 60 per cent, its rates on freight lowered 36 per cent, in order to conform to this constitutional provision. Now, the Visalia and Tulare Railroad will not, at that time, be earning $4,000 per mile. It will only be earning $3,000 per mile under the most favorable auspices, and with the most favorable results, and yet it must also, by reason of the law of competition, lower its rates to the rates which will be charged by the Visalia Railroad, because it is in direct competition; and it cannot do any business if it charges more than the Visalia Railroad, under the provision.

And if the Visalia Railroad, under the constitutional provision, charges only 22 cents for people to go to Visalia, the Visalia and Tulare Railroad cannot charge you more than 22 cents, either, because if it does charge more, it will do no business. If the Visalia Railroad reduces its charges 36 per cent, as it will necessarily be obliged to do, immediately the Visalia and Tulare Railroad must reduce its rates 36 per cent, in order to compete with it, and then the Visalia and Tulare Railroad, which at that time earned, if it earned as much as its projectors hope it will, which will be $3,000 per mile, under those rates it will be reduced immediately down to $1,200 or $1,300 per mile, and will be obliged to suspend business. It will simply have to quit, to use the language of the street. It will have to stop, being brought into competition immediately with this other road—in direct competition. The rates, as you know, are always regulated by competition, for we are told here by every person—we are told here by the gentlemen who favor this bill, as well as those who oppose the bill—that competition is the surest thing to regulate charges of railroads. We are told that in the East one reason why rates are different there is because of the great competition. We all recognize it. It is the same with the railroad business as with any other business. If it was not for the competition between lawyers, it would be almost impossible to pay their exorbitant charges. And so it is with railroads. Competition is what makes business; and I don't care how politic a man may be, I don't care how much a man may desire to have a little railroad he believes in succeed, if he can ride over an opposition road for 22 cents he is not going to pay 50 cents to ride over a road owned and controlled and operated by his friend.

It is not human nature, and this Visalia and Tulare Railroad will be obliged to reduce its rates of freight and fare to meet the competition of the Visalia Railroad, which has been obliged to reduce its rates by reason of this constitutional provision. Now, is that fair? Is it right? Is it just? I don't speak of any vested rights. I don't wish you, gentlemen of this committee, to understand me as saying that I think any man has the right to stand up here and say, "you can't take this away." I grant that you can do it. I grant, and I understand that you have the power to confiscate this road. I grant that you have the power to kill this road. But what I say is, that if you do pass this bill, if the people indorse your action and make it a part of the Constitution, you do kill this road; and I ask, is it right to do it? Is it right to ruin it, even? Is it right to pass any bill which will have a tendency to cripple or kill any interest, particularly an interest like this little road, which has no enemies, against which no complaints have been made, which is neither an object of envy nor an object of hate to anybody within the State of California? Is that doing what will advance the interests of the people? Is that in accordance with the oath that every man took as a member of the Legislature, to support the Constitution, which guarantees equality to all? If so, where are the facts? Where is the evidence which authorizes and demands that such be done?

Of course, we are informed through the newspapers, which sometimes get things right, we are informed through the medium of Mr. Leeds, who I understand to be the real author of this bill, that they are not seeking to make war upon the little roads; that they are only anxious to grapple the large road; to throttle the monster, as they call it, and to seize hold of the Southern Pacific Company, and, metaphorically speaking, to choke it, and compel it to submit to wholesome legislation. Inasmuch as the author of this bill, inasmuch as the friends of this bill, inasmuch as the newspapers that favor this legislation, inasmuch as all the people who seem to favor this legislation, are united in one voice, and say that they don't wish to injure any little road, we are here representing a little road, and ask you to protect us. We ask, if you feel compelled, either by your own feelings or the quality of the evidence that may be brought before you, if you feel that it is due to the public opinion, if you feel that there has been built up in this State a sufficient anti-railroad feeling to justify you in voting for such an amendment as this, if you feel that you can go home and justify it to your constituents, if you feel that it is the opinion of the people of the State of California, that are always right, although they may at times make mistakes, if you feel that the people will sustain you, then I ask you, in the name of every man who says he favors this, to protect the little road, and get the big road that you want to hurt. Protect us. The little road cannot protect itself against competition. The little road cannot protect itself against the big road.

If you are going to make class distinctions, if you are going to make arbitrary distinctions, make them in such a manner that all the little roads will be safe from injury; and unless you can do that, we say it is not right to pass a law which will have a tendency to injure them. The strong can take care of themselves. The weak need protection from the Legislature. It is good to have a giant's power. It is wicked to use that power like a giant. You gentlemen have a giant's power. You can kill these little roads. We ask you not to do it. We ask you to study this matter carefully before you pass any measure which will have the tendency named, which will simply result in killing these little roads.

We ask you, before you make any such radical changes in the Constitution of this State, which change is so great that the very mention of it makes people shudder, we ask, before you revolutionize the Constitution of this State and reform the laws pertaining to railroad legislation, we ask you to be careful and eliminate from it everything that will injure the weak, and if you desire to strike at the corporation that is deemed powerful, strike directly at it. You have the power. If you have the power to pass this, you have the power to pass a resolution directed solely at the Southern Pacific Company. And I say, why not meet the question fairly? Why seek behind a general law and a general purpose to cover the real design? Assail the Southern Pacific Company. It will welcome you. Assail it in any way you choose, but leave the little roads alone. If the Constitution of the United States will permit the passage of a constitutional amendment in the State of California, such as is here proposed, it will permit the passage of a constitutional amendment to strike directly at one road and leave all others alone. Of course, that would be class legislation. Of course, they won't ask you to do that. Why? "Because," they would say, "the people won't stand that. The people would say that you are actuated by the desire to crush one particular company." But the result of this legislation, if you pass this bill, is exactly the same as if you assail the Southern Pacific Company alone.

Now, I haven't a word to say against Mr. Leeds. He has devoted a good deal of time to this matter. I wish he were here to-night, that he might ask me a few questions, and I might have the privilege of asking him one or two questions on this matter. I grant he has given many years of study to this tariff question, and I grant his honesty of purpose. I believe him when he says he is working for the benefit of his employers. I grant he can present their views to this committee with ability second to none. I grant he is doing the best he can. But I seriously object to the conclusion he draws. I most seriously object to his proofs, and I do deny the logical deduction he seeks to draw therefrom. Now, it is admitted, gentlemen, that this new Constitution, that this amendment to the Constitution—it is admitted that it is an anomaly—that it is an innovation. If this bill is correctly represented, it is an innovation upon the Constitution of the State. Leaving out of the question whether there is any great public clamor in favor of this particular amendment to the Constitution, let us for a moment ask ourselves a question. Is it dignified to put a mass of figures like that in the Constitution of this State? Is it statesmanlike to do so? Is it in accordance with the intention of the framers of this Constitution? I believe you know, and I believe every one in the State believes it is not. Was he following out the designs of the public, the wishes of every community or not? It should contain direct statements, plain propositions and figures. Figures are exceedingly proper in reports, but out of place in the Constitution. A Constitution should contain something that everybody can understand—lawyers and laymen—whether he is a railroad expert or a mere citizen, paying for his travel on the railroad and paying for the transportation of his freight.

But if we grant for the sake of argument that it is a good plan to put a mass of figures in the Constitution—if we grant for the sake of argument that a mass of figures such as here contained in three pages of this bill, that we shall put that in the Constitution—whether it is plain, or whether it should be made plain; if figures are to be placed in the Constitution, they should be there so that the common people can understand them. I have as great regard for the people as you have and we all have. I think everybody should be able to understand the Constitution which governs him, and if you are going to have figures in the Constitution, let them, as I said before, be such that everybody can understand them.

What man can memorize such a mass of figures as that classification? What man, whether familiar with figures or not, can memorize that classification and tell what it means? The putative author of this bill, the Honorable Senator Gesford, cannot do it. The real author of this bill, Mr. J. S. Leeds, cannot do it. There is not a man on earth that can take those figures and memorize them, or read them and understand them. Why? Because they are not complete—because they are not complete. Because it requires an outside book or a paper to explain them. Because it requires something besides the figures. For it so says here, in section three, that this Distance Tariff shall be applicable to all freight traffic between all stations in the State of California now established, or that may be hereafter established:

"The classification of property provided for in this Distance Tariff is based on the Western Classification, and rules governing the same, adopted and issued by the Western Classification Committee, of which J. T. Ripley was Chairman, and which took effect January 1, 1893, to which said classification reference is hereby made; provided, however, that no rule or rules governing said Western Classification, providing for any change, modifications, or additions to the classifications mentioned in this California Distance Tariff, shall have any application hereto."

Let us consider now—laying aside the question whether J. T. Ripley is deserving of so much of the people of California, that he should be immortalized by having his name inserted in the Constitution of the State of California, as being the only man in the United States of America that deserves having his name printed in the Constitution that is to govern us for any and all time to come—leaving that out, leaving that out of the question as to whether this classification committee is composed of men of such standing and ability that they are to be immortalized in the State of California—leaving out of view, any and all questions as to whether figures should be put in the Constitution or not, you will see, gentlemen, from the reading of these figures, they are meaningless. They are like unto the hieroglyphics of the Pyramids of Egypt that remained for centuries unsolved, until they discovered the "Rosetta stone;" they remained unknown until the "Rosetta stone" was resurrected. The inscriptions on the Pyramids could not be read until the resurrection of the "Rosetta stone." And when a man takes the Constitution of the State of California and tries to read it, he says, "What does it mean?" He cannot read and understand the figures, but he looks at it and tries to make it intelligible. He observes the name of J. T. Ripley. "Who," he says, "Who is this J. T. Ripley? I don't know. Where did he come from? What has this J. T. Ripley done that he should be immortalized in this Constitution, without any reference to his great achievements? How did he acquire this preference?" But, we have a "Rosetta stone" in the book published by the Western Classification Committee, with which to read our Constitution. Is not that a terrible state of affairs? A terrible state of affairs for the Constitution of this State.

Now, a man hereafter elected to the Legislature of California appears in the Senate Chamber, and there, before the Superior Judge in this country, swears that he will support the Constitution of this State—swears that he will support the Constitution of California, and the book prepared by J. T. Ripley! That is our Constitution! That is your Constitution, and you are asked to make that Constitution. You are asked to label that Constitution as being a proper one for the people of this State to live under, and you are responsible for it. If anybody hereafter finds fault with this Constitution, it will be you, gentlemen, who will receive all the blame. Of course you will receive all the praise if this proves a benefit to the State, but can you afford to run such a chance? Now, is that right? Is that good policy? Is that good law? Is that good sense? Is it American? Is it constitutional? We are told in history that the old Sibyl of Rome came to the Emperor with certain books to sell; there were nine of them; she demanded a very large sum; he would not pay it, and she went away. Then she came back with only six books, and demanded a still larger sum, but he would not pay it. Then she went off and returned again with three books, and demanded a still larger sum, which he refused to pay. She went away, and the books were lost.

Now, suppose this book were lost—where would we be? They say that railroad companies are wicked. They say that the railroad would corrupt members of the Legislature. They say that gentlemen who are now present in this room have been hanging around the halls of Legislatures for the past twenty years for the purpose of corrupting members of the Legislature, and they say that they have succeeded in doing it. They say that the railroad companies of this State, particularly the big railroads, maintain people for the express purpose of corrupting members of the Legislature. Grant it all. They say also that they have corrupted the newspapers—that they have even soiled the judicial ermine of this State—not only of this State, but of the United States—and that they have even invaded the precincts of the gubernatorial home and the presidential hall, and corrupted them all. Grant it that they have done so; and if it be true, how long would it take for the railroad companies to steal all these books and burn them up, and then where would we be?

If the book issued by the Western Classification Committee were destroyed—if every book issued by that committee were burned up (and I tell you it is an easy matter to do so, for no man except a railroad man has possession of those books—no man save a railroad man has them) the railroad companies of this State, and this nation could destroy in twenty-four hours every book issued by the Western Classification Committee.

Have any of you gentlemen ever lived in the State of Nevada? If so, you know there existed there in its early history men who were known as the "inside" prospectors; they would come into Court at any time and swear to any lie about any mine, if reasonably paid for it. They relied upon their memory. So if we are to become a profession of "inside" prospectors, it will be far ahead of those of the Comstock Lode, who, we are told, were willing to swear from memory to the lies of the various mining corporations. Now, if you grant everything that is said against the railroad companies—for if they do what they say they have done in the past, what they say they are trying to do now—why, there is no limit to their wickedness, and these books would be gobbled up so quick that no man would be able to even keep a leaf.

Now, has there been any evidence produced here that would justify you in running such a chance as that? If so, where and when and how? If there is any testimony here of experts; of any common, plain every-day ordinary citizen; if any testimony of any shipper in the land, if any testimony of any man who has been charged extortionately for rates of freight or fare; if any testimony presented here in the reports of any authorized Commissions; where is it? Answer where? It exists simply in the brain of one man. And yet, you are asked to change the Constitution without anything to base the change upon. We say that is not right. We say that is not a mere temporary measure. It is law—it is not a law that can be later amended or repealed. It is a Constitution made to last for all time; not to be changed with the next breath of public opinion. We know that political parties of California are nearly equally divided; we know that the Legislature of one session is Democratic and the next Republican. All this because the people change their politics. We read of a certain party in power one session, and the next changed. But these are mere temporary changes that can be made without injury to the mass of the people. The Constitution is a solemn and sacred instrument; the Constitution is made for all time, and it should not be changed except upon the very best of reasons; and unless the man who votes to change it can say, I gave my vote because of evidence introduced which was overwhelmingly in favor of the change.

Now, again; are these figures set here in this Constitution—these five pages of figures—are those figures as low as they should be? If so, where is the testimony to prove it?

Has any man on this committee heard any testimony to show these figures are as low as they should be? Remember, you are called on to legislate for the people; still, they tell you the people want low rates; are these rates as low as they ought to be; ought they not to be reduced? If so, why? Ought they not to be raised? Has any man introduced testimony to show these rates are as high as they ought to be? I understand not; but I understand, on the other hand, there have been a dozen or twenty men here giving evidence, showing from facts and figures that these rates are not high enough; why, then, should you adopt these figures?

Again, if we admit, for the sake of argument, that these rates are correct for the present time, let us admit for the sake of argument, that if these rates are put into the Constitution, all railroads in the State are compelled to charge these figures, and no more; let us admit to-day it is the proper amount to charge. Will the same conditions always exist in California? If not, then should we take these figures as a basis; will we always have the same number of railroads, too? Will there not be competition? We hope so, we believe so—almost know so; then should these figures be fixed? If so, why?

Who made these figures? A railroad man. Who vouches for them? A railroad man. Where is the sworn testimony that supports them? They are based arbitrarily; they are made without reference to the condition of affairs in this State; they are made by the Western Classification Committee, which is not composed of the railroads of this State as an entirety; the railroads of this State form but a very small portion of that Western Classification Committee, and have very little to say in fixing those rates.

Where is the sworn testimony, then, which proves to you these rates and figures are what they should be? Who vouches for their being correct? There is not any Court in this land that would mulct a man for fifty cents without testimony. Shall this committee strike the millions invested in railroads in this State without some sworn testimony to justify the action? We say it should not be. Now, we say also, that this legislation is absolutely and entirely unnecessary. I shall not take up the time of the committee, as it is growing late, and I know your time is valuable. I shall not take up the time with what we know to be correct. We don't believe there is any public clamor in this State in favor of this particular bill; we think it has been engineered by one person—by one association—and they have built up a fire and flame. What is its real intent? What is its real strength? It amounts to nothing. It is not the feeling of the people, because if it were, it seems to me there would be more complaints presented than there are at present. But this resolution, we say, is entirely and absolutely unnecessary.

The theory of the Railroad Commission is a good one. It's execution, let us admit, is poor in California. Let us admit for the sake of argument that it is poor in California. It would be almost in contempt of Court to say that it's execution were not poor in California, because it has been decided it was inefficient in California, and I feel the respect due the Court, therefore we will admit for the sake of argument that its execution is poor in California—admit that the present Commission has not done right.

Admit everything that can be said in regard to it; let us admit it in its strictest and broadest sense. Let us take the pledges made in the Assembly in favor of that resolution as the basis, and see if their word was true, for the sake of argument. What of it? Whose fault is it, the railroads? No, it is the fault of the people; it is the fault of the people who elected the men to office. It is the fault of the law. Let the people elect better men to office. If we are going to change the Constitution at all, change it so the Commission can have the power to enforce their decrees. I have lived in California for twenty-seven years, and have heard members of Boards of Supervisors denounced as strongly as this Commission has been denounced. I have heard the Legislature denounced; I have heard—I have seen members of the Legislature burned in effigy; having served in both branches, I can say, all this I saw, and part of this I was. But who ever heard of abolishing the whole Legislature simply because some of the members had done wrong? It is claimed that most of this Commission have done wrong, and, therefore, you must change entirely the Constitution, change the execution of it. Where will the control be placed if you abolish this Commission? Where will the control be placed? Part in the Legislature, part in the Constitution; a divided body.

I will submit whether it is a good plan to put the power into the Legislature again. I served in the Legislature when the railroad question was before the Legislature. I served in the Legislature when the railroad question was not before the Legislature. We did not have any friction; we devoted our time to work. I believe in keeping this matter out of the Legislature; it is a good way to handle it. The experience in other States demonstrates that Railroad Commissioners, if they are men who will do their duty, is the best way; the remedy is with the people. If the people elect good men to the Legislature, they are all right; if they elect bad men, they get the worst of it; if they elect bad Justices, they get the worst of it, and the remedy is to get rid of them. If it is sought to change it—if it is sought to change the Constitution in reference to the Railroad Commissioners—give them more power. You say you want to change the Constitution. I say, as one speaking his humble opinion, I say it is not necessary to change the Constitution to do that. I believe the Legislature has power to enforce their decrees; I think you have the power to give this Railroad Commission ample, unlimited power to say to the railroads, these are the rates for freight and fare; we have prepared them for you, and you must obey them; and give that Commission power to enforce their decrees; let the responsibility rest with them; change the Constitution so as to give them the power, if they have not got it now; but in the name of common sense, in the name of this State, in the name of equal rights to all, in the name of that safety which is voiced by the Constitution of this State, let us have no more class distinctions, no more arbitrary distinctions.

Let this railroad question, if it is to be tinkered with at all, be tinkered with by giving the Commission power. The reason they have not done their duty in the past, they say, is because they have had no power to enforce their decrees. Give them the power. Admitting as I do, although I deny it as a matter of fact, the proposition that the Railroad Commission in the past has not done its duty, for the sake of argument, then I say, the reason given by themselves—and it is a good reason—is that they did not have the power to enforce their decrees, and if it is necessary to amend the Constitution in order to make up for the damage done to the State by reason of the failure of the members of the Railroad Commission to do their duty, amend the Constitution so as to give them power to do their duty, and then elect good men as members of the Railroad Commission, and all will be well. Give the little roads a chance. If you are to pass this, leave them out. But do not pass this at all; do not put such an anomaly in the Constitution of this State. We are all proud of our State; if I may be pardoned in saying a word in favor of the State to members here, some born in the State and others living here for many years; and in the course of travel this year, and we all expect to attend the World's Fair, we all expect to go there and boast of the State of California as all true Californians do—I venture the assertion that even the respected and honored gentleman who represents the county of Napa in the Senate with so much ability, and whom I have known and honored so many years—I venture the assertion, if Senator Gesford, the putative author of this bill, was in Chicago visiting the World's Fair, and this should become a part of the Constitution, and he was asked "Who put this mass of figures in the Constitution?" he would say: "I do not know, really I have forgotten." He would not be proud of his own work, because it would be such an anomaly, this Constitution; and the results are not too far-fetched, for it would ruin every little road that has come up here and given your committee facts and figures to show that it would be dangerous.

The Southern Pacific Company, I speak not for. I have no affiliation with them, except that of friendship to some of the men connected with it. I represent it in no way, shape, form, or manner. I know not its views on this matter, and care not for them. I speak here as the representative of the little roads, as a citizen and taxpayer of California, and say that if such a measure is ever passed (and voicing the sentiments of the gentlemen before me), it would turn back the wheels of progress in this State for twenty years. We are all looking forward to the time when the headlight of the competing railroad shall be seen flashing its rays upon the hills and valleys of this State, carrying the music of the competing railroad into the ear of every shipper of the State, reducing the rate of fares and freights, not by the Constitution or by oppression of law, but by the higher, broader, stronger, grander, and more impressive law of competition; and unless you allow the railroad people to manage their business in a reasonable way, unless you invite capital here, and unless you refrain from putting iron bands upon capital, as this would be, the day is very far distant when a competitive railroad will enter California. If things are left as they are; if the people are permitted to go on in their own way, I venture the prophesy, Mr. Chairman, that at the next session of the Legislature, when you return here to resume your seats, you will be met at the entrance to the depot at Sacramento with the headlight of a competing railroad in this State, and that will solve the question of fares and freights in California.

Gentlemen, I thank you for your attention.

Sacramento, February 1, 1893—8:30 p. m.

Mr. Earl: At the adjournment of Constitutional Amendment Committee last evening, we had arrived in order of the programme at the Eel River and Eureka River Railroad. Mr. Dolbere—is he here to present any matters in that regard?

Mr. S. M. Buck

Appeared in behalf of the Eel River and Eureka Railroad Company, and spoke as follows:

Mr. Chairman and Gentlemen of the Committee: On behalf of the Eel River and Eureka Railroad, I desire to call your attention to a few facts in regard to the condition of that country, and also of the condition of the road, that you may the better understand how we are situated up there. I have listened to many of the reports in regard to the short roads, and I find that there is a similar condition existing in regard to all of them throughout the State. However, we are somewhat peculiarly situated up there. Of course, Humboldt County is a large county—commences about the 40th parallel of latitude, lying on the shore of the Pacific Ocean, running about 100 miles, and is about fifty miles on an average wide, making a very large territory; and it is peculiarly situated in this, that it is surrounded by a very mountainous, hilly country, and its only outlet for the purpose of transportation, either of passengers or freight, is by way of Humboldt Bay and the Pacific Ocean, and has been for years. Now, under these circumstances, and considering the fact that navigation has been considered rather hazardous across the bar—Humboldt Bar, as it is called—the county has had a very slow development.

It has, we claim, great natural resources. It has boundless forests of very fine timber, and fine grazing land, and really is a country that ought to have invited some railroad to penetrate there long ere this; but it never has. And the business of the county has developed very slowly, yet still steadily. It never has gone back. But the necessities, the absolute necessities of the business of the county, demand the building of railroads. Of course, business men there after they had attained considerable wealth and standing in the community, found that they could not compete in their business with other portions of the State, except that they made use of this modern means of transportation. Now, then, about ten years ago several of the citizens of Eureka, which is the county town of Humboldt County, and contains a population of perhaps eight or ten thousand inhabitants, conceived the idea that they would build a railroad to Eel River Valley, about twenty-five miles long. Now, this railroad would point to Ukiah, where it would naturally connect with the San Francisco and North Pacific Railway. To them, at that time, it seemed to be an enormous undertaking. Of course they were men who had had no experience in railroad building, and they subscribed a sufficient capital stock and paid in sufficient to start the road, and in the course of a couple of years they even completed it, and after having completed it, of course they found that it had cost them about several hundred thousands of dollars to build that road. The most of the capital that built that road was borrowed capital, so that now the financial condition of the road may be tersely stated to be about this: The bonded indebtedness of the road is $488,000, represented by four hundred and eighty-eight bonds of $1,000 each, bearing interest at six per cent per annum, payable semi-annually.

Now, when they built this road, of course they had no idea that they were building it for profit. They believed that their money would be lost for many years, and it has proved so; that is to say, the original stock has never paid any dividends, except a small dividend, I think;

this year our dividends started in. It has kept up the repairs of the road, and made such small necessary betterments as had to be made; and it is completed and paid for, and some day the enterprising citizens who built it have hoped to secure from it, that is, from their original investment, and for the time and energy expended in its construction, some recompense. However, the people along the route that reaches Eel River Valley have reaped an enormous benefit. Of course they risked nothing; they gave nothing to the road. Here was a road built to their doors by the enterprising citizens, and they found that they could send their property to market—they could go themselves to Eureka for one half what they had been accustomed to expend for that same purpose. They found that the value of their property had nearly doubled by reason of the building of this road, and they realized that they had been benefited in a great many ways. Besides, it created a great deal of business that otherwise would not have been done.

Now, much of the freight over this road is lumber, and of course while the earnings of the road have been considerable, considering its length and its cost, the earnings have principally consisted of the transportation of lumber, which has been transported under special contract, and not upon any regular rates. Of course, they have a schedule of rates for ordinary freight, such as produce, grain, potatoes, and freight of that description, but all of the lumber that comes from these large mills is carried upon contract. And they now have, as I learn, contracts with the two principal mills that they carry lumber for, to carry for so much a thousand under these contracts, which extend over a number of years.

Now, this railroad is earning—but I will first call your attention to the rates. The rate for lumber is from $1 per thousand up to $2, according to the difficulty of getting it. The rate for passengers is 5 cents a mile. The other freight rates I do not know, the schedule rates, but they are about in the same proportion to these. The road is doing very well; that is, it is doing a large amount of business. It is well built, well stocked with rolling stock, sufficient to accommodate all the traffic offered. Now, the gross receipts per mile per annum is about $5,000. Of course that would bring it within the prohibition of the $4,000 restriction, as I understand it, of this constitutional amendment.

Now, coming back, may it please the committee, to our overland connection; that is what we need, and what the people of the county have been longing for for years—connection with the railroad system of the State and the United States. The distance or gap between the end of the road already built (because there is a small extension forming a junction with the Eel River road, up Eel River) is about one hundred and fifty miles. To build that we will say in round numbers will cost about four million dollars.

In order to build that, of course it will be necessary to furnish bonds to the extent of about three million dollars. Now this is a great necessity for our people. They all feel it. None of them complain of the charges upon this Eel River road—and I shall call your attention in a few moments to other roads of the county. They are all happy and pleased; they have been greatly benefited by it, and of course with a short road built by their own neighbors and friends there is no need to have any difficulty, because if any difference of opinion arises, they can easily consult with each other. But this connection with the railroad system of the State has been longed for for years by these people; and, as I said before, it has become a burning necessity. They feel they must have it. Now then, they naturally feel very timid; they feel very anxious over this constitutional amendment introduced in the Legislature, and they say to themselves, if such a thing as that passes, how would it be possible for us to furnish bonds? It must necessarily destroy the confidence in railroad securities, especially in the building of new roads. In other words, it would arrest the development of that county for years; that is, we feel it would; we fear that it would, and we may say that we are positive that anything of this kind would do us an immense amount of harm, in fact utterly ruin us.

Now then, may it please the committee, take a general view of it. In Humboldt County we have about one hundred miles of standard gauge railroads—a little over—consisting of short roads, leading from the main bay, Humboldt Bay, out into the main valleys. More roads must be built.

Any legislation tending to cripple railroads built would injure the people there vastly. Now, it has become, may it please the committee, in these days, an absolute necessity to have railroads; in other words, our civilization depends upon railroads. The railroad, the telegraph, the telephone, and electric lights, have all come to stay. There is no such thing as going backward—we must constantly go ahead. The whole ambition, the whole feeling of the people, is to advance, to go forward; and any person, or any set of persons, who attempts to stem this tide of prosperity, must necessarily be buried. They cannot meet the masses that are pushing forward, and if they undertake to stem that tide, they are bound to be trampled under foot. Now, you take this very proposition. It is a move in retrogression of the progress of the people—it is an attempt to put a block under the wheels of progress. But it cannot possibly be. Now, I feel, may it please your committee, somewhat diffident in addressing you. I have heard several addresses here, and this ground has been gone over so thoroughly, that it seems to me, if I undertake to elaborate on it, I will only touch on the old ground over again, and it must become somewhat stale to you, to have this thing hammered and dinned into your ears. To give you some idea of our necessities for a connection with the railroad system of the State, I will say that we have about thirty thousand inhabitants in that county, and they are entirely isolated from the world, except over this ocean route; and for myself, I have traveled over this, back and forth, so often, that I feel like a regular old shell-back sailor.

There is the Eel River road, 25 miles; the Pacific Lumber Company road, about 15 miles; the Arcata and Mad River road, about 15 miles; the Fresh Water railroad, about 15 miles; Vance's railroad, about 15 miles; Macabe & Co., about 10 miles, and other short lines aggregating about 140 miles of railroad in that county. They are all short roads, but they have cost a great deal of money, and there has been no money made on them except in this way: many of them have been built by business men, who found that they were a necessity in order to do business. That is to say, regarding lumber manufacturers—they had to have their logs—they found it necessary to run these railroads into the forests, and penetrate into the different valleys, rivers, and creeks in order to draw the logs to their mills; in other words, they became a necessity to the doing of business in the county.

Of course, there are many objections to this proposed constitutional amendment. Not only will it destroy and retard the progress of railroad building, which seems to me is a great necessity, not only to our people there, but to the whole State; but so far as we are concerned, I believe that we really need it more than any other portion of the State; and we think that this bill, if it could possibly become a law, would injure us more than any other portion of the State in proportion, because there is hardly any part of the State but that has some railroad connection; that is to say, they don't have the same distance and the same obstacles to overcome in order to reach a railroad connection with the system of the country.

Of course, I can't conceive, may it please the committee, that one hundred and twenty intelligent gentlemen, such as compose this Legislature, can be assembled from different portions of the State, who could seriously consider this proposed constitutional amendment. I don't believe it, and never shall. I presume that all the time and trouble that we have been to in coming here, have made no difference as to the final result of the vote upon this amendment; but, after all, since the agitation has been commenced, I hope, and I believe, and pray that good may come of it. The different roads, represented by different gentlemen, have come up here and have given you facts and figures, and made you acquainted with the reasons why agitation of this kind should cease, so that you can not only present it to your fellow members, so that they can all intelligently act upon it, but your proceedings being public, and being published and spread broadcast over the land, everybody derives information in regard to it. In other words, it is an educator of the people. The people ought to be educated on this subject, and they ought to understand that all persons who agitate a fight against the railroads are not their friends—in other words, they are not doing that which is advancing the interests of the people of this State. No man who fights the great improvements of the age is doing his fellow men good. Every man who wants to benefit the people of this State, or any other State, or any other country in which he lives, must advocate and must throw his influence in the direction of progress. He must not resist the great improvements, the great educators, the building up of the country. The rail-civilizers—they bring the people together; they make us all neighbors; they bring the people of the East right in close neighborhood with the people of the West. They are the peace-makers of the world. They make neighbors of men separated thousands of miles in distance, who without these railroads would be strangers; would be jealous of each other; would hate each other; they bring the people together, and they make a brotherhood; they make a nation of brotherhood.

Now, suppose this should pass—and I don't wish to go over the ground of the gentleman who addressed you last evening, Mr. Johnson. I had some ideas which he expressed much more aptly than I could, and much more forcibly, but I would like to make one or two suggestions. Now, suppose if this were possible to pass, what would be the result in a legal aspect? I quote from the case of the Chicago, Milwaukee, and St. Paul Railway Company against the ———, 134 U. S. 459, a brief synopsis, or rather a brief extract from the decision of Mr. Justice Miller, who speaks of legislation of this character, and he says this—it is only a few lines:

"And neither the Legislature, nor any Commission acting under the authority of the Legislature, can establish arbitrarily, and without regard to justice and right, a tariff of rates for such transportation, which is so unreasonable as to practically destroy the value of property of persons engaged in the carrying of business on the one hand, nor so exorbitant and extortionate as not to have regard for the rights of the public for the use of such transportation on the other."

In other words, then, suppose this were to pass. It is an entirely arbitrary measure, and it must necessarily be. This Legislature can not try and fix tariffs for any particular road. If it should undertake to do anything of the kind, it must make an arbitrary rule, an arbitrary regulation, and if this must be done, what would be the result to all these little roads—they would be virtually confiscated under this proposed amendment. Of course, if the doctrine enunciated by the learned Supreme Court decision of the United States be correct, why, these lines must resist; in other words, the consequence would be that it would open up a Pandora's box of litigation. Now the vast extent to which these roads would be thrown into litigation of course wouldn't benefit the people. It would be, may it please the committee, like all titles to land that are entirely unsettled. We all recollect the effect of the old Spanish grants in this State, and until these titles became settled, and until the people could feel that their title was good, that they were the owners of the soil upon which they settled, they couldn't make permanent improvements. No man will do it. He hasn't confidence to do anything of the kind, nor will people build railroads if you check the confidence in their ability to control the property after they get it. Now these are considerations that all ought to be looked to. They ought to have their weight.

But, may it please the committee, without going over, and without going into detail in this matter, I take it that this is the understanding of the committee, that no Legislature has the power—they may have the legal power, but they have not the power to do impossible things, and I undertake to say if this thing pass it would simply be an impossible thing. and what I mean by that is that it would be an impossible thing to enforce it. No Legislature, nor any set of officers ever could enforce it. It would simply stir up strife; it would simply raise commotion; it would simply throw open a Pandora's box of litigation all over the land; progress would cease for a season, but mark you, gentlemen of the committee, progress will never cease for any great length of time; all those who throw themselves in the way of the wheels of progress will be crushed sooner or later; they cannot stop it; you nor I nor any one else can control this question. It is to be for advancement; it is going ahead; no Jack Cade can control it, and there are many of them in the land who say to the people, if you will give me the power, I will do this and I will do that, but no more than the Jack Cade of old can you, by legislation, do this thing at all. Of course, true, the only way that you can do this is by a Court something like the Commission; may be that the Commission has been a failure so far; I think myself to a great extent it has; in other words, my idea of a Railroad Commissioner would be a most intelligent man, and one who was willing to devote his whole time and attention to the great object of investigating the condition of the different railroads of the State—investigating their relations to the people, investigating their rates of freights and fares, and if they found any injustice and they did not have the power to correct it, report it to the Legislature and obtain the power.

Now, we have never had a Railroad Commission that has done that thing, although I believe that the Railroad Commission has been a very great benefit to the State; the very little that they have done has benefited the people, and all the time this thing is being discussed, all the time this Railroad Commission is being arraigned before the people because they did not devote their time and attention to the duties which are imposed on them by the Constitution. I say that the Commission itself and the people are being educated up to it, and the Commission will become what it was meant to be and what it ought to be. There is no other way. It is impossible for the Legislature to deal with this thing; it is impossible, I say, because I believe you are all intelligent, honorable gentlemen. I say it is impossible for them to pass this thing; it is impossible for them to seriously consider it, in my judgment. I understand from some of the members of the other branch of the Legislature that there has been a report something like this: that it has been reported back without recommendation; but I am satisfied, from conversation I have had with different members of that branch of the Legislature, that many men who came here prejudiced in favor of some measure of that kind, upon consideration, when their thoughts had been directed to it, they have entirely changed their impression as to the feasibility of anything of this kind, and necessarily they must.

Now, I don't feel like elaborating upon this thing, because I feel, as I said before, I should simply be going over the ground that has been so ably gone over by others, and I think I have given you something like a general idea, and I hold in my hand here a type-written report in regard to the road, which I will file with your committee, which gives a little more succinct statement and perhaps a little more in detail than what I have given you; but I think I have given you a general idea of our situation up there; of our needs and necessities, and we hope, and believe, in fact I have no doubt in my own mind as to the result of your investigation of this matter that you will recommend that it is impracticable and tell your fellow Senators so; and I know that your report, which you can easily make up from all these reports which have been handed in to you, when it goes forth to the people, I am satisfied, will convince the people that they have been ably and well represented, and on further consideration that your report and your action is correct. Of course I can understand this, that there is always some question between the railroads and the people; there necessarily must be; the railroads are managed by people who desire to make money; it is very natural, and sometimes, perhaps through thoughtlessness, perhaps through inadvertence or ignorantly, they do that which may wrong somebody, and the person who is wronged becomes antagonistic to the railroad at once. True, it may be that wrongs have been committed, but there is no business in the world, may it please the committee, that has been conducted where there is not more or less friction and more or less wrong committed, and we cannot expect railroads shall be an exception. We cannot expect that they shall always be controlled by men of intuition or men of godlike qualities; so that they may always do exactly the right think at the right time; and these things, it seems to me, ought to be disseminated among the people at large, and I know of no place where matters of that kind can be presented and spread throughout the land better than from this Senate.

Now, gentlemen, I will not detain you longer, so far as I am concerned, and I thank you.

BURKE: When was your road completed?

BUCK: In 1885.

BURKE: What is the amount of the bonded indebtedness at the completion of the road?

BUCK: Something like over $500,000. They have paid off some portion of it.

BURKE: How much are you paying off per annum?

BUCK: There is no special amount to be paid off; the bonds have some fourteen or fifteen years to run, and they can only be paid off to such as are willing to take their pay.

BURKE: Do you make any provision from your gross earnings to meet your indebtedness?

BUCK: This is the first year that the law required a sinking fund to be commenced. The bonds had so many years to run, and after that they are required to commence a sinking fund for their redemption at their maturity.

BURKE: Your gross receipts, as I understand you, amount to about $125,000 per annum; do you know what your expenses are, independent of the interest on your bonds?

BUCK: I could not tell you that; I did not have the data to make it up, and Mr. Dolbere, who is the only Director, is here. We are trying to make this up as well as we can. We had to do it somewhat hurriedly. I can't answer that exactly.

STATEMENT OF MR. JOHN DOLBERE.

(Representing the Eel River and Eureka Railroad.)

To the Chairman and Committee on Constitutional Amendments:

GENTLEMEN: In 1882, a few prominent business men of Eureka united to build a railroad connecting that city with the Eel River Valley. The people living on the proposed route were anxiously waiting for better facilities of travel and transportation. Under those circumstances, the Eel River and Eureka Railroad was pushed to completion by its projectors at a cost of $700,000. It was completed and in running order some time in 1885. Since then the rates paid by passengers and shippers for transportation has been thereby reduced at least 50 per cent, besides the great advantage of speed and safety. It is about twenty-five miles long, and is a standard gauge railroad, fully equipped with rolling stock sufficient to handle all traffic offered.

The funds for constructing this railroad were mostly borrowed, and the present bonded indebtedness of the railroad is $488,000, represented by four hundred and eighty-eight bonds of $1,000 each, bearing interest at the rate of 6 per cent per annum, payable semi-annually.

The building of the Eel River and Eureka Railroad was not undertaken by its projectors with the expectation of making money; they hoped for some remuneration for their time and money expended, but their principal inducement in building the railroad was to improve the city of Eureka, and accommodate the inhabitants of the rich Eel River Valley, and also to commence a railroad pointing in the direction of Ukiah, in Mendocino County, where it would connect with the San Francisco and North Pacific Railroad, and thus afford Humboldt County railroad facilities which would unite it with the railroad system of the State and United States, and with the city of San Francisco.

This railroad now extends from Eureka a distance of twenty-five miles on the direct line towards Ukiah. The Pacific Lumber Company have built an extension of about fifteen miles further up the main Eel River. This leaves a hiatus of about one hundred and fifty miles to be built in order to make railroad connection with the San Francisco and North Pacific Railroad at Ukiah. To build and equip this extension will require, in round numbers, say $4,000,000. From what I have already said, it must be apparent that this extension of the Eel River and Eureka Railroad to Ukiah is a burning necessity to the people of Humboldt County. In addition to this, local extensions and branches must be built in order to properly accommodate the growing business of the county and develop its vast resources. To build these necessary railroads it is absolutely necessary to borrow large sums of money, and this upon bonds secured by mortgages upon the roads to be built. The people interested are fully informed upon this most important, and to them vital subject. They feel, and we all feel, that any legislation tending to cripple the short local roads now in operation in that county, must of necessity have a tendency to impair railroad securities, and render it very difficult, and perhaps impossible, to borrow money on them. The resolution now pending before the Legislature to amend the Constitution of this State, and incorporate therein a fixed schedule of rates and fares and freights applicable to all railroads in the State, if passed and adopted, must necessarily cripple all short roads in the State. It would virtually shut the county of Humboldt in from the outside world for many years to come, and this, upon the very eve of a prospective railroad outlet.

It will therefore be readily seen that the proposed measure would not only virtually put a stop to the investment of private capital in building railroads in this State, but it would cripple the energies of the people and discourage thousands of business enterprises dependent in whole or in part upon railroad facilities.

The passenger fare on the Eel River and Eureka Railroad is 5 cents per mile. Rates for freight are in about the same proportion. The patrons of the railroad have never complained of this, as they appreciate the great advantages which have accrued to them from the building of this railroad. While they have not invested nor risked a dollar in aiding the enterprise, they have seen other men, citizens of the same county, jeopardize their money and devote their energy to building a railroad to their farms, bringing to their very doors a market for everything they can produce, and doubling in value everything they possess.

As the gross earnings of this road amount to about $5,000 per mile per annum, it would fall within the class of railroads to which the schedule of rates in the proposed constitutional amendment would apply. The most of this freight is, however, on lumber and shingles, which are handled over this road at a very low rate, increasing the volume in a greater proportion than the profits of the road. If allowed to run on its present schedule, it would, from this time forward, pay the projectors of the enterprise some interest on the money originally invested by them. For the first nine years, the road did not pay the investors a single dividend for their time, energy, and the risk required in undertaking and carrying through the enterprise. Any legislation that would at this time deprive them of all chance of any profits that might otherwise accrue, and possibly oblige them to go deeper into their pockets for the means of paying the interest upon the bonded indebtedness of their railroad, would be exceedingly unjustand oppressive. The stockholders of this railroad believe that they have vested rights in this property, and also in the use thereof, that are just as sacred as if their money had been invested in any private manufacturing enterprise.

But over and above private rights of property, and what is of paramount importance to the great northwest of California, is the blighting effect such a measure would have upon every projected railroad. The days of munificent subsidies are among the things of the past. Private enterprise alone can now be depended upon to construct new railroads, and open up and develop the vast resources and riches of large portions of the State that are now lying untouched; but legislation of the kind now contemplated, would strike a deathblow to all railroad extension, by killing the railroads that have been built wholly by private enterprise, and by bringing financial ruin upon those enterprising and public-spirited citizens who have come to the front and risked their money and credit in building and constructing railroads, thereby enhancing the industries of different portions of this great State.

Respectfully submitted.

Mr. William Collier.

(Representing the Los Angeles Terminal Railway Co., and also the Southern California Railway Co.)

Mr. Chairman: While I have no statistics in regard to the Los Angeles Terminal Company, I can only say for them that they operate something over forty miles of road in Los Angeles County, and they desire to be understood as objecting, in connection with other companies, to this proposed legislation; and while I have before in a former meeting made some suggestions to your honorable committee in regard to the results of this legislation in former States, since that time I have been able to procure some figures in regard to the results, which I think are practical, and which I think ought to be taken into account by this company. I have pursued my investigation somewhat further than the State of Iowa that I mentioned formerly, and I find that in the State of Wisconsin, in 1874, a statute was enacted fixing a maximum of rates of fares and freights. I find also in Minnesota in 1871 a statute was enacted in like manner, and also in Iowa in 1874. If there be others than these, I have failed to discover them. I have traced this legislation through the sessions and laws of these several States, with the result which I will give, and will take them in order.

I have prepared, with the aid of the assistant in the State Library, a schedule of the railroad construction in those States prior to and during the existence of those statutes, as follows:

This, as I believe is throwing the clearest light upon the result of such legislation as is proposed by this amendment:

In the State of Minnesota there were built in 1869 two hundred and sixty-eight miles of road. In 1870, two hundred and seventy-seven miles. In 1871, five hundred and forty miles. During this year a law was passed fixing maximum rates of freights and fares in that State—Chapter XXIV, Laws of 1871—a law covering, or attempting to cover, practically the same ground as that proposed by this amendment. In 1872 there were built two hundred and ninety-four miles of road in that State. In 1873, forty-four miles. In 1874, forty miles. They got weary then and repealed the law, but they left, however, some very stringent features of the statute. In 1875 there was not a single mile of railroad built in that State. That year they wiped out the thing almost entirely, and passed a more favorable and liberal law toward railroad companies. In 1876 there were thirty miles built, in 1877 one hundred and seventy-four miles, and in 1878 three hundred and forty-one miles.

In the State of Wisconsin in 1873 there were four hundred and eighty-two miles of road built. In 1874, one hundred and eighty-six miles. The agitation was pending then, and during that year the Potter law was passed in that State, fixing the maximum of fares and freights. In 1875, the next year, there were twenty miles built. In 1876, seventy miles. That year they repealed the Potter law. In 1877, sixty-five miles—takes a little while to get over the disease, you will observe—and in 1878 one hundred and nine miles.

In the State of Iowa, in 1871, there were built four hundred and seventy-seven miles of road. In 1872, four hundred and eighty-six miles. In 1873, eighty-two miles. Now you will observe, gentlemen, that the conventions of the anti-monopoly element were being held during the year 1873. The grangers were organizing throughout the State. The agitation was fermenting. The conventions were held during the summer time—August or July. The election was held in November. The Legislature met early in December, or late in December, and the law was passed in March of 1874, so that pending the decision of the people upon this question there was a falling off from four hundred and eighty-six miles in 1872 to eighty-two miles in 1873. In 1874, in March, the result of this agitation in the Legislature took place, and what was known as the Granger law was passed. That year, 1874, there were thirty-seven miles of road built in the State of Iowa. In 1875 there were eighty-five miles. In 1876 there were eighty-nine miles. In 1877 there were ninety-five miles. In 1878, in March, the law was repealed, and there were in the year one hundred and thirty-two miles built in the State, and in 1879 there were five hundred and thirteen miles built.

It seems to me, gentlemen, that these figures, taken from Poor's Manual, which I take it is authority, speak very loudly to us in this particular matter. It seems to me that comment is almost unnecessary—and yet there are one or two matters I desire to mention.

I don't believe agitation ever came at a more inopportune time than at this. We have not reached the point in the State of California when we can afford to discourage investments in railroad enterprises in this State. We are all hoping for great things as a result of the magnificent appropriation made by this State to make the California exhibit at Chicago during this year a success. We expect to have our State there magnificently represented, and to attract great attention—hoping to receive great results from that exhibit, in the increase of our population, and in capital to invest itself within our border. It seems to me it would be a very dangerous move, in the light of what we desire, and what we expect as a result of that national exhibit, for representatives of the State of California to appear there in Chicago with a law or a constitutional amendment such as is proposed here in one hand, and point to that exhibit with the other; it seems to me that if it were possible at all, that one would entirely neutralize the other.

In regard to the Southern California lines and their purposes, I have no knowledge. What their profits may be I am unable to state. I know this, however, that for the past six or seven years they have been continuously expending money south of the Tehachapis, until they have more than five hundred miles of road in that section. What the purposes of the Santa Fe system are, I don't know; whether they propose to extend these lines from Mojave north, I am unable to say. But I do say this, that if it be their desire—if it be within their ability to do this—to reach the bay of San Francisco, I can say, for I believe it to be true, that it cannot be done. The funds cannot be procured to carry forward this enterprise if such legislation as this is placed in our Constitution. It makes no difference to me whether it was in the Constitution or in the State statutes, it would have a like effect. I do not know—it is not for us to say—the matter is entirely in the discretion of you gentlemen and your associates, what is required and what is needed in this State; but I do believe, in the light of this showing, in the face of the figures that I have read to you, and the experience of other States, we ought to be wiser than they. We ought not to allow ourselves to fall into the same error, and cripple the progress of our State by the same means that it has been done in other States, who have repented and learned a lesson after some four or five years.

These remarks, gentlemen, are all I desire to make, and I thank you very kindly for your attention.

WEDNESDAY EVENING, February 1, 1893.

EARL: Mr. Fulton, do you wish to add anything to what you have said?

MR. FULTON: I don't like to use the committee's time. I presume you are tired of the question; but I have waited here since last Friday evening, supposing that Mr. Leeds would be in Sacramento. Our interest is such, and he seems to be the gentleman who has had the honorable Senator to introduce this bill; he seems to be our only accuser; he seems to have deluded the merchants of San Francisco into the belief that they are abused and robbed by all the railroads in the State, or, at any rate, a bill has been introduced taking in all the railroads. Mr. Leeds, I see, and I presume we may believe, says to-day in the "Bulletin" that if there isn't special legislation in regard to the smaller roads that they will be taking the property away from them without any due process of law; that it is necessary to discriminate in regard to the railroads of California. He says plainly to a reporter of the "Bulletin" that it is necessary to discriminate between the Southern Pacific Company and the other railways of California, or take the property away from them without due process of law.

Mr. Leeds made assertions here in regard to the ties of the road. He made assertions in regard to the fuel consumed by the roads. He made comparisons of the operating expenses of California roads, comparing them with Eastern roads, that are absolutely false, either through ignorance or misapprehension. I am willing at any time to come before this committee, in the interest of our people, and by further testimony prove the assertions I have made, or meet Mr. Leeds before this committee; but if Mr. Leeds' assertions are to be taken for one bit of strength before this committee, I claim the right for people that don't owe one dollar—that have brought their money into this State for its development, and to add to the taxable property of this State—I claim I have the right to have an opportunity to question Mr. Leeds, and let him prove his assertions that he has made, or to permit me to say and to prove to this committee that he has falsely asserted things in regard to ties, fence posts, fuel, and many matters that are of great importance.

After he made his assertions in regard to the operating expenses of railroads, and your committee adjourned to Tuesday evening, I went home, and had a table made of some of the purchases that it had been necessary to make in the operation of our railroad. In the past month or six weeks we have bought rails in the State of Illinois. When we bought them they were $32 a ton, when they reached us they were $52 a ton; an increase of 60 per cent over Illinois, Iowa, or Kansas. We have bought a little material in Kansas and had it loaded, and when it arrived to us for the Nevada-California-Oregon Railway, the increase over and above the expense for the Eastern lines was 53 per cent.

Wheels and axles in carloads, at Chicago, f. o. b. cars, when they come to us have an increased cost over and above the Chicago price, or for the Eastern roads, of 86 per cent. This is spot cash. There is no thirty days; there is nothing. It is spot cash. Take iron. Iron in carloads for building trucks for our cars comes to us with an advance of 52 per cent. Brake-beams I have bought in Detroit, Michigan—carloads—come to us with an increase of 33 per cent. Car seats from the Kilburn Car Seat Manufacturing Company, in the city of Philadelphia, come to us with an increase of 25 per cent. Waste in St. Louis or Boston comes to us with an increase of 41 per cent. The articles enumerated show a cost over and above what would naturally be the cost to the Eastern roads, an average cost of 52 per cent over the average cost of these articles to the Eastern roads.

I have nothing further to say to the committee, unless it be an opportunity presents, before I go home, to meet Mr Leeds.

Southern Pacific Company.

(Statement of J. C. Martin, Attorney.)

Earl: Mr. Martin.

Mr. Martin: It is not the desire of the Southern Pacific Company to be heard before this committee by its counsel; it is the purpose of that company to present to the committee a truthful statement of the present condition of affairs; to present to this committee the facts concerning their operations and earnings, and take the judgment of the committee as to whether this bill or this resolution should pass or not.

The hour is late, and as the parties will necessarily be occupied some time in the presentation of the case of the Southern Pacific Company, I will, with your permission, endeavor, for the better understanding of the witnesses who will be produced, to give an outline at this time of what the Southern Pacific Company intends to show. And yet, before that, if I can be of some service to this committee in pointing out what I conceive to be grave defects in this bill, both in its principle and its wording, I shall be satisfied; and with your permission will endeavor to do so. The first point—in the first place I desire to say that any criticism that has been made or may be made on this bill or the principle involved in it, is not applicable, according to our understanding, to the honorable Senator from Napa, who stands sponsor for it in the Senate. The bill was not drawn by him, but has been drawn by others, and he has presented it, possibly without thought or time to investigate the matter in the way he himself would desire before becoming entirely responsible for a measure of this character. It is of the first and highest importance that every law which affects a great number of people, and great interests, should be so carefully and plainly drawn that it may, in the first place, express the intent of the Legislature; and may, in the second place, be readily interpreted and understood by those to whom it is intended to apply. This bill does not do so. That it has not received the attention that a measure of this importance should receive, has been demonstrated by the numerous amendments that have been suggested and proposed in the short time that this measure has been before the committee. This is a bill of the Traffic Association of San Francisco, drawn, I presume, by their manager, attorney, or by their legislative committee.

The Traffic Association is an organization of merchants and gentlemen of San Francisco, as we understand it, whose names are not given to the public, but who believe that the profits of their business are too small and should be increased, and that the profits of the railroads are too great and should be diminished. I presume that is the principle on which they are organized. As you know, they have an executive committee, whose names are given to the public—honorable and respected merchants of San Francisco—and they have a legislative committee, whose duty it is, I suppose, to draw laws, and that committee has arbitrarily drawn up this law.

When the matter of legislation was first presented to the public by the Traffic Association, and I speak now of a matter which is common knowledge to all of you, the plans and purposes of legislation were disclosed in what was called the "Traffic Association's pledge," which was sent out to all candidates to the Legislature of all parties, with a hint of support in case that pledge should be signed, and with a suggestion of opposition to any one who should refuse to sign it in writing.

That pledge, Mr. Chairman, as you know—for I presume you received a copy of it—called for a legislative proposition entirely different from this one. There is no similarity between the legislation proposed in that pledge and the legislation as represented in this resolution first before this committee; and so strong was the demand made by the Traffic Association of the gentlemen who were candidates for the Legislature, that—if I recollect right, and if I am wrong you will correct me, Mr. Chairman—the signers pledged themselves not to adjourn until the particular plan outlined in the pledge should be, I believe, successfully accomplished; or at all events, they should not vote to adjourn until something was done in the premises. The legislation outlined at the time when the resolution to amend the Constitution was first presented here, was entirely different from that outlined in the pledge, and while that resolution has been before this committee it has been subjected to at least two changes by the proponents of the measure.

We have a committee substitute for the original bill, so-called, and we have pencil memoranda and amendments to the committee substitute; at least one such amendment, possibly more. I remember but one. This committee substitute changes the plan of the original bill in this: An attempt was made to divide the roads into two classes: those whose gross earnings exceeded $4,000 per mile and those whose gross earnings were $4,000 per mile or less. Those whose gross earnings exceeded the sum of $4,000 per mile were to be subjected, or to be by this bill, subjected to, by legislative action, certain maximum rates on both fares and freights; and those whose gross earnings are $4,000 or less, were not to be subjected to that constitutional limitation.

Now, a Constitution is, as was stated last night by Mr. Johnson in his very able and interesting address, a declaration of principles, a rule of conduct, binding on the people, and, of course, on the Legislature of the State, and is supposed to last for all time. It is difficult to amend. It may be amended, but it is supposed to be so skillfully and perfectly drawn that it will meet all conditions that now exist, and all conditions that can reasonably be anticipated. Now, the committee substitute, as it was first read, and under the $4,000 proposition—and I believe it was line 17, page 2—I think the amendment suggested by Senator Gesford was this: After the word "mile" insert "as shown by the Thirteenth Annual Report of the Railroad Commissioners of the State of California." Now, Mr. Chairman, I suggest to you that that proposition is not in proper form, either for a statute that makes laws for two years, or a Constitution that makes laws for many years. As amended, it will then read as follows:

"Until the Legislature shall prescribe rates, as aforesaid, or in the event that any such prescribed rates shall, from any cause, become inoperative, the rates of charges for the transportation of passengers on all railroads in this State, whose annual earnings are more than $4,000 per mile, as shown by the Thirteenth Annual Report of the Railroad Commissioners, shall not exceed three cents per mile."

It is in evidence before you that there are a number of roads whose gross earnings now approximate closely to $4,000; but as in the Thirteenth Annual Report of the Railroad Commissioners their earnings are not equal to $4,000, if this constitutional amendment or provision should be adopted as now amended and as it stands; if those roads—and they all have great hopes—should within two years be earning $10,000 per mile, they don't come under the provision of the section, because in the Thirteenth Annual Report their earnings are shown to be less than $4,000 per mile. And yet, if by misfortune, a railroad that is earning more than $4,000 per mile, and it has been so shown in the Thirteenth Annual Report, should have its earnings reduced to $1,000 per mile, it would still be subject to this constitutional limitation, because in the Thirteenth Annual Report the earnings were shown to be $4,000 per mile. Is that right? Is it the understanding that that shall be the gauge for all time; that measure as shown by the Thirteenth Annual Report of the Railroad Commissioners; that those figures shall be at all times the measure of whether or not a railroad shall be subject to constitutional limitations? If there can be any reasonable answer given to this objection, Mr. Chairman, from any gentleman, I would like to hear it now.

Gesford: You will recollect I said in presenting that bill that the schedule of rates of fares and freights was only for a temporary purpose, only until the Legislature could fix the rates; they could not fix them in a year, and they were for that purpose, at the outset; that was the idea.

Mr. Martin: But that does not relieve the bill from the difficulty. Remember, you are making a constitutional provision in which you declare that certain roads shall have fixed limitations; you have a maximum limit for what kind of roads? For roads whose gross receipts, according to the Thirteenth Annual Report of the Railroad Commissioners, are shown to be $4,000 per mile and over. What will you do with a road which earns $3,900 per mile, and in two years from now it amounts to $10,000 per mile gross earnings? What will you do with it? Is it subject to the constitutional limitation or not? How can it be? Will the Thirteenth Annual Report of the Railroad Commissioners of the State of California show $10,000, or will it show less than $4,000?

Gesford: Well, can you fix on a basis? You can't do it until you refer to some particular basis, can you?

Mr. Martin: Of course I am not fixing the bill; I am trying to point out what I conceive to be defects in what has been proposed. If these defects exist, and if I or you cannot make a better schedule than that, we should abandon the principle, because it is unreasonable to fix it so, and take some other method of fixing the limit on the roads, and when they come under the maximum of the Constitution. It is not fixed now. The absurdity is apparent upon the face of the bill, that for all time roads may come and roads may go, but this constitutional provision goes on forever, and the question is, when the railroads are exceeding the limit of three cents per mile, and exceeding the California Distance Tariff, and are called upon to answer for it, the question is, what did the Thirteenth Annual Report of the Railroad Commissioners show your gross earnings to be? If that report shows your gross earnings to be $4,000 or less, they are forever exempt under the Constitution as changed. Remember, this is a constitutional provision, not fixed for eighteen months or for two years, but fixed until the people shall change it. I am sure the committee appreciates, without further dwelling on this point, the point I present—the objection I present to this amendment. And it is no answer to this objection to ask, what would you suggest in the place of it? Nor would it be an answer to it if I said I can suggest nothing. It would be an argument against a principle that has been adopted that leads to such absurd and unfortunate results.

But, again, what would you do with a competing road, the road that is to be built (and the only popular road on earth is the road that is to be built); what will you do with the railroad that is coming after awhile, that everybody is in love with and in favor of; what will you do with it? It comes in, and, receiving the favor of the united people, in their business, of this State, it gets all the traffic, and its rates exceed the constitutional limit everywhere, and you try and regulate them, and say: "Here, you are charging too much. You ought to be bound by the Constitution; you ought to be limited by this constitutional provision of three cents per mile and the California Distance Tariff." And they say: "Oh, no; that only applies to roads which, according to the Thirteenth Annual Report of the Railroad Commissioners, were earning $4,000 per mile, and that report does not cover us."

Under this constitutional provision, and by every fair construction of it, only those roads are regulated by it whose gross earnings appear in the Thirteenth Annual Report of the Railroad Commissioners of this State, and there is not any other conclusion to be drawn from it.

But if the maximum were different; if the Senator or myself were able to fix some better plan to escape this difficulty, what would be the result?

Take Colonel Kidder's road (the Grass Valley road, I think it is called), that has a gross earning now per mile of $3,900, and they have hopes next year to come within the limit. They are ambitious to get out of the class of roads that are called the "little roads" before this committee.

Suppose this were amended now, so as not to limit this report of the Railroad Commission, but to make it general for roads whose earnings may hereafter equal four thousand dollars, or exceed it; make it that way and the Grass Valley road climbs up until it reaches four thousand dollars and more. What does the Constitution do then? It is all right until it reaches that point, when the Constitution comes in and cuts its rates in two, diminishing its revenue fifty per cent; down goes Colonel Kidder's road from under the constitutional provision, and it climbs up again, because they are ambitious; they fix their rates until the Constitution drives them back; they can fix their rates, and when they do that, they climb up again and they get within the constitutional provision, but just as soon as its head is poked in that limit, the Constitution strikes it again with this load, and down it goes again from under the constitutional provision. Isn't that a fair construction of the operation of that provision? If there is any answer to that, I would like to receive it now.

Gesford: Mr. Martin, I didn't suppose you were talking to me; I don't want to go into critical argument on that proposition; I propose to make a little argument at the close, and I will then try and reply to them if I can. If I cannot I will try to propose something in place of it.

Mr. Martin: Well, we would like to be heard, because this is an important matter, and we present these points so that while we are here we would like to have them answered, because if you trust to Mr. Leeds and the Traffic Association's Legislative Committee, judging the future by the past, where you have fallen into one error you will fall into another. Of course we are at a disadvantage, we cannot be here always; we cannot stay here always, cannot be here to hear the answer to these questions, and I am sorry that the gentlemen who are the real authors of this bill are not here, when we point out difficulties of this character so plain, objections so grave, that they are not here to give us some light on the subject.

But, Mr. Chairman, there is another—it seems to me to be—a serious objection to the bill. The first resolution that was proposed by the bill or resolution, whichever it is properly termed, provided the same California Distance Tariff that is now inserted, and I understand there has been no change in the figures of this distance tariff, no changes in that. And it also provided for this Western Classification, signed by Mr. J. T. Ripley, who, if he does not become immortalized by having his name inserted in the Constitution, will certainly be so by the speech of Mr. Johnson last evening; but it was proposed in the first bill that this classification, too, was subject to change; and while I think it was suggested—I think by one of the members of the committee, or the Senator at one of the meetings of the committee—that this amendment does not permanently fix that classification in the Constitution, making it a part of the Constitution—I have read it carefully, and while there may be some possible doubt on that question, I think the fair construction of that instrument, while it gives the Legislature the power to change rates within the maximum of roads to which the maximum applies, I am of the opinion that a fair construction of that instrument permanently fixes that Western Classification, with all its benefits or demerits, in the Constitution, itself.

Now, a classification is one thing, and the making of rates another thing; and while classification necessarily lies at the very basis of rate-making, on account of the great number of commodities subject to transportation, yet it is entirely a different thing, a distinct thing, a distinct matter from the fixing of rates. Classification is this: It is a determination of what commodities shall have the same rate. That is all a classification is. And it is made because it is almost impossible to make a rate-sheet big enough, broad enough, so that people could read it, to cover the thirty-five hundred or four thousand different articles that are now the subject of railroad transportation. And to avoid this it has become necessary to group certain commodities together, and, we will say, a certain number being grouped, they are such commodities as should take equal rates, and they all should be first-class, and the rate is fixed for the first class; and so with the second class. Rate-making, then—I mean classification—is but the grouping of commodities so that the rate may be applied to them. Now, I think, Mr. Chairman, that if this constitutional provision is adopted in its present form, that Western Classification, signed by Mr. Ripley, becomes a fixed portion of this Constitution, and is not subject to legislative change.

Now, there are many defects and difficulties in the Western Classification outside of the difficulty and absurdity of placing it in the Constitution, which will in the proper time be explained to you more in detail than I can give it to you now, by Mr. Smurr; but my attention was called by him to-day to one proposition, and there are others, and I wish Mr. Leeds were here to answer it. If this classification becomes a part of the Constitution, and it could be proved in Court when questioned, it would not be proved by these books, it would have to be proved by original records published by State authority—it would have to be fixed by the original records of the Western Classification Committee.

But there are commodities, there are articles that are not classified at all, and important ones to the industries of this State. As I said, my attention was called to one—ore—by Mr. Smurr, and instead of being classified, that important commodity to the transportation companies and to the people of this State, instead of receiving a classification and a rate, is, if I have not misunderstood Mr. Smurr—and he will correct me when he comes on the stand if I have mistaken him—is by the Western Classification referred to a special rate. Now, what will you do with the Western Classification? You have got to take that special rate, to which that classification applies, and it does not apply to California, because the ore is not carried under the special rate of that Classification Committee. And there are other commodities of the same kind. Let me just explain for one moment, Mr. Chairman, how these classifications are made. The roads interested desire, each road, to protect and foster the industries of the line of its own road; but there are conflicting industries, and for that reason when the Committee on Classification representing the various roads merits, the classification is made by a system of compromises and concessions until they agree upon that classification which will best serve the roads who are members of and represented by the committee.

East of Chicago there is entirely a different classification from the Western Classification. It is called the Trunk Line, or the Official Classification, and no road east of Chicago uses the Western Classification. Efforts have been made—strenuous efforts—to get the trunk lines east of Chicago to unite with the roads west of Chicago on a common classification, but they won't, because it would affect the industries of those roads in a manner so variously that they are not willing to yield, and there is no compromise. To-day from Chicago east is the Official Classification, and from Chicago west is the Western Classification. Naturally, the Western Classification would more approximately represent the commodities of this State, because to some extent it is used under it. But while the Western Classification is in use, I am informed by Mr. Smurr there are a thousand or more commodity rates which are taken from that classification and all other classifications as well. You can't do it if you adopt this Western Classification, because when you adopt it as part of the Constitution, or as a law, the goods which are classified there must take the same rate; and if you take one man's commodity out of that class, you would discriminate against the other man's commodity which was left in the class, and you could not do it under other provisions of your Constitution, and therefore that most important thing to the industries of this State, the commodity rate, would be abolished, except in so far as the distance schedule itself does provide for some three or four commodity tariffs; the rest would be abolished. And among other things, and while I am not familiar with this matter, and it will be further explained by the gentlemen representing the Traffic Department of the Southern Pacific Company, the maximum rate upon the industry which greatly concerns the special district of Senator Gesford, the wine industry, is placed by that classification in the second class. Why? Because they don't make wine on the line of those roads which control the Western Classification. They don't ship it, except to dealers generally in the higher class wines, and this wine comes in the second class, and the maximum rate fixed by this schedule would raise the wine rate from Napa, and the points further up the valley, over and above what the commodity rate which the Southern Pacific Company is now giving the valley. Of course, generally, it would not raise the rates, but you can see where the danger is of adopting a fixed classification, taking away the right to make these commodity rates, taking out these things which are of special interest to the people of this State, taking them out of the commodity class, which is always a lower rate than the class rate, and fixing them formally and forever, until the Constitution is changed, in the second class. It would be a harm to the wine-makers of this State, which the railroad company is not disposed to inflict on them, but which it would be powerless to avert, if wine were to remain forever in the second class, and it must so remain if the Western Classification were to become a part of the Constitution; but aside from that, Mr. Chairman, at the close of the bill is a singular provision, and it comes under the head of "Additional Rules:"

"Railroads shall be considered independently in computing distances; except, however, that a system of railroads consisting of leased, operated, or independent roads controlled under a common management, although working under different charters, shall be considered and treated as one road, and the distances shall be computed over the shortest operated line composed of two or more of said roads."

Now, that was supposed to be a master stroke against the Southern Pacific Company. That is what it was intended for; intended to reach the small roads of the Southern Pacific Company; and while the Southern Pacific Company is operating a great many miles of road in this State, it has some little small branches that are about as weak as any that can be presented here. But it was the design of the framer of this Constitution to except these little lines if they belonged to the Southern Pacific Company from the operation of the maximum clause of the Constitution, and place them under it.

The result would be, of course, that provision could easily be avoided by any company which would be disposed to avoid the law, but the Southern Pacific Company is not. It could be avoided at once by canceling its leases of the little roads and letting them become operated under their own management, and it would not be much more trouble than a stroke of the pen to do it; but let us see how that would work:

If the gentlemen who have the little road running up to Yreka, which was built by the men, women, and children of that town, become tired of operating their road, and they want to sell it to get their money out of it, or they want to lease it to some one so as to have a connecting road, they would probably apply to the Southern Pacific Company. But when they come to the Southern Pacific Company we will say, "What are your earnings?" They will say, "$1,500 per mile." "Well, then, you are not subject to the limitation of 3 cents per mile." "No." "Well," we will say, "we cannot take your road, because you can run it under the maximum fixed by the Constitution, and we can't. While you own it you can fix your rates regardless of this constitutional maximum, but if you sell it to us or lease it to us, we can't do it." And they have to keep on running their road.

It might be said it is an advantage in compelling these people to hold on to the road; but the principle is wrong; it does not make any difference who owns the road. If roads are to be classified according to their earnings, are you not, by this amendment, instead of classifying roads, which you probably could reasonably and properly do, are you not classifying owners, and can you do that? Can you say that any of these small roads, which, while in their present ownership, can be operated regardless of the constitutional limitation, if it should pass into another ownership, could not be so operated? This Constitution, then, would not apply to roads; it would apply to persons; it would apply to ownership, and not to the roads at all. We say it is not right, even if it can be done.

EARL: Mr. Martin, could that be done under the Federal Constitution?

MR. MARTIN: I don't think so; but, Mr. Chairman, of course it is not my purpose to raise constitutional questions here. It is proper for this committee to consider them, and they should, because the committee is bound to support the Constitution of the United States applying in this State, and it is proper for you to consider it. It would be well enough for me as the attorney for the Southern Pacific Company to say, when you come to the proposition, which the Constitution of the United forbids, pass it; you can't harm us much, because we are protected by the Constitution; pass it and you can't enforce it; it would become to us a matter of indifference, but it is a question of the Legislature and of this committee, because under the Fourteenth Amendment of the Constitution of the United States, corporations are persons, and no State can deny to any person within its limits the equal protection of the law, and that is the declaration of the Fourteenth Amendment to the Constitution; and while you class railroads and class property, you can't class ownership; it is contrary, and it is indefensible and improper of itself; it deprives the gentlemen who own the road of the opportunity of selling or leasing it. It does not apply to the Southern Pacific Company's lines, because it would let those roads alone if the occasion occurred; but it does apply to those gentlemen, because they could neither lease nor sell, and so the Fourteenth Amendment to the Constitution, which protects the strong roads and the big roads, applies also to the owners of the short roads, and you are interfering with the right of the disposition of property of these small roads when you say: "If you run them and own them yourselves you shall not be subject to the constitutional limits; but if you sell them to another, that person shall not have the use of the property which you had; you cannot confer upon them the privileges which you have secured, to the property which you have secured to yourself by investing your money;" and doesn't that debar them of the power of disposing of it? And it is often so, that where an unjust effort is made to reach particular persons under the form of law, that the effort overreaches itself. And this is a fair illustration.

It was desired and intended that if a small road was operated by the Southern Pacific Company, or any other company, for that matter, whose gross earnings exceeded $4,000 a mile, that they should not have the power to use the property as the original owners had. Now, as I have said, the Southern Pacific Company have got just as many little roads in this State as the rest of them, and the effect would be, while they are extending and building these lines, such as the branch road in Colusa, out to Fruto, such as the numerous little branch roads that are being built in the San Joaquin Valley; while they are doing this, your constitutional amendment would compel them to charge upon these little roads the same maximum that applies to the main line of the company; they couldn't build their roads, and they couldn't operate them, and they couldn't do it. I do not believe that railroad men, as a rule, build railroads as a matter of charity; they build them just exactly as every other business man conducts his business, to make money out of it. And if you put a bar, if you could do it, in this provision, upon the small branch roads of the Southern Pacific Company, it would not build any more, and they could not operate them without a loss, and it is not so charitable to the public, I believe, as to operate these roads for the benefit of the public at their own expense entirely. Now, you can see from any fair construction of this matter that the law itself is defective. It is badly drawn; it was aimed at the Southern Pacific Company, but it is like the blunderbuss loaded with scrap iron; it shoots everybody in the neighborhood, and that is why the gentlemen representing these small roads are here. It was not aimed at them, and they were told it was not aimed at them, but it reaches them all the same.

Does not that show that this bill has not been drawn with that care which a property law, much less a constitutional amendment, should be drawn? But, Mr. Chairman, this is an endless subject, and I am not going into the details of this matter further than to call your attention to these, which I conceive to be the defects of this law; and if there could be an answer shown to us now, or if there could be an opportunity for us to reply to the answer, or at least consider it, we should feel better satisfied than we are to have to leave this committee without an opportunity of hearing the answers to be made to these objections. We can see no answer to them. Perhaps it is our fault, but it is our misfortune that we will not have the opportunity of being enlightened.

I don't know, Mr. Chairman, what you will think about this matter when it is submitted; but the Senate would like—I know the Senate would give us every opportunity, and would only be too glad to have this, or any other objection pointed out; but as I have said, Mr. Chairman, there have been so many changes from the beginning, it shows clearly, or ought to show to every one, that the attention to this matter has not been given that its importance demands. And after the pledge that I have referred to, under which some members of the Legislature were elected and some were not, after that pledge was given out as being the plan and purpose of the Traffic Association, it wasn't but a few weeks until entirely another but different form from this was also announced. And I would like to call your attention, if you will pardon me—I didn't mean to keep you so long—to what was announced that the California Traffic Association contemplated. They have charged about so much, that it is hard work to keep up to the pace. Now, this is from a paper by no means unfriendly to the Traffic Association, and I read an extract from it, because it is given out to the public for the purpose of informing the public of the plans and purposes of the legislative committee:

"We find, too, that there is in force in Kansas a schedule of railroad charges, termed the Kansas Local Distance Tariff, based substantially on the idea of a terminal charge, and a rate per mile per movement. It is found to be (that is, the Kansas Distance Tariff) fair and sufficiently remunerative to the railroads in Kansas, and we believe it can safely be adopted in this State as a substitute for existing rates, to be in force until others are lawfully adopted."

Now that is a plain, square declaration that they have drawn the law, based upon the Kansas Distance Tariff, which they believe to be fair and remunerative to the roads in California; that is the proposition. Now you would naturally expect that if a statement was given out to the public in that form, that when the bill of the Traffic Association was presented, that it would be strictly in accordance with this declaration, the Kansas Distance Tariff which they believe to be fairly remunerative to the roads in Kansas, and sufficient for the railroads in California. Now, before the rates in Kansas could be a fair measure for the roads in California, the conditions of construction and operation would have to be the same, together with the density of the traffic. It would be only when all of these conditions were the same that the rates of one road could be measured by the rates of another. It was stated by Mr. Leeds that the roads in California could be operated and constructed as cheaply as the roads in Kansas. Now, that was a singular statement to make—that the roads in California, over which every member of the Legislature has ridden, and some of you over the roads in Kansas—to announce, as Mr. Leeds did, that the roads in California were as cheaply constructed and as cheaply operated as in Kansas. Is there a tunnel in the State of Kansas? Is there a mountain in the State of Kansas?

But, what do you do when you start from San Francisco? When you go north, you go to the cañon of the Sacramento, and reach the vicinity of the Siskiyou Mountains; if you go east, you have to cross the Sierras before you reach the State line. If you go south, you encounter the Coast Range and Tehachapi Mountains. There are no mountains on the west, because there is no land; but there is no direction that you can go from San Francisco without going over grades and through tunnels and around curves, and yet the statement is made to this committee, and in the presence of the assembled gentlemen, that the roads of California can be as cheaply operated, as cheaply constructed, as the roads in Kansas. Now, we have some showings on these matters; showings made by Mr. Curtis, who is in charge of the tracks of the roads, the maintenance of way; to be made by Mr. Gray and Mr. Smurr, who are in charge of the traffic of the road; to be made by Mr. Lansing, the Secretary and Controller, who has charge of the finances of the road; and we are glad of this opportunity of showing to you, and showing to the public, so far as we may be able to show the public, the true condition of the finances and earnings, and operating expenses and cost of that road, and they will be shown to you; and while it is an easy matter to sneer at the figures presented by railroad men, I undertake to say that they are entitled to equal consideration with other men in other business. And these figures which they will bring to you, and these statements, are those which are made to the Directors of the road; they are from their reports, which are made to their stockholders and bondholders, and they must be exact, because there are more people interested in them than the persons engaged in operating the road.

We will show you these things in order to demonstrate that the railroads could not be constructed and operated as cheaply in this State as in Kansas. Now, would you not expect to find the Kansas Distance Tariff, which they say is sufficiently remunerative to the roads in Kansas, and they believe ought to be in California; wouldn't you expect to find it; don't you expect that bill is drawn from the Kansas Rate Tariff? Anybody, most, would believe it. Senator Gesford, if he has read this announcement of the Traffic Association, must, too, believe it; that the bill is drawn substantially from the Kansas Distance Tariff. Now, Mr. Chairman, have you got the bill?

EARL: Yes, I have it here, Mr. Martin.

MR. MARTIN: Now, the Kansas Distance Tariff runs in limits of five miles and under; ten miles and over five; fifteen and over ten. Now, Mr. Chairman, have you got the place for the first class? The Kansas Distance Tariff, which is believed to be fairly remunerative to the roads in Kansas, and believed to be the same for the roads in California, gives merchandise in cents per hundred pounds, five miles and under, 13 cents. What is it there?

EARL: Three and three quarters.

MR. MARTIN: Thirteen cents in Kansas and 3¾ cents in this State. The Kansas Distance Tariff for ten miles and over five gives a rate of 15 cents. What does it give in California?

EARL: Four and a half cents.

MR. MARTIN: Four and a half cents against 15 cents! And the Kansas rates are presumed to be fairly remunerative. Twenty miles and over fifteen; fifteen miles and over ten is 18 cents. What is it there?

EARL: Eight cents.

MR. MARTIN: Eighteen cents against 8 cents. Twenty miles and over fifteen is 20 cents in Kansas. How much here?

EARL: Twelve cents.

MR. MARTIN: Twenty-five miles and under twenty is 22 cents here. How much is it with you?

EARL: Fifteen cents.

MR. MARTIN: Well, Mr. Chairman, I do not wish to take your time, but there is the Kansas Distance Tariff, and you have the California Distance Tariff, and the Traffic Association announced that they had founded their bill upon that distance tariff, notwithstanding the fact that the roads in this State, to our own knowledge, to the knowledge of every man in this room, are far different in the cost of construction. far in excess of those in Kansas. That is the California rate that you have read, and this is the Kansas Distance Tariff which I have. Is it fair? Is it right, to give out to the public in the name of the Association or any member that they are adopting the Kansas Distance Tariff and bring that in after that assertion without an explanation—and even the Senator, the Senator who introduced the bill, until this moment has rested under the belief that he was introducing the Kansas Distance Tariff instead of that one. Eighteen cents, 8 cents; 13 cents against 3¾; and it runs up to the distance of 500 miles, not perhaps so great, but always below, and materially below, the Kansas Distance Tariff. Now, why is that? It is not right in a business way; it is not proper.

But, we will show you not only that the cost of construction and of operating roads in California is of necessity far in excess of the cost of construction and operation in Kansas, and for that reason that this State ought to have, by reason of this condition and that excess, a much larger rate; yet it is reduced all the way through, and reduced in material proportion. Now, it would simply be ruinous to the roads in Kansas even; the roads in Kansas could not operate under it, and we will show to you by the proper showing of these officers of the Southern Pacific Company, the roads in Kansas to a great extent are bankrupt; there is not a mile of construction going on, because their rates are reduced; and then with all these conditions and differences in the cost of operating the roads in California, and with the principle that the Kansas Distance Tariff is remunerative, fair, and believed to be sufficiently so here; instead of being introduced, why, it reduces the figures; but I am going over ground that will be more properly, more amply shown by the gentlemen who will come after me, and who will not present principles, but will present facts.

We are much obliged to this committee for the opportunity of being present and presenting the railroad situation of this State, so far as the Southern Pacific Company is concerned. And we thank you for your patience, and the attention which you have given, and which you will give to the conclusion.

BURKE: Has the Western Classification a different rate from the Kansas Distance Tariff?

MR. MARTIN: Let me explain. The Western Classification classifies commodities into the first, second, third, and fourth classes, as you will see by the bill. Now, in California, under what is called the Local Classification, you will find that articles in the lower classes here are in the first class; some of these articles by reason of that classification have a much higher rate than they would have if they were in the lower class. Articles in the lower classes, two, three, and four, in California would be in the first class; so that commodity has a higher rate by reason of its being in the first class and in the second there. That changes the rate, it changes the class.

BURKE: I understand that, but my question was, Mr. Martin, whether the Kansas Distance Tariff applies to this Western Classification, or whether there was a difference, a different one.

EARL: The Western Classification applies to the Kansas Distance Tariff, as Mr. Leeds told you.

BURKE: But I understand that the Western Classification does apply in California.

MR. MARTIN: Mr. Leeds correctly stated that the Southern Pacific was using the Western Classification, but it is used in the southern part of this State; but it is not used in the simple form as it appears in this book that you have.

EARL: In other words, the Western Classification to-day does not use the rates set down here in that bill?

MARTIN: It does use the rates set down in that bill, because the Western Classification applies to all the rates in Kansas.

EARL: Do you mean, Mr. Martin, that the Western Classification which is proposed to be adopted here applies to the roads in Kansas? The classification of the commodities therein applies to the thirty-five hundred commodities, but the rate that these commodities are to be charged by the roads are not the same as the first class here, and second class here, and third class here, as set forth in this distance tariff; the Kansas tariff is different from the distance tariff which you have just now read.

MARTIN: It is different from the distance tariff shown in this, that there are higher rates in Kansas than there are in the California tariff, and there is no other difference.

BURKE: There is no such rate, and the differences in Kansas are there?

MARTIN: No, not that I know of; I have the tariff of the road that Mr. Leeds refers to, the Atchison road, and that which is the schedule; you understand that the Western Classification applies to this rate sheet, and if the Western Classification is adopted it will apply to this.

MONDAY, February 6, 1893—7:30 P. M.

Committee met pursuant to adjournment.

W. S. WOODS, attorney for the Nevada, California, and Oregon Railroad, addressed the committee as soon as it was called to order. He said he appeared for J. M. Fulton, Master of Transportation of the Nevada, California, and Oregon, who could not be present. He had a letter from Mr. Fulton, addressed to the committee, and read it. It was as follows:

"RENO, NEVADA, February 4, 1893.

"*Senator Earl, Chairman Senate Committee on Constitutional Amendments, Sacramento:*

"DEAR SIR: I notice by the press that Mr. Leeds, of the Traffic Association, intends being in Sacramento at the next meeting of your committee. He states his willingness to answer any question put to him by any one representing the small railroads of California, and particularly myself.

"Mr. Chairman, I waited in Sacramento from Tuesday, the 24th day of January, until late on Wednesday night, February 1st, for Mr. Leeds, that he might explain to me certain assertions he has made.

"I only left then on account of having waited eight days, and no Leeds. I gave up all hopes, and now do not believe he will come before your committee, or I assure you I would be present Monday evening to meet Mr. Leeds and attempt his entertainment for a time.

"I ask your honorable committee to notice with what perversity Mr. Leeds asserts that the small roads are not affected by his bill. He should explain why they are not, and whether they would be when their earning power increases to the sinful point of $4,000 per mile per year gross earnings.

"Our table of certain commodities purchased in St. Louis, Chicago, Philadelphia, etc., with freight added, has been criticised by Mr. Leeds. The table was given to your committee, believing that it might assist you in coming to a just conclusion upon this vexed question, which I believe you and your committee desire to do.

"In the criticism alluded to, Mr. Leeds says, I am 'howling against our own interests;' that 'the Southern Pacific Company is robbing us.' Perhaps so; and even if it were so, my statement of the cost of those commodities is still a fact, and, therefore, does it not show that it costs us more to operate our road than it does Eastern lines? Mr. Leeds says 'No;' I say, 'Yes.' Again, does the Southern Pacific Company's line run to Philadelphia, St. Louis, or Chicago? Will Mr. Leeds deny the fact that the rates paid by us on the shipments enumerated, and which he criticises, are not now lower than when he was Chairman of the Transcontinental Association; did we then hear his voice commanding a reduction of rates?

"Mr. Leeds has made statements before your committee that are not founded on facts. Perhaps—through ignorance, perhaps—he has deceived the Traffic Association, and is trying to stir up a fuss where there is little cause for it. Mr. Leeds has said that he does not see the justice or fairness of the criticism he is receiving by the small roads of this State. Let us see about it. Mr. Leeds, an employé of certain San Francisco merchants, personally having no interest except the salary he receives, comes before your committee and advocates that you recommend for passage to the Senate an amendment to the Constitution of the State of California, whereby the maximum charge of any railroad in California shall not, for passengers, exceed two cents per mile, and that the proposed distance tariff affects every road, large or small, up hill or level, exactly alike. You, Mr. Chairman, by your incisive questions, of which Mr. Leeds did not answer one half, showed the bill to be so devoid of common sense that your committee adjourned, that it might be changed and printed. It came again before you with a clause reading that roads earning over $4,000 gross per mile per year must not charge to exceed certain rates for passengers or freight. Roads earning less than $4,000 per mile were to be subject to laws yet to be made by the Legislature. Why did Mr. Leeds attempt to have a law passed giving the small roads of the State but two cents a mile? If it were right and honest, why did he change it? Was it done through ignorance, or was it intended to do wrong? If the former, he is not worthy of consideration; if the latter, he committed a crime. The fact, however, remains, and should be considered by your committee, that he did succeed in getting the honorable Senator from Napa to introduce the proposed amendment, which would ruin every small, or large road, for that matter, in California, if it became the law of this State; and in speaking upon the question he said, if the small roads did lose money, it was a bad investment they had made, and no one was at fault except the investors. Now, he objects to our criticism, and says we are unjust. Mr. Chairman, I think we are not; but that Mr. Leeds, in introducing or proposing, or causing to be proposed or introduced, such a measure, has shown either an evil mind or the most dense ignorance.

"Mr. Chairman and gentlemen of the committee, Mr. Leeds scatters —he scatters badly—he is truly no good as a railroad expert. I do not believe he is good for the Traffic Association of San Francisco, and I think all will bear me out in the assertion that he is a rank failure as a framer of amendments to the Constitution.

"Now, with what you have not heard from Mr. Leeds, and with what you have heard from Mr. Burgin, Mr. Wade, Mr. Kidder, Mr. Bender, and other gentlemen who have appeared before you, I think you will, when considering this very important subject, place Mr. Leeds' utterances in the niche where they properly belong. His assertion that the Southern Pacific officials are handling the representatives of the smaller roads to its (the Southern Pacific Company's) advantage, or attempting to do so, is not worthy of notice. It is not a fact. It compares favorably, however, with other assertions made by Mr. Leeds, and I ask you to remember the axiom, 'false in one thing, false in all.'

"Should Mr. Leeds be present Monday evening, I shall regret not having been there to have heard the wisdom flow from the tongue of the mighty fence-post, water-logged Traffic Association expert.

"I am, Mr. Chairman and gentlemen of the committee,

"Yours, most respectfully,

"J. M. FULTON,

"Master Transportation Nevada, California, and Oregon Railway."

SOUTHERN PACIFIC COMPANY.

(Statement of W. G. Curtis, Assistant to General Manager.)

SACRAMENTO, February 1, 1893.

To the Senate Committee on Constitutional Amendments:

The gentlemen who are credited with formulating the papers now under consideration by your honorable committee, proposing an amendment to the Constitution of the State of California, regulating the rates for the transportation of freight and passengers to be charged and the classification of various commodities to be made by the railroads of this State, have, as we understand from the testimony they have presented before you, based their action upon the broad assumption that the existing rates are unreasonably high, and the classification of commodities arbitrary and unjust.

The plain truth of the matter is that the railroads of California are now occupying, and, if left unhampered by arbitrary and unjust restrictions, will continue to occupy their true and proper position in relation to the commercial and industrial development of this State. Although the classifications of freight may differ in some respects from the classifications in the Eastern States, the differences, whatever they may be, are justified by the difference in conditions surrounding the operations of the railways. The existing rates, as compared with rates prevailing in other States of this Union, are not higher in California, nor out of a fair proportion to the greater value and cost of commodities in every department of industry.

No industry requiring the coöperation of railway carriers has languished, nor has the progress of any legitimate enterprise been impeded through the failure or refusal of railway people to provide the needful facilities at fair rates and under conditions reasonable and just. On the contrary, every project looking to the development of the State, and to the increased prosperity of its people, is fostered and encouraged by the railway.

It has been given out by the gentleman representing the Traffic Association of San Francisco, who, we are told, formulated the proposed amendment to the Constitution, and testified before you in favor of its passage; who has not been in the State of California, I believe, more than a year, and whom, we believe, has traveled but little throughout the State, but has spent the most of the time of his residence here in the city of San Francisco; who, when asked by you, Mr. Chairman, was unable to name all of the railroads in this State other than the Southern Pacific—

that the Southern Pacific Company is the especial object of attack by himself and the people he represents. We cannot believe that he represents the views of the merchants of San Francisco or the people of this State. The principal owners of the Southern Pacific lines, Mr. Huntington, Senator Stanford, and their associates, were among the earliest of California pioneers, and their interests have been identified with this State ever since. They have certainly done much to advance the general interests of the State; they have done much more than any other individuals or associations to induce the investment of foreign capital in the railroads of this State, which have done so much to build up California. These railroads have so stimulated production and facilitated transportation that not only California wheat, but California wine, California fruits and vegetables, dried and in cans, find markets in the Old World. The experiment of shipping green fruit to England has been tried. It is not quite yet a success, but it will succeed, and shipments of California commodities to the eastern side of the Atlantic will increase until England and Germany will, if indeed they do not now, pay back to California for its productions far more than they are entitled to demand from the States, on their capital invested within its borders. We submit to you that the Manager of the Traffic Association does not represent the views of the people who are identified with the permanent and enduring interests of this State; and we believe the majority of the members of the Traffic Association agree in this view.

With your kind permission, I shall speak only of the operating service, that is to say, the conditions affecting the work of maintenance of equipment, maintenance of way and structures, and conducting transportation, including the train and station service of the railroads operated by the Southern Pacific Company, formerly thirty-seven in number (see page 362 of California Railroad Commissioners' report for 1892), but now consolidated into six companies. Officers of these companies will ask your indulgence to present various other matters. We have nothing to conceal from our patrons or from you gentlemen. Our only desire is that you shall know the exact and literal truth with respect to our roads, their operating conditions, and relations to the public.

Railway operation in California is more expensive than in Eastern States; first, because of the difference in physical characteristics. The physical characteristics of California are, as compared with the Mississippi Valley and Atlantic Coast States, peculiarly adverse to railway construction, maintenance, and operation. The State of Kansas typifies the great valley States west of the Mississippi; there are no mountains in that State. The general surface is an undulating plateau, with a gentle slope downward from the western to the eastern border. The State of Indiana, in its topography, typifies the prairie States generally; at least two thirds of the State is level or gently undulating land. There are no mountains, or even hills, of any size in that State.

California has an area of one hundred and fifty-six thousand square miles, or about one hundred million acres of land surface, which has been classified topographically as follows:

Mountainous	82,000 miles, or 52 per cent.
Rolling, or "foothills"	12,000 miles, or 8 per cent.
Valleys	25,000 miles, or 16 per cent.
Marsh, or tule	2,000 miles, or 1 per cent.
Desert	35,000 miles, or 23 per cent.
Total	156,000 miles, or 100 per cent.

For the industrial development of California, railroads must be built and operated to traverse the sterile desert regions, and ascend over barren mountains, where the expense of operation is costly, and where no traffic can be furnished to contribute toward the expense of operation and maintenance. The country along nearly 25 per cent of the Southern Pacific lines in California furnishes no local traffic to be carried. Railroad lines connecting the central basin region of California with other parts of the State, and with adjoining States and Territories, must cross high mountain ranges, where the necessary cost of construction and maintenance of the roads is many times greater than in the States east of the Rocky Mountains. The railroad line of the Southern Pacific, connecting Northern and Southern California, crosses the Tehachapi Pass, at an elevation of four thousand feet; the Soledad Pass, at an elevation of three thousand two hundred feet; passing through twenty-seven tunnels, one of them one and one quarter miles long; and between Southern California and Arizona, the San Gorgonio Pass, at an elevation of two thousand six hundred feet. The line connecting California and Oregon crosses Black Butte Pass, at an elevation of three thousand nine hundred feet, and the Siskiyou Mountains, at an elevation of four thousand one hundred feet, and passes through twelve tunnels. The Central Pacific line, connecting California and Nevada, crosses the Sierra Nevada Mountains at an elevation of seven thousand feet, passing through seventeen tunnels and thirty-three miles of snowsheds. The total rise of strictly mountain grades on the railroads operated by the Southern Pacific Company in California is over thirty thousand feet, in a distance of a little over five hundred miles, and on the entire system, west of Ogden and El Paso, the total length of mountain grade is over seven hundred miles, and the total rise nearly forty-two thousand feet.

The power required to move a given quantity of traffic over these mountain grades is from five to seven times greater than on the comparatively straight and level lines of the Eastern so-called prairie States.

The profiles before you [various important profiles and a relief map of the United States were here exhibited to the committee] indicate the difference in grade of the systems of roads east and west of the Rocky Mountains more clearly and forcibly than can be expressed in figures, but it may not be out of place to state that, for the roads operated by the Southern Pacific Company in California, covering a mileage of 2,895 miles, the length of level track is only 548 miles; the length of curved line, 646 miles; the number of degrees of curvature 128,319°, equal to 356 complete circles; the sum of ascending grades in feet, 42,862; descending grades, 26,035 feet; total rise and fall of grades, 68.897 feet.

There are 86 tunnels on the Pacific System lines of the Southern Pacific Company, aggregating 66,701 feet; 54,000 feet is in the California railroad system, which includes the Siskiyou Mountains along the boundary line between California and Oregon; 69 of these tunnels, aggregating 49,448 feet in length and costing over $4,500,000, are within the State boundaries of California. These tunnels have been costly to construct and are expensive to maintain. There is practically no similar expense for either construction or maintenance work in the Mississippi Valley States. Taking the snowsheds and tunnels of the Southern Pacific lines in California together, their aggregate cost is over $6,000,000, or probably a sufficient sum to build and equip over 200 miles of railroad in Kansas. If invested in Kansas railroads, and if the San Francisco Traffic Association's estimate of uniform distance tariff covering railroad rates in that State is correct, it might be expected that interest at a fair rate might be earned upon this $6,000,000 investment; but the investment as it stands in California brings no direct returns. It is an extra cost connected with the construction of something less than 40 miles of railroad, and a constant expense is required for maintenance of the heavy timber work required in a great portion of this tunneling.

The damage consequent upon washouts, landslides, and snow blockades, is also exceptionally great in the mountain regions. From these causes, not longer than three years ago, railroad communication between California and Oregon was suspended for more than two months at a time.

At present, on the South Pacific Coast road, between San Francisco and Santa Cruz, there is a great landslide in the Santa Cruz Mountains, which has crushed down a tunnel timbered and braced as strongly as possible. A large force of extra men, as many as could be placed on the work, employing shifts to carry along the work continuously night and day, have not succeeded in reopening the road for traffic, which has now been interrupted thirty-four days. This road has been so damaged by other slides and washouts that it is more than probable that, taking into account the increase in operating expenses, together with the decrease in earnings, consequent upon the interruption of traffic, the road may not this year earn enough to cover its operating expenses. This line has heavy mountain grades, and considerably more tunnels—at least 50 per cent more—than on the Pennsylvania Central Railroad, and is one of the roads mentioned by the gentleman representing the Traffic Association as showing excessive gross earnings as compared with Eastern lines. Another road mentioned by him in the same connection is the California Pacific, operating 115 miles of line, from Sacramento to South Vallejo, from Davisville to Knights Landing, and from Napa Junction to Calistoga. This road crosses the tule lands between Sacramento and Webster, being subject to overflow and damage by floods, which, from year to year, show a tendency toward a greater height. This particular road, for over eight miles, is protected on both sides of a high embankment with a granite face wall, very costly to construct. If the high-water plane of the Sacramento River continues to rise, as is probable, it will become necessary to build up the embankment supporting the track to a greater height, and, in consequence, remove and replace this walling. The floods of the present winter have been right up to the grade, and the drift deposited by them now lies at the end of the ties for several miles. The timber work on this line is extensive and costly to keep in repair. More than $100 000 will have to be expended this year in repairs to the bridge over the Sacramento River. Knowing, as I do, the requirements of this road for maintenance, I will say that it needs every dollar that it can earn.

LABOR EXPENSES.

The labor expense on the railroads in the Southern Pacific System in California generally averages more than 30 per cent greater than on the roads east of the Rocky Mountains.

It may be noted that, in the State of Kansas, according to the Railroad Commissioners' report for 1891, page 291, the average daily compensation paid railway employés is $1 73, while in California and contiguous States and Territories, the rate is about $2 57, or 49 per cent greater than in Kansas. (On the Southern Pacific lines alone, it is at least $2 59.) It is to be understood that the daily rate of compensation is computed on 313 days in a year, the basis commonly adopted by Railroad Commissioners in various States.

As nearly as can be estimated, the payroll of the Southern Pacific Company for services rendered in California is $9,700,000 per annum for about 12,000 employés. Could the rate of compensation be reduced to the Kansas figure ($1 73 per day), this would become $6,470,000, or $3,230,000 less than now paid, or 13 per cent of the amount earned annually in California from transportation of passengers and freight. At the Illinois rate of wages ($1 93 a day), the saving would be $2,400,000, or about 10 per cent of the Southern Pacific Company's earnings in California.

The difference between the rates of railway wages, as between the Mississippi Valley and Pacific Coast regions, is well typified by the so-called Atchison properties. For their Chicago, Santa Fe, and California line, the Railroad and Warehouse Commissioners' report, State of Illinois, for the year 1891, shows the average daily rate of compensation for all classes of employés to be $1 06; for the Atchison system in the State of Kansas, the Railroad Commissioners in their report for 1891, show a rate of $1 87; for the Atlantic and Pacific Railroad, extending from eastern New Mexico westward through Arizona into California, the rate is $2 01; and on the Southern California Railway properties the rate of wages is $2 71, as shown by the California Railroad Commissioners' report for 1892.

In this connection, the attached table (Exhibit A) is presented, to show the average compensation paid and class of railway employés on the Southern Pacific and San Francisco and North Pacific roads in California, as compared with the Atchison and Illinois Central roads in Illinois.

The efficiency of railway employés—that is to say, the number of tons of freight transported to each person employed—is somewhat less in California than in the Eastern States.

FUEL.

The principal sources of coal supply for use in California are Colorado, Wyoming, Washington, British Columbia, Australia, and England. There is no coal in California suitable for use on locomotives, while, on the other hand, roads east of the Rocky Mountains generally run through coal mines, not only producing coal for their own operations, but being an important item of commercial tonnage to be moved.

The cost of fuel on Pacific Coast roads, being fully 20 per cent of the total expenditure for maintenance and operation, is a very important item to be considered in fixing railway rates. The total cost per ton for coal, delivered on locomotive tenders, for the past five years, on the Southern Pacific Company's lines in California, is between $6 40 and $6 50. This is a lower rate than the similar average prices paid by other roads in this State, for the reasons, first, that through the ownership or control of coal mines and of ocean steam colliers by controlled or friendly companies, the Southern Pacific is able to secure the output from such mines at a minimum rate, and to so maintain its standing in the market as to prevent combination by other mine or ship owners, or "cornering" by dealers to unfairly raise the price of fuel required by the Southern Pacific Company.

For the year 1891, the cost of fuel per mile run by locomotives on the Pacific System lines of the Southern Pacific Company was 19.12 cents, which is somewhat lower than the cost in California. As against this, we find the corresponding cost on various Eastern roads to be:

Road.	Cost Fuel per Mile Run—Cents.	Year.
Denver and Rio Grande Railroad	4.55	1891-2
Chicago, Rock Island, and Pacific Railway	5.78	1890-1
Lake Shore and Michigan Southern Railway	5.18	1891
Missouri Pacific Railway	5.89	1891
Wabash Railway	4.50	1890-1
Chicago and Northwestern Railway	6.89	1890-1
Atchison, Topeka, and Santa Fe Railroad	8.57	1891-2
St. Louis and San Francisco Railway	6.42	1891-2
Average	5.96	

The gentleman representing the Traffic Association of San Francisco has testified before you that on account of the equable climate in California there is required only fifty-six pounds of coal to run a locomotive one mile, while double the quantity is required to perform the same service in Eastern States. He has taken, in support of this assertion, the report of the Atchison, Topeka, and Santa Fe Railroad System for the year ending June 30, 1892, and the annual report of the Southern Pacific Company for the year 1891. In connection with the figures he has produced from these reports, he carefully avoided to state to you that although the quantity of fuel used per mile run appeared to him greater, the cost of fuel per locomotive mile on the Atchison, Topeka, and Santa Fe Railroad system is shown, on the same page with the other figures he considered, to be 8.57 cents, while on the Pacific System lines of the Southern Pacific Company the cost of fuel per mile run is shown to be 19.12 cents.

Neither did he tell you, which is true, that those statistics, instead of representing the conditions east of the Rocky Mountains, apply to seven thousand one hundred and thirty miles of the Atchison System, covering railroads in the Republic of Mexico, the Atlantic and Pacific Railroad in the Territories of Arizona and New Mexico, and the Southern California Railway in this State, only about one seventh of the mileage being located in the State of Kansas.

Further, there is a blunder in computations, leading to grossly erroneous results, but apparently the gentleman lacked the judgment and practical experience in railway operation to detect the error. As shown by their 1891 report, the Southern Pacific Company (Pacific System) locomotives ran 20,356,680 miles, consuming against this mileage 570,102 tons of coal, and 141,793 cords of wood. This 141,793 cords of wood was not taken into consideration in Mr. Leeds' calculations, but it was used largely in locomotives running over the Sierra Nevada Mountains, over the Siskiyou Mountains, and on the lines in Oregon. He simply ignored the wood altogether, and took the total engine mileage running with wood as well as coal, and divided it into the coal alone; thus producing his figure of fifty-six pounds of coal per locomotive mile. From one and a quarter cords of wood to two cords are required to enable a locomotive to perform the same service as with a ton of coal. The rule commonly used by Eastern roads is to compute one and one half cords of wood equivalent to one ton of coal. Making that allowance in this case, we find that sixty-five pounds of fuel, instead of fifty-six pounds, are required to run a locomotive one mile on the Pacific System lines of the Southern Pacific Company. Now, as to the gentleman's figures on the Atchison, Topeka, and Santa Fe road: Page 82 of the annual report of the Atchison, Topeka, and Santa Fe Railroad Company, for the fiscal year ending June 30, 1892, shows the miles run by locomotives to be 34,383,445; the tons of coal used, 1,354,-693; cords of wood used, 31,565. Again, figuring the wood at one and one half cords equal to one ton of coal, we have the equivalent of coal of 1,375,603 tons, or 2,751,206,000 pounds, used by locomotives running 34,383,445 miles. Dividing this mileage into the fuel, we find the Atchison lines in question, including, with the lines in Kansas, those also in California, Texas, and Mexico, used eighty pounds of coal to run a locomotive one mile, instead of one hundred and eight pounds, as stated by Mr. Leeds. It would appear that his figures were computed by taking the total quantity of fuel as above used by locomotives in all classes of service and dividing it by the mileage only of those locomotives which run in revenue train service; while the correct comparison on the face of the figures is, for the Atchison lines under consideration, eighty pounds of coal per locomotive mile, and for the Pacific System lines of the Southern Pacific Company sixty-five pounds of coal per locomotive mile. It is not true that the Atchison lines in question correctly typify the coal consumption of the Mississippi Valley region.

By further investigation, Mr. Leeds might have found that the consumption of fuel to move a car one mile on the Southern Pacific Company, Pacific System, was 7.18 pounds; on the Missouri Pacific Railway, operating mainly in Kansas and Missouri and entirely in the Mississippi Valley, 6.8 pounds; on the Atchison, Topeka, and Santa Fe, 7.8 pounds; this slightly higher figure being undoubtedly due to the fact that a very large portion of the Atchison line here considered lies in Mexico, Arizona, and California, where, as a matter of fact, and by reason of the difference in physical characteristics, more coal is required to haul a car one mile than is necessary in the Mississippi Valley. The truth of the matter is, as is well known to practical railroad men, that if there is any difference, more coal is required to perform a given amount of train service in California than in the Eastern States. The following figures for various lines, including the Atchison, Topeka, and Santa Fe, and the Northern Pacific, both of which extend to the Pacific Coast, corroborate this fact:

Road.	Year.	Pounds of Coal per Car Mile.
S. P. Co. (Pacific System)	1891	7.18
D. & R. G. R. R.	1892	8.8
C. R. I. & P. Ry.	1890–91	6.18
Mo. Pac. Ry.	1891	6.8
Wabash Ry.	1890–91	6.5
C. & N. W. Ry.	1890–91	7.3
A. T. & S. F. Ry.	1891–92	7.8
St. L. & S. F. R. R.	1891–92	7.5
Nor. Pac. R. R.	1891	7.2
Chicago & Alton	1890	6.75
Penn. R. R. Co.	1891	5.52

Average Eastern roads, 7.06; Pacific System, 7.18.

I should not fail to mention in this connection that many Eastern roads running over coal fields and taking their coal supply to locomotives from the mouth of the mines, find it to their advantage to burn screenings and coal slack, which is either purchased at a low figure, or in many cases, given to them by the mine owners, who are desirous of getting rid of this, to them, unsalable material, this slack going into the fuel account, ton per ton, with the good coal, while its cost is merely nominal.

The average cost per mile run for fuel for the Southern Pacific Company's lines in California for the past five years averages 21.5 cents, which is from 15 to 25 per cent higher than the total cost of running a locomotive one mile on many Eastern roads, including the expense of fuel, repairs, service of engine men, oil, waste, storage, etc.

COST OF MATERIALS.

The average cost of materials for railway construction and maintenance is generally higher in California than in the Mississippi Valley. Pig iron, suitable for the manufacture of wheels and many classes of castings used for rolling stock, bridges, etc., must come from the East, and the handling charges laid down at our machine shops here in Sacramento increase the cost from 30 to 40 per cent, as compared with similar cost to Eastern manufacturers of railway supplies. The insurance, freight, primage, and handling charges on steel rails make the cost of this material here more than 30 per cent higher in California than in the East. Many other materials for railway construction work, as fishplates, bolts, nuts, spikes, as well as tools, machinery of all kinds, either manufactured in the East, and shipped out, or manufactured here, are relatively more costly here in about the same proportion, that is to say, from 30 to 50 per cent higher. It costs, for instance, at the present time, $1,000 to bring a locomotive from Eastern works to California. The Pacific Coast produces no coal suitable for foundry uses or blacksmith work, nor anthracite coal, required for heating cars. Both Lehigh and Cumberland coal, for these purposes, are brought from the Atlantic States, the transportation and handling charges more than quadrupling its cost to California, as compared with Eastern railroads.

Oak lumber for draft timbers for cars, and for many other purposes in building and repairing rolling and floating stock, costs, f. o. b., in Kentucky and Indiana, from $12 to $15 per thousand feet, board measure. The expense of freight and handling brings the minimum cost in Sacramento up to $70 per thousand feet, board measure. The current market quotation in San Francisco is, I believe, $90 per thousand feet, board measure.

With the existing and prospective volume of traffic to be moved, the rates for the transportation of freight and passengers in California should, on account of the higher cost of labor, fuel, and miscellaneous supplies, to say nothing of the greater requirements for fixed charges on account of the higher cost of the roads in California, be at least 35 per cent higher than similar rates which would be fair and equitable in Eastern States.

In this connection, it is proper to state, that because the States and Territories adjoining California on the east do not produce lumber or hardly anything that is required in the maintenance of the Southern Pacific line in those regions, many classes of materials are bought in California for operations outside the State, and many articles are manufactured in California from crude materials purchased here and shipped over for the operation of the road and maintenance of its way and structures in adjoining States. For these reasons, the amount paid out by the Southern Pacific Company to California dealers and producers exceeds the earnings of the company on freight and passengers taken up and laid down in California.

In summarizing his views, the Manager of the San Francisco Traffic Association stated, in effect, that the railroad earnings per mile in California were greater than in Nebraska, Kansas, and contiguous States, and that the cost of operating roads in California was not greater than in those States. As a matter of fact the cost of operating railroads in California is very much higher than in the region he mentioned, and railroad men who have made a study of these things will all agree that, aside from the higher cost of other items of expenditure, if the railroads in that region were obliged to pay for labor and fuel the rates which apply on the Southern Pacific lines in California to-day, they would not earn their bare expenses of operation. Figures are not necessary to prove this proposition to railway experts, who, from practical experience and personal observation, have informed themselves as to the difference in operating conditions. As corroborative of this fact, however, we present to your consideration a statement compiled from the Railroad Commissioners' report of the State of Illinois for the year 1891; also a similar statement of the five principal roads in the State of Iowa.

[See exhibits marked "B" and "C."]

Permit me to quote to you from the last published report of the United States Interstate Commerce Commission on "Statistics of Railways of the United States," commenting on the statistics compiled under authority of the Commission, which are believed to be the most complete that have yet been prepared, the railways of the United States being therein divided into ten territorial groups:

"It is believed that the attempt to group statistics will be completely justified by the facts presented in the present report, for the comparisons which it renders possible throw new and important light on the operations of railways in the United States. They show, for example, the great divergence in the conditions under which railways are operated. Thus, whether we consider the gross earnings per mile of line, the operating expenses per mile of line, number of locomotives per one hundred miles of line, passenger mileage per mile of line, freight mileage per mile of line, revenue per passenger per mile, revenue per ton per mile, per cent of passenger earnings to total earnings, per cent of freight earnings to total earnings, value of railway property per mile of line, or any other prominent fact pertaining to railway economy, the variations are so great as to dispel the thought that there is any approach towards uniformity in the conditions under which railways are operated or in the administrative rules to which they conform."

Among other comparisons made of those groups, the statistician shows that, out of 76,207,000,000 tons of freight carried one mile in the United States, only 1,944,000,000, or 2.7 per cent, were moved in group number ten, including California, the largest in area of all the groups. Out of 11,347,000,000 passengers carried one mile in the United States, only 631,000,000, or 5.8 per cent, were in group ten. Of the 62,625,000 people reported by the census of 1890, only 2,350,000 were in the States and Territories of Washington, Oregon, Idaho, Nevada, California, Arizona, and the western portion of New Mexico, or 3.7 per cent.

OPERATING EXPENSES.

Of the total expense of operating and maintaining a railroad, about 9 per cent is for general and miscellaneous expense, including administration expenses, printing, taxes, etc., commercial agencies; 22 per cent for maintenance of way and structures; 15 per cent for maintenance of locomotives, cars, and other equipment; 24 per cent for wages of engineers, firemen, station expense for agents, clerks, and laborers, telegraphers, wages of conductors, brakemen, switchmen, flagmen, and watchmen; 30 per cent for fuel for locomotives, steamers, train and station supplies, roundhouse labor, fuel, station attendance, heating, lighting, and inspecting cars and stations, lubricating cars, loss and damages to freight and other property, expense of sleeping cars, parlor cars, etc.

The tendency of many people to overestimate the earnings, and undervalue the expenses of a railroad, most probably arises from the fact that the patrons of a railroad company in their various transactions connected with transportation are chiefly concerned with the rates charged; they are not called upon to inform themselves with respect to the cost of transportation and expenditures other than that which may come under their direct notice, as necessary for the receipt and delivery of freight, the sale of tickets, and the running of trains. In other words, it is probable that the most of railway patrons have some appreciation of the 24 or 25 per cent of the total operating expenses required for engineers, firemen, conductors, brakemen, telegraph operators, station agents and clerks, switchmen, flagmen and watchmen, as above, but understand little or nothing about the 75 or 76 per cent of the expenditures which, so far as they are concerned, do not enforce themselves upon their attention in any way, seeming to go on easily, and to be conducted with so little visible effort as apparently not to require a great expenditure of money.

MAINTENANCE OF SNOWSHEDS.

In California there is something over thirty-four miles of snowsheds which must be maintained. The average annual cost of snowshed maintenance for the past four years has been in round numbers $194,000. On the Eastern roads in question, there is nothing comparable with this expense. The snow service is also excessively costly on the California lines. For the past four years the average yearly cost has been in round numbers $137,000. In 1890, in the last snow blockade, the cost of snow service, including the construction and purchase of new snowplows and other appliances for clearing the track, was in round numbers $500,000. No roads east of the Rockies are obliged to remove snow under such great difficulties as the Southern Pacific. The snowfall with us is deeper and heavier on the Sierra Nevada Mountains than anywhere east of us.

The snowsheds are at all times exposed to damage by fire. Our losses last year from this cause were not less than $75,000.

TIES.

I must not omit mention of the railroad tie question in order to confess that, when we can no longer utilize them in the track, we do use some of them for fence posts, and some to kindle fires in locomotives; some few we sell to farmers, and I suppose we must save as much as $5 per mile of road by doing so, instead of burning them up, which is the common way of disposing of them, and is the manner we get rid of our pine ties, and by the way, about one third of these ties we use are pine.

We also practice many other economies not thought of in the Eastern States in our struggles against adverse physical conditions surrounding our operations. A prominent railroad expert once said to me, after spending some seven weeks in a thorough and critical examination of our lines, that from the great care and economy he observed in the use of all our materials, he was satisfied that we must have a place somewhere, where we made things no longer useful for railroad purposes into soap, and he wanted to see that soap factory before he left us. Redwood ties do resist decay better than the oak, cedar, and chestnut ties commonly used in the Eastern States, but they crush down under the rail, and on many of our lines are thus worn out in a shorter time than required for pine and fir ties to fail by decay. By reason of the softness of these ties, their life on curves, of which we have many, is shorter than on straight track. Our ties are transported long distances and are handled over a good many times on their way from the forests on the northern coast of this State, via the ocean, to point of use. On a general average, the cost of tie renewals is a little more in California than in the Mississippi Valley. The following figures corroborate this:

Comparative Cost of Tie Renewals.

Road.	Mileage of all tracks, including sidings.	Ties used in renewals per mile of track.	Mileage of main line track.	Cost tie renewals per mile, main line.	Year.
S. P. Co., Pac. S.	5,639	240	4,711	$130	1891
Nor. Pac. R. R.	No data.	No data.	4,349	124	1891
A., T. & S. F.	No data.	No data.	7,130	90	1891-2
St. L. & S. F.	No data.	No data.	1,893	113	1891-2
D. & R. G. R. R.	No data.	No data.	1,640	105	1891-2
Tex. & Pac. Ry.	No data.	No data.	1,499	114	1891
C. & N. W. Ry.	5,581	214	4,273	110	1890-1
Wabash Ry.	4,070	171	No data.	No data.	No data.
C., R. I. & P. Ry.	4,197	135	3,409	73	1890-1

Average, except Southern Pacific Company (Pacific System), $104.
Southern Pacific Company (Pacific System), $130.

At San Francisco the expense and maintenance of ferry and transfer steamers, and docks and wharves, is much greater than in the Mississippi Valley States. The cost under these headings to the Southern Pacific Company annually is about $753,000.

Water supply for locomotives, train and station supplies, and many items other than those I have mentioned, are higher with us than in the East.

SLOW DEVELOPMENT OF CALIFORNIA.

California, in many things other than its physical geography, is an exceptional State, and it is just about as difficult to force its industrial development along the same lines as have been followed in the development of the Mississippi Valley, as it would be to level down the mountains and fertilize the deserts to make all of California as level in surface and as productive throughout its area as the State of Illinois. The rights of ownership in the soil, the methods of its cultivation, and the commodities produced from it, are widely different from the Eastern States.

In 1870 the population of California was five hundred and sixty thousand two hundred and forty-seven; in 1880, eight hundred and sixty-four thousand six hundred and ninety-four; in 1890, one million two hundred and eight thousand one hundred and thirty. The miles of railroad in California in 1870 were nine hundred and twenty-five; in 1880, two thousand one hundred and ninety-five; in 1890, four thousand three hundred and twenty-eight. Thus, from 1870 to 1880, the increase in population was 54 per cent; in railroad mileage, 137 per cent. From 1880 to 1890, increase in population, 40 per cent; railroad mileage, 100 per cent. For the two decades from 1870 to 1890 the increase in population was 115 per cent; in railroad mileage, 357 per cent.

Other statistics bearing closely upon this subject will be presented for your consideration by Mr. Richard Gray, our General Traffic Manager, and will show that, when fairly contrasted with other States, Californians have reason to congratulate themselves on their progress, and the railroads of this State have no reason to be ashamed of the results of their efforts to promote its progress.

After a village existence of some ten years as Fort Dearborn, the birth of Chicago as a town dates from August 4, 1830, when it was surveyed as the town of Chicago, and a plat of the survey published by James Thompson. In 1870, forty years later, the population had grown to two hundred and ninety-three thousand nine hundred and seventy-seven. The town of San Francisco, existing theretofore as a small village, began its existence as a city in 1849 and 1850. On its fortieth birthday, or in 1890, it numbered two hundred and ninety-three thousand nine hundred and ninety-seven people, outranking Chicago when it had reached the same age by twenty inhabitants.

Taking into comparison with California the so-called Northern, Central, and Northwestern States, as shown by the first census taken in those States after their admission into the Union, in comparison with the census figures forty years later, we find that, by the census in 1890, forty years after the first census, in 1850, California had increased its population to thirteen times, while the average of the States of Illinois, Indiana, Ohio, Iowa, Michigan, and Wisconsin was only eight times, the rate of increase in each State being as shown by the following table:

Illinois, population in first forty years increased	30 times.
Ohio, population in first forty years increased	8 times.
Indiana, population in first forty years increased	9 times.
Iowa, population in first forty years increased	10 times.
Michigan, population in first forty years increased	8 times.
Wisconsin, population in first forty years increased	5 times.

It is commonly assumed that dense rural population forms the basis of real and enduring prosperty in any State. This may or may not be true. Many facts can be adduced to show that the cultivation of land in great ranches founded largely upon the Spanish grants is, under the peculiar climatic conditions of California, beneficial rather than detrimental to this State. Be this as it may, railroad managers would like to see more people settled in California, and no inducement offered, for example, to emigrants who in recent years have settled in the State of Washington, have exceeded in liberality the similar inducements offered by the roads leading into California. In fact, the Washington roads merely copied the rates previously offered, and duplicated the emigrant cars previously built by the California lines. The Central Pacific Railroad was the first road in this country to design and build emigrant cars. People immigrating to the State of Washington, and settling there, did so merely because land was plenty, and cheap, for sale by the Government and the railroads, at not more than $2 50 an acre. This class of people, generally without capital, did not come to California, because desirable land was not offered so cheap here. Nevertheless, there are many people who appreciate the great productive value of lands in California, and are coming to us all the time; but unfortunately, this class of people is small as compared with the immigration that is attracted only by cheap lands, and consequently California's increase in population is in the very nature of things comparatively slow, though all of us who are familiar with the capabilities of our wonderful State of California know that in the light of a permanent investment, California lands, whatever may be their price, are always cheap in comparison with the lands of Oregon and Washington.

There are three classes of large landholders in this State. First, those who cultivate their own land, raising grain on a large scale, plowing by steam, or with great teams of animals propelling gang plows, turning over many furrows at a time, and harvesting the grain with combined heading and thrashing machines that take the grain from the stalk and drop it into bags in wagons alongside or upon the field behind; thus doing nearly all the cultivation by machinery, and employing only a very little labor, and that not continuously, but for short periods at seed time and harvest. This method largely prevails in the Sacramento Valley, in the north end of the San Joaquin Valley, and, to a less extent, in other localities.

Another class of large landholders rent out their land to tenant farmers, taking as their rent a certain fixed proportion of the crop. These farmers are generally able, independently of transportation companies, or all other outside influences, to so adjust their rental as to fix the conditions of living among their tenants. Many of these landlords are broad and liberal-minded men, who see to it that their tenants who are up to or over the average of men in thrift and diligence, reap their fair share of the rewards of industry, and consequently prosper in their work. Others are said to be more exacting.

In this connection I know of a case, where a railroad was built, affording transportation facilities to a fertile country, but at such a distance from the markets that, up to the time the railroad was built, it was merely used as a cattle range. It is now one of the most productive grain regions in the State. The grain rates, when the road was first built, were placed at figures then deemed to be fair. As the grain tonnage increased, the rates were constantly lowered. A gentleman who owns one of the largest ranches along this line, who rents his land to be farmed by tenants, at first took as a rental one fifth of the crop. When the first reduction in grain rates was made, he demanded and received one fourth of the crop. When the next reduction to the existing rates was effected, he demanded and now receives one third of the crop. Though large quantities of grain are now produced along this line, the ranches have not been divided up, the increase in population has been small, the growth of towns along the line has been slow, and the railroad rates are now down to bedrock. This gentleman, who has raised his rent as the railroad rates have been reduced, has more than once applied to us to make a further reduction in rates, because he says the homes of some of his tenants lack the ordinary comforts of life, and he is even obliged to advance them money to buy the prime necessaries in the way of food.

While this may be an extreme case, I personally know of other land owners who raise their rent whenever a reduction in railroad rates can be secured. This may be only good business policy on their part; but, under such circumstances, the railroads must not be blamed if an industrious and thrifty population of small and independent land owners does not establish itself along every new road built in this State. Where land is not for sale at some price, even though it be a high price, in small tracts to suit the purchaser, a dense population of independent land owners cannot be established, no matter how many roads we build, or at what figures the rates for transportation are fixed. One of our company's new roads in the San Joaquin Valley, built a little over a year ago, runs for over fifty miles through the lands of one firm. We hope and believe that the firm will construct irrigation ditches or sink artesian wells, both being feasible, fitting the land to be handled in small tracts, and proceed to cut it up and offer it for sale at such figures as will bring people into that region; but the matter rests with the land owner, not with us, and he will be guided by his own interests. We can only offer him transportation at reasonable rates for anything that may be produced on his land.

In regions where the annual rainfall is insufficient to produce crops other than the cereals, and where, consequently, irrigation is required—and this is true of a greater portion of our State—the natural sequence of events is perhaps for the land to be first held in large tracts, in order that capital may be safe in bringing the water from the rivers and mountain streams, so that the cultivation of land on a small scale may be profitable, even though its price is high. Doubtless this is true, and, as I said before, we have no complaint to lodge against the large land owners, or others who believe that they are doing what is right to build up this State. But these conditions do affect the railways, and their managers cannot change them. They must adapt their operations to them, and only ask that they be not blamed that, because of the difference in conditions which affect railways in common with all other interests, the State of California is, in its progress and development, different from States east of the Rocky Mountains. I have said that the railroads of this State are fairly and honestly adjusting their operations to the needs of their patrons. In this connection, I desire to call your attention to some facts that, to my mind, are of great significance in corroboration of this statement.

The counties of Sacramento, Solano, Yolo, Sutter, Yuba, Colusa, Glenn, Butte, and Tehama, covering the Sacramento Valley, with navigable waterways, affording the most effectual protection against unreasonable railroad rates that can possibly be provided in any country, traversing every one of these counties, showed an increase in population in 1890 over 1880 of only 9,438, or 7 per cent; 5,778, or more than half of this increase, being in the cities of Sacramento and Woodland; leaving for the rural population, including the smaller towns and villages, an increase of only 3,571, or 4 per cent. Some of the counties have lost in population, and to some slight extent, this may be due to the fact that there has been a decadence in the mining industry in those which extend up on the western slope of the Sierras. In Yuba County, for example, where the loss in population in the last ten years was 1,648, 330 being in the city of Marysville, which is located upon a navigable river, and in Butte County, which in the ten years lost in population 782 people (406 of the loss being in the town of Chico, the county seat), the fruit grower has gone upon the foothills to replace the miner, and oranges are already being produced on a commercial scale in these counties. The county of Tehama shows in 1890, as compared with 1880, an increase in population of 615 people, but this increase is all in the towns, the town of Red Bluff alone showing an increase of 502, the village of Vina 129, and the village of Corning 210.

San Joaquin County, one of the most fertile in the State, and perhaps in a position to be the most independent of railroads of any county in this State, the San Joaquin River, with its tributaries and navigable sloughs, offering transportation to market in easy competition with the railroads throughout the county, shows an increase in population, in 1890 as compared with 1880, of 4,280 people; 4,142 of this increase is in the thriving manufacturing city of Stockton, leaving for the country and smaller towns an increase of only 138 people in ten years. The same condition of things exists in Stanislaus County, also served by the navigable waters of the San Joaquin River.

Why is this so? The explanation is simple. In these portions of the State, large ranches, based mainly on the original Spanish grants, exist and are profitably cultivated by their owners. Now, I am not prepared to say that these counties are less prosperous than they should be because of these conditions. But if it be thought that progress in population, as well as in taxable wealth and area of land under cultivation, is to be measured by the mere increase in population, let me point you to some portions of the State of California that depend exclusively upon the lines of the Southern Pacific Company for the transportation of their products to the general markets, to the extent of requiring the railroads to transport deciduous fruits from 2,500 to 3,000 miles from the point of production, to be there marketed in competition with fruits produced in the immediate neighborhood. It is to be especially noted in these cases that every intending settler can in these counties obtain land in small holdings at some price. I do not mean to say that this is not true of the other counties I have mentioned, but that in these counties, there was in the beginning fewer Spanish grants—which, by the way, in their aggregate area of nearly 9,000,000 of acres, cover over 25 per cent of the arable area in this State (when we count in as "arable" every acre of desert and mountain side that can probably be reclaimed)—and it has been considered more profitable to work the land in small than in large farms.

Merced County, in 1890 as compared with 1880, shows an increase of 2,429 people, or 43 per cent, only 600 of this being in the towns. It is true that the San Joaquin River affords some transportation to this county, but in the main it depends upon the rail lines. Fresno County, which practically has no navigable waterway within its borders, shows an increase in 1890 as compared with 1880 of 22,548 people, or 238 per cent; 9,706 of this increase was in the city of Fresno, the remainder in the country and smaller towns. Tulare County, depending entirely upon the railroad for transportation, shows an increase of 13,293, or 118 per cent, 2,250 being in the town of Tulare, the remainder in the country and smaller towns. Kern County, at the head of the San Joaquin Valley, depends absolutely upon the lines of the Southern Pacific Company for the transportation of its products to the market. This county shows, in 1890 as compared with 1880, an increase in population of 4,207, or 75 per cent; 1,825 of this is in the town of Bakersfield, the remainder in the country and smaller towns.

As will be shown by the testimony of others, the average railroad earnings throughout the State per ton hauled and per passenger carried one mile on the Southern Pacific Company's lines, have been steadily reduced, and railroad construction continued from year to year, both the reduction in rates and the extension of mileage being out of proportion to the increase in volume of traffic offered to be carried. An arbitrary reduction in rates would bring the same results as in Kansas, bankrupt a majority of the roads, and absolutely stop railroad construction, greatly to the detriment of the State.

Many people suppose that Mr. Huntington has only to ask for money to have it freely furnished. Mr. Huntington to my certain knowledge has endeavored to obtain capital for large extensions of roads in this State, which bankers have been unwilling to furnish. They have been all over the State; they see these conditions which I have attempted briefly to describe; they see the land holdings; they compare the conditions here with the conditions surrounding other States East in which they have loaned money; they observe the differences here, and they do not understand them, and they are cautious and conservative.

Our railroads and their equipment are now well maintained, but many things beneficial to the public remain to be done, such as ballasting more of the track, the substitution of heavier steel rails for the lighter in certain sections as the latter wear out in service; the construction of masonry culverts and bridge foundations; the substitution of iron bridges for wood; new stations and depots; new side tracks; new and improved cars and locomotives; and additional main tracks to convert the roads into double track lines. The money for all these and other improvements, all to the advantage and safety of railway patrons, must come from the earnings; there is no other way for us to obtain it; and we ask of you that you will not, by giving your sanction to the measure presented for your consideration, deprive us of the means to maintain and improve our property to proper and desirable standards. You have been asked by their owners not to kill the little roads. We respectfully submit that the Southern Pacific System in California is made up of lines originally built by 37 independent companies; and, whatever advantage has accrued to the companies by their consolidation and aggregation of their lines into one system, that advantage has been fairly and squarely shared with the public by the furnishing of additional facilities and improved service. Do not, we beg of you, kill either the lines that remain as little roads or those which have, to the mutual advantage of themselves and the public, been combined with each other into a larger system.

BURKE: You speak, Mr. Curtis, of two groups of railways in the East, and their earnings?

MR. CURTIS: Yes, sir.

BURKE: And also their operating expenses; now, will you be kind enough to furnish us with similar information about the Southern Pacific system of consolidated lines you speak of—of the six consolidated lines?

MR. CURTIS: That information, and all that you can desire in this connection, will be furnished by Mr. Lansing, our Secretary and Controller, who has all these things at his fingers' ends. I have the data now in my possession, but it will take too much time, and Mr. Lansing can answer.

BURKE: I would like to ask one other question in relation to your payroll, and the payrolls of these companies you have spoken of. Who do you include in the payroll?

MR. CURTIS: All classes of employés.

BURKE: From the Superintendent down?

MR. CURTIS: Down to the track walkers and section men.

BURKE: Is there a difference in the rate of wages for conductors, engineers, brakemen, firemen, track walkers, and section men, as compared with Eastern men?

MR. CURTIS: Yes, sir. The firemen, for instance—I have before me comparative statements of wages paid on the principal roads in Illinois, and upon the Southern Pacific Company's Pacific System in California. Firemen with us earn an average of $3 40 per day. In Illinois, the rate is from $2 01 to $2 07 per day. You ask about conductors: With us their average wages are $4 11 per day; in Illinois it runs, on the Illinois Central and the Atchison System, two prominent roads which I have taken, from $3 11 to $3 42, against our $4 11. These figures are from the Railroad and Warehouse Commissioners' Reports of Illinois, on the one hand, and our people's reports on the other.

You ask about trackmen. Section foremen in the East earn from $1 48 to $1 80 per day. Our section foremen earn an average of $2 74 per day. Other trackmen, that means section hands, or the laborers, in Illinois earn from $1 16 to $1 28; while our section men earn $1 61.

I will place this table, if you desire, with the report filed with the clerk.

EXHIBIT "A."

Comparative Wages Paid on Principal Roads in Illinois and California. Average Compensation per Employé per Day (313 Working Days to Year).

Class.	In California.		In Illinois.	
	Southern Pacific Co.	S. F. & N. P. Ry.	Atchison.	Illinois Central.
General officers	$14 10	$16 02	$9 04	$12 45
Superintendent		10 50		
Attorney		11 02		
Chief Engineer		11 50		
Master Mechanic		6 60		
General office clerks	3 47	3 42	2 59	2 37
Soliciting agents		4 36		
Station agents	2 59	2 48	1 80	1 82
Other station men	2 44	2 16	1 59	1 85
Enginemen	4 32	4 04	3 98	3 74
Firemen	2 40	2 02	2 01	2 07
Conductors	4 11	3 67	3 42	3 11
Other trainmen	2 91	2 29	1 93	2 15
Machinists	3 34	2 88	2 50	2 33
Carpenters	3 15	3 36	2 18	2 21
Other shopmen	2 31	2 67	1 66	1 56
Roadmaster		4 28		
Section foremen	2 74	2 32	1 48	1 80
Other trackmen	1 61	1 76	1 16	1 28
Switchmen, flagmen, and watchmen	2 86	2 33	2 06	2 03
Telegraph operators and dispatchers	3 26	3 26	1 72	1 75
Employés floating equipment	2 77	2 51		2 83
All other employés and laborers	3 59	2 25	2 47	2 05
Storekeeper		3 43		
Average	$2 59	$2 68	$1 66	$1 98

EXHIBIT "B."

EFFECT ON OPERATIONS OF FIVE IOWA RAILROADS (COMPRISING ABOUT 65 PER CENT OF THE ENTIRE MILEAGE IN THE STATE) IF OBLIGED TO PAY FOR FUEL AND LABOR AT THE RATES PREVAILING IN CALIFORNIA AND ON THE SOUTHERN PACIFIC COMPANY (PACIFIC SYSTEM), IN CONNECTION WITH THEIR EXISTING TRAFFIC RATES. (Authority, Railroad Commissioners' Report for Iowa, year ending June 30, 1891.)

Road.	Miles Operated June 30, 1891.	Earnings From Operations.	Operating Expenses.	Labor Expense.		Coal Expense.		
				No. of Men.	Wages.	Tons Used.	Per Ton.	Cost.
(Reference)	p. 80ff.	p. 80p.	p. 80m.	p. 80u.	p. 80u.	p. 80gg.	p. 80gg.	computed.
Burlington, Cedar Rapids, and Northern Railroad	901	$3,310,479	$2,293,225	2,748	$1,352,169	124,242	$1 50	$186,363
Chicago, Burlington, and Quincy Railroad	755	6,274,348	4,406,001	3,636	2,158,988	739,048	1 37	1,012,596
Chicago, Milwaukee, and St. Paul Railway	1,553	7,501,489	4,787,675	5,390	3,383,803	275,148	1 95	536,539
Chicago and Northwestern Railway	1,163	7,212,720	4,799,673	4,116	2,528,433	340,952	1 75	596,666
Chicago, Rock Island, and Pacific Railway	1,066	8,524,427	5,358,454	3,659	2,173,573	541,388	1 89	1,023,223
Totals	5,441	$32,823,463	$21,645,028	19,549	$11,596,966	2,020,778	$1 66	$3,355,367
At Pacific System prices, figures would be: Labor, 6,118,837 days, at $2 59					15,847,788	Coal, at $6 40		12,932,979
Excess expense at Pacific System rate					$4,250,822			$9,577,612

Total increased operating expense at Pacific System prices for fuel and labor	$13,828,434
Present operating expenses of the five Iowa lines above	21,645,028
What operating expenses would be at Pacific System prices for fuel and labor	$35,473,462
Present gross earnings of the five Iowa lines above	32,823,463
Operating expenses over earnings at Pacific System fuel and labor prices	$2,649,999

EXHIBIT "C."

Effect on Operations of Ten Illinois Railroads (Comprising About One Third of the Entire Mileage in the State), if they were Obliged to Pay for Fuel and Labor at the Rates Prevailing in the State of California, with the Existing Tariff for the Carriage of Freight and Passengers, which now Produces to these Roads an Annual Gross Earning per Mile of Road Operated in Illinois Greater than that Earned by the Pacific System of the Southern Pacific Company. (For authorities, see reports of the State Railroad Commissioners of Illinois and California, for the year 1891).

Road.	Miles Operated June 30, 1891.	Earnings From Operations.	Earnings per Mile Operated.	Operating Expenses.	Labor Expense.		Coal Expense.		
					No. of Men.	Wages.	Tons Used.	Cost.	Per Ton.
(Reference)	p. 23, c. 15	p. 43, col. 16	p. 56, c. 12	p. 49, col. 18	p. 65, c. 19	p. 65, col. 20	p. 84–87	computed	p. 87, c. 29
Chicago, San Francisco, and California Ry.	294.79	$3,012,691	$10,219	$2,727,419	1,770	$921,519	142,612	$248,145	$1 74
Chicago and Alton Railroad	586.06	5,638,658	9,621	3,056,386	3,086	2,010,399	192,847	336,430	1 75
Chicago and Eastern Illinois Railway	202.55	2,186,216	10,793	1,166,667	1,465	907,655	73,262	70,331	96
Chicago and Grand Trunk Railway	30.65	431,093	14,065	281,931	261	160,530	17,799	35,598	2 00
Chicago, St Paul, and Kansas City Railway	172.16	1,383,747	8,037	1,126,791	554	381,365	61,056	103,795	1 70
Chicago, Rock Island, and Pacific Railway	236 18	4,329,418	18,331	2,715,714	3.457	2,255,503	139,346	250,826	1 80
Cleveland, Cincinnati, Chicago, and St. Louis Ry.	482.75	3,940,331	8,068	2,728,473	3,418	1,815,104	163,258	176,319	1 08
Illinois Central Railroad Company	1,285.28	9,692,696	7,562	6,408,104	8,158	5,066,091	467,143	467,143	1 00
Terre Haute and Indiana Railroad	158.34	1,773,333	11,199	1,197,894	1,203	646,923	65,831	72,414	1 10
Wisconsin Central Railroad Company	56.56	891,864	15,768	702,814	202	131,845	17,982	42,977	2 39
Totals	3,505.32	$33,280,047	$9,494	$22,112,193	23,574	$14,296,964	1,341,106	$1,803,978	$1 34

Summary.

Day's labor in Illinois, based on 313 days per year, 7,378,662. Average wages per day, Illinois roads, $1 93; Pacific System, $2 59. Additional expense at Pacific System rate of wages to Illinois roads	$4,867,277
Price coal per ton, Illinois roads, $1 34; Pacific System in California, $6 40. Additional expense at Pacific System coal price to Illinois roads	6,780,936
Present operating expenses of above Illinois roads	22,112,181
Operating expenses of Illinois roads at California fuel and labor prices	$33,760,394
Present gross earnings of Illinois roads	33,280,047
Operating expenses over gross earnings at California fuel and labor prices	$480,347

STATEMENT, OF RICHARD GRAY.

(General Traffic Manager of the Southern Pacific Company.)

The distinguished Senator who introduced the bill now before your honorable committee, which was framed by the San Francisco Traffic Association, on further consideration withdrew his proposition for 2 cents per mile as maximum passenger fares, stating that he had been informed that 3 cents per mile was the rate charged by a large number of the principal roads in the United States, and was therefore willing that 3 cents be fixed as the maximum.

It has been shown that the Act of the Legislature under which the Nevada County Narrow Gauge road was organized allows a charge of 10 cents per mile for passengers, and 20 cents per ton per mile for freight.

So anxious was the community to secure this road, that the Legislature agreed not to interfere with its rates until after it had been shown that the road earned more than 12 per cent per annum on the investment.

If 10 cents per mile is considered reasonable for the line from Colfax to Nevada City, which, while having steep grades, is practically below the snow line, surely 5 cents per mile is reasonable for the line from Auburn to Truckee, with its heavy grades, numerous tunnels, and continuous snow galleries for thirty-eight miles.

If 3 cents per mile be reasonable and the average fare charged, as we were told, on the great railroads of the Western States, connecting large centers of population in such States as Illinois, Iowa, and Nebraska, will any one contend that 5 cents per mile is extravagant on the Colorado Desert, between Banning and Yuma, where the road is subject to periodical inundations from the Colorado River, numerous cloudbursts, which make it very difficult to maintain a roadbed, and where there is no local traffic of any kind, and which, for all business purposes, might as well be a bridge or a tunnel?

If three cents per mile be reasonable and the customary charge between centers of population in Eastern States, will any one contend that 4 cents per mile is an extravagant rate between Redding and the Oregon boundary, through the tortuous Sacramento River Cañon, and over the Siskiyou range of mountains, with maximum grades of one hundred and seventy-four feet to the mile? Or that 4 cents per mile is unreasonable between Bakersfield and Saugus, over the Tehachapi range of mountains, and the Mojave Desert?

I think you will admit, gentlemen, that different circumstances and conditions prevail in this State from other States; that variety and not uniformity is the rule, and particularly is this the case with railroads, in their operations as well as their construction; that the proposed uniform rate per mile, regardless of character of road, would be unjust in the extreme to mountain roads and roads in desert or thinly settled districts.

Since coming before your honorable committee, the framers of this bill have learned that 2 cents per mile, as originally proposed, was unreasonable, and have admitted this fact. Would it not be well for them to again investigate, when they will doubtless find that 3 cents, which is the maximum charge on the Southern Pacific lines through the great valleys of the State, is also an unreasonable rate to apply to mountain and desert districts of California; that such a rate adopted as the maximum would be unjust, and sure to cripple small roads and branch lines now in existence, while effectually preventing the building of new roads in the future?

In view of the evidence already presented on the subject, I think it would be insulting the intelligence of this committee to dilate further on this point. The facts as to our passenger rates, to which we invite the investigation and criticism of all fair-minded men, speak for themselves.

The Manager of the San Francisco Traffic Association, in his hearing before this committee on the evening of January 23d, argued in favor of a constitutional amendment embodying a distance tariff and classification to apply on freight, which he would have put in force on the railroads of this State.

Mr. Leeds has repeatedly compared our rates with those in force in Kansas, which seems to be his favorite State; but I notice that in constructing a distance tariff which he would have adopted for California, he does not use the official Kansas Distance Tariff, but rates very much lower. We have not had time since receipt of copies of this bill to apply the new tariff to our business, or judge accurately of its effects thereon. But I can assure your committee that the rates proposed would be disastrous in the extreme.

It is proposed to ingraft in the Constitution of the State, to govern this tariff, a classification which is made by Eastern people to apply on Eastern roads, whose conditions and circumstances differ widely from those in California.

The proposed rates can be shown to be lower than those now used on any road on the Pacific Coast, or on any road similarly situated as to grades, cost of construction, or any of the elements which enter into the expense of maintenance and repairs.

The Manager of the Traffic Association has made certain statements which have been, or will be answered by other officers of the company; but there is one statement or allusion which has been reiterated in certain San Francisco newspapers to which I will refer, which I think was altogether uncalled for. He, Mr. Leeds, reminds your honorable committee you are considering rates, which, as he understands them, apply to roads which are within the limits of California alone; that it has been insisted that the Pacific System of the Southern Pacific Company should be considered as a whole, including Arizona, Oregon, and other States. He tells you the Supreme Court of the United States has held that each State is an integral part by itself, and as such the State has power to fix rates on all State business; that you must not call on California to support a business in other States or Territories.

These strictures are altogether unnecessary, because, while it might justly do so, the Southern Pacific Company has never asked California to support roads in another State or Territory. Facts indicate the reverse. Our printed annual reports will prove that our lines through Nevada, Utah, Arizona, and New Mexico, are self-sustaining. On the other hand, our lines in the States and Territories referred to, are feeders of the California line, bringing to it business which it would not otherwise receive, and but for which it would not be able to operate as economically for, or furnish as good train facilities to, the citizens of this State.

Were the California roads not connected with the East, their earning power would be very much diminished, as can be readily shown to any one who will take the trouble to look into the matter. A little thought on the subject will readily convince any investigator that the States are interdependent—that no State is, as Mr. Leeds puts it, "an integral part by itself," or can afford to be so—least of all, California. Up to the close of 1869, California might be called an integer, because it had no direct communication with the rest of the country; but was it happy or prosperous in that condition? We know it was not. But California now has railroads, and the principal of these is on trial. We are told that it has oppressed and is oppressing the citizens of the State, who are now seeking relief. Let us see. The old adage is a true one: "By their fruits ye shall know them."

The Manager of the San Francisco Traffic Association has repeatedly stated that he looks with suspicion on railroad figures; that his experience leads him to be dubious of them; but I do not think he can accuse the United States Census of being partial, or made up to favor any particular interest. It may therefore be well to make a few comparisons from the Census by way of illustration:

California had in 1870, the first year in which the overland railroad was in operation, real estate valued at $169,536,546; with a population of 560,000; that being $303 per capita.

This was her population and development after twenty years of Statehood, including a gold excitement and production such as the world has never seen.

In 1880, with mining values steadily decreasing, the valuation of real estate had increased to $491,885,079; and her population to 864,000; being $569 per capita.

An increase of $322,348,533 in ten years, or nearly three times.

In 1890, her real estate was valued at $930,822,650; her population had increased to 1,208,000; being $770 per capita.

Being an increase of over $761,000,000, or $467 per capita, or nearly five times in twenty years.

Now let us glance at Kansas, with which State we have been frequently compared for several months past:

Census Bulletin No. 104, issued August 22, 1891, gives valuation for 1890 of Kansas, including personal property, as $290,593,711; being $203 68 per capita; while the valuation of California, including personal property, was $1,071,102,327, or $886 per capita.

Thus the wealth of the people of California is 4.36 times as great per capita as the people of the State with which Mr. Leeds would compare us.

The total valuation of Kansas in 1880 was $160.891,000; which in 1890 had increased to $290.293,000; or an increase of $129,402,000.

With which compare California in 1880, $584,578,000; and in 1890, $1.071.102,000; or an increase of $486,524.000.

The Census of 1890 shows Kansas had 9,000 miles of railroad within her borders, while California had but 4,336 miles, or less than half as much; but we find in twenty years, the enormous sum of $761,000,000 added to the taxable value of real estate in California, not to mention an increase of over $60,000,000 in her personal property, all of which I maintain is directly traceable to the construction and operation of railroads, which give her communication and direct connection with 65,000,000 people on the eastern side of the continent.

To one not familiar with the facts, or hearing them for the first time, this may sound like a startling claim; but we need only refer to the recently published reports of the California State Board of Trade to prove the truth of our assertion. Since the decadence of gold mining and previous to the construction of transcontinental roads, and the development brought about thereby, California was essentially a pastoral and wheat-growing State; her average yield of wheat ranging from fifteen to twenty million centals, most of which, as at present, reached tidewater on the bay of San Francisco.

General N. P. Chipman, in his address before the State Horticultural Convention, at San José, November 15, 1892, states that in the year 1890, the value of fruit and fruit products exceeded by over half a million dollars, the value of wheat and flour exported within the year. In 1880 he says the export of fruit may be said to have commenced, and yet, "in ten years, we added twenty million dollars annually to the wealth of this State, without diminishing the possibilities of wheat growing by so much as a bushel." Still quoting from the same report, we find that in 1891, a comparatively small acreage in Southern California received $1,796,000 for oranges alone, and this will be very largely increased the present year. Riverside, he says, shipped fifteen carloads in the winter of 1880–81, and in 1889–90 shipped one thousand five hundred carloads. And I would say right here, while not abating a jot from the debt we owe our Santa Fe friends, it should be borne in mind that the Santa Fe was not completed to San Bernardino until 1886, and did not have its own line into Los Angeles until June, 1887; therefore, the wonderful development about which we have been talking was due to the Central Pacific and Southern Pacific, who created it and fostered it. In 1870 shipments of deciduous fruits, mainly from the central portion of the State, were only about four million pounds. In 1880 these were quadrupled, being sixteen million pounds. This latter in 1891 was increased over five times, aggregating eighty-three million pounds; while in 1892, shipments exceeded one hundred million pounds. Still quoting the same report, we find in 1880, Fresno County had less than ten thousand population; in 1890 it was over thirty-two thousand. Fresno is the center of the raisin industry, which previous to 1873, may be said to have had no existence. In 1880 her shipments were less than two million pounds, and in 1891 had increased to over twenty-seven million pounds. What is said of Fresno County, may be said of Santa Clara, Kern, Butte, Tehama, and other counties, as well as Los Angeles and San Bernardino.

It is needless to say that this wonderful development of our fruit culture would have been impossible without the overland roads, as well as the local system within the State. Without cheap and rapid transportation, the business would not have been possible, and the State could not have attained anything like her present degree of prosperity, to say nothing of the great and brilliant future which awaits her.

But, it may be suggested, it is not through, but local rates, which are under consideration. My answer is, the revenue from starting point to State line is a local earning, and this charge is, on all the staple products of California, the lowest rail transportation in the world.

Even under rates established by the defunct Transcontinental Association, that great bugbear of the San Francisco Traffic Association, rates on the principal products of California, which while intrinsically much more valuable than wheat, were, to enable them to reach the great centers of population at the East, transported at rates which were lower per mile than rates on wheat from points in the Dakotas and other Western States to Milwaukee or Chicago.

I maintain it makes no material difference to the farmer or consumer what rates he is asked to pay from San Francisco to the interior on his tobacco, tea, whisky, and other luxuries; that it makes no difference whether these articles are jobbed by a merchant living in San Francisco, Los Angeles, Sacramento, or elsewhere, so long as the rates on staple products of his orchard and vineyard are low enough to enable him to compete with and lay his fruit down in competition with similar products of the Eastern States and of Europe.

What is true of green fruit is also true of raisins, canned fruit, and other commodities, which it is possible to ship by water, but which, to be profitably marketed, must reach promptly and in good season all the great cities East, South, and West, in much shorter time than they could be transported by the most rapid water communication.

That the State has prospered since the advent of the transcontinental railroad, the above figures, showing $761,000,000 increase in land values, proves beyond question. Railroad construction in some parts of the State has kept pace with, as well as promoted, this development. Will any fair-minded man demand that the instruments of all this prosperity shall not have a fair share of the same?

There are yet several counties of this State, notably Lake and Humboldt, anxiously crying out for railroads, and demanding railroad connection with the rest of the State. Any one visiting the fair now in progress in San Francisco, will find the Humboldt County exhibit, which is one of the most interesting in the Pavilion, displaying sun-dried prunes and other valuable products. He will also find a sign conspicuously displayed reading as follows:

"Humboldt has one hundred and twenty miles of railroad, and yet there is not enterprise enough in the State of California to give this great county railroad communication with the outside world."

I will call the attention of Mr. Leeds and the Traffic Association of San Francisco to this sign. It is a standing reproach to them.

It is safe to assume that within a year from the construction of a railroad into Lake and Humboldt, the taxable value of land in those counties would have increased at least 100 per cent. But what is this "Traffic Association?" Let us look into it a little.

I maintain it is not, as its title would indicate, a traffic association of "California." I have it on the authority of a gentleman who helped to organize it, that ninety-eight per cent of its members reside in San Francisco; the other two per cent consists of citizens of other parts of the State, whose names were put on for effect, who take no interest in its proceedings, and contribute nothing to its revenues.

These San Francisco merchants, during a period of dull trade, and looking around for some means of bettering the situation, imported from the East a gentleman whose name came before the country in connection with the Transcontinental Association, and they put him in charge of their association. This gentleman immediately, from his office in San Francisco, began to "reform" matters, and in one of his public speeches at a dinner of the Chamber of Commerce, announced what he no doubt in his freshness candidly believed, that the State was languishing under what he was pleased to term "Your ONE Railroad."

I am glad my friend Leeds has come to Sacramento, because he has certainly learned since coming that instead of one railroad, there are more than thirty railroads in the State. He has learned something of the greatness of California; that there are mountain roads as well as valley roads; that there are circumstances under which one road may live and earn fair interest on its investment, while other roads languish and starve; that no uniform distance tariff can be just or reasonable, as applying to all roads in this State; and what is true of *all* roads must be true of roads forming parts of a system of roads; that while his favorite State of Kansas has nine thousand miles of railroad, much of which is bankrupt, California has as yet but half that mileage, though with double the area. He has learned, I hope, that the crying need of California is "more railroads;" that railroads have been the cause of her present prosperity and are indispensable to her further development; that, if instead of pulling down and trying to cripple railroads now existing in the State, which have done so much for the State, the San Francisco Traffic Association would inaugurate and encourage railroads to Humboldt, to Lake, to Del Norte, to Lassen, to Modoc, and to other counties holding out their hands and seeking railroad communication, they would accomplish far more for the State and for San Francisco than by any amount of rancor and defamation of the men who have invested their own capital and that which they have been able to borrow, for the building of railroads and development of the country.

San Francisco has no real quarrel with the Southern Pacific Company, and should have none. Individual members of this company are among her leading and most public-spirited citizens, who have done their part towards building up the city; self-interest alone would lead the Southern Pacific Company to cultivate the most friendly relations with San Francisco and her citizens. While endeavoring to maintain such relations, the company cannot discriminate to the detriment of growing inland cities, but, nevertheless, has enabled San Francisco, so far as it could consistently with the interests of the other localities it serves, to distribute merchandise to remote interior points in competition with like merchandise from Eastern cities. In short, the Southern Pacific Company does not now, and never has sought to deprive San Francisco of any of the commercial advantages which naturally should come to her by reason of her location on the sea.

But I maintain this complaint of the city which has had a portion of its trade curtailed by natural causes, and by the building of competing lines of railroads to the north of us and on the south, is not an index to the true situation, but is a libel on the State, which, if allowed to pass unchallenged, may do it serious injury.

My duties require me to make frequent visits to the Eastern States, and I can say from personal observation that California is to-day the most prosperous State in the Union, and her development is, and has been steadier, her wealth greater, her happiness and prosperity better assured than any other State; and if our San Francisco friends would devote some of the two hundred million dollars lying idle in her banks, or loaned only at low rates of interest on city real estate, for the development of railroad, irrigation, and kindred enterprises, we would have such a season of prosperity as would leave in the shade the famous "boom" in the southern counties. San Francisco would see her trade revive, and would be too busy attending to her legitimate business to send a Traffic Manager to Sacramento with a proposition to insert in our organic law a scheme of rates and classification which, to put it mildly, is absurd and ridiculous, and which even the distinguished Senator who presented it, apologizes for as an "innovation."

This enormous increase of $761,000,000, a sum nearly three times the total wealth of Kansas, speaks louder than any words of mine. It places the burden of proof on those who, in their ignorance and short-sightedness, defame and belittle our fair State.

I respectfully submit, no evidence has been produced to show affirmatively why there is any necessity for reducing or in any way changing the existing railway rates of this State. No representative of any industry has appeared before you to complain, or produced any evidence tending to show that the railroads of this State have not in the past occupied, and are not now occupying, their true and proper place in the industrial development of the Commonwealth; that they are not now doing all that the State has power to compel; that the growth of California, the development of its agricultural, mineral, or industrial resources are being in any manner restricted or impeded by acts of transportation companies.

No representative of any industrial interest has appeared before you to make a showing of this character, for the simple reason that no good cause for complaint against the rates or methods of the railroads exists. On the contrary, it is true that the railroads are doing all in their power to make the State great and prosperous. It is to their interest that this should be done. If in their power to exact rates, the enforcement of which would result in distress and poverty to communities along the lines, no one interest would feel the harmful effects more quickly or forcibly than the railroads themselves. The business interests of a railroad company are best promoted by prosperity in every branch of industry which in any way employs transportation; and it is a fact, so far as the influence of railroad companies can contribute to this end, the State to-day is prosperous, and no arbitrary reduction in the average rates now charged for the transportation of freight or passengers should be made.

EARL: I notice the accredited agent of the San Francisco Traffic Association, Colonel Barry, is present. Colonel Barry, would you like to make any statement to the committee?

MR. BARRY: Mr. Chairman, I think, although I can hardly say I replace Mr. Leeds—it is absolutely necessary for other matters of great importance to that association, that Mr. Leeds should depart from the State of California, and he left to-day, and I am therefore, although not entirely fitted for the task, substituted for him before this committee in so far as the Traffic Association is interested in this matter, and in so far as that interest should be represented here.

We introduced this measure. Senator Gesford made an opening statement which outlined the character of this bill. Mr. Leeds has given certain testimony, I believe. In so far as we have acted at all, we have laid our case before you. I think it is only fair, instead of making any statement this evening, that after these gentlemen, representatives of the various roads, have made their statements, that the Traffic Association shall receive that courtesy from this committee.

Possibly, as we have introduced this measure and have made our statement in full, we might be permitted to reply, and for that reason I do not desire to say anything this evening, but I shall beg of the committee at some future time the opportunity of either replying or submitting an argument to the committee in reference to what has been said by the representatives of the various railroads.

It seems to me that thus far this measure is on trial. These gentlemen come here with statements and arguments, and it seems it would interfere with the logical consideration of the subject if anything I should say, or any representative of the Traffic Association, should be interjected at this time, and it would be better that all that can be said against the measure, either as to its general scope or plan, or as to its details, be said, so that we may make a comprehensive reply, and therefore, Mr. Chairman, if agreeable to the committee, I should prefer not to say anything, but wait until the closing case is presented against the measure.

EARL: Certainly; the opportunity will be given to all to be heard, and we will be glad to hear from you, Colonel, at any stage of the hearing—at any time during the hearing.

MR. BARRY: I shall say here, Mr. Chairman, that I shall be present here at all of the meetings hereafter, and shall give that attention to the arguments of the gentlemen that their importance demands, and then I shall ask a hearing.

STATEMENT OF C. F. SMURR.

(General Freight Agent Southern Pacific Company.)

Regarding the proposed constitutional amendment now under consideration by your honorable body, I would say:

As the documents thus far introduced read, it is clearly the intention that in the absence of legislation, the Constitution shall provide specifically what classification shall be employed, to wit: the Western Classification; and what table of rates shall be employed as a maximum, to wit: that set forth therein as the California Distance Tariff; thus wiping out all existing classifications, rate-sheets and rates, and that from date of adoption, or thereafter, as may be provided, all property must be transported under classes, as set forth in said Western Classification, and at rates not exceeding those set forth in said "California Distance Tariff."

Practically speaking, given a railroad within the State of California, its fixed expenses known, its operating expenses approximately known, although there are many disturbing factors that make this feature a constantly variable one, leading among which is climatic conditions, disasters incident to fire, snow, and flood, and in addition, given the volume of traffic, direction of movement, its character or description, length and direction of haul, freedom from competition of markets and freedom from competition of carriers, it would not be a difficult matter to devise a freight tariff to be applied thereto that would be sufficient to meet the fixed and operating expenses of such a road.

On the other hand, given a railroad within the State of California, its fixed expenses unknown, its operating expenses only approximately known, and subject to the variable conditions before named, its traffic wholly unknown or undeveloped, competition of markets and carriers existing in active degree, and the proposition of making freight tariffs is no longer to be regarded as simple and one easy of solution. This latter condition is what has prevailed from date of the completion of each and every railroad within the State, and the tariffs as applied to-day are the outgrowth of the experience of a quarter of a century or more; and the idea that any single individual, without local knowledge and exact information, within slightly more than a twelvemonth, can proceed to evolve one uniform distance tariff that will meet the variety of commercial conditions existing within this State, and that will do justice to the people as well as the carriers, is in my humble judgment, to say the least, ludicrous presumption.

In practical working we are called on to consider the question of making changes in or establishing new rates daily, and necessarily must have due regard for bulk, likelihood to damage (for the rail carriers are insurers), value, volume of traffic, direction of movement, length of haul, return empty haul, competition of markets, competition of carriers, and cost of service. The propositions requiring such consideration come to us from the commercial communities served, and as a rule may be regarded, and are, in the public interest; and it may be said, we believe, with propriety, that whensoever it can be demonstrated that a modification of rates is necessary to development in a general or specific way—that such modification will bring about improved results—the emergency is met; the aim in general being that, on the whole, rates shall be such as to bring about the maximum development of production in all its different forms, and at the same time bring enough revenue to enable continuance of the service of the roads already established, and encouragement in direction of construction of new roads, and the consequent development resulting therefrom.

Touching the assertion made by the Traffic Association of San Francisco's representative at your first meeting, in effect, that an inflexible classification as a part of the Constitution or statutes of the State of California, by reason of inability to make changes therein save once in two years, would work no hardship on the commercial community, and assigning as one of the reasons therefor that the local classification of the Southern Pacific Company had not been changed "within the past two years or within the past ten years"—I am compelled to characterize said assertion as being, to say the least, extremely reckless Had the Traffic Association of San Francisco, through its representative, wished to present the facts to you, it could have obtained them from the files of the State Board of Railroad Commissioners, where the various changes as made within the past one year, two years, or ten years are to be found. The fact is, there were numerous changes made in the local classification, as used by the Southern Pacific Company on its Central California traffic, during the year 1892—forty-five in number. During the same period commercial necessities required changes in the Western Classification, aggregating 265 in number. When you take into consideration the vast area over which the Western Classification is in operation, to wit, practically all the territory west, say, of the Chicago meridian, you will at once see that relatively there have been more changes in the Southern Pacific Company's local classification than in the Western, which is set up as the inflexible standard, and which it is proposed to adopt, regardless of commercial requirements.

Again, for the term January 1, 1883, to January 1, 1893, ten years, as referred to by the Traffic Association's representative, the local classification of the Southern Pacific Company has been changed as follows: Additions to, 365; removals from, 59; modifications of the current classification, 254; total changes, 678. These general changes, and, in addition, thousands of individual commodity changes from and to given points, have been made necessary within the period named, and because of the ever-changing commercial and competitive conditions.

One word more with respect to the proposed rigid Constitution classification: The document referred to in the resolution indicates rating as follows: Coke, carloads—coke tariff rates. Ore, n. o. s., released to valuation not exceeding $100 per ton—special ore tariff rates.

Query: Which one of the differing coke and ore tariffs, as in use by each of the seventy-four railroads that have adopted and use the Western Classification, will, under this proposed Act, become a part of the Constitution of California?

It may not be amiss to present for your information a brief history of the document known as the Western Classification, first called Joint Western Classification, and issued April 16, 1883, and used thereafter by the following railroads:

Atchison, Topeka, and Santa Fe Railroad.
Burlington and Missouri River Railroad.
Central Iowa Railway.
Chicago and Alton Railroad.
Chicago, Burlington, and Quincy Railroad.
Chicago, Milwaukee, and St. Paul Railway.
Chicago, Rock Island, and Pacific Railway.
Chicago and Northwestern Railway.
Chicago, St. Paul, Minneapolis, and Omaha Railway.
Denver and Rio Grande Railway.
Des Moines and Fort Dodge Railroad.
Illinois Central Railroad.
Kansas City, Fort Scott, and Gulf Railroad.
Missouri Pacific Railway.
Minneapolis and St. Louis Railway.
Sioux City and Pacific Railroad.
Union Pacific Railway.
Wabash Railroad.

It was a classification of articles carried by the roads named, and was added to from time to time as the necessities developed, and its adaptation to the freight traffic of the particular territory served by the roads named was a comparatively easy matter. April 1, 1887, the name was changed from Joint Western Classification to Western Classification, and the work of adding thereto, or taking from, or making changes in, as necessities developed, proceeded in the usual course. About the same time, to wit: April 5, 1887, the Interstate Commerce law became effective. Then the document was in such wide range of use that it was deemed advisable to utilize it as the fundamental or foundation principle of rate making on transcontinental interstate traffic. A schedule or table of class rates applying to and from the Pacific Coast and what is known as Atlantic seaboard territory, Buffalo-Pittsburg territory, Detroit-Cincinnati territory, Chicago territory, Mississippi River territory, and Missouri River territory, was finally arranged for and published, the Western Classification applying thereto, and it has continued in use as the foundation of freight rates on transcontinental traffic up to this time.

It was apparent from the start, however, that it could not be relied on exclusively to meet the requirements of commerce. As a consequence, the roads engaged in transcontinental traffic issued commodity rates, which aggregate to-day on west-bound business some 1,329 in number, and on east-bound business some 332 in number. From this you will perceive that the Western Classification, with its table of rates, comes far from being a perfect document, and such a one as to meet all the requirements of commerce. The same conditions with respect to necessity for commodity tariffs that prevailed on transcontinental traffic, prevails in practically all territory where the Western Classification is now in use. As it was extended westward to—Colorado, for example—

the leading industries there were so different from those of Iowa and Illinois that it could only be partially utilized, and naturally a large number of commodity rates were necessitated. And this same experience has been found wherever it has been put into effect—Utah, Montana, Washington; the varying conditions of production, consumption, etc.—more especially the former—necessitating radical departures from the Western Classification and its table of class rates. The consequent tendency throughout the country to-day is, instead of restraint and rigidity of classification, in the direction of flexibility of classification.

Regarding the statement made by the Traffic Association of San Francisco, through its representative, that the Southern Pacific does to-day apply the Western Classification on certain portions of its California traffic, I have to say that this is technically correct. When the Santa Fe System built into Southern California, it brought with it the Western Classification, tariffs, rules, and conditions that governed its business elsewhere, and it adopted the Southern Pacific Company's schedule of the merchandise and numerous commodity rates without material change or reduction therein. Instead of graduating its merchandise to first, second, third, and fourth-class rates, the same rate, as a rule, was used by it for each of the four classes—the result of this adjustment of tariff to the Western Classification in Southern California being to practically produce the same revenue as would result from what is known as the local classification and merchandise rates of the Southern Pacific Company; or, to make it clear to you, in practical operation the use of the Western Classification, when applied to the schedule of rates as above described, is in no material features different from the local classification that was in use in Southern California, and is now in use in Central California.

The theory of the local classification of the Southern Pacific Company being to simplify in fullest degree, consequently it starts out with the announcement, in effect, that all articles not named specifically therein will be charged for at merchandise rates—then proceeds to indicate the exceptions, enumerating articles that are light, bulky, of excessive value, liable to damage, inflammable, or hazardous in any measure, and provides higher ratings, ranging from one and a half to double first class thereon—the same in principle, in this regard, as the Western Classification. It also enumerates various staple articles on which carload rates are made—similar in principle to the Western Classification. The chief difference between the local classification of the Southern Pacific Company referred to and the Western Classification, is that the Western undertakes to enumerate practically each and every article known to trade that is transported by rail and other carriers. This makes of said Western Classification a very voluminous document. Of course you appreciate that the classification, no matter whether it be the local classification of the Southern Pacific Company or the Western Classification, or any other classification, does not within itself make the tariff; it is simply the key to the tariff; or it is the index to the charge that should be made, said charge represented by the rate corresponding to the class named and found in the table of rates. The classes are: On less than carloads, first, second, third, and fourth; on carloads, fifth, A, B, C, D, and E. You will perceive that if all less than carload quantities of each and every article named in the Western Classification takes either first, second, third, or fourth class, and the same rate is used for each of these four classes, that it is equivalent to a rate made by using the Southern Pacific Company's local classification, wherein, as before stated, it is set forth that all articles not named specifically therein will be charged for at merchandise rates.

The Western Classification is also used in conjunction with a table of graduated class rates between Central California points, San Francisco, for example, and Southern California points. This has been the principle of making rates to and from that territory since completion of the rail lines joining the two communities. Originally, however, the classification as applied to the graduated table of class rates was one devised and adopted by the Southern Pacific Company of its own motion, adopted with the intention of enabling San Francisco to compete by rail in that territory as against the water carriers. When later the Western Classification became prominent, it was deemed expedient to apply it to the table of graduated rates that had been in force for a term of years to and from the territory mentioned, the particular desire being to place San Francisco merchants in position to enter that territory in competition with merchants of other commercial centers that were using a similar classification.

It may be proper to say here that as a classification, in the ordinary acceptation of the term, not as a constitutional or statutory provision, making it a rigid or inflexible instrument, the Southern Pacific Company has no material objection thereto, and is not averse to its application where it can be made without such loss in revenue as will embarrass or make it impracticable to continue operating the various railroads in the State of California now under its control.

The State of California embraces about 156,000 square miles. Of this, 25 per cent (or 39,000 square miles) is valley and foothill, 22½ per cent desert, 52½ per cent mountains. The State of Kansas embraces about 81,700 square miles, the whole of which is practically a level and productive country. The people of the State of California have within its boundaries, radiating from San Francisco, say 900 miles of navigable inland waters, over which established steamer and sail lines are now operating, and the whole of its coast line, from Oregon to Mexico, approximately 700 miles of ocean front, where they have like competitive advantages. The railroads operated by the Southern Pacific Company compete with the waterways above described in greater or less degree throughout the whole of the State, and directly at all the principal towns about the bay of San Francisco; with the numerous navigable inlets and sloughs, on the Sacramento and San Joaquin Rivers; with the Pacific Ocean at Santa Cruz and Monterey Bays, Santa Barbara, Ventura, and Santa Monica and San Pedro Bays. In other words, water competition affects in greater or less degree practically every rate made by the Southern Pacific Company's roads within the State of California to-day. This, coupled with the fact that a large portion of the State's area is mountainous, desert, non-productive, costly of operation, should bring conviction to the minds of your honorable committee of the impracticability of introducing and applying the California Distance Tariff, or any other uniform distance tariff, whether it be subject to the Western Classification or any other classification.

For example: The distance by the shortest operated rail line from Napa to San Francisco is seventy miles. California wine in wood, carloads, per Western Classification, takes second class. The proposed California Distance Tariff makes second-class rate for seventy miles 25 cents per 100 pounds as maximum that could be charged. In fact, the Southern Pacific Company, forced by the water competition from Napa to San Francisco, charges on this commodity to-day but 5 cents per 100 pounds, which produces but a trifle, may be one mill per ton per mile, above the actual cost of the service; but the business is taken in the face of the cheapest known mode of carriage, and is regarded as desirable because of its ability to contribute that one solitary mill toward meeting the other or commonly called fixed expenses incident to the conduct of transportation, and to that degree it lightens the burden or reduces the charge that must necessarily be imposed on all the remaining traffic. Under the terms of the proposed amendment, the Southern Pacific Company could not make effective a commodity or independent rating on any article that is classified in the Western Classification.

The only method would be to reduce the class rate in cases where it is found necessary in order to meet competition or any peculiarity of condition that might control. Should the Southern Pacific Company desire to continue in the business, and, having been compelled by influences beyond its control to establish this as its second-class rate for the seventy miles from Napa to San Francisco, it thus fixes 5 cents per one hundred pounds as second-class rate for any given seventy miles between any two given points within the State of California on any commodity the Western Classification names, and there are several, as taking second-class rate. Having established this as the rate for seventy miles, you will at once perceive that for seventy-five miles distance, preserving the same differential as the California Distance Tariff observes, the second-class rate would be 6 cents, as against California Distance Tariff provision of 26 cents; for eighty miles it would be 8 cents, as against California Distance Tariff provision of 28 cents; for one hundred miles, it would be 16 cents, as against California Distance Tariff provision of 36 cents. The injustice of such requirement you will at once appreciate, and that its effect will be to remove the Southern Pacific Company's roads as competitors with water or other rival carriers, for this very essential reason: that it cannot continue in business as a common carrier and base its rates throughout the whole State of California on the extreme competitive conditions that exist between Napa and San Francisco; and its withdrawal from the field means an advance in the rates of its water-carrying competitors, just as surely as the tides rise and fall. There are scores of instances where similar conditions prevail, and where just such results as outlined in the Napa wine rate would follow the adoption of a rigid classification and the California or any other distance tariff.

In the State of Kansas, where the adverse physical conditions existing in the State of California do not have existence, where the country is practically level, no inland waterways worthy of the name of competitor, no coast line, no mountain ranges or deserts to traverse—even there, and without a rigid classification being imposed, a uniform distance tariff does not meet the requirements. The Santa Fe, as well as other roads in Kansas, have in addition to the distance tariff numerous special tariffs and commodity tariffs and rates issued from time to time to meet the commercial requirements of the various communities they serve. In fact, however, as has been presented, it is not intended that California, with its unfavorable physical conditions as compared with

Kansas, is to have as its maximum rates the Kansas Distance Tariff, but it is proposed that it shall have as its maximum rates a distance tariff as compiled by the Traffic Association of San Francisco, and which is lower than the Kansas Distance Tariff in the following degree:

	Per Cent.		Per Cent.
First class	20	Class A	10
Second class	27	Class B	12
Third class	25	Class C	10
Fourth class	28	Class D	25
Fifth class	31	Class E	16

The representative of San Francisco's Traffic Association has seen fit to mention particularly the California Pacific Railroad, commenting on its earnings, with evident intent of creating in your minds, that by reason of said earnings undue or excessive rates are imposed. The facts are that no railroad in California or any State in the Union has more active competition, and that by the very cheapest known carrier, than has the California Pacific. This road, as you know, parallels the Sacramento River and the upper bays; reaches from Knights Landing to South Vallejo, with branches, one from Napa Junction to Calistoga, and from Davisville to Sacramento, every foot of which is in direct competition with water, save north of Napa, and that, too, in only slightly modified degree. Three regular steamer lines are plying on the Sacramento River, besides outside steamers, and in addition sailing craft that reach Suisun, Cordelia, South Vallejo, and Napa. With this unsurpassed competitive condition as the controlling factor in the regulation of rates, it is simply an impossibility for the Southern Pacific Company to impose rates that can reasonably be regarded as excessive or exorbitant, and its patrons can for all time rest easy in their enjoyment of the very lowest minimum rates consistent with operation and maintenance of the property.

The explanation of the earnings referred to lies in the fact that the territory served by the California Pacific Railroad, the Sacramento River, and the upper bays, is exceedingly fertile and productive, and the further fact that the California Pacific Railroad is, in practical operation, the stem of that portion of the railway system radiating from San Francisco Bay northward and eastward—in other words, the small end of a funnel through which the larger proportion of the traffic of the system of railroads operated by it in California, and adjoining States and Territories, flows. Further, with respect to the mention made of the earnings of the South Pacific Coast Railway, the evident intention being to create in your minds that by reason of said earnings undue or excessive charges are imposed, I desire to say that the same class of competition exists. This road parallels San Francisco Bay from San Francisco to San José, and its southern terminus is on Santa Cruz Harbor, where it meets water craft, both steam and sail, and being so situated that the controlling factor, to wit: water, or the cheapest known method of carriage, makes its rates, I may with propriety again urge that excessive or undue charge for services rendered is beyond the possibilities.

Reference has been made by the Traffic Association of San Francisco, through its representative, to a 15 cents per ton per mile maximum rate as being in use by the Southern Pacific Company. The facts are, there was a statute that did so permit, and the same was in full force prior to the new Constitution, which became effective January 1, 1890. Since then there has been no maximum provided by law, other than as might be made by the State Board of Railroad Commissioners, and it is a fact that the average rate charged by the roads operated by the Southern Pacific Company in the State of California on their local traffic to-day is less than 2¼ cents per ton per mile, and that their average pro rata earning on through traffic is less than one half that earned on their local traffic—the reduced earning on the through traffic being attributable to the absolute necessity of providing abnormally low rates in order to enable the marketing of the products of California in the thickly populated States which are found two thousand miles and farther distant.

With these figures, then, as indicating the average rate necessary in order to meet the fixed and operating expenses of the roads operated by the Southern Pacific Company, you will at once appreciate the embarrassment that would result from the adoption of the proposed California Distance Tariff as a maximum provision governing every class and every distance, it being self-evident, given an average rate necessary to earn, that the higher the maximum the lower may be the minimum; in other words, holding the carrier down to the maximum proposed will necessarily raise the minimum in order to enable it to earn the average. The result in practical operation will be that the rail carrier will go out of the transportation of many low grade commodities, and be compelled to raise the rate on many staple products.

I have carefully compared rates as proposed by the Traffic Association of San Francisco with rates in effect, and my conclusion is that the adoption of the proposed amendment will carry with it a reduction of revenue as derived from freight traffic, of say 40 per cent, which means absolute inability of the several railroads operated by the Southern Pacific Company to continue rendering service of a grade as at present given to the people of this State. And in conclusion I beg to submit if the railroads now serving the people of this State should be hampered by a rigid classification, and in addition a uniform distance tariff, that must be applied regardless of physical or competitive conditions, as a maximum, thus depriving the carriers of opportunity or ability to consider and thus be guided by the varied fluctuating but controlling factors that enter into the conduct of transportation within the State of California? It is my judgment that such requirement will prove a veritable boomerang, and bring about such depressed commercial and industrial conditions, not only as applied to the railroads, but as applied to each and every enterprise within its borders, as has never been felt since its organization as a State.

Southern Pacific Company.

(Statement of G. L. Lansing, Secretary and Controller.)

The mileage of railroads in this State, as shown by report of the Railroad Commission for December 31, 1891, was as follows:

Operated by the Southern Pacific Company	2,894.36 miles
Operated by other companies	1,483.82 miles
Total	4,378.18 miles

The companies not controlled by the Southern Pacific Company thus owned on the date named 34 per cent of the entire mileage. Of the effect on these roads of the proposed tariff, its author has stated that he had no knowledge or information. But when his attention was thus called to the matter, the form of the bill was changed, excluding nearly all of the lines excepting those of the Southern Pacific Company from its present operation. Mr. Leeds further explained that, though he had not examined the effect of the tariff on the smaller roads, he had examined as to its effects on the Southern Pacific Company's lines. His statement of the results of that examination furnish the principal, if not the entire fund of facts, on which the adoption of the proposed tariff and classification is justified. A fair and just judgment of the conclusions which this bill assumes, therefore, requires a careful consideration of the relevance and application of Mr. Leeds' statements as to facts, their correctness, and their sufficiency. As the measure rests on the statements of this man, a fair judgment of its merits requires also to be considered, that the bill is avowedly framed and proposed in the interest of a society of men engaged in business in San Francisco, the membership of which is secret, and one of its purposes has been stated to be to fight the Southern Pacific Company whenever and wherever it can do so.

The proposed tariff is based on those in effect in some of the agricultural Western States, and notably the State of Kansas. Its rates are lower than those of the Kansas Distance Tariff, and will, as stated by Mr. Leeds, reduce the earnings from local freight in California on the Southern Pacific Company's lines 25 or 30 per cent. The person responsible for its introduction as a proposed portion of the Constitution of our State is lately from Kansas, was at one time Traffic Manager of the Missouri Pacific Railway, operating a large system of railroads in that State, and as such is familiar with the effect on that State of the Kansas Distance Tariff. His statements on this subject convey the impression, as I understand it was intended they should, that Kansas and its roads have been prosperous, and that railroad construction has been encouraged, with corresponding development and advancement of the resources of the country. The intended inference would follow that a similar tariff for California (though the tariff proposed has been found to be lower than that of Kansas) would bring like prosperity and development to the people and the railroads of this State. Let us inquire into the railroad prosperity of Kansas.

In their report for 1890 (pp. IX., *et seq.*) the Railroad Commission of that State, in a general review of the railroad situation there, says:

"We have fifteen hundred miles of railroad which is worse than worthless to its owners, and a burden upon the commerce of the State as a whole, though a blessing to the country along its line. It came by invitation, encouragement, and support of the people; it cannot be ignored in the discussion of rate-making for the rest."

At the commencement of 1885 there were in Kansas four thousand and thirty-eight miles of road. From 1885 to 1887, inclusive, two thousand five hundred and eleven miles were constructed. Since then the annual construction has been as follows: 1888, one thousand nine hundred and sixty-seven miles were constructed; 1889, two hundred and thirty-nine miles were constructed; 1890, one hundred and thirty-six miles were constructed; 1891, ten miles were constructed; 1892, one mile was constructed.

The conditions in Kansas controlling rates and traffic have thus brought railroad construction in that State to a stop.

In 1890 the Kansas Commission had under discussion the adoption of the Iowa Distance Tariff, the rates of which were lower than those in Kansas, and decided to maintain the higher tariff for the following reasons (Rep. 1890, pp. 117 *et seq.*):

1. The population of Iowa is greater than in Kansas.

2. Freight tonnage is correspondingly greater. For the year ending June 30, 1889, the freight tonnage over all the roads operating in Iowa was 36,645,038; in Kansas, 21,454,367. Tons per mile of road in Iowa, 1,452; in Kansas, 1,321.

3. Expenses in Kansas more than in Iowa. Operating expenses and taxes per mile in Iowa, $3,144 40; in Kansas, $3,347 88.

The Commission then conclude: "As to those roads whose sole or chief dependence is local traffic, the reports show that they are far from being self-sustaining. What the people living in the agricultural States of the West are chiefly interested in, is low rates to points where the great bulk of the surplus products must go to find a market for consumption; there the prices are fixed. Rates of charges for transportation to intermediate points do not affect the prices to the producer, but the cost to the consumer." (p. 118.)

If the items of this comparison made by the Commission as between Kansas and Iowa were applied as between Kansas and California, the result would prove a greater argument against the proposed California Distance Tariff than even that shown by the Commission against the Iowa Distance Tariff.

Compared with Iowa, Kansas shows less freight traffic by one hundred and thirty-one tons per mile of road, with an increase of $203 per mile for expenses, or 6½ per cent. The returns for all California roads are not summarized so as to afford a comparison; but comparing the Pacific system lines of the Southern Pacific Company with the Iowa lines, shows for the California system a less freight traffic by one hundred and six tons per mile of road, with an increase of $2,144 per mile for expenses, or 68½ per cent.

A comparison of results for all roads in a State can clearly be used only in a most general way, and to one not familiar with all the conditions is apt to mislead. Thus, the fifteen hundred miles of road which the Kansas Commission characterize as worse than worthless to its owners, but a blessing to the country along its line, would, if its returns were added to those of a prosperous system, modify the total result so as to give the false impression that the prosperous lines were poor. Railroad systems similar in size, traffic, and general conditions, so far as such are available, furnish the fairest and most reliable basis of comparison possible. Such a comparison can be made between the Pacific system of the Southern Pacific Company and the Missouri Pacific system. As shown by the maps published in the annual reports of these companies, the former consists of main lines, with numerous branches and feeders extending through the State of California, and into neighboring States and Territories, and the latter occupies a relative position to the State of Kansas. As the author of the proposed amendment to our Constitution was an officer of this Kansas company, he will be able to exercise a careful criticism of my statement of facts regarding that system, and save your honorable committee from error in founding upon them any false conclusions.

The following is a comparative statement of the operations and the cost thereof for the systems named:

MISSOURI PACIFIC SYSTEM VS. SOUTHERN PACIFIC COMPANY.

Comparative Statement of Operating Expenses per Unit of Traffic.

Year, 1890.	Missouri Pacific System.	Southern Pacific Co. (Pacific System).
Operating expenses	$18,096,951 00	$21,976,218 00
Revenue train miles	17,558,465	16,436,398
Operating expenses per train mile	$1.030	$1.337
Freight and passenger car miles	247,847,050	180,587,114
Operating expenses per car mile, in cents	7.302	12.169
Freight cars to a train	20.00	15.41
Tons of freight to a train	160.7	136.8
Tons of freight one mile	1,744,226,042	1,260,513,051

Year, 1890.	Missouri Pacific Excess.		Southern Pacific Excess.	
	Amount.	Per Cent.	Amount.	Per Cent.
Operating expenses			$3,879,267	21.43
Revenue train miles	1,122,067	6.82		
Operating expenses per train mile			$0.3070	29.80
Freight and passenger car miles	67,259,939	37.24		
Operating expenses per car mile, in cents			4.867	66.65
Freight cars to a train	4.59	30.00		
Tons of freight to a train	23.90	18.00		
Tons of freight one mile	483,712,991	38.37		

From Annual Reports of railroad companies, 1891.

It will be seen that on the Missouri Pacific, revenue trains ran 1,122,067 miles, or 6.82 per cent more than on the Pacific System. At the same time the cost to the Pacific System was for operating expenses, $3,879,267, or 21.43 per cent more; and the cost of operating expenses per revenue train mile was 29.80 per cent more than on the Missouri Pacific lines. But these items do not furnish a full comparison of the relative cost for the service performed, as the operating expenses alone do not indicate the work done, and the train miles do not show how many cars the trains hauled, nor the amount of traffic they carried.

The statement further shows that the Missouri Pacific freight trains hauled an average of 20 cars to the train, to 15.41 cars on the Pacific System, or an excess of 30 per cent; and carried an average of 160.7 tons of freight to a train, compared with 136.8 tons on the Pacific System. Considering the work done by all revenue trains in the transportation of freight, passengers, express, and mails, and that the operating expenses are incurred in the performance of this combined service, the natural basis of comparison for the cost of the service performed by a railroad is the mileage made by cars in revenue trains, including both freight and passenger. This affords, in fact, the only fair and complete unit of measurement, as it embraces on the one hand the earnings from all classes of traffic carried, and on the other the operating expenses which have been caused in part by each class of the earnings. On this basis of comparison, then, the statement shows that the car mileage on the Missouri Pacific exceeded that on the Pacific System by 67,259,939 miles, or 37.24 per cent, and at the same time that the cost per car per mile for operating expenses for the Pacific System exceeded that for the Missouri Pacific by 4.867 cents, or 66.65 per cent.

If the Missouri Pacific were subject to the conditions of operation which prevail on the Southern Pacific lines, the operating expenses of that Kansas system would have been increased 4.867 cents per car mile, or the annual amount of $12,062,714. This sum added to the present operating expenses would make $30,159,666 as the operating expenses of the Missouri Pacific system; and as the gross earnings of that system amount to $25,473,583, it would have failed to pay its operating expenses by $4,686,083, instead of having earned a net amount of $7,376,631, as was the case.

Or, reversing the comparison and applying the cost of the service on the Kansas system to the Southern Pacific lines, the expenses of the latter would have been reduced by the amount of $8,789,175. Thus, if the conditions of operating here were as favorable as in Kansas, the operating expenses of the Southern Pacific lines would have been less than they were by $8,789,175—a sum which would represent an annual dividend of 5 per cent on $175,783,500.

The data for this statement is taken from the annual reports of the companies named. The figures used represent with both systems the same items. The operating expenses are in each case prepared under the printed detailed rules prescribed by the Interstate Commerce Commission and the State Railroad Commissions of California and Kansas. The principal causes of this contrast in the operating expenses of the two systems are the following:

1. The large amount of mountain road in California having heavy grades and curves, requiring greater power to haul a given load, or requiring lighter loads to a train, compared with the Kansas system, the roads of which are comparatively on a level.

2. The greater volume of traffic carried by the Kansas system, which, other things being equal, reduces the rate of cost per car mile or per ton mile, as the expenses of administration, supervision, maintenance, and repairs are imperceptibly increased by an increase of traffic, and the more direct expenses of conducting transportation are not increased in proportion to the increase of business.

3. The greater cost of labor in California, which has been shown by Mr. Curtis to be about 30 per cent, and all material and supplies in which labor is an element of production, including locomotives, cars, machinery, rails, and all other manufactured articles which are manufactured in the Eastern States and have the transcontinental transportation added to their cost in California.

4. The greater cost of fuel in California, making the comparative cost for fuel consumed by locomotives as follows:

Year 1890.	Cost for Fuel.	Locomotive Miles.	Cost per Mile Run—Cents.
Missouri-Pacific System	$1,549,797 04	23,165,875	6.69
Southern Pacific Co., Pacific System	4,016,254 59	19,697,178	20.39

If the cost of fuel per mile run on the Pacific System were as low as on the Missouri Pacific, the cost of fuel consumed by locomotives in the year named would have been $1,317,741 20, as compared with the actual cost of $4,016,254 59. Or, if the average rate for the Missouri Pacific were as great as on the Pacific System, the cost for fuel consumed by locomotives for the year would have been on the Missouri Pacific $6,273,318 95, as compared with the actual cost of $1,549,797 04.

Mr. Leeds has suggested here that the greater cost of coal on Southern Pacific lines is due to that company's manner of accounting, in adding to the cost of coal transportation charges over the company's own lines. This company's practice in this respect is that common to all systems consisting each of several railroads belonging to different companies. To make a proper accounting of earnings and expenses for each railroad, materials shipped over one road for use on another of the same system, are charged with freight at a nominal rate to cover the bare cost of the service. The same practice is followed on the Missouri Pacific system, as is noted in the Annual Report of that company for 1891, page 104.

Nor are the results shown by this comparison exceptional or peculiar. A similar comparison between the Southern Pacific Company's lines, and the lines of any other large system in the Western agricultural States, will give like results.

The rates of cost per unit of service for the systems named are as follows:

Year 1890.	Operating Expenses Per Car Mile —Cents.	Excess of Cost for S. P. Co. Per Car Mile—Per Cent.
Southern Pacific Company, Pacific System	12.169	....
Missouri Pacific System	7.302	66.65
Union Pacific System	8.194	48.51
A. T. and S. F. System	6.884	76.77
Northern Pacific Railroad	8.784	38.53

The rate of cost per car mile for Southern Pacific Company is 12.169 cents; the highest except this is 8.784 cents for the Northern Pacific Railroad. The difference in these rates is 3.385 cents per car mile. Thus, compared with the system least in contrast with the Southern Pacific Company, the excess of cost for operating expenses on this company's lines amounts for the service performed to the annual sum of $6,093,000.

MR. LEEDS' STATEMENTS.

These facts are in direct contradiction to the results reached by the proponent of this constitutional amendment, and upon which the tariffs in the amendment are justified. Mr. Leeds has said, "They (the Southern Pacific Company) claim that operating expenses are higher here than in the East, owing to the high price of coal; I believe I have shown that one half the amount of coal here provides the same service as in Kansas."

And again, he states the following summary of his testimony: "The operations, earnings per mile of road, the comparison of operating expenses, the information that California is paying to this road about twice or more than twice as much per mile as is earned by roads in other portions of this country, also the proposition that it is no more expensive here to operate a road, or should not be, than in that territory, should be quite sufficient, it strikes me, and demonstrates the necessity for some reduction."

This summary of alleged facts deserves careful examination, for if it contain errors, or facts irrelevant to the issue, the demonstration would fail and the Traffic Association amendment would rest only on assertion. The statement resolves itself into four propositions, which I will consider in turn.

First—One half the amount of coal here provides the same service as in Kansas. This is a point of the first importance, as the cost of fuel is the largest single item of expense in the operation of a railroad. It has been shown by Mr. Curtis that the proposition has no foundation in fact, and that it was based on a blunder made by Mr. Leeds in his calculations. In his comparisons of the relative economy in the use of coal on the lines of the Southern Pacific Company and the East, Mr. Leeds has selected and has used solely for the latter territory the Atchison, Topeka, and Santa Fe system. This system operated on June 30, 1892 (Annual Rep., 1892, pp. 10, 11, 69), 7,130 miles of road, including in this the Atlantic and Pacific, Southern California, and other railways, aggregating 1,933 miles in California, Arizona, New Mexico, and Mexico. Thus covering for these part of the same territories and where the conditions are the same as for the Pacific System lines. Had his comparisons, therefore, proven that the cost of coal was greater on the Atchison system than on the Pacific System of the Southern Pacific Company, that result would have been irrelevant in a comparison of cost as between California and Kansas.

But taking even the Atchison system, as quoting from the reports and the same pages as were used by Mr. Leeds, the results shown as to fuel are as follows (reports Atchison, Topeka, and Santa Fe Railway Company, 1891–92, page 82; reports Southern Pacific Company, 1891, page 66):

	A. T. & S. F. System.	S. P. Co. Pacific System.
Locomotives, miles run	34,383,445	20,356,680
Cost per locomotive mile run for fuel	8.57 cents.	19.12 cents.
Cost of coal, per ton, average	$2 11	$5 79

The total cost to the Atchison system for fuel consumed by locomotives was thus $2,946,661 23. The cost to that company would have been, at the rate which it cost the Southern Pacific Company, 19.12 cents per locomotive mile, $6,574,114 68, an increase of $3,627,453 45, or 123 per cent. In other words, the fact is that it costs to perform an equal service on the Atchison system less than one half as much for fuel as it costs the Pacific System of the Southern Pacific Company.

Second—Comparisons of operation and expenses show that it is no more expensive here to operate a road than it is in other portions of this country. This proposition embraces also the preceding one, and is partly answered under that head. It has been fully answered and refuted by the statement of Mr. Curtis. There remains, however, an item that deserves notice, not from its intrinsic importance, but from the importance given to it by the author of the proposed amendment. Mr. Leeds, in his assertions that the cost of operating railroads in California is less than in other portions of this country, lays special stress and dwells at length upon the percentage of operating expenses to earnings, and he argues that as the percentage of operating expenses to earnings is less as a rule on the California roads than on some of the Eastern lines, it follows that the cost of operation here is less than there. This is not an uncommon fallacy. But that a railroad man of Mr. Leeds' experience should entertain it, is only explicable by his statement before the Railroad Commission in the Shively case, that he knew nothing about the operating expenses of railroads, his experience having been confined to the traffic department. The fact is that the percentage of operating expenses to earnings proves nothing as to the cost of operation. It being a ratio to the earnings depends as well upon the amount of earnings as upon the cost of operation. For illustration: The gross earnings of a road amount to, say $10,000 a mile, and the operating expenses $6,000, or 60 per cent; by a reduction in earnings to $9,000 a mile, due perhaps to new sources of competition and with no change in the cost of operation, the ratio of expenses to earnings would be increased from 60 per cent to 66.66 per cent.

It is a rule to which I know of no exception that the most prosperous roads, those particularly which pay not only their fixed charges but dividends to their stockholders, have the highest percentage of operating expenses to earnings. I take at random for illustration the following Eastern lines:

Name of Road.	Dividends Paid—Per Cent.	Percentage of Operating Expenses to Earnings.
Lake Shore and Michigan Southern	5.00	68.15
Pittsburg, Fort Wayne, and Chicago	7.00	66.22
Pennsylvania Railroad	5.50	67.94
New York Central and Hudson River Railroad	4.50	66.09

Compared with the dividend roads, the ratio of operating expenses on the Pacific System lines is 58.93 per cent. Yet none of these California lines, excepting the Central Pacific, has ever paid a dividend to its stockholders. The increased ratio of operating expenses on the Eastern roads named is not due to the greater cost of the service of operation, but on the other hand is due to the much greater volume of traffic, which is accompanied by a much cheaper cost of operation, considering the service performed, and results in a larger net profit, notwithstanding their lower rates.

In contradiction to Mr. Leeds' conclusions, it is also true that a road with a low percentage of operating expense may be unprofitable to its owners and be operated at a high rate of cost for the service performed. For illustration, the Pacific Coast Railway has shown that its gross earnings for 1891 were (Report of California Railroad Commission, 1891), $194,034 50; operating expenses, $94,680 87; ratio of operating expenses to earnings, 49 per cent. Notwithstanding this low percentage of operating expenses, compared with say the Lake Shore rate as above of 68 per cent, it costs to haul a train a mile on the California road $1 19, and on the Eastern road $1 06, and the traffic in the train is many times greater in the latter case. (Statistics of Interstate Commerce Commission, 1890, p. 639.)

The percentage of operating expenses to earnings thus proves nothing as to the cost of operating in one State compared with another State, and it has been here demonstrated that the *results* reached by Mr. Leeds in the use of such percentages are directly contrary to the facts. Notwithstanding the lower ratio of operating expenses to earnings here, the actual cost of operation is much greater than in other portions of this country.

Third—California is paying to this road (the Southern Pacific Company) twice as much per mile as is earned by roads in other portions of this country. In this proposition Mr. Leeds cannot of course mean literally what he says, for he must know that some roads in other portions of the country earn per mile as high as three times as much as the Pacific System. Compare for instance the above mentioned dividend paying roads:

	Gross Earnings per Mile of Road.
Southern Pacific Company, Pacific System	$8,001 00
Lake Shore and Michigan Southern	14,137 00
Pittsburg, Fort Wayne, and Chicago	25,582 00
Pennsylvania Railroad	26,981 00
New York Central and Hudson River Railroad	24,457 00

As the Southern Pacific gross earnings per mile are about one third that shown on these roads, Mr. Leeds must mean to confine his comparisons to other roads. He has, in fact, named the Atchison system and the Missouri Pacific system in this connection. The fairness of such comparisons, or, in other words, the truth of the deduction which may be obtained therefrom, depends on the fullness of the numerous other facts to be considered. A high average earning per mile indicates in itself neither high rates nor large profits. The largest earnings per mile, as a rule, are received where the rates are lowest; thus the Eastern roads above quoted have larger earnings and lower rates than the Pacific System. And the Pacific System has larger earnings and lower rates than the other roads in California. On the Pacific System it is a fact, also, that on those roads where the earnings are largest, the rates are the lowest. This results from the common relation between a large traffic and low rates. Under natural conditions, and without arbitrary interference, rates are reduced wherever it is believed that it will induce sufficient additional traffic to give on the whole an increased net profit. Thus commodities which are produced in the largest quantities are taken out of the body of the tariff and given special rates. This ap,"it is to all the principal products of this State. Applied to the country ·me large, it affects with the greatest force the staples of life, and results in the lowest rates: first, on the necessities of life, which are consumed by all; second, on the common comforts, consumed by a less number and to a less amount, and third, to the luxuries of life, which take the highest rates and are enjoyed by the few. The reductions of rates, under natural conditions, with the object of securing an increase of traffic with a lower rate but a larger net profit, thus results in the greatest good to the greatest number. On the score of rates there is nothing to be feared here from large gross earnings per mile of road. Where the earnings are largest, the rates are lowest. For any increase in earnings per mile which the railroads may secure, the patrons of the road and the people of this State will be benefited to a much greater degree. What is wanted here is more such roads, not discrimination against them such as this measure proposes.

Neither can the profits of a railroad or the reasonableness of its charges be judged by the gross earnings per mile, nor by comparing this with the percentage of operating expenses to earnings. There must be considered, also, other necessary expenses, interest on the bonded debt, and a fair return on cost of the property. These charges are all greater for the railroads in California than in the States of the Mississippi Valley, for reasons similar to those stated in explanation of the increased cost of operation. The cost of construction is much greater here now than east of the Rocky Mountains. It was still greater a number of years ago, when the Central Pacific was built. The characteristics of the greater portion of California railroads are snowsheds, trestles, bridges, tunnels, grades, and curves. Under equal conditions of cost for labor and materials, the character of the country would greatly increase here the cost of construction, compared with the level plains of the other territory named. But it has been shown that the cost of labor and materials here is much greater than in the East. Again, the use of capital has always demanded and still requires higher interest here. These conditions combined, greatly increase the actual necessary cash cost of railway construction in this State compared with the State of Kansas and its neighbors. On these points, which are paramount, because they are necessary to consider before railroads can be constructed here, Mr. Leeds has offered no evidence. He has in no case shown what were the profits of the roads here, or whether the gross earnings afforded a fair return upon the actual cash investment.

Fourth—These three propositions being proven, should be quite sufficient, and demonstrates the necessity for some reduction. This is Mr. Leeds' conclusion. With full confidence I rest the judgment of the proof of his propositions, and the demonstration he would draw from them, on the honesty, the justice, and the patriotism of this committee and the Legislature of this State.

CAPITALIZATION.

As to the capitalization of the Southern Pacific lines, Mr. Leeds has furnished your committee with the following information:

"The earnings of the roads within the State of California, including the entire system of the Southern Pacific Company, were $9,021 per mile; that covers 3,498 miles of road; that the interest on bonded debt paid by the Pacific System on some of that was $8,675,587 42. I have since learned that the capitalization on that 3,498 miles of road was, for funded debt, $144,494,500, or $41,305 per mile; the capital stock of the same, $165,311,300, or $47,255 50 per mile; and an aggregate capitalization for the two, $88,560 50 per mile."

Again, in referring to these figures, he states: "That represents 3,498 miles of railroad for which you are expected to put up the necessary money to pay the interest on capitalization amounting to $309,805,800, or $88,560 average per mile." And in another reference to the subject, he says: "I believe that the bonded indebtedness of these roads is very much in excess of the cost of construction."

Mr. Leeds' confusion of facts, errors of figures, and false conclusions in these statements are fairly characteristic of the popular misinformation and prejudice which exist on this subject. He confuses his remarks regarding the roads in California, the entire system, the lines covering the 3,498 miles of road, and the interest on bonded debt "paid on some of that;" so that to understand his statements one must refer to the source from which he has derived them and try to locate the figures. From such a reference to the annual report of the Southern Pacific Company for 1891, I find that the interest on bonded debt stated as being "paid by the Pacific System on some of that," $8,675,587 48, covers not only some, but all the Pacific System lines in the States and Territories of Oregon, California, Nevada, Utah, Arizona, and New Mexico. The 3,498 miles of road includes the lines operated by the Southern Pacific Company in California, Nevada, and Utah. The capital stock named covers these last-named lines, and in addition thereto the 242.51 miles of the Atlantic and Pacific Railroad between Mojave and The Needles. The bonded debt named is apparently intended to cover the same lines as the capital stock, but by an error it overstates the amount to the extent of $12,786,000. Through the error of dividing the amount of capital stock by the wrong mileage, the rate of capital stock per mile is in error. Correcting the errors, both in the wrong mileage and the wrong amounts for the bonded debt, it should be reduced from $41,305 to $35,209 per mile of road. But aside from the errors of his figures, Mr. Leeds' statement that "you are expected to put up the money to pay the interest on capitalization amounting to $88,560 per mile," is not true in fact, and conveys a grossly erroneous impression. This sum (if not in error as to the amount) would represent the issue of both bonds and capital stock on all lines operated by the Southern Pacific Company in California, and the Central Pacific lines also in Nevada and Utah. None of these California companies have ever paid a dividend on their stock. This stock, amounting to $97,311,390, has therefore no more relation to the past or present earnings of the roads than if not a share of it had ever been issued. The only dividend paid by the Pacific System is 2 per cent for the Central Pacific line. The much greater portion of the earnings of this road are from through traffic, the rates on which are fixed by competition, and so are entirely unaffected, whether dividends are paid or not. During the past seven years the dividends paid for this road have only been earned in one. Operated on its own merits the dividends could not have been made; they were paid from the guaranteed rental under the lease to the Southern Pacific Company.

As to the bonded debt of these roads, Mr. Leeds believes that "it is very much in excess of the cost of construction." This is but an extreme expression of a common belief which Mr. Leeds found upon his advent here, and adopted on hearsay evidence, as he has testified in the Shively case. But like some other forms of faith, investigation will show that its foundation is not on fact. There seems also to be a quite common belief abroad, that the bonded debt of the Southern Pacific Company's lines is increasing from year to year, so as to make the interest charge on them an increasing tax to be collected from the traffic carried. The following statement showing the original and the present bonded debt of each of the lines comprising the Pacific System of the Southern Pacific Company, will throw some light upon this subject:

Southern Pacific Company, Pacific System. Summary of Funded Debt of Railroad Companies, December 31, 1892.

Miles of Road Owned.	Name of Issuing Company.	Total Amount of Bonds.		
		Issued.	Redeemed.	Outstanding
1,741	Southern Pacific Railroad of California	$54,335,000	$8,398,500	$45,936,500
390	Northern Railway	10,111,000	192,000	9,919,000
54	Northern California Railway	945,000		945,000
104	South Pacific Coast Railway	5,500,000		5,500,000
115	California Pacific Railroad	6,848,500	23,000	6,825,500
2,404	Total lines wholly in California	$77,739,500	$8,613,500	$69,126,000
1,360	Central Pacific Railroad	$74,586,000	$15,449,000	$59,137,000
393	Southern Pacific Railroad of Arizona	10,000,000		10,000,000
167	Southern Pacific R. R. of New Mexico	4,180,000		4,180,000
568	Oregon and California Railroad	17,036,000		17,036,000
58	Oregonian Railroad	No bonds.		
28	Port. & Will. Val. R. (P. & Y. R. R., October 1, 1892)	No interest charged.		
2,574	Total other lines	$105,802,000	$15,449,000	$90,353,000
4,978	Total Pacific System	$183,541,500	$24,062,500	$159,479,000

Miles of Road Owned.	Name of Issuing Company.	Bonds per Mile of Road Owned.			Reduction in Interest Charges.
		Issued.	Re-deemed.	Out-standing	
1,741	Southern Pacific Railroad of California	$31,209	$4,824	$26,385	$551,760
390	Northern Railway	25,925	492	25,433	32,760
54	Northern California Railway	17,500		17,500	
104	South Pacific Coast Railway	52,885		52,885	
115	California Pacific Railroad	59,552	200	59,352	58,785
2,404	Total lines wholly in California	$32,338	$3,583	$28,755	$643,305
1,360	Central Pacific Railroad	$54,843	$11,360	$43,483	$1,033,060
393	Southern Pacific Railroad of Arizona	25,445		25,445	
167	Southern Pacific R. R. of New Mexico	25,030		25,030	
568	Oregon and California Railroad	30,000		30,000	
58	Oregonian Railroad				
28	Port. & Will. Val. R. (P. & Y. R. R., October 1, 1892)				
2,574	Total other lines	$41,104	$6,002	$35,102	$1,033,060
4,978	Total Pacific System	$36,870	$4,834	$32,036	$1,676,365

Taking all the lines that are wholly within the State of California, which includes the Southern Pacific Railroad of California, Northern Railway, Northern California Railway, South Pacific Coast Railway, and the California Pacific Railroad, they comprised on December 31, 1892, two thousand four hundred and four miles. The original issue of bonds on these roads amounted to $77,739,000, but under the laws of the State of California every railroad mortgage, or all railroad mortgages under which bonds are issued, must provide that a sinking fund be established for the redemption of the bonds, to be paid entirely from the income of the road. The sinking fund has been used with some of these roads; it is accumulating with others, and has been used, although there is a large accumulation invested in these very bonds, although it is not shown here as a reduction. What I wish to show is that in these roads comprising the Pacific System there has been a material reduction in the amount of bonded debt, running along through years of their history, and it has resulted in a material reduction of the interest charge on the roads, which Mr. Leeds says you are expected to pay. Now, for the lines that I have stated were wholly within the State of California, of this $77,000,000 bonds have been redeemed to the amount of $8,600,000, leaving outstanding $69,000,000. Now, the original issue of these bonds averaged for all the roads something over $32,000 per mile; some of them were issued as high as $40,000 per mile, some at higher rates, and some at $17,500; but they averaged $32,000. Since then, by redemptions, they have been reduced so that the present average bonded debt of the railroads wholly within the State of California—the railroad companies whose lines are wholly within the State of California which are controlled by the Southern Pacific Company—amounts to $28,755 per mile of road. The reduction of interest, the annual interest charge, which has been effected by the retirement of these bonds, amounts to $1,436,000. Now, taking the lines of the system; there is the Central Pacific, Southern Pacific of California, and of Arizona and New Mexico, the Oregon and California, and a couple of other little roads in Oregon. The total redemption of bonds for all these roads amounted to something over $24,000,000, and the issue, which at the original rate, averaged $37,000 per mile of road, has been reduced to an average of $32,000; that includes the high rate on the South Pacific Coast Railway, which has only one hundred and four miles of road, and has a very high rate of issue per mile, owing to the fact that its principal properties are the ferries and ferry properties in Oakland, Alameda, and San Francisco, so that it is not a fair way to show that rate.

For the California Pacific the average is $59,000 per mile, owing to the fact that that road was constructed by interests different from those at present controlling it, and at the reorganization it became bankrupt, and the reorganization was effected to save the old creditors as far as possible, resulting in scaling down the interest; so they have first, second, and third mortgages. Now, the third mortgage only pays 3 per cent; those are the roads whose bonds are highest on the system, not excepting the Central Pacific, and were issued before the control by the present proprietors over these properties.

Earl: That is the Napa Valley line? A. Yes, part of the Napa Valley line; but the principal line is between Vallejo and Sacramento.

EARL: Was that built by the present owners? Was that not built through the swamp by the present owners? A. Yes, across the swamp; but it has been reconstructed, almost entirely, at great expense.

MR. CURTIS: Been reconstructed three times?

MR. LANSING: It was washed out badly, as stated, three times. I mention that to show the highest rate. The present proprietors are not responsible, and their interest in this matter has been to reduce that rate.

As before stated, it will be seen that for the companies wholly in California, there were on December 31, 1892, 2,404 miles of road, on which bonds were originally issued to the amount of $77,739,500; but that of this amount $8,613,500 have since their original issue been redeemed, leaving outstanding at the present time $69,126,000, or $28,755 per mile of road. The redemption of bonds on those roads, wholly within this State, average for all lines $3,583 per mile. For the Central Pacific, both within and without the State, bonds have been redeemed to the amount of $15,449,000, or $11,360 per mile of road. For all the Pacific System lines, the bonds redeemed amount to $24,062,500, which with such as have been refunded at lower rates of interest, have reduced the total interest charge by the sum of $1,676,365 per annum. The average bonded debt per mile for the entire system, including the Central Pacific Railroad, is at the present time $32,036, and for the roads wholly in California, $28,755. The bonded debt on these lines and the interest charged thereon, have thus not been increased, but materially reduced during the years of their operation. It has been shown that the cost of construction for the Pacific System lines has been much greater than for the roads of the Mississippi Valley and the East. This is common to all lines here, on account of the greater cost of labor, materials, and supplies; and has more or less additional application to each, due to its proportion of mountain and desert road. When these known conditions of relative cost are taken into consideration, a comparison of the bonded debt of railroads here and in the East will satisfy an unbiased mind that the cost of construction on the Pacific System has been greatly in excess of the amount of their bonded debt.

In the most thickly settled portion of our country, on the Atlantic Coast, the capitalization is the greatest. For the group of States designated in the statistical report of the Interstate Commerce Commission as group 2 (reports 1890, page 46), which includes New York, New Jersey, Pennsylvania, Delaware, and Maryland, the average bonded debt per mile is $58,275. These roads also have issued capital stock to the amount of $51,698 per mile, on 52.73 per cent of which dividends are paid. The greater capitalization in this group of States is due to the more expensive roadway, terminal properties, and larger equipment required to conduct their greater volume of traffic. An equal standard of construction there would cost much less than here. Coming west to a territory of lighter traffic, though greater than our own, we find in Kansas a standard no higher, and I believe not so high as that of our Pacific System lines, with which a comparison may be made under conditions fairly equal as to the standard of construction, but differing materially as to the relative price of labor and materials, and the topographical features of the country through which the roads run.

The Railroad Commission in Kansas seems by its course in that State to have inspired the confidence of the San Francisco Traffic Association and its Manager, so that its testimony on this matter may be quoted with confidence as having at least no undue bias in favor of the railroads. In considering this subject of the returns upon capital invested, in their annual report for 1890 (p. 20), they say: "It is quite common for inflated orators to assert that from $8,000 to $10,000 a mile is all that a railroad legitimately costs, and that all capitalization above that is water. We have an itemized statement of the actual cash cost of 1,388 miles, 1,055 being in Kansas. We refer to the Chicago, Kansas, and Nebraska Railroad. All of this road was built within the past four years, under most favorable conditions as to cost of labor and material, and built by or under the auspices of a company whose financial credit was high, enabling it to place securities upon the market upon very favorable terms; yet the actual cost and outlay for road and equipment up to June 30, 1889, was $29,264,497 33, or $21,083 93 per mile. There is no water in this.

"It is true that all the railroad mileage in the State has not cost so much per mile as the Chicago, Kansas, and Nebraska line, but some has cost a great deal more. Railroads that are cheaply built in the beginning cost more before they are finished than they would if well constructed at first. A railroad thrown down on the prairie at a cost of $10,000 or $12,000 per mile is no criterion of the cost of a road over which immense trains run with safety thirty and forty miles an hour.

"It would, in our judgment, be a moderate estimate to put the actual average cash cost of the total railroad mileage of Kansas, including equipment, at the cost of the Chicago, Kansas, and Nebraska line, per mile."

Of the roads over which immense trains run with safety thirty or forty miles an hour, which the Commission say "cost a good deal more per mile" than the average prairie road of the State, I find the following lines, with the bonded debt per mile of road, issued on the lines in Kansas (Rep. R. R. Com. Kas., 1891, p. 266):

Name of Road.	Bonded Debt per Mile of Road in Kansas.
Atchison, Topeka, and Santa Fé Railway	$32,780 00
Missouri Pacific Railway	27,888 00
Missouri, Kansas, and Texas Railway	39,404 00
St. Joe and Grand Island Railway	34,537 00
St. Louis and San Francisco Railway	30,143 00
Union Pacific Railway	38,891 00

The mean issue for these principal lines in Kansas is $33,940 per mile. With the Southern Pacific Company lines in California we have shown it to be $28,755, and for the entire Pacific System, including the Central Pacific, with its mountain grades, tunnels, snowsheds, and war prices for labor, material, and capital, but $32,036 per mile.

Mr. Leeds is wrong, Mr. Chairman, in saying, "You are expected to put up the necessary money to pay the interest on capitalization, amounting to $88,560 50 per mile;" for the lines of this company, which are wholly in California, are paying interest only at the rate of $28.775 per mile, and are paying no dividends. The large capitalization of the Central Pacific is due to the great natural obstacles which had to be overcome in the construction of that road, and to the much greater cost of labor, materials, supplies, and equipment, due to construction in time of war and before the completion of this line had furnished the present low rates of transportation across the continent. The bond issue was provided by Act of Congress, the United States bonds being based on $16,000 per mile on the plains, $32,000 in the foothills, and $48,000 per mile crossing the Sierra Nevada Mountains. The company was then authorized to issue its bonds for the same amount. After paying annually the 25 per cent of net earnings required under the provisions of the Thurman Act into the United States Treasury, the earnings of the Central Pacific lines are not sufficient to meet the accruing interest on the issue of the United States bonds. These bonds were loaned by the Government to this company in the same way that loans are made by private parties to the company on the issue of its bonds. They were made payable in United States currency, and accepted by the company at par, amounting to $27,855,680, interest on which at 6 per cent is an annual charge to the company; and it may be of interest here to note that, during the time of construction, all payments made on the Pacific Coast were in gold, which was then at a high premium. In order to convert these bonds into gold to pay its payrolls and bills, the company was compelled to sell them for $20,735,000, or at a discount of $7,120,000.

Earl: Then it is erroneous to think the Government put up money, gold coin, to the amount of the debt that it holds against the Central Pacific? A. Yes, sir.

Q. They put up bonds and then took a mortgage to secure the face value of them as a debt? A. The Government never put up a dollar in coin. They issued their currency bonds at 6 per cent, and loaned the bonds to the company on condition that the company should repay the bonds with interest. They being currency bonds, and currency at that time being at a great discount, everything here being in gold, the company had to utilize them at a great loss.

Lansing: I would submit to the committee a statement showing the income from operations of the Central Pacific Railroad for the past five years, and each of them, showing gross earnings from other sources of income to the company; that is, other sources in connection with the operations of the property—not land sales; not for sales of their property—the operating expenses and the other charges which are necessarily a charge against the income of the road, and which would be a legitimate and proper charge required from the road before a justification of a reduction in its rates reducing its income would be allowed under the recent rulings of the United States Courts, fixing what is a reasonable rate, or establishing the principle of what is a reasonable rate.

For 1887 the gross earnings or income of this line amounted to—I will read in round figures—say, $14,000,000; the charges against it, the whole item of charge, a little more than that.

In 1888 the income was nearly $16,000,000, and the charges about $16,500,000.

In 1889 about $16,000,000, and the charges $16,500,000.

In 1890 the income $16,000,000, and the charges $16,750,000.

In 1891 it earned a net of $473,000.

For the whole period—five years—together, the result was a net deficit of $2,228,000. This is without payment of any dividend; the dividend, as I have stated, being payable under contract or lease to the Southern Pacific Company, and guaranteed.

BURKE: What road was that?

A. The Central Pacific Railroad. That is the largest system of lines, and, as every one here knows, the most important to the Pacific Coast. I would like to say something about the Southern Pacific Railroad of California. This is probably, by a great deal, the most important company in the State of California.

BURKE: I am sorry, Mr. Lansing, that I cannot stay any longer, as I have a pressing engagement.

LANSING: It is the most important road, because it has a greater mileage in this State than any other line; it has about fifteen hundred miles in operation, and has in contemplation the construction of about fifteen hundred miles additional, making something over three thousand miles of road.

I have a statement showing the growth of this company—showing, in similar form to that which I have given for the Central Pacific, the earnings and expenses and fixed charges for each of the past five years, which show an increasing condition of prosperity. This company consists of a number of lines that have been consolidated from time to time with a view of effecting economy in their operation, and of having them stand together as a system to protect each other—for the better lines to help the weaker, and so strengthen their securities that additional capital can be secured for the extensions that have been contemplated.

The income has been increasing from year to year, until in 1890 there was a surplus of about $14,000 out of gross earnings amounting to $8,896,000. In 1891 there was a surplus of $937,000; and in order to carry out the contemplated extensions that the proprietors of this property have in view in the State, they amended their articles of association, providing for quite a number of new lines, making in all about fifteen hundred miles proposed to be constructed, as I have stated.

I would like to file the amended articles of association, which describe all the lines and their terminal points. And it was hoped and is still hoped that the increasing prosperity would allow the controllers of the company to issue bonds on the proposed lines, or to make a contract with bankers for supplying them with funds as the bonds were issued on constructed road, and they have laid their plans with that object in view.

For the whole period of five years, which I have before me, there is a net deficit of $1,765,000; but as I have said, the latter portion of the period shows better than for the former portion.

MR. EARL: How long? A. Five years; 1887 to 1891, inclusive.

Now, the bonds which have been issued by the Southern Pacific Railroad, of which this is simply the continuation, were under conditions existing at that time of the cost of construction, and character of the road, and the requirements of capital, fixed at $40,000 per mile at 6 per cent. On the lines which have recently been constructed, the issue has been limited to $22,500 per mile at 5 per cent. They have issued no more bonds than with the capital stock which they pay in, on which they pay cash, is required to carry on the work; that is what has been planned, and what is hoped for the extension of these lines.

I submit this statement also, with blue print for a map, showing the contemplated lines in dots. This is the blue print map that was made for the information of the bankers interested in furnishing the capital for the enterprises.

[Mr. Lansing here filed blue print and statement.]

I wish to say that one branch of this company's projected line is now in process of construction, running down the coast from San Francisco to Santa Margarita, thence to San Luis Obispo and Santa Barbara; and there is a line contemplated crossing the mountain range separating the coast from the San Joaquin Valley; there are a number of lines—branch lines—on the coast and throughout the San Joaquin Valley.

I wish to say that there is no question but, if from the investigation which we have made into the operation of this proposed constitutional amendment, if a California distance tariff of that kind is imposed upon these roads, there is no possibility of their being constructed by the present proprietors, and all work at present on them must cease.

I would like finally to add a note on the subject of reductions in rates.

REDUCTION IN RATES.

The business of railroad transportation I hold to be a legitimate business, and one on which the welfare of this State in a great degree depends. It involves the control and use of a vast amount of capital, which is of necessity a permanent investment in this State. It cannot be operated to the injury of the State without operating to its own injury. The interests of the communities which it serves and the patrons of its lines are also its interests, and to wrong one of these would be bad policy, as well as unlawful. Such differences as may exist between the company and its patrons as to rates that are unreasonable or discriminations that are unjust, it would be the company's paramount interest to remedy if wrong, or rest the settlement with a proper Commission or Court if agreement were not otherwise possible. Its business can only be prosperous if conducted on business principles. To the best of the judgment of its proprietors and officers, it has been guided by these principles in the past. I believe the best results for all concerned will follow from adhering to them in the future, and with the growing wisdom of experience, which is as useful to the railroads as to the people. Mr. Curtis and Mr. Gray have illustrated the remarkable growth and development of this State, and the dependence of such prosperity on the railroads. I wish to strengthen their testimony by showing the reductions which have been made by the Pacific System lines under natural conditions of regulation and competition in charges for the transportation of passengers and freight.

Statistics, first, show the average rate of charge for transportation of the Pacific System lines in 1872; for this year the average rate of freight per ton per mile was 3.66 cents. In 1891 it had been reduced to 1.835 cents. These figures do not include company's freight. The reduction during this period thus amounts to 1.825 cents, or half the entire rate. This means, that if the average rate of 1872 were collected on the tonnage of the present time, the freight earnings of 1891, which were $21,500,000, would have been $43,000,000.

But, during this period named of twenty years, great changes have affected these lines by the construction of other and competing transcontinental railways, and as both through and local traffic are included in the tonnage shown, it may be naturally claimed that the reduction is chiefly due to the competition on the through and does not much affect the local traffic in the State. To answer this, the statistics for the past ten years have been made to show separately the local tonnage and the through. The following are the statistics for both freight and passenger traffic for 1881 and 1891, which afford a more detailed comparison for this period:

FREIGHT STATISTICS—SOUTHERN PACIFIC COMPANY (PACIFIC SYSTEM).

(Not including company's freight.)

	1891.	1881.	Increase or Decrease.	Per Cent.
Through Freight.				
Miles road operated	4,625	2,707	*1,918	70.85
Earnings	$7,972,452	$3,423,499	* 4,548,953	130.28
Tons carried	738,914	309,329	*429,585	138.89
Tons one mile	669,634,362	259,684,517	*409,949,845	157.8
Ton miles to one mile of road	144,786	95,931	*48,855	50.93
Average rate per ton per mile (cents)	1.190	1.318	†0.128	9.71
Earnings per mile of road	$1,724	$1,265	*$459	36.
Local Freight.				
Earnings	$13,536,142	$12,418,640	*$1,117,502	9.00
Tons carried	4,949,142	1,862,712	*3,086,430	165.6
Tons one mile	502,437,824	373,170,214	*129,267,610	34.64
Ton miles to one mile of road	108,635	137,854	†29,219	21.20
Average rate per ton per mile (cents)	2.694	3.328	†0.634	19.05
Earnings per mile of road	$2,926	$4,588	†$1,662	36.23

* Increase. † Decrease.

PASSENGER STATISTICS—PACIFIC SYSTEM, SOUTHERN PACIFIC COMPANY.

	1891.	1881.	Increase or Decrease.	
			Amounts.	Per Cent.
Through Passengers.				
Miles of road operated	4,625	2,707	*1,918	63.43
Earnings	$2,793,295	$2,048,090	*$745,205	36.39
Passengers carried	163,517	77,998	*85,519	109.64
Passengers carried one mile	136,625,120	63,721,671	*72,903,449	114.41
Passenger miles to one mile of road	29,540	23,540	*6,000	25.49
Average rate per passenger per mile (in cents)	2.04	3.21	†1.17	36.45
Earnings per mile of road	$603 95	$756 56	†$152 61	20.00
Local Passengers.				
Earnings	$8,538,485	$4,644,738	*$3,893,747	83.83
Passengers carried	17,701,359	6,884,936	*10,816,423	157.77
Passengers carried one mile	387,057,215	145,106,283	*241,950,932	166.74
Passenger miles to one mile of road	83,688	53,604	*30,084	56.12
Average rate per passenger per mile (in cents)	2.21	3.20	†0.99	30.94
Earnings per mile of road	$1,846 16	$2,543 38	†$697 22	27.40

* Increase. † Decrease.

It will be seen that for the past ten years the through freight shows a reduction in average rate of .128 cents, or 9.71 per cent, while the local rate has been reduced .634 cents, or 19.05 per cent. With passenger traffic there has been a reduction in the average rate on through of 1.17 cents, or 36.45 per cent, and with local an almost equal rate, or .99 cents, or 30.94 per cent.

If the average rates of 1881 had been collected on these roads on the traffic of 1891, it would have increased the earnings of the latter year by the following amounts:

Through freight earnings	$853,328 80	
Through passenger earnings	1,598,513 90	
Total through		$2,451,842 70
Local freight earnings	$3,184,988 78	
Local passenger earnings	3,831,866 42	
Total local		7,016,855 20
Total reduction		$9,468,698 99

There have thus been greater reductions affecting the local traffic during the ten years past than there have been for through. This has been caused by following the conservative and wise policy of developing the resources and building up the territory local to the company's lines. As there is no State which during the past ten years has shown a more prosperous growth than that of California, so I believe there is no system of railroads in this country that has made concessions and reductions in its local rates aggregating so great an annual sum.

VOLUME OF TONNAGE.

At a recent meeting of this committee, Mr. Martin informed the committee and the proponent of the resolution that the proposed California Distance Tariff for freight rates was not the same, but was materially lower than the Kansas Distance Tariff. This fact, thus for the first time being made public, was acknowledged by Mr. Leeds in a published interview in the San Francisco "Examiner" of February 3d, where he says:

"Martin has commented on the fact that my rates are much lower than those in the Kansas Distance Tariff. I admit that such is the case. I intended that such should be the case. The Kansas roads have not so much tonnage per mile as is the case here."

The last sentence is intended as a justification by Mr. Leeds of the lower tariff for California. If it were true (and other things were equal), it would be a strong argument for such a difference, for it is a fact with which all railroad men are familiar that an increase of tonnage can be carried by a road without a corresponding increase of expense. So the roads under the regulation of natural conditions study to reduce their rates where there is a fair premise that the traffic will be thereby increased in sufficient volume to produce a larger net result. If, on the other hand, it should prove that the volume of tonnage is greater on the Kansas lines than in California, such fact would afford an equal argument in justification of higher rates here. Indeed, laying aside the facts which have been proven as to the excessive cost of operations in California, and admitting for the sake of argument that the service of transportation costs no more here than in Kansas, this factor of the volume of tonnage is of sufficient importance in itself, that if it is found to be less on the Southern Pacific Company's lines than on the Kansas systems, to condemn the California Distance Tariff in its application to the lines of this company as unfair and unjust. This is the comparison which Mr. Leeds invites. Now, what are the facts? The following data, covering all the principal railroad systems in Kansas, and for those having the largest traffic, is taken from the report of the Railroad Commission of that State for 1891 (p. 301).

The corresponding data for the Pacific System of the Southern Pacific Company is taken from the annual report of that company for 1891 (p. 68).

MR. LANSING: So that the average in California, taken by itself, is a little lower than for the Pacific System, and the Pacific System is 93.00 ton miles lower than Kansas, or 37 per cent lower than the roads in Kansas, which I have mentioned; those roads are not confined to the State of Kansas, but include the systems running in and out of the State, like the Missouri Pacific.

EARL: And what is the average reduction, as shown by the California Distance Tariff, from the rates prescribed in the Kansas Distance Tariff? 20 per cent, you say in your opening statement. A. Mr. Leeds stated that applied to the local business of California, as I understand him, that his first statement was 25 or 30 per cent, that is on the local business; but, applied to the total business, amounted to something like 21 per cent.

EARL: No, I don't mean that. I mean this: You say that you have calculated the average reduction shown by the California Distance Tariff with reference to the Kansas Distance Tariff—you yourself had, and you found the average to be about 20 or 25 per cent? A. No; you misunderstood me.

EARL: Well, then I guess it was Mr. Smurr, perhaps.

MR. SMURR: Ranges from 10 to 31 per cent.

LANSING: It is hard—in fact, impossible—to make a correct estimate of the effect of a tariff of that kind upon the whole tonnage of a road. We have to apply it to the various commodities in such a way that it takes a great deal of time and labor to make it up, so that, as Mr. Smurr has applied it to the different classes as closely as he can, it gives a different rate for the different classes. Then the effect upon the whole revenue would depend upon what the volume of traffic in each of those classes—the proportion—was to the whole. It is very material; that is sufficient.

The following statement shows the volume of tonnage of the Pacific System lines in each State and Territory, and the proportion of through and local in each case. This is an interesting document, and verifies the fact which I have stated, that for the California lines, the volume of tonnage is less than for other lines. For instance, in California, the proportion of through you will see the explanation in that, is 103,000 tons; while in Nevada the through was 409,000 tons, and Utah 411,000 tons, that is larger than the whole average of California; taking the through and the local in this State, it is only 59,000 and 55,000 respectively, and so in Arizona, the average for through is 216,000, and for New Mexico, 214,000, which, added to the local they have there, makes a higher total average for the line in those desert territories than the average in California, when it is applied to all the little branch lines of the system in this State:

STATEMENT SHOWING VOLUME OF TONNAGE.

PACIFIC SYSTEM, SOUTHERN PACIFIC COMPANY VERSUS KANSAS SYSTEM.

	Mileage.	Tons—Rev. freight one mile.	Tons one mile, per mile of road.
A. T. & S. F.	4,582.12	1,456,057,989	317,588
C. B. & Q.	5,284.25	1,645,745,417	311,419
C., R. I. & P.	3,408.56	1,082,223,392	317,492
K. C., Ft. S., & M.	670.60	405,362,003	605,605
Mo. Pac.	3,176.82	877,751,584	276,282
M. K. & T.	1,670.36	585,272,713	351,150
S. L. & S. F.	1,326.93	357,170,350	284,224
U. P.	1,821.86	1,209,224,850	663,673
Total	21,941.50	7,618,808,298	347,225
Pa. System, S. P. Co.	4,625.17	1,172,072,186	253,421

These figures include only revenue tonnage. It will be seen that the volume of tonnage for the Pacific System averages 253,421 tons per mile of road, compared with the average for the Kansas lines of 347,225 tons per mile, and that the volume of tonnage here is 93,804 tons per mile, or 37 per cent less than with the Kansas lines. From these facts it follows that the Kansas Distance Tariff, if reasonable to the railroads there, would be unreasonable here, and Mr. Leeds' tariff being still lower, would be still more unjust if applied to this State.

But the volume of tonnage above quoted is the average for all Pacific System roads, including those in Oregon, Nevada, Utah, Arizona, and New Mexico, as well as those in California. It has been intimated here, and would be readily believed unless one were familiar with the traffic, that the California lines had a much greater volume of tonnage than those in the other States a ıd Territories named. This, however, is not the fact. The larger number of small local branch lines in California, compared with the main trunk lines of which the mileage of the other States and Territories is compose l, with the exception of the State of Oregon, reduces the volume of tonnage in this State to 238,090 per mile of road, compared with 267,084 for the remaining roads.

The following statement shows the volume of tonnage for the Pacific System lines in each State and Territory, and the proportion of through and local in each case:

Territory.	Through Freight—Ton Miles.	Local Freight—Ton Miles.	Total—Ton Miles.
California	103,072	135.018	238,090
Nevada	409,102	69,052	478,154
Utah	411,418	55,168	466,586
Oregon	17,205	35,397	52,602
Arizona	216,921	67,461	284,382
New Mexico	214,755	98,857	313,612
Average	143,843	105,422	253,421
Average, California excepted	208,855	58,229	267,084

EARL: Will you file those statements with the committee?

MR. LANSING: Yes, I will file all of them.

EARL: I hoped to see some one of the Traffic Association with us—Colonel Barry—or some one to-night, so as to fix a time to adjourn to.

Martin: I understood Mr. Barry to say that he was going to attend the meetings from this time on, and he would have something to say when we got through.

Earl: So I understood. I am at a loss to set a time for the next hearing on account of the Traffic Association not being represented here to suggest an hour and time that will be convenient.

Martin: I hope that whatever hearing may be had, that sufficient notice may be given so that we may be represented here. Of course, we cannot get here in a day; we ought to have sufficient notice.

Earl (to clerk): Send for Senator Gesford.

Earl: Mr. Lansing, have you a duplicate copy of any of this matter that you have presented here this evening?

Lansing: Yes, I have, but not here; I can furnish you a duplicate.

Earl: Could you furnish me a duplicate? A. Yes, sir.

Earl: About when? A. Think I could send it to you to-morrow.

Earl: Senator Gesford, the hour of adjournment has arrived, and we would like to know what time would be satisfactory to yourself, as proponent of this measure, and the Traffic Association, for you to meet again, when any statement that Mr. Barry would like to make and yourself, can be made.

Gesford: Any time will suit me after Thursday. You are a member of that other committee, and I suppose you will be engaged there for two or three evenings, and probably we can't reach this till the latter part of the week.

Earl: It is getting so late in the session it seems too bad to defer it; but we will be too busy in that committee to-morrow night and the next night, and possibly any other night; would say Monday; next Monday night.

Gesford: Next Monday night; that would be agreeable.

Earl: Very well; the committee stands adjourned until next Monday night, at 7:30; either to meet at this place or down stairs, Department Two; you will ascertain from the Sergeant-at-Arms—Monday night, 7:30 o'clock.

Monday Evening, February 13, 1893.

Mr. Earl: Committee will come to order. Mr. Martin, at the last sitting of the committee did the Southern Pacific Company finish its showing?

Mr. Martin: Yes, sir; we finished everything we have to say.

Mr. Earl: Is there any one else that desires to be heard? Colonel Barry?

Mr. Barry: In deference to the notice that has been taken of the mere suggestion on my part that, representing the Traffic Association, I desire to present a written statement of Mr. Leeds', in so far as he could make one, answering what has been testified to or suggested by way of argument to the committee before he departed. I say I simply made that suggestion, but apparently more heed was given to it than I expected, and more than was anticipated on the part of the Traffic Association—because the committee was apparently inconvenienced by my absence at the last meeting.

This has been a source of regret to me, because the committee has been very courteous not only to representatives of the Traffic Association, but to every one who has appeared before them, and I know the pressing duties of legislation weigh on you all the time, and you cannot devote all of this session to this one particular subject. I therefore desire to say to you that it was absolutely unavoidable on my part, and further that there was nothing to indicate at the previous meeting of the committee that the case would be closed at this time.

Now, I desire very briefly to say a few words myself after I shall present what is the real main object of my appearance before you, the communication written by Mr. Leeds prior to his departure for the East on business of even equal importance to the State of California as the consideration of this subject. It was by no means the result of faltering on the part of the Traffic Association or loss of confidence on the part of Mr. Leeds in this Legislature, or inability to comprehend the momentous question presented to you as the representatives of the State of California that caused him to depart in the midst of this discussion. But there are many sides to the methods of relieving the State of California from the oppression of the railroad corporations that have a monopoly.

There are many methods of relief, other than by abolishing this Railroad Commission, and establishing a maximum tariff, even on the lines of the Kansas or any other traffic lines. There are other methods of relief coming outside of competing railroads, even by the use of that great natural highway which God gave the State of California, and which if the Central Pacific Railroad did not prevent it, would have made us a happy, prosperous, and wealthy community. The establishing of a competing steamship line—the natural use of the water, which so long the Central Pacific Railroad Company has prevented the State of California from enjoying the benefit of—that was the subject in the judgment of the Traffic Association, and also the judgment of Mr. Leeds, their representative, the importance of which caused him to depart; and unless there should be any question about the absolute confidence of the Traffic Association in Mr. Leeds, and the absolute interest it feels in this measure and all measures that will give relief to the oppressed industries of California, I desire to present to the committee, with its permission, a duly attested resolution of the Traffic Association, expressing its confidence in Mr. Leeds, and indicating that in every respect he has carried out their wishes in this regard. I will not read it, because it has already appeared in the public press, Mr. Chairman, and therefore, I will hand it to the clerk.

[Mr. Barry here handed the resolutions referred to, to the clerk.]

Now, therefore, having expressed these preliminary observations, I desire to say that it is necessary to a proper understanding of this communication of Mr. Leeds, that from his enforced departure, not the fullest and amplest answer could be made to those suggestions daily made here since his absence. It will be obvious to the committee that his answer therefore can only go into those general principles and those general ideas, anticipatory to any special information that might be brought before the committee after his departure; and I say for him, as also is my own idea, that it was not necessary for a comprehension of this question to have the time of this committee taken up with this bill from roads that had a purely speculative interest in it—roads not directly affected by this tariff regulation at all, and who speak simply for the purpose of, and with the view of occupying the time of this committee and confusing this issue.

Nor is it necessary, Mr. Chairman and gentlemen of the committee, to a full understanding of the fact that something must be done for California, in the way of giving her reasonable railway facilities; it is not necessary to comprehend that the clamor of the people is not without cause, to become thoroughly conversant with railroad matters in every item and detail, as is the knowledge of those who have made it their lifetime study; it is not necessary for this committee, in the brief space of time allotted to it, to go outside the question presented in this constitutional amendment, and take up the time with matters that may be better understood and appreciated if the legislation outlined in this constitutional amendment ever comes before the people of the State of California. Much of it would be proper and necessary if the Legislature two years from now—the Railroad Commission having been abolished—should be confronted with the question of having to establish railroad rates of fares and freights by means of a schedule to be adopted and enforced. Therefore, with these preliminary remarks, I will read the communication, as follows:

Office of the Traffic Association of California,
San Francisco, February 4, 1893.

Hon. Guy C. Earl, *Chairman Committee on Constitutional Amendments, Sacramento, Cal.:*

Dear Sir: It has become necessary for me to go East on business which, in its nature, is imperative, and which will render it impossible for me to appear before your committee in person to further urge the merits of Senate Constitutional Amendment No. 8, introduced by Senator Gesford on January 11th, and now pending before your committee. I therefore beg that you grant me the privilege of submitting some of the points I would desire you to consider in writing. Before I enter upon the subject I want to mention a report which, it appears, has been given some currency (evidently by the opponents of the measure), to the effect that there is a difference of opinion between myself and the Executive Committee of the Traffic Association as to the methods adopted in our work, and with particular reference to this amendment, which is understood to be inspired by the said association. I desire to say that, so far as I am aware, there is not a dissenting member of the committee, and I assert here, that I am in full sympathy with the movement; and further, that there has never been a time since the organization of the association when the committee have been more unanimous than at this time. If there is a dissenter, the fact has not been developed in any of the deliberations of the committee. I therefore pronounce all such reports, from whatsoever source, as false in their entirety. I refer to this matter only because of the possible effect it might have upon your committee or the legislators who will be called upon to consider this amendment. With reference to the abandonment of the conflict (in the way of legislation) with the railroad monopoly of California by the Traffic Association or by myself, there is at this time no intention of such a course, as time will doubtless prove.

This amendment, as at present before your committee, contains virtually all of the principles which were set forth in the original draft;

the alterations in details have been arrived at after consideration with Senator Gesford and others, as defects were pointed out, and it would be strange if none were found in a measure affecting the whole transportation interest of the State. The amendment, as it now stands, is entirely practicable. I assure you that in the use of it the plan of a distance tariff, as a general basis, is no experiment. Outside of Central and Northern California the use of distance tariffs, made upon practically the same plan as the one submitted, is almost as universal as railroad transportation. I know of no other exception to the rule. It certainly possesses the merit of equity, in that the practice of discriminations between shippers and between places are less liable to occur, and are more difficult for the carrier to conceal; besides it insures at least a reasonable rate to all shippers, which it can be easily demonstrated is not true of California at this time. It enables a manufacturer to establish a business at any point without first going into partnership with the carrier. It also admits of the development of the resources of one point as well as another, even though the carrier may be an interested party, and under present conditions discriminating as between points and individuals.

The plan of introducing this tariff into the organic law of the State I admit is an innovation, and has been the source of some ridicule on the part of the opposition, but I desire to say that ridicule is not argument, and they have not been able to show that it is unconstitutional. The plan certainly possesses the merit of placing the carrier in the position of supplicants for legislation (instead of obstructionists), provided that changed conditions of a road under the operation of the law may show it to be necessary; my view of the measure being, that its operations upon a road earning over $4,000 per mile would be arbitrary only until the following term of the Legislature if by chance they in the meantime earned less. The fundamental principle being, that the Legislature shall fix the rates of charges of all roads in the State at all times. That the maximum rule shall apply only to roads which earn more than $4,000 per mile. That this tariff shall cease to be operative on all roads in the State as soon as the Legislature shall have performed the duty imposed upon them under the Constitution as amended. I hold further, that by the adoption of any tariff of uniform application to the roads of the State, at least as much time as the period at which this tariff could become effective, until the following Legislature would be necessary to develop the full effect of its operation upon the roads, and the commerce in the territory in which it is applied.

The plan of putting the Western Classification in effect in this State and making it practically a part of the organic law of the State, has been subject to some criticism, and some ridicule has been indulged in by some of the opponents, because reference is made to J. T. Ripley, Chairman. This, however, refers to the title only, and is to make the description of the document perfect and unmistakable. As to the merits of the classification, I will say the universal use of it in all of the States and Territories west of Chicago and the Mississippi River, California included, except the Southern Pacific Company's roads in the central and northern portions of the State, also that they use it on through traffic on all portions of their system of the road, ought to constitute a reasonable assurance that California could, with a reasonable degree of safety, accept it, in lieu of such documents as are at present in use, particularly as there is no reason why exceptions to it may not be made where it is found to be too high, and it is hardly probable that the people would suffer any material damage by reason of its being too low. There is also another reason why it should be adopted. You now have in effect in the State three classifications, the Western, and the two (so-called) local classifications of the Southern Pacific Company, all of them governed by widely different rules. The free business intercourse between different portions of the country require as uniform rules and classification as it is practicable to have (I refer to the local, or State traffic), and it is well known that it would only be practicable to adopt the Western, for universal application, if the convenience of the carriers is at all considered, as no one except the Southern Pacific Company would think of using the locals now in use by them; they have been the subject of criticism and ridicule in railroad circles for many years. Objection will be urged that the adoption of that classification for a period of two years, arbitrarily, and that the changes made by the Classification Committee will interfere with its use here unless such changes are adopted currently.

It must be borne in mind that those changes may apply, as now, on through traffic, and that there has never been any common rule or similarity between the classifications in effect in the State and those in use on through traffic; hence the grounds of such an objection cannot be well taken. As to necessary changes to meet the local requirements of the tradé in the State, it does not appear that the State Board of Railroad Commissioners have been especially industrious in their revisions of classification or the rules governing the same. I believe I would be borne out by the facts if I were to state that no Commission, since the organization of the Board some fourteen years ago, has ever revised a classification or actually made a tariff without the assistance or the guidance of the road which was to use it. All of the tariffs and classifications which I have examined since I came to the State bear pretty conclusive evidence in their general characteristics of such supervision. In general use the changes in classification in what may be called staples—such as agricultural products, staple groceries, machinery (such as is in common use), implements, hardware, and iron goods—have not been very frequent or very arbitrary. It is certain such technical objections are only raised for the purpose of obstructing progress on this amendment, especially when viewed in comparison with the past methods of California roads. There would be no great necessity to make classification changes within the period of the arbitrary application of this classification as provided.

The Western Classification is used over such an extended territory, that it covers about all conditions of commerce, there being about five thousand articles named in it, and it will be found that many of the changes are made to meet the requirements of manufacturers and would not materially affect this State, which for good reasons has made no very rapid strides in manufacturing. Some reference has been made to my recent advent in this State as a reason why I am not prepared to recommend a proper tariff for use in the traffic of California. I believe I had a fair knowledge of the general principles of tariffs and the rules which apply to the handling of traffic, before that period, and have made a pretty diligent study of the conditions and requirements here since then. I believe the recommendations which have been made by the introduction of this amendment are reasonable to the public and just to the carriers; it has been our purpose to present only such a proposition. I have been supplied with what purports to be a comparison of the proposed tariff and the existing tariff of the San Francisco and North Pacific Railroad. I have examined that tariff in the light of the annual report of that road, and find that the lowest class named in their alleged tariff would yield a higher rate per ton per mile than the earnings reported in their report to the State Board of Railroad Commissioners. They may have such a publication, but it is evident they do not use it in their business, hence the introduction of it as evidence before your committee is a deception and is insincere. No business which is at all dependent upon the item of transportation could exist under such a tariff as the one which is submitted by them.

The rate per ton per mile as reported by them as earned in the year 1891 is abnormally high, it being in the aggregate over four and a quarter cents per ton per mile; and it is not strange that there is not development enough along the road to justify a reduction below such a figure—a slight advance would naturally kill off that which must now exist under extreme difficulty.

I have been furnished with a comparative statement of replacement of cross ties which was presented before your committee. While the statement shows that the tie lasts at least two years longer in California, the comparison is an unfair one, and the party who presented it evidently selected the roads which he did for that reason. In the first place, I suppose, he informed your committee that the roads, except the San Francisco and North Pacific, belong to the same system. They run through large areas of the finest timber in the country; a great deal of it oak of the finest quality, and I presume nothing but white oak ties are used, and by reason of its location on the road and much of it more remote from market than some other white oak districts, ties are very cheap and of the very best quality to be had east of the Pacific Coast.

By taking time to digest the different arguments set up by the roads (if life were long enough to do so), they will either be found distorted, like their capitalization, or based on false premises, or upon purely technical grounds, introduced for no other purpose than delay, and to envelop the question in a cloud of mystery too indefinite to be clearly comprehended by any one except by those whose trade it is to obstruct legislation, that they may continue to oppress the people. It is good evidence of the utter insincerity of these roads to look back upon the history of the past, with reference to all of their dealings with the public in every department of their organization.

It ought to be enough to know, if their own figures are taken as a guide, their earnings are nearly double those of other roads in the country which meet their obligations; and further, that their own figures show they consume from ten to twenty per cent less of their gross earnings in the operation of the property, and their net earnings within California are largely in excess of other States on their own properties, and largely in excess of other roads. It has been repeatedly shown in evidence in the Courts and elsewhere, that the roads of the Southern Pacific Company were bonded largely in excess of the whole cost of the property and equipment—that not only did the capital stock represent no tangible investment, but as a matter of fact the promoters put into their own pockets a large profit upon the building of the roads, but still retain possession of them, and have the hardihood to set up the claim that they should have a profit from the operation of the property in which they have not now—nor did they ever have—a dollar of actual investment.

I hope your committee will look at results, and not at the technical methods introduced in order to conceal the actual state of facts. You are called upon to pay a rate of transportation which will yield an income on a funded debt, aggregating $41,305 per mile, and pay a dividend on a capital stock of $47,255 per mile, on roads which in actual outlay did not originally cost more than one third the amount—if honestly constructed—and which can be duplicated to-day, and fully equipped ready for traffic, for a much less figure. And this is not all—you are asked to contribute to the support of their poor relations, the non-paying property in the outlying States and Territories; and then, I understand, their attorney, Mr. Martin, has suggested the propriety of a profit from the operation of the property, the expenses of which are paid out of current receipts, and in which the Southern Pacific Company have not one dollar of invested money.

Possibly if it were found that it were not proper for them to put on a percentage or commission for the operation of the roads, there might be a compensating factor in the profits of the Pacific Improvement Company, the nominal assets of which have been reported to be $200,000,000 or more. I hope your committee will not allow your minds to be diverted from these governing facts by the small technical objections raised, as they are simply subterfuges. It makes no difference as to the details of how the operating expenses are made up, whether an item costs $1 or $2, so long as the aggregate proves that the premises upon which they argue are false.

Consider the burden, if you please, which they seek to lay upon this State, at least two thirds of which is unjust, and represents absolutely nothing which was ever invested, and then turn, if you please, to the lately completed road of the Great Northern Company, which is said to have a funded debt obligation of twenty-four thousand dollars per mile, and it will be apparent that this State is expected to assume a burden of more than a thousand dollars per mile of road annually more than will be necessary to meet the obligation of the Great Northern Company, and consider what are the prospects for immigration to California as against Washington and Oregon. Lack of time prevents a further argument by me of this question, except to say that the basis of four thousand dollars per mile is a very liberal allowance as exemption from the application of the proposed tariff. A majority of the small independent lines of the whole country it will be found earn less than that amount, and yet meet their obligations, while many of them have a surplus afterward, being conclusive evidence that the whole argument against the four thousand dollar limit is based on false premises. I would further state that in none of the States, so far as I am aware of now, where rates are fixed by law, is any exception made in favor of the local roads, while in almost all cases conditions of competition, either between carriers or upon commodities, renders it necessary for them to compete with the larger systems of road. I submit reference to a few of the smaller roads, hurriedly selected, and without any effort to secure those which favor the argument I desire to set up. They are as follows:

Louisville, Evansville, and St. Louis, 359 miles; gross earnings, $3,975 36 per mile; operating expenses, 64.38 per cent.

Louisville, New Albany, and Corydon, 12.5 miles; gross earnings, $1,244 per mile; operating expenses, 65 per cent.

Chicago and Fort Madison, 45 miles; gross earnings, $556 70 per mile; operating expenses, 80 per cent.

Chicago, Iowa, and Dakota, 26½ miles; gross earnings, $1,577 per mile; operating expenses, 90 per cent.

Chicago, Kansas City, and Texas, 20 miles; gross earnings, $1,343 per mile; operating expenses, 85 per cent.

Cincinnati, Georgetown, and Portsmouth, 42 miles; gross earnings, $1,645 80 per mile; operating expenses, 80 per cent. Paid interest on bonds and had $36 19 balance.

Cleveland and Marietta Railroad, 104 miles; gross earnings, $3,430 57 per mile; operating expenses, 71.11 per cent. Paid all obligations, interest on bonds, and had surplus $42,623 02.

Such examples can be produced without limit, where the business is done on a legitimate basis and with a view to development of the resources of the country served by them.

Notwithstanding technical objections raised by those opposed to this measure, as to the practicability of the scheme, I will say the plan, so far as the tariff goes, is nominally the same as is in general use in the territory where there is much less discrimination than is practiced here in California, and with a disposition on the part of the carriers to put in effect an intelligible system of tariff, the plan will work admirably.

There has been no argument advanced by the carrier up to this time which shows any sincere desire on his part to treat this question equitably, nor can any be produced which will show that the present basis is equitable, nor can any be produced, because equity is not one of the elements which enter into the present plan upon which the transportation business is conducted in this State. Time forbids an argument of the case of the Commission. I will only say they have failed utterly in the performance of their obligation in every particular as provided by the law. So far as can be discovered they have done absolutely nothing which has amounted to anything, which has not been submitted to them for ratification by the carriers. The system is certainly wrong which admits of a possibility of such dereliction of duty by any servant of the people.

Very respectfully,

J. S. LEEDS.

CAPITALIZATION PACIFIC SYSTEM,

Exclusive of the Oregon lines; also excluding the United States Government obligations of the Central Pacific.

SOUTHERN PACIFIC OF CALIFORNIA, 1,474.54 miles.

Funded debt (bonds)	$47,375,000 00, or	$32,128 67	per mile.
Capital stock	65,135,300 00, or	44,173 30	per mile.
Total	$112,510,300 00, or	$76,301 97	per mile.

CALIFORNIA PACIFIC, 115.44 miles.

Bonds	$6,825,500 00, or	$59,126 00	per mile.
Capital stock	12,000,000 00, or	103,950 00	per mile.
Total	$18,825,500 00, or	$163,076 00	per mile.

NORTHERN RAILROAD OF CALIFORNIA, 390.38 miles

Bonds	$9,919,000 00, or	$25,408 00	per mile.
Capital stock	12,896,000 00, or	33,026 00	per mile.
Total	$22,815,000 00, or	$58,434 00	per mile.

SOUTH PACIFIC COAST, 104 miles.

Bonds	$5,500,000 00, or	$52,884 00 per mile.
Capital stock	6,000,000 00, or	57,692 00 per mile.
Total	$11,500,000 00, or	$110,576 00 per mile.

NORTHERN CALIFORNIA RAILROAD, 53.6 miles.

Bonds	$945,000 00, or	$17,600 00 per mile.
Capital stock	1,280,000 00, or	23,835 00 per mile.
Total	$2,225,000 00, or	$41,433 00 per mile.

CENTRAL PACIFIC (Exclusive of Government obligation), 1,360.26 miles.

Bonds	$73,930,000 00, or	$54,349 00 per mile.
Capital stock	68,000,000 00, or	50,000 00 per mile.
Total	$141,930,000 00, or	$104,349 00 per mile.

SOUTHERN PACIFIC OF ARIZONA, 388.10 miles.

Bonds	$10,000,000 00, or	$25,773 20 per mile.
Capital stock	19,995,000 00, or	51,533 50 per mile.
Total	$29,995,000 00, or	$77,306 70 per mile.

SOUTHERN PACIFIC OF NEW MEXICO, 171.06 miles.

Bonds	$4,180,000 00, or	$24,444 00 per mile.
Capital stock	6,888,800 00, or	40,285 00 per mile.
Total	$11,068,800 00, or	$64,729 00 per mile.

TOTAL CAPITALIZATION (Exclusive of Oregon, Arizona, and New Mexico), 3,498.24 miles.

Bonds	$144,494,500 00, or	$41,305 00 per mile.
Capital stock	165,311,300 00, or	47,255 50 per mile.
Total	$309,805,800 00, or	$88,560 50 per mile.

SAME EXCLUDING CENTRAL PACIFIC, 2,138 miles (all California).

Bonds	$70,564,500 00, or	$33,005 00 per mile.
Capital stock	97,311,300 00, or	45,515 00 per mile.
Total	$167,875,800 00, or	$78,520 00 per mile.

NEW MEXICO AND ARIZONA COMBINED, 559.16 miles.

Bonds	$14,180,000 00, or	$25,366 72 per mile.
Capital stock	26,888,800 00, or	48,092 68 per mile.
Total	$41,068,800 00, or	$73,459 40 per mile.

Southern Pacific of California—earnings, $9,279,822 50 ($6,611 54 per mile); net, $3,851,547 85; operating expenses, 58.50 per cent.

California Pacific—earnings, $1,528,747 72 ($13,242 79 per mile); net, $759,525 09; operating expenses, 50.31 per cent.

Northern Railway of California—earnings, $2,914,444 34 ($7,465 66 per mile); net, $1,375,131 31; operating expenses, 52.82 per cent.

South Pacific Coast—earnings, $1,107,772 87 ($10,651 66 per mile); net, $393,807 54; operating expenses, 64.45 per cent.

Northern California Railway—earnings, $95,824 26 ($1,787 68 per mile); net, $8,333 49; operating expenses, 91.30 per cent.

Central Pacific—earnings, $16,629,104 36 ($12,244 76 per mile); net, $7,407,354 90; operating expenses, 55.40 per cent.

Southern Pacific of Arizona and New Mexico—earnings, $3,077,947 58 ($5,506 16 per mile); net, $1,023,322 84; operating expenses, 66.75 per cent.

Oregon Roads—earnings, $2,302,650 24 ($3,502 87 per mile); net, $390,118 80; operating expenses, 83.06 per cent.

Pacific System, except Oregon, Arizona, and New Mexico—3,498.24 miles.
Southern Pacific of California
California Pacific.
South Pacific Coast.

Northern Railway of California—earnings, $31,555,716 05 ($9,020 45 per mile); net, $13,805,700 18; operating expenses, 56.25 per cent.
Northern California.
Central Pacific.
Same, excluding Central Pacific—2,138 miles.
Southern Pacific of California.
California Pacific.
South Pacific Coast—earnings, $14,926,611 09 ($6,981 57 per mile); net, $6,388,345 28; operating expenses, 57.20 per cent.
Northern Railway of California.
Northern California.
Whole Pacific System—earnings, $37,010,078 16 ($7,856 10 per mile); net, $15,201,282 94; operating expenses, 59 per cent.
Atlantic and Pacific System, 6,375.53 miles—earnings, $50,449,815 88 ($7,913 07 per mile); net, $19,286,203 94; operating expenses, 61.77 per cent.
Comparison: Atchison, Topeka, and Santa Fe Railroad Co., 7,124 miles—earnings, $36,438,188 97 ($5,114 57 per mile); net operating expenses, $11,227,255 15; 69.19 per cent. Missouri Pacific Co.—($4,965 81 per mile); operating expenses, 70.96 per cent.

Rate per Ton per Mile.

Southern Pacific Company, Pacific System, through freight .. 1.119 cents per ton per mile.
Southern Pacific Company, Pacific System, local freight ..... 2.699 cents per ton per mile.
Southern Pacific Company, Pacific System, all freight .... 1.835 cents per ton per mile.
Local 226.6 per cent of through or more than two and a quarter times as much.
Atchison, Topeka and Santa Fe System, all freight .... 1.219 cents per ton per mile.
Atchison, Topeka and Santa Fe System, difference .... .616
Missouri Pacific System, all freight .... 1,024 cents per ton per mile.
Missouri Pacific System, difference .... .811

Engine Statistics.

Miles run per ton of coal, Southern Pacific Company ...... 29.74 miles; cost per ton, $5.79
Miles run per ton of coal, Atchison, Topeka and Santa Fe. 26.12 miles; cost per ton, 2.11
Miles run per ton of coal, Missouri Pacific .... 25.43 miles; cost per ton, 1.35
Tons of freight carried per train, Southern Pacific Company .... 124.63 tons.
Tons of freight carried per train, Atchison, Topeka, and Santa Fe .... 118.84 tons.
Tons of freight carried per train, Missouri Pacific .... 161.18 tons.
Pounds of coal used by road per mile run by locomotive, Southern Pacific Co..... 56 lbs.
Pounds of coal used by road per mile run by locomotive, Atchison, Topeka, and Santa Fe .... 108 lbs.
Pounds of coal used by road per mile run by locomotive, Missouri Pacific .... 83 lbs.
Gross cost of coal to Southern Pacific Co...$3,300,800 58, or 8.9 per cent of gross earnings.
Gross cost of coal to A., T. & S. F. .... 2,858,402 24, or 7.8 per cent of gross earnings.
Percentage of empty to loaded cars moved, Southern Pacific Company..... 24.79 per cent.
Percentage of empty to loaded cars moved, Atchison, Topeka & Santa Fe. 28.32 per cent.

Passenger Rates.

Southern Pacific Company, exclusive of ferry and suburban, per mile .... 2.50 cents.
Atchison, Topeka, and Santa Fe, exclusive of ferry and suburban, per mile.. 2.39 cents.
Distance traveled, Atchison, Topeka, and Santa Fe .... 65.91 miles.
Distance traveled, Southern Pacific Company .... 68.2 miles.
Average receipts per passenger, Southern Pacific Company $1 704
Average receipts per passenger, Atchison, Topeka, and Santa Fe 1 57

Southern Pacific Company, ferry and suburban number of passengers carried in one year, 11,845,443—earnings, $1,121,763 45. Average distance traveled by each passenger, 9.6 miles; average receipts for each, 9.47 cents.

Local passengers, Southern Pacific Company, pay 2.73 cents per mile, excluding ferry, suburban, and through.

Interest paid on funded debt, Southern Pacific Company, Pacific System, $8,675,587 42; funded debt, $144,494,500, or $41,305 per mile of road.

Now, Mr. Chairman, there was a document prepared by Mr. Leeds summarizing and placing in condensed form the figures which he used in his opening statement to the committee, and which has been filed with your Secretary, but I have a separate copy here, and if the members of the committee care to have it, outside of the Secretary, I shall be happy to afford it to you.

Mr. Earl: When was that filed?

Mr. Barry: It was some time before Mr. Leeds' departure for the East. Mr. Kavanagh received it, I think, and lest it may be mislaid,

I take the liberty of replacing it. The items, the figures, the facts, are summarized by Mr. Leeds, if I may direct the attention of the committee to it, as to the funded debt and capital stock of the various branches of the Southern Pacific system, and showing the capitalization. Your committee remembers the figures that were read before you, and their intent, for instance:

The Southern Pacific of California, distance 1,474.54 miles, has a funded debt of $32,128 67 per mile, and has a capital stock of $44,173 30.

Now, the California Pacific, with 115.44 miles, has bonds (not reading the aggregate, but simply the amounts per mile) of $59,126 per mile, and a capital stock to the extent of $103,950 per mile, making a total capitalization for each mile of that road of $163,076.

The Northern Railroad of California, 390.38 miles, has capitalization of $54,434 per mile.

The South Pacific Coast, which was obtained from Senator Fair, has now, under the administration of the Southern Pacific Company, a capitalization of $110,576 per mile. It is hardly necessary to say that Senator Fair never received any price like that per mile for his road.

The Northern California Railroad is capitalized at $41,433 per mile.

The Central Pacific, exclusive of the Government obligations, of the mortgages of the Government, should the necessity arise of paying back some of its indebtedness to the Government, has a capitalization of $104,349 per mile.

The Southern Pacific of Arizona, 388.10 miles, has $77,306 77 capitalization.

The Southern Pacific of New Mexico, 171.06 miles, has a capitalization of $64,729 per mile.

A total capitalization, exclusive of Oregon, New Mexico, and Arizona, and covering a distance on this system of 3,498 miles, and which is the one we so often refer to, has $88,560 50 per mile for this system of roads.

Excluding the Central Pacific, the capitalization would be $78,520 per mile.

New Mexico and Arizona combined, with a distance of 559.16 miles, has a capitalization of $73,459 40.

The earnings, briefly, are as follows:

The Southern Pacific of California earns nine millions and over, which is an aggregate—which is an average per mile of $6,611, as gross earnings. Its net earnings for the whole distance are $3,851,547, and its operating expenses are ——

(These figures are not correct—they are manifestly incorrect—the copyist has evidently made a mistake; it reads 85 per cent. It is probably 58.85 per cent.)

The California Pacific has earnings of $1,528,747; gross earnings per mile, $13,222 79, and has operating expenses of 50.31 per cent. The operating expenses of the Southern Pacific of California are 58.50 per cent.

Northern Railway of California has gross earnings of $7,465 66 per mile, and has net earnings of $1,375,131, and operating expenses, 52.82 per cent.

The South Pacific Coast had gross earnings per mile of $10,651 60; has $393,807 54 net earnings; and has 64.45 per cent as operating expenses.

The Northern California Railway earns $1,787 68 gross per mile; it has net earnings on the whole road of $8,333 49, and its operating expenses 91.31, per cent.

The Central Pacific has gross earnings per mile, $12,644 76; has operating expenses, 55.40 per cent, and has net earnings, $7,107,354 90.

The Southern Pacific of Arizona has $5,506 gross earnings per mile; has net earnings, $1,023,322 64; operating expenses, 66.75 per cent.

The Oregon roads have $3,502 87 gross earnings per mile, and have net earnings of $390,118, and operating expenses of 83 per cent; which clearly establish, Mr. Chairman, the fact that the Southern Pacific roads operating within California are actually supporting and contributing to the revenue of the Southern Pacific of Arizona and New Mexico and the Oregon roads, and the people of California are paying for the burden and responsibility of railroad development in those two neighboring States.

Earl: Colonel Barry, in reading that, you say the Oregon roads, for instance, the earnings are so much, and the rate per mile so much, and you say the net earnings are so much. What do you mean by net earnings? A. Net earnings on the whole road, Mr. Chairman. The difference between the operating expenses and the gross earnings is the net earnings. We have not given the operating expenses in amount; we have simply given the percentages. The difference between the operating expenses and the gross earnings would give the net earnings; in other words, if you choose to take that last figure there, 83 per cent, being the operating expenses, the total gross earnings being $2,302,650 24, 17 per cent, which would be the remainder, is the net earnings, you see, would be just about equal to $390,118, which is the net earnings.

Earl: That would not be paying the fixed charges? A. No; well, it is paying the fixed charges, all except the interest on the debt.

Q. Paying taxes and other expenses, that are not included in operating expenses? A. No, sir; not taxes.

Burke: They do not put in taxes, because they do not pay them, is not that it? A. No; yes, that is the reason, I suppose, Mr. Burke. That is my impression; you merely suggested it, and I suppose it is correct. That is Mr. Burke's suggestion.

Now, the Pacific System of California, I mean the Southern Pacific system, excepting Arizona, Oregon, and New Mexico, has a total mileage of 3,498.24 miles; consisting of the Southern Pacific of California, the California Pacific, the South Pacific Coast, and the Northern Railway of California; and its gross earnings are $31,555,716 05; and its gross earnings per mile are $9.020 45; and the net earnings for that combination are $13,805,700; and the operating expenses are 56 per cent of the gross earnings.

Excluding the Central Pacific, with its distance of 2,138 miles, the remaining roads, the California Pacific, the South Pacific Coast, the Northern Railway of California, and the Northern California, earned $14,926,611 69, with an average of $69,181 77 per mile; and the net earnings are $6,388,345 28, with operating expenses of 57 per cent of the gross earnings.

The whole Pacific System, then, has a gross earnings of $37,000.000 and over, with gross earnings per mile of $7,800 and over; and with net earnings of $15,000,000 and over; and operating expenses of 59 per cent.

The Atlantic and Pacific System, within the same jurisdiction, under the same conditions—that is to say, taking the total mileage of 6,375.53 miles—has a gross earnings of $50,449,815 88; and its earnings are $7,913 07 per mile; and it has a net earnings of $19,286,203 91; and its operating expenses are 61.77 per cent.

The Atchison and Santa Fe—that is the Atchison, Topeka, and Santa Fe Railroad—with a distance of 7,124 miles, has earnings of $36,438,188 97, and its earnings per mile was $5,114 57, being over $2,000 less than the whole Pacific System, and its net earnings are $11,227,255 15; so that the gross earnings only—less than a million less than the whole Pacific System—in fact of only half a million, the difference in favor of gross earnings for the whole Pacific System being half a million over the Atchison, Topeka, and Santa Fe, the Central Pacific has the benefit and advantage on net earnings of $4,000,000.

The Missouri Pacific Company has an average earnings—of gross earnings—of $4,965 81, and its operating expenses are 70 per cent and over.

There is more, following up this, Mr. Chairman. I will not take the time of the committee further, as it is possible for you to follow out and look over at your leisure. There is here a showing that on rates per mile, on engine statistics, tons of freight carried per train, pounds of coal, gross cost for coal, etc., percentage of empty to loaded cars, passenger rates, and all of those matters that are necessary and proper elements in determining the question, that if anything, the advantage in all these matters is in favor of the Southern Pacific system as against similar roads in the East.

Earl: Colonel Barry, from what source did you get these figures? A. They were taken from Poor's Manual.

Q. Well, the Missouri Pacific, you say, is $4,965 81; is that it? A. Yes, sir. That is from Poor's Manual, also. Poor's Manual, I may explain, Mr. Chairman, contains full details and statements, received everywhere as correct on the part of all railroads with reference to all these matters. Now, Mr. Chairman, this discussion that has been going on before the committee for some time, in the main is wholly foreign to the principal object of this constitutional amendment now before the committee; and what is really the proper subject for discussion, as of most importance to determine any action on the part of this committee. I shall endeavor to show you, Mr. Chairman and gentlemen of the committee, that the establishment of a tariff rate in the interim between the adoption of this constitutional amendment and the action of the Legislature was merely an instance to this legislation, and not its main character. A moment's reflection will enable you, gentlemen of the committee, to understand why the force and strength of the opposition has been placed upon the incident and not upon the principle of it. The principal object of this constitutional amendment, Mr. Chairman, is to get rid of the Railroad Commission of the State of California. Get rid of it, because it is not fit to be imposed upon the people of this State, or even permitted to hold office and receive salary from the State; and in every clause of this measure—in its central character, as originally constructed—the Constitution of the State of California in this particular was monstrous and absolutely destitute of good sense, and without any support in any other State in the Union.

It was in line, Mr. Chairman, if I may be permitted briefly to go over some facts which we forgot, that all the railroads in the State of California had ever done in connection with this subject, from the time when the growing roads, from 1862 on, gradually extended themselves over the State, that all legislation which we have ever had on the statute books of the State of California was a law passed in 1861 that there should be made a report to the Secretary of State in reference to certain matters by railroad corporations, and that was all that it was necessary for them to do. That was about the only provision that the laws of the State of California carried up to the time that the first transportation committee was established here, up to the time that by the Act of 187—I will ask your indulgence for a minute, Mr. Chairman. Mr. Chairman, in the Act of May 20, 1861, to be found in the Statutes of 1861, page 601, were the only provisions in reference to a railway system in this State that at all pretended to make any provision for the people for the regulation of railway freights and fares; and that was, they made an annual report to the Secretary of State, which none of them ever complied with or paid any attention to, and next or subsequent section or paragraph, the maximum, which so far as prevailed in the State of California, ten cents per mile for passengers and fifteen cents per ton for freight, was established; and notwithstanding the efforts of the people, as shown in the Archer bill, and the Freeman bill, and other bills of that character, it was not until the third day of April, 1876, after fourteen years of struggle, that the railroad company gave us one of its Dead Sea apples, one of the effects of continuous and ——— legislation, which is so often now extended to the people of the State of California, since it gave us a Board of three Railroad Commissioners, that were to last for two years; these Railroad Commissioners were men of the very highest character, and I say it without fear of contradiction, the best Railroad Commission the State of California has ever had, consisting of John T. Doyle, Isaac W. Smith, and Governor and General Stoneman.

The Commission entered upon its duty; it served notice upon the railroad that it desired certain information the Act called for. This Act, Mr. Chairman, was modeled upon most modern ideas of the great States that had been successful in their contests with railroads. It avoided the extreme form which has often been called the Western or violent idea, which prevailed in Iowa and Illinois for awhile, and it was formed upon the more lenient, more genial and kindly method of Massachusetts, and those other States that relied upon public sentiment and public opinion, and achieved results of the proper character; appealing to the sentiment of decency, if any there existed in railroad corporations; appealing to the sense of justice, if any one could ever cause it to arise; and gentlemen, what did they do?

They refused to comply with the request of the Commission; they denied their authority, and when taken into Court and it was determined by the Judge of the Third District Court that a mandamus would apply against them, and they would be compelled to comply with this statute, they went to the Supreme Court of the State and the appeal was pending in the Supreme Court of the State when the so-called Grangers decision, in the Supreme Court, was the handwriting on the wall to these people, and then, to this extent, they complied with the requirements of the Commission; complied in words, but not in acts; promised to send reports, reports which for some extraordinary reason never materialized; and when that Commission was abolished two years afterwards by the succeeding Legislature, that appeal was still pending, and they were still defiant of the authority of the Railroad Commission.

When these Commissioners came to the Legislature and made their report, that Legislature refused to give them any assistance, and that was the Legislature which, in derision of the people, repealed this Board of Transportation Commission because their personnel was unsatisfactory, and substituted another and single Commissioner with nearly all the powers, although some extension was made; and, at the same time, in 1878, in April, they passed that amendment to the law, wiped out that Commission, and gave a new Commission, consisting of a single Commissioner of Transportation. They also adopted a call for a Constitutional Convention to come together the same year, which Constitutional Convention, carrying out certainly the hopes, if not the wishes, of the Southern Pacific Company, and the Central Pacific Railroad Company, formed a method of reaching and controlling these roads that had been repudiated through the Union, appointed an irresponsible Commission that was above the law, and that against the protests and rights of the people. They thus having made this creature, they pretended to fear they would be rent and torn by this Frankenstein, this bogie, this monster; they thus pulled, and puffed flame and fire through him to scare the people of the State apparently, and thus stood aghast at their own oppression.

Since that time, gentlemen that have come here, and during the whole of this discussion, they have not told you once there is no such Commission as that in existence in the United States, and there was not then at that time among all the other States of the Union, and there are many of them that have Railroad Commissions, and had then. I call your attention to the fact, Mr. Chairman, that in the report of this very Railroad Commissioner, B. F. Tuttle, as Transportation Commissioner appointed under the Act of 1878, in his first report to them, to the Legislature and to the people of the State, he called attention to the fact that out of seventeen States in the Union that at that time had Railroad Commissions, there was but one State, and that was Illinois, that gave the absolute right of fixing rates for freights and fares absolutely. That the States either as a class resorted to the Courts for the method of enforcing the decrees of the Commissions, or that they relied on public sentiment and appealed to the common sense of the railroads and to the great force of public opinion that would stand by the right and truth if the people maintained it. And now, gentlemen, it was under these auspices and these circumstances that this Railroad Commission of ours was ingrafted on our Constitution, fixed there in all its enormity, so that we have to come when we desire to get rid of it to appeal to the Legislature and obtain against this powerful influence in legislation, feared by every one who has tried to stand up against it; we have to appeal against the insidious methods of this Commission to get two thirds of your votes for the proper privilege of going and asking the people of California whether they are dissatisfied with this organic law wrung from them by fraud and imposition. Why, gentlemen, what could be expected from a measure that was originated in that way? What could we expect from a constitutional provision of that character, inflexible, indurated into the Constitution and requiring so much labor to get rid of it?

How could we expect to prosper alongside of those other States that in wisdom had created their Commissions by legislative Act, so that the same hand that created them could also destroy them, and as the people felt the necessity for amendment and change, extension or repression, for giving ampler authority to the Commission or relying more on the Courts than simply the blind fiat of a few men, there was still power on the part of the Legislature to accomplish something? But here, with us, that Legislature has been tied hand and foot, and we have nothing upon our statute books, when the whole series of the States in the Union have most beneficent and wise provisions in reference to legislative control; provisions that enable the people to have depots when insufficient accommodations are given to them; provisions that compel the roads to make proper crossings, to keep their tracks in proper repair, to continue the roads in operation after they acquire them, rather than buy them solely to destroy them; to make proper bridges, and in a thousand ways, even to the very extent of compelling them to carry hatchets in case of fire, and other paraphernalia and implements of use, so that they may be provided with some means at least to secure the safety of those who travel. In the most minute details, the most practical legislation in the States of the Union, with the exception of California, and even in the civilized world, they are certainly liberal and appreciated both by the railroads and the people.

SEAWELL: Excuse me in bothering you, now don't you think that it is a pretty good reason for keeping this Constitution? A. Yes, sir; but I think we ought to abolish the Railroad Commission. I am talking about abolishing the Commission, and that is the real subject at stake here and of equal importance for you gentlemen in taking up matters concerning the progress of California, for the fact remains that this Railroad Commission is against the progress of California. Restore the power to the Legislature to do something.

EARL: Your idea is if the clauses of the Constitution were abrogated as to the Railroad Commission and its powers, that the Legislature could then by legislative enactment, if this amendment were carried, provide for a Commission here as in Eastern States? A. Yes; that is about it.

Q. But it reads: "The Legislature shall have the power and it shall be its duty to establish rates of charges for the transportation of passengers and freight by all railroads operated in the State, and to enact such laws as may be necessary for the enforcement and carrying into effect such rates." It says, it shall be its duty. I don't see how they could delegate the power to any one else. A. I would like to call your attention, Mr. Chairman, to the fact that the subject was very fully discussed before the Transportation Commission, consisting of all these Boards of Railroad Commissions of the Union.

SEAWELL: We don't want to break into your argument or idea. A. Well, I just wanted to answer Mr. Earl's question, because it is much better now. After the meeting of the various members of the State Commissions with the Interstate Commerce Commission last year, and a very lively discussion, by a vote of 24 to 7—and these men are perhaps the best informed on this subject in the United States—the various Railroad Commissions and the Interstate Commerce Commission—it was adopted as an expression of sentiment on their part that it is within the power of Congress and the State Legislatures to delegate the power of reasonable regulation to Boards of Commissions; and whether they are——

EARL: That was not exactly the point. By the decision of the Dougherty case, as laid down in this State, when the Constitution says the Legislature must do a thing it must do it. It cannot delegate to any Commission, or Board of Supervisors, or anybody else——

A. That is not my impression in relation to a Commission fixing freights. In the report to the Legislature of the original Transportation Commissioners, such legislation is suggested as the Legislature can act upon afterwards. It would not be necessary in case the committee did not see fit to directly authorize the Legislature. If the committee should not be of the opinion that it would be wise for the Legislature to endeavor to fix rates, it would not be necessary for the investigation to take place in the Legislature; but a Commission could be appointed to gather facts and statistics and make a recommendation, just as do the Commissions in Massachusetts and Michigan. They have no power to make rates; nor in New York; or lower rates. It can hear complaints and refer them to Courts, and make recommendations to the Legislature. Nearly all legislation in Massachusetts since 1884 has been made in consonance with and in direct execution of the suggestions made by the Railroad Commissions from time to time, as to proper amendments in the law; but I will come to that again, Mr. Chairman, if you will indulge me one moment.

Therefore, I say, Mr. Chairman, it is not at all singular that the real object of this bill, in its great relations to the people, has been entirely obscured in this discussion and this position of Mr. Johnson, who laid out in his argument and stated that he did not believe there was any general public demand for the removal of the Railroad Commission, or the change of this law, and who, in some manner, which I cannot understand the force of, ridiculed and commenced to talk about legislation of a private character as opposed to general legislation and general laws; that we should not change our Constitution in this regard, because, in some way, it would be making a special case of it, and the people would be going back of the general proposition.

Now, Mr. Chairman, this constitutional provision provides first in reference to the Railroad Commission, and no one supported the idea that the people, after fourteen years of bondage, do not wish to do away with this Commission. For fourteen years we had something different from anybody else, and having derived no benefit from it, it is about time that we provide a Commission more in accordance with the wisdom expressed by those in other States. Therefore, I say, Mr. Chairman, I trust and believe, that after the knowledge you have of what the State of California demands—now, I do not mean any senseless clamor, any talk on the street corners, nor voicing any expressions in the journals, except in so far as they may embody and typify the patriotism and intelligence, hopes, and aspirations of California. It is not to those things I allude.

Now, I say you recognize the demands of California; you recognize that she, unprogressive, loitering behind in the march of progress on this western shore, notwithstanding her enormous advantages, her wealth, her grandeur, that in forty years she has grown so little, and Washington, and the Dakotas, and all those other States are leaving her in the lurch; that is the situation, gentlemen, and that is the demand I hope you will listen to; and looking across this State of ours, give to the people the first section of this law. Repeal these two provisions that provide for that Railroad Commission. I trust that the sentiment of the committee will be unanimous on that point.

Now, Mr. Chairman, next after that—I am taking the bill—it was thought wise, Mr. Chairman, that the Legislature, as in many States of the Union, should fix a maximum rate of tariff. As a matter of fact, nearly all the States of the Union, either through their Courts—that have Commissions—either through their Courts or the Legislature, do carry out what we have laid down here as the duty of the Legislature. There are, Mr. Chairman, nineteen States and Territories of the Union that in 1891 had no Commission; of those, two, I may say in passing—that of those nineteen, two, Delaware and Florida, after having Commissions in use, had abolished them by legislative enactment. Texas, which passed a constitutional amendment in 1891, which, Mr. Chairman, is in some respects similar to what has been suggested here in this committee —and which, in fact, in some respects, was modeled after it—passed in 1890 the following provision to its Constitution:

"Article II: Railroads heretofore constructed or which may hereafter be constructed in this State, are hereby declared public highways, and railroad companies, common carriers. The Legislature shall pass laws to regulate railroad freights governing railroad business to prevent unjust discrimination and extortion."

Although that is a constitutional provision of Texas, Texas has not as yet seen fit to adopt the Railroad Commission, and it manages to make the railroads behave themselves in that State with the authority of the Legislature. Now, of the States that have Railroad Commissions, twenty-eight in number, twenty of them in one form or another, actually fix the rates—either maximum, as in some of the States, like Illinois or Iowa, or absolutely, as in many of the States—and ten of those States of the twenty, in one form or another, legislate through their Commissions and prescribe rates for their railroad organizations; ten of those States make those rules and regulations subject to ratification by the Courts.

Martin: Did I understand you to say that Texas had no Railroad Commission? A. Not as I find shown in 1891; it may be so now. I was unable to find in the library here, any publication for 1892, and I had to rely on that last authority I could get, I had to take that for 1891; it may have been since; it may have been appointed since that time, Mr. Martin.

In these ten States where they fix the rates of charge, and absolutely impose them on the corporations, they all express in the statute that they are subject to examination of the Courts, and practically since the decision in the Minnesota case, I presume it will be understood that all rates of freights and fares as established by Commissions, whether so expressed in the organic Act or not, would be subject to examination by the Courts, if the charge were made that they were not reasonable rates, or whether through passion or prejudice. Now, then, Mr. Chairman, it being deemed wise to restore to California a position similar to that of certainly twenty-nine States in the Union, to operate through our Legislature in its channels, it was found that there would be an interim in this redress offered to the people through the constitutional amendment, for about two years, which could not be filled in except by calling a special session of the Legislature.

If the constitutional amendment, which, I say, is in substance the contention of the Traffic Association here, which is most important, and which the interest of California demands, should it, at a special election, be adopted, coming in a few months from now—coming through the people—there would be until the next session of the Legislature, in 1895, the absolute maintenance and continuance of the present system, from which the people are suffering. Therefore, you can appreciate, Mr. Chairman, this State, which, after much discussion, it became necessary in some manner to provide some method of extending redress to the people; and, therefore, as I say, this maximum tariff—this tariff of the Western Traffic Association—is the understanding in this constitutional amendment. And if I have any force or any ability of expression, I desire to urge on this Commission that all discussion of this tariff, and all the facts and figures appearing here, have certainly had the appearance of avoiding the main controversy by the railroad company, which is: First, shall you abolish the Railroad Commission, as fixed by the Constitution, and, secondly, shall we give to the Legislature the right to fix freights and fares? And then, in order that the people shall not be detained and kept away from this benefit, we have, we believe, provided a just and proper method.

Now, Mr. Chairman and gentlemen, I presume—and I shall not indulge in very much discussion of it—from the objections which have been urged to this measure, which is simply temporary, and your committee will understand a mere incident to the legislation promised the people, because even if the Railroad Commission were impeached and the Legislature authorized to take this subject under its control, the omission of any further action on the part of the Legislature would, I think, in view of the great boon that they had conferred on them in doing so much, would not be viewed in any censorious spirit; but, if in addition to this great boon, the people could get the great benefit of it, then whatever stricture and whatever ridicule may be put forth to drive away from the real subject in this incident, why, we care nothing about it. We are anxious to say to you that we believe, if the committee, will indulge in a few moments' reflection on this subject, it will be observed we are urging no other method but to give, in the interim during which this Commission was abolished, and the meeting of the Legislature, some regulation for the railroads in California. It was necessary somewhere to establish maximum rates; it was necessary to do something. Is there anybody in California who believes that the Commission ought to be abolished, who believes it is wrong in its present personnel and consequently wrong in its origin, and perhaps also that the Legislature can be better intrusted with this matter than this Commission, will he not only believe, but that there must be a demand for these things, and that that demand cannot be postponed for two years?

EARL: Well, Colonel, is it the idea that the Legislature could fix different rates than those prescribed in the so-called Distance Tariff? A. Yes, sir.

EARL: You mean less but not more? A. I think they could fix less; and I think by changing the classification, and making the classification flexible, I believe they could make higher rates.

EARL: It says in the amendment the Legislature has "no power to prescribe rates of charges for the transportation of passengers on any railroad or system of railroads whose gross annual earnings are more than $4,000 per mile to exceed 3 cents per mile; *and provid*nterest on that the Legislature shall have no power to prescribe the rates ot"e than for the transportation of freight on any railroad, or system of railman, whose gross annual earnings are more than $4,000 per mile, to exceed the rates specified by the California Distance Tariff, as in this section set forth." How can the Legislature under the language of this Act there, where it is expressly declared it shall have no power to prescribe in excess of this —— A. No, sir, not in excess of 3 cents per mile, nor the California Distance Tariff rates, I do not think so.

Q. So you put the power in the Legislature and make it different in other States? A. There are a number of States where the maximum rates, Mr. Chairman, are in the Constitution.

Q. No, sir; no, sir—— A. I think there are one or two.

Mr. Martin: You say there is one? Which one? A. I think there is; think there is one State in the Union has a constitutional provision in reference to passenger but not as to freight. But that, Mr. Chairman, that brings us back to this point that we desire to obtain a measure of relief that must be self-executed in the Constitution. If the Legislature, as it did very frequently in time gone by, refuse to act at all, after all this agitation, we would simply have got rid of the Railroad Commission.

Earl: But, you were saying the matter presented here by these railroads in opposition to this amendment was not germain to the main features; was not germain and pertinent in itself, and material to the general matters. If the maximum rate prescribed in this California Distance Tariff is burdensome on these roads, if it is wrong, and they shall come in and show the fact? A. That would make no difference, Mr. Chairman, as to the main idea, that the Railroad Commission be abolished and the Legislature should be vested with authority. If it should be in the judgment of the committee thought unwise for the Legislature to be clothed with so important a matter as the maximum rate, why that would not, of course, in any manner throw any light upon the necessity of abolishing the Commission.

Earl: What, but Colonel, if the maximum rates of freight, Colonel, were such as to be oppressively low on these carriers, are they not justified in coming in here and showing that fact, that this proposed schedule of tariff, this California Distance Tariff, is oppressive and burdensome in its nature, is not that showing highly pertinent and a good argument against the adoption? A. It is a good argument against the adoption of the incident to the constitutional amendment, but in no manner affects the main purposes of the constitutional amendment. I do not see if it was shown that it was any burden—that it is oppressive; but, as I said, the whole strength and force of this discussion so far has been on the mere incident, which I have endeavored to show to the committee came from the necessity first of abolishing the Commission, and the providing a method of legislative enactment, and for providing in the interim some redress. There are three ideas embodied in the constitutional amendment, each one separate and independent, and certainly the first two are more directly connected than the last.

Now, Mr. Chairman, it has been suggested by the Chairman, if the showing here was of the character spoken of, that it would be proper and pertinent. In the first place, there have been a number of objections made; some of them by roads which it was sought to pacify and quiet. Why, there are only three railroads in the State of California that are earning more than $4,000 a mile, as shown by the last annual report of the Railroad Commissioners of this State, also by Poor's Manual. It would seem as if those were the roads directly affected, and that all the other small corporations referred to were put forward here rather for the purpose of being the shoulder and bulwark of these three roads than from any interest they felt themselves.

Earl: You know this maximum of $4,000 was not in the amendment as it came from the printer originally? A. Speaking now for the bill as it is at present, that was not in it before; it was suggested—this wise course was taken, when the departure was made, in the interest of the small roads. I say the main object of the endeavor should not escape. Now, these small roads have a degree of immunity and consideration that they would not receive in other States, where they must all conform to the general provision. Still, I say the very concession made them has been used as an argument against this measure, as indicating want of thought. I simply desire to say that it was simply on the ground of policy, so the people of the State of California would understand what was the aim and endeavor of this measure.

The small roads of the State of California have awakened to a degree of hostility; they have done very little to injure the people of California. Why, gentlemen, the real object of California's interest on this subject arises from the extortions of the Southern Pacific system; there is no need of disguising it, and there would be no such agitation in this State were it not for the continuous and oppressive disregard for the most ordinary consideration for the community in which it is transacting its business. If it was not for the absolute defiance of all that is good in politics and all that is just in law by this corporation, this measure would not be occupying your time here, and the great State of California would not be wasting the substance and the energy of its legislators in endeavoring to settle these complicated and difficult questions. Therefore, I say when every measure of relief extended to the people is used as a reflection upon this measure as indicating a want of thought in its formation and in its preparation, it is foreign to the subject. This measure, gentlemen, as I have said, is looked upon as the necessary consequence of other measures that were formed in due propriety, and it makes no difference, gentlemen, as to its propriety, if made at the last moment or the first moment.

Now, as to the fact, Mr. Chairman, the earnings of these roads—I shall say nothing about the Southern Pacific system—I say, very frankly, a road that is capitalized at $88,000 per mile, and expects to pay interest upon it when it is actually in competition with systems that are capitalized at only $44,000, or where, for instance, the excess of funded debt amounts to something like $25,000 per mile——

Earl: You have heard the testimony, did you not, that the roads of the Southern Pacific system have paid no dividends in their history, excepting a slight dividend paid on the Central Pacific at one time. A. Yes, the Central pays dividends.

Q. That the bonded debt of the roads in California does not exceed about $30,000, or $31,000, or $32,000, whereas the Atchison road's bonded debt in Kansas is $34,000, and $37,000 or $38,000, some of them, the rates now being such as not to pay dividends. Colonel, is it a correct statement to say that the capitalization is $88,000 per mile, and that we are expected to allow them to charge rates that will pay interest on that capitalization when they show that they do not pay more than their operating expenses and fixed charges? A. Oh, well, Mr. Chairman, they do pay considerably more than their operating expenses and fixed charges, because they have a very handsome net surplus here. Why should the people be compelled to pay interest on a road with capitalization of $88,560 per mile, when it can be duplicated here, as Mr. Leeds says, for at least $40,000 per mile, and where it is in competition with others, constructed upon a much simpler and better basis?

EARL: Would you take it as a basis, then, in figuring on the cost to duplicate the road? A. I desire to say, Mr. Chairman, that the principle upon which railroads are conducted and which is shown by the testimony of the Cashier of the then New York Central and Hudson River Railroad, and the management of the Michigan Central Road, at the same time, taken before the United States Senate Committee, which was investigating the question in 1875 or 1876 of transportation to the seaboard; he testified that their capitalization had nothing to do with railroad rates and charges, that the true principle on which all railroads were conducted—and a moment's reflection will show—is whatever the traffic will bear. If an article cannot afford to pay what is asked, it will not be transported, no matter whether the road cost $10,000 or $1,000,000 per mile, and they pay no attention to that element themselves; I say it is a mere myth, a fiction, and something for the purpose of confusing and disguising the real question; it is not a proper element of charge. If it cost the Southern Pacific Railroad Company $120,000 per mile to construct it forty years ago, and a similar road could be built to parallel it for $20,000 per mile—I say, Mr. Chairman, the Central Pacific Railroad Company has no more right to come and ask that the charges shall be made on its line on the basis of $120,000 per mile than a grocer who bought provisions here and shipped them around by sea in 1849 and at that time retailed them at fabulous prices in those times, and who still has them in store, and says his customers must pay out so much for those things, with interest running up to this amount. Wouldn't you deem this an imposition upon the people, and one which they would not accept?

EARL: Colonel, you know the Interstate Commerce Commission has laid down, as an element or basis for fixing rates, the cost of the road—— A. I do not so understand it.

Q. Well, it is so. I have seen the reference recently myself. A. It says simply the value of the property; it does not say the capitalization.

Q. It says interest on the capital invested; that is the way it reads, Colonel. A. Well, gentlemen, the capital invested may be an element of that character in conjunction with other things. I question that that is the sole element of determination, Mr. Chairman. The true method of fixing railroad freights by themselves, is upon what the traffic will bear.

EARL: Well, Colonel, but when a State exercises the power of fixing rates, it is laid down by statute that the rate so fixed must be just and reasonable—just and reasonable, as determined by a rate fixed upon the cost of the plant itself—that is, the construction, the interest on the bonded debt, and a reasonable income—reasonable profit on the investment.

A. Mr. Chairman, the question is what would be the just capital; what would be the investment of capital here; what would be the method of determining the cost? I shall insist, I say frankly to the committee, I say there is no investment of capital in the line of the Central Pacific Railroad, or the Southern Pacific, other than that which is fictitious, and even if it were necessary to consider that cost, there is nothing to consider—nothing of that sort; they have simply gone to work and swelled the amount of it. Of course, it is not an element if this company has an exorbitant capital in comparison with similar roads. I want to say also that a reasonable rate as determined by the theory of railroad management internally, cannot be very different from a reasonable rate as determined by railroad management considered from the outside.

BURKE: Let me interrupt you, Colonel——

BARRY: I think, Mr. Chairman, the figures show conclusively—the figures we have shown here—of those roads constructed in the United States since the completion of this road, are meeting their just obligations, and are carrying freights at much lower rates than the Central Pacific. I say we are entitled to the benefit of similar considerations, and the mere fact, if it were true, that this road had paid so much more, should be of no consideration as against the other principle that a similar road could now be constructed for so much less, and we should have the benefit of the new investors rather than follow round the claims to a bad investment.

EARL: Would it not be a fair proposition to say to them, "Build a road, if it will cost less, rather than take other people's property, and, say, depreciate it one half?"

BARRY: I do not consider that we are depreciating their property, Mr. Chairman. We do not understand that, in comparing this system, with its extraordinary capitalization, with other systems, we are doing anything more than calling attention to a well-known fact in this State; a fact that was pointed out conclusively in the report of the first Transportation Commission ever organized here—that the system of expansion was indulged in. I was not going to speak about the Central Pacific, because I consider that matter will be finally disposed of elsewhere.

I propose to take up a road that has assumed a very extraordinary position here, which is fully understood by all of us. It occurred recently, and we know all about it. I propose to show that the San Francisco and North Pacific Railroad Company, in its claims that it is entitled to any consideration, is absolutely almost forgetting, I think, that it is only a few years ago that all these circumstances and facts happened that go to show that its position is absolutely untenable. Now, the Donahue and Cloverdale line, and the other lines owned by Peter Donahue, were in existence in 1878. They had a total mileage of one hundred and six miles, including the steamer route. Their earnings for that year—the consolidated road was opened July 1, 1876—were $467,501 52, and their operating expenses, $220,103 43, less than 48 per cent, as you will observe; and their net earnings were $247,398 07. Their capital stock at that time was $5,000,000, and it so appeared in their statement at that time. The paid up stock was $3,750,000; their floating debt, only $20,000 36.

On the other hand, they expended in construction $2,871,503; for equipment, $366,000; for other permanent investments, $433,307 44; for materials and fuel, $31,500; for various accounts, $25,888; and they had cash on hand of $41,247. So that, in order to get the matter up to a proper position, they had a profit and loss account for only a few years' management of that road, with no bonded indebtedness at that time, and a floating debt of only $20,000—they had $638,606 on account. That was due to the management of Peter Donahue. That was due to the fact that the road was conducted on principles that made it profitable to them.

In 1888, ten years afterwards, just about the time he died, and when his system had not been destroyed, its earnings were then $620,685; its operating expenses $399,146, and its net earnings, $221,539 53. At that time its profit and loss account had swelled up to $1,235,547; when, in 1889, Mervyn Donahue (I desire to say nothing except what is kind) got control of the road and wished to absolutely obtain it for his own property, so bought out his family, he purchased those various roads. The mileage was then 166 miles; and although, as you have seen, of this value of $5,482,070, there was only an original subscription of paid in stock of $3,750,000, with, perhaps, $200,000 in the Sonoma road. There was then $1,235,247 charged to profit and loss. He issued stocks to purchase those roads to the extent of $6,000,000, swelling it up about one third on the original investments, which represented the fruits of his father's accurate and correct management; but, not having the ready money, and the stocks not being available for sale, he issued bonds to the extent of $4,000,000, so that that road represented, with its bonded debt and stock, $10,000,000. Is it right that the State of California should be compelled to pay rates upon that sort of management?

EARL: When was the Ukiah branch built?

BARRY: The Ukiah branch was built in 1889. It was only extended from Cloverdale to Ukiah.

EARL: About thirty miles, is that?

BARRY: About twenty-eight miles; from twenty-eight to thirty miles. Well, gentlemen, they could have put silver ties all the way from Ukiah to Cloverdale for that $4,000,000. The road has been sold recently, and was not sold on any such basis, through the Probate Court of Marin County, that is, for $10,000,000. That was a fictitious value given to it for the purpose of floating bonds and of making rash and unwise extensions of the road that would not pay. I say this road that comes in here and says, although its earnings are $6,000 a mile notwithstanding all those things, and which I shall contrast, gentlemen, to show how they do things under similar circumstances in the East. I shall take a road that in some respects very much resembles that road; a small road in Ohio, one hundred and sixty four miles long—the Cleveland, Lorraine, and Wheeling Railroad Company, that runs from a point on the West Virginia side, up through northeastern Ohio up to the lake and to Lorraine, which is one hundred and sixty-four miles long. That road earned $1,291,471 83; or it earned as gross earnings $7,860 45 per mile; whereas, the North Pacific earned $5,131 88. But the operating expenses of this road in Ohio—these roads that are run so much more cheaply than the California roads—those operating expenses were $5,631 43, whereas the Donahue road is $3,191 70; so that, although the Donahue road had only gross earnings of $832,647 54, as compared with $1,291,471 for the other road—a difference of $400,000—the profits or net earnings of the Ohio road were about $366,225, as against $314,795, or the $400,000 had shrunk to $355,000.

But, gentlemen, the Ohio road does not pay $206,000 interest upon the funded debt, created in the manner as is the case in this other organization. Therefore, it put away for that year a surplus of $275,012 out of a net earning of $366,225, while this other road, out of a net earning of $314,000, had a surplus of $356,000. Why was the surplus so small here? Gentlemen, because of these $4,000,000 of bonds, created in this manner and the origin of which I have not put out as fully as I might, for the reasons known to every one here. There is no reason, I say, that indicates that these gentlemen should be entitled to so much consideration as has been given them when coming with claims for the consideration of this committee.

Further, Mr. Chairman, I say that, in so far as the roads earning from $1,200 to $2,800, I think that a complete answer to their position is, first of all, that the comparative statement with similar little roads shows that similar roads did prosper under this tariff in other places; and, secondly, that if we could not get redress in any other manner from the injustices the Southern Pacific system is inflicting upon us, it would be cheaper for the Legislature to buy every one of these roads, so they may be removed from the problem, and so that we may stand face to face with the real antagonist in this case, unconfused and unconfounded with other side issues.

Now, Mr. Chairman, the proposition has been made here, leaving out of consideration the attack on these small roads, that this small road, which is now called a less than $4,000 road, which, because it does not appear in the report, the Thirteenth Annual Report of the Railroad Commissioners, would have to stay there permanently, and that roads organized afterwards would not be affected at all.

I need not call your attention to the fact that that amendment introducing the Thirteenth Annual Report there as a basis, was not in the bill as presented; and while, at the suggestion of the author of the bill, or the introducer of it, it may be necessary, when criticism of that character is made, it can be determined that reports shall be made annually, as in Iowa, so that this thing will be very simple to overcome. That would, I think, where a provision is made that roads earning $4,000 a mile shall be included, that the expression of such a classification carries with it the ability on the part of the Legislature to prescribe such methods of determining whether such $4,000 road shall be included. I do not think there is anything in the point that, really, there was any necessity to inintroduce that provision in reference to the Thirteenth Annual Report. I think, whenever the road got $4,000 a mile, there would not be any difficulty on the part of the Legislature afterwards in applying the proper tariff. It is said also, Mr. Chairman, that some of the classifications in this tariff are different from the Kansas classifications. Of course, I need not say to you, Mr. Chairman, nor to the very learned array of gentlemen representing the railroads, that I don't claim to be an expert on tariff regulations. I don't claim to understand all about the varied minutiæ of charges—the varied minutiæ of charges of different commodities, of the 5,000 of them, that enter into a tariff; but I do know that a classification system that is used in some portions of California, that is used generally in the regions west of the Rocky Mountains, cannot be such a dreadful thing as has been pictured here. I will also say that the roads operating in the regions spoken of, managed with their operating expenses in every case higher in percentage than the California roads, to get along with these rates. It is quite possible that even with the difference in conditions—it is quite possible that these roads in California, benefited and privileged as they are, with lower operating expenses, should submit to the same tariff.

As far as this wine business in Napa is concerned, it is not necessary to say it is not any beneficent desire on the part of the railroad that fixes the rate, for, if Napa Creek did not exist, and if transportation by water did not afford the wine growers in that region some redress, I assure you they would soon find out that they were paying all the traffic would bear. I do not believe these little considerations should in any manner affect the general proposition.

It has also been suggested, Mr. Chairman, that the small road operated to-day by individuals, might fall into the possession of a large aggregation of roads. Well, if it did so, Mr. Chairman, it would do so with the full knowledge of this Constitution here, if it is adopted, and it would become part of that system, and it would be subject to the rules governing that system, and it would be subject to the rules governing that system and this classification, Mr. Chairman, is according to the character of the road, and not according to the ownership, because it does not depend on anything else except the fact that it don't make any difference who owns the roads, whether it is one corporation or otherwise; it is there. It in no manner conflicts with the United States Constitution or any other Constitution. It seems to me, Mr. Chairman, that, therefore, even if we consider that, from little difficulties, sometimes a road may not pay $4,000 this year, and will the next year, those matters are very simply rectified by themselves. In answer, Mr. Chairman, finally, to this suggestion in regard to tariffs of this character, diminishing the rates, as I believe Mr. Leeds suggested, probably from 20 per cent to 25 per cent, and especially in response to my friend, Mr. Collier—I simply read his statement in the paper—I would like to call his attention to Iowa since he left there. On page 9, of the most recent report of the Commissioners of Iowa, under the heading of "Commisioners' Rates," it says: "The Commissioners' rates have now been in force since February, 1889, and while they materially reduce published tariff rates in effect at that time, yet experience shows a steady increase in tonnage and revenue on the roads doing business in Iowa, under the operation of the said rates.

"The fiscal year 1891 shows a net increase in tonnage of 1,369,882 tons over 1890. The result of earnings is even more marked. From tabulated statements found below, it will be observed that, while for the years 1887, 1888, and 1889, there was a steady decrease in the revenues on Iowa business under the rates fixed by the railroads, yet, since the legal rates have been in force, there has been a marked improvement, and a steady increase in the revenues of nearly all the roads in the State, the aggregate earnings on Iowa business climbing from $37,-148,399 75 in 1889 to $43,102,399 35 in 1891."

Now, as you observe, Mr. Chairman, this is practically 16 per cent. "That the rates have benefited Iowa is evidenced by the increased business thereunder. The testimony of the railroad officials in the Courts was that they caused a reduction of about 26 per cent on local rates, which had been exorbitant. The effect has been to stimulate Iowa industries by giving them cheap fuel and low rates for getting their produce to market. It has caused the opening of new coal mines," and so on.

It also shows, Mr. Chairman, in response to the suggestion of the gentleman respecting railroad construction, it shows that between 1889 and the Commissioners' rates, when the Commissioners commenced to be active and establish their rates, that the increase was over 100 miles in a State that had been already crowded with railroads and almost the whole State gridironed, so much so that the Commissioners say, it is almost impossible—speaking of the subject, they say:

"The gain in mileage in 1891 for the fiscal year ending June 30th, is but little more than the loss by the Ottumwa and Kirkville and Clarinda and St. Louis. The gain for the calendar year is 36.35 miles. Iowa is at present so covered with railways that no spot can be found within our borders that is not within fifteen miles of a railroad. With this fact facing them, it requires great faith in the future of our State and people for capitalists to elbow their way into our midst and plant new enterprises in competition with and against the stern opposition of those already established, and yet railway construction still goes on in Iowa."

Now, gentlemen, if it be true, on what basis are we told in California here, that, if we attempt to regulate rates, that we will stop all enterprise, when in this State so covered with railways that there is not a single space of fifteen miles from a railroad, where competition is so intense that capitalists can hardly see an opportunity to reap a benefit on the investment, and that, between the establishment of these rates, between 1889 and 1890, there has been built over one hundred miles of road in that State?

Now, gentlemen, speaking further on this point, I want to call your attention also to a matter to which little attention is paid. As an illustration, I will read:

"The twenty-third General Assembly of Iowa enacted a law empowering and requiring the Commissioners to establish joint rates on continuous shipments of freight over two or more roads, where said roads failed to put in said rates required by law. The Board promulgated a schedule of rates, fixing the rate to be charged by each road for such service at 80 per cent of the Commissioners' rates."

The representatives of the Mason City, and Fort Dodge, and Crooked Creek road came before the Commissioners and appealed for higher rates, stating that they could not live under the new joint rates. The Board heard them patiently, and called their attention to the fact that the Dubuque and Sioux City road was hauling the bulk of the coal into northwestern Iowa from Illinois on a low interstate rate, and supplying a market that properly belonged to them, but from which they were practically shut out by the high rates over the two roads to market. That with an 80 per cent rate over their roads, they could successfully compete with the Illinois coal. An understanding was finally arrived at to give the joint rates a fair trial for say, sixty days, the Commissioners expressing a willingness to revise the rates if there was not shown a sufficient increase of business to make up for any deficiency caused by the use of those rates. Of course, naturally, the powerful big roads of that State refused to pay any attention, and I notice the matter is before the Supreme Court of the United States, the Iowa Courts having decided against them.

EARL: Colonel, what report is that?

BARRY: This report is for 1892, and is dated December 1, 1892—the roads have not been heard from since. They are quite satisfied. It has been going on now over a year, and are now quite satisfied with that general rate, though they assured the Commissioners that, if once established, it meant ruin.

Now, gentlemen, that is illustrative of the fact that you can't always believe these statements that are founded upon a narrow view of the possibilities of a great State. I do not think, Mr. Chairman, that any great injury can arise from establishing a tariff that has proven of advantage in other States of the Union—that is even working, also, in the State of California some benefit. I do not believe that these roads exactly appreciate the great State of California, never feel that her development and her increasing prosperity will not be of advantage to them. I cannot imagine that those principles which have been followed by other corporations in other States can possibly, even in the extraordinary conditions of California, work such irreparable harm and mischief. I cannot understand that, if they kindly consent to unite with others who have made their homes in California, to extend and promote the development of the State, to advance and develop her resources, to assist our neighbors in moving over our borders to take up homes, to enable those on the outside to look with longing eyes on the wealth and treasures of this great commonwealth, and who are unable to participate in the blessings which this railroad has shut them away from; that, if they would take by the hand the population that is now fast filling up the bleak and almost sterile plateaus of the Northwest, if they would extend a welcome to that population which, notwithstanding the rigors of the blizzards which sweep along the northern portion of the continent, have made their homes there rather than come to this genial land of California; possibly, gentlemen, you would find it to your advantage to accept a tariff which has been found of benefit to those less favored regions. If Kansas, with occasional utter destruction of her crops by grasshoppers and other devastating causes, is enabled, notwithstanding these great disasters—even if favored by her level surface—to enjoy a degree of railroad prosperity under this tariff which we offer you here, California, with no such blights upon her, with these immense fertile valleys that are now unoccupied because the population has been denied them; if you will assist this State, that has none of those destructive influences, as in the more crowded regions in the Northwest, now, why, gentlemen, you will reap your reward, not only in the advancement of the interests of California, but in a financial and substantial one—one that will not be disagreeable to you, and that may possibly add to the satisfaction you will feel in promoting the prosperity of California.

Mr. Chairman and gentlemen, I thank you for your courtesy.

CHAIRMAN EARL: Is there any one who desires to make any statement or showing to the committee. Mr. Martin, do you wish to make any further statement for the Southern Pacific Company?

MR. MARTIN: Are the proponents entirely through?

Statement of Senator Gesford.

Gesford: I suppose, we being the proponents of this bill, that we are also called upon to close; whatever the committee desires in the premises. I don't care to reopen the matter. Mr. Leeds, in his testimony and statement before the committee, stated those facts which are germain to the subject. All the roads of the State, I believe, have been heard, and I believe there was one came from out of the State, from Nevada, who also had his say. And now, Colonel Barry has closed the case for the proponents of the bill. I might add one or two thoughts to what he has suggested in respect to wine rates in my county—a bugaboo that has been raised in respect to wine rates in my own county. I have seen, in the 4x6 publication in my city, called the "Napa Register," a statement from some one signing himself "Index," who I presume to be some railroad attorney, because it is written in railroad language and bears the earmarks of the Southern Pacific Railroad Company; and when I read it I at the same time remembered that the editor of that paper rides on a free pass, furnished him by the Southern Pacific Company. I am called upon simply to refer to this wine rate proposition.

This article has also been copied in the railroad organ, known as the "Sacramento Union," from which I have received a few blasts of locomotive smoke since this matter came up. And I simply want to refer to those wine rates made by my friend, Mr. Martin, the other evening. I have taken particular pains to write down and ascertain about the rates on wine in Napa Valley; and permit me to say, gentlemen, that I believe that if we had competing lines of railroad in this State there would be very little necessity for legislation upon the subject of railroad freights and fares, because I believe that competition would regulate that matter. A misapprehension exists with reference to the purposes and object of this proposed constitutional amendment. This constitutional amendment has not for its primary purpose the fixing of passenger and freight rates; that is a secondary consideration. The main purpose has been very truly stated by Colonel Barry, that this proposed amendment is to abolish those provisions of the Constitution providing for a Railroad Commission, and, in the interim, providing for a schedule of freights and fares; that is, pending the meeting of the Legislature, to which body it is proposed to relegate the fixing of freights and fares. Now, it has been argued by some that this constitutional amendment would raise the wine rates, for instance, in Napa County. It does nothing of the kind; it provides for a maximum rate, beyond which, of course, the Legislature cannot go.

In the interim a classification is adopted, and a schedule of rates is adopted, so that we may have something to operate under until the Legislature shall have fixed a schedule of freights and fares. Now, in Napa County, this question of competition is illustrated very nicely by the rates the Southern Pacific people charge on wine, and I want to read to the committee a statement I have received from that point with reference to the charges on wine in my county. The distance from Rutherford, in the county of Napa, to San Francisco, by way of Suisun, is about seventy-five miles, and the rate per ton for wine is $1 95, or $19 50 on a car of ten tons. This rate per car of ten tons makes 26 cents per mile for carrying a car from Rutherford to San Francisco. From Rutherford to Napa City, a distance of fourteen miles, the rate per ton is $1 20, and the carload rate of ten tons, $12. or 85 cents per mile. From Napa to San Francisco the distance is sixty-one miles; the ton rate is $1 and the car rate $10, or 16⅔ cents per mile. Of course, Napa River is only navigable to Napa City. Now, gentlemen, I submit to you, if it pays to haul wine from Napa to San Francisco for 16⅔ cents a mile—if it pays the Southern Pacific Company to haul wine from Napa City to San Francisco for 16⅔ cents per mile—why not extend the rate all the way up the valley? If that was so, the Napa people, instead of paying the exorbitant rates that they do now from Rutherford to San Francisco, would pay $2 30 per car from Rutherford to Napa. From Rutherford to Napa they now pay $12 per car.

In other words, if they would fix the same rate from Napa to San Francisco as they now fix from Rutherford to Napa, we would now get our wine hauled for $2 30 per car, where we are now paying $12 per car. Now, it is not possible, gentlemen, I do not believe—it is not probable that the Southern Pacific Railroad Company, if this amendment shall be adopted, that they will raise the rates on wine from Rutherford, or that they will raise the rates on wine from St. Helena to Napa, or from Rutherford or St. Helena to San Francisco. They are charging now every cent the traffic will bear, and they are only kept in line by the little river that runs from San Francisco Bay up to Napa; in other words, they are brought into competition there with navigation, and by that means we have reasonable rates from Napa to San Francisco. Now, this idea of competition is very nicely illustrated, I say, in the wine rates of Napa County, and the Legislature, if called upon to fix the wine rates of Napa County, would undoubtedly fix it on the basis that is now charged from Napa to San Francisco. But Mr. Martin suggested the other night that there was nothing in this amendment which would permit the Legislature to provide a classification on wine in Napa County, and I see that, whoever has written this article, has said that there is nothing in the Western Classification providing for wine in wood and wine in glass or mixed cargo.

I don't so understand this constitutional amendment. I don't understand that it compels the Legislature to adopt the Western Classification, but, gentlemen, if there is any doubt in your minds as to that proposition, it is very easy to insert in the amendment that the Legislature may fix rates and fares, and in doing so, they may fix any classification that they see fit. They may provide a classification for ore. Mr. Martin suggested the other evening that there was nothing in the Western Classification relating to ore. I take it there is nothing in this constitutional amendment that will prohibit the Legislature from fixing the classification, or from providing the rates upon ore, or upon wine, or upon any other commodity. This classification is only to be used in the absence of the Western Classification—in the absence of any legislation, and we can well afford to wait a year and a half, providing we have some reasonable assurance that, when the next Legislature convenes, we shall have the rates remodeled and reconstructed in the interests of the people. Now, another suggestion made by Mr. Martin the other evening. I want to say, at the outset, gentlemen, I will say, that I am an attorney and don't desire to be anything else—I don't know anything about railroad rates and fares. I don't pretend to know. It isn't my trade, it isn't my business. I have introduced this bill, gentlemen, in good faith, at the suggestion of the Traffic Association, and if it has done nothing else, I believe it has educated the people of the State of California, and this committee, and this Legislature, and I know it has given me a few ideas about railroad freights and fares. I never did know much about railroads—never had a free pass, and don't think I ever saw one.

But if this constitutional amendment provides a wrong basis for determining what the gross earnings of any road are—that is, if the Thirteenth Annual Report is not a proper basis, then this constitutional amendment can go further, and provide that the railroads of this State shall report, say on or before the 15th day of January, 1894, to the Governor of this State, what their gross earnings were for the year 1892, and that shall be the basis for passenger and freight rates for the following year, the Thirteenth Annual Report being made to govern for the year 1892; this is a very easy thing to arrange. The objection that was made by Mr. Martin—I will not say it was Mr. Martin, but some one—as to what railroads were meant when we referred to railroads in this constitutional amendment. It is a very easy matter to incorporate that "Railroads doing business in the State as common carriers;" that will cover that proposition.

There was another objection made, that the latter portion of this amendment provides that all lines should be considered independently in fixing these rates.

I refer to additional rule 1:

"railroads shall be considered independently in computing distances; except, however, that a system of railroads, consisting of leased, operated, or independent roads controlled under a common management, although working under different charters, shall be considered and treated as one road, and the distance shall be computed over the shortest operated line composed of two or more of said roads."

I was surprised at the Southern Pacific people objecting to that rule, as it is really in their interest, because, if they lease several roads, the rates are fixed over the shortest operated line of leased roads, and hence they would get larger freight rates than if controlled independently, because five, ten, or fifteen miles on a short mileage are higher there than on longer miles of road; therefore, I can see nothing in that objection on the part of Mr. Martin; but this rule is really in the interest of the Southern Pacific Railroad, if it could be in the interest of anybody at all.

Now, as to these rates being reasonable—I don't care to discuss that; but it is in evidence here, and it seems to me it is a matter worthy of consideration, that if roads in other parts of this country, having a gross earnings of $4,000 per mile can make money, they ought to in the State of California. That looks like a common sense principle to me; and the idea that we are to fix our rates and have no redress because of our high capitalization, seems to me ridiculous. It makes no difference whether one road is capitalized for $100,000 a mile or $40,000 a mile.

EARL: You take a mountain road, for instance, which costs much more to construct.

GESFORD: Well, I would make it uniform—that is the idea; no matter what the road costs.

EARL: That's the point I was getting at. That is the point which is not to be escaped. You take a road built to-day, say in the mountains, which, unavoidably, by reason of tunneling, grading, etc., will cost a great deal more than one in the level Sacramento Valley, and yet this is uniform; and a rate reasonable for roads here in the valleys must be reasonable for one constructed at an enormous outlay—perhaps four or five times as much as the other.

GESFORD: Well, this maximum rate is provided only in the interim, that is all.

EARL: But, Senator, the Constitution says you cannot exceed that maximum.

GESFORD: If they earn $4,000 per mile.

EARL: They cannot exceed it.

GESFORD: But if they make money on $4,000 per mile in other parts of the country, it seems to me they ought to do so here—possibly more.

EARL: There they may have a level road, as level as a table, while here are the Sierra Nevadas. While for all railroads in operation, this amendment, Senator, says for five miles and under, first-class merchandise, per one hundred pounds, would be 3¾ cents.

GESFORD: Yes.

EARL: Yes, that is the maximum; whereas, in the mountains, with heavy grades, etc., that might be excessively low, in the valley it might be reasonable. There is the very difficulty in attempting to fix a uniform rate.

GESFORD: Of course, there are a great many mights in this case. You might suppose anything.

EARL: Yes, but Senator, is it not inevitable—how can you escape it?

GESFORD: Well, we do escape it. That $4,000 per mile is enough to make up for the additional cost of operating.

SEAWELL: Senator, allow me to interrupt you a minute. Do you mean to say—I think you did, if I understood you correctly—do you mean to incorporate, Senator, these pages, 3, 4, 5, 6, 7 in the Constitution?

GESFORD: Yes, those distance tariffs; if that is what you refer to.

SEAWELL: Yes, those are what I refer to.

GESFORD: Yes, that is what the Traffic Association proposes to incorporate in the Constitution. If I may be permitted to state what my opinion as a lawyer is, I would prefer first to wipe out this Railroad Commission. That is the great proposition in this case, and I take it, gentlemen, that this thing is one of the things, above all other things, that the railroad companies of this State do not want wiped out.

SEAWELL: Do you understand, Senator, that these pages, 3, 4, 5, 6, and 7——

GESFORD: That is, the distance tariff. Yes, these pages of figures go in.

SEAWELL: What, go into the Constitution?

GESFORD: Yes, they are to go into the Constitution, certainly, because you have got to have a distance tariff.

BARRY: You must have something in the interim to work under.

GESFORD: Yes, in the interim. What are you going to do from the time it goes into effect until the time the rates are fixed? What I would suggest as a lawyer would be this, and it only suggested itself to me to-day—and I may say this distance tariff has given me no little concern and trouble, because it was such an innovation and it would look so strange in the Constitution, which is already filled with statutes on every conceivable subject. But if this Railroad Commission could be wiped out, abolished, then this Legislature could enact a law providing for a Commission to fix a schedule of freights and fares. The

Railroad Commission to be subject to the Legislature, and the Legislature could wipe it out whenever it saw fit. Let the Governor of this State, immediately after abolishing this Commission, appoint three Railroad Commissioners to act temporarily, and at the next general election, let them fix a system of freights and fares; and provided that at the next general election, a Board of three Railroad Commissioners from the State at large, shall be elected by the people—that Railroad Commission to be subject to the Legislature, so that we would not have to get rid of it by compelling a two-thirds vote of each house and then by ratification over again by the people of the State. Some such system as that, I conceive, would be more lawyer-like than this; but this is a war measure.

BARRY: Yes, it is a war measure.

GESFORD: It is a war measure—like Lincoln, when he called for troops and it was said he hadn't authority, he replied, "But, gentlemen, this is a war measure."

BARRY: Certainly, it is a war measure.

SEAWELL: Oh, then, it is a war measure? I am in accord with you in much that you say, but here, these pages, 3, 4, 5, 6, 7, and 8, must be voted for by the people if you put them in the Constitution. I don't think they would ever be able to make them out—to understand them.

GESFORD: I don't think they would, either. That is what we are here for, Senator, to give them something, and then, when we get out of here—I don't think we are any the less through with it when we get out. I think it is our duty to explain these matters to the people of the State of California.

BURKE: Let me ask you, Senator, if it would be any worse to allow the interim to go quietly along until the next election than it is now.

GESFORD: I am glad you asked me that question, Senator. I believe there is enough decency left in the railroad companies of this State, and I refer particularly to the Southern Pacific Company, to compel them to maintain a fixed and reasonable rate of freights and fares until the Legislature shall have convened. It cannot be any worse than now, for these Railroad Commissioners have not given any relief. The railroad companies fix every tariff before it is published anyway. It could not be any worse even if embodied in the Constitution. If there is any reason why they should not be embodied in the Constitution—that distance tariff and that reference to the Western tariff—abolish the Railroad Commission and leave the people of the State without any Railroad Commission.

SEAWELL: Do you believe, as a matter of fact, and as an attorney—do you believe these pages, 3, 4, 5, 6, and 7, should go in the Constitution, that cannot be changed readily?

GESFORD: You are asking a very pointed question. Not—that is—we understand——

SEAWELL: No, I am simply asking a question. I have not attended all the meetings. But do you really think that these pages, 3, 4, 5, 6, 7, should go into the Constitution? Is that statesmanlike?

GESFORD: Well, I don't think that Thomas Jefferson, or Daniel Webster, or John C. Calhoun would have put it in the Constitution. No. But I do say, and I repeat it, I do not care how it may look in the Constitution, if it will give the people the relief asked for. I don't see that it will make the Constitution any worse off if it will only do the work.

SEAWELL: That's right, Senator.

BARRY: I say as a lawyer, it is fitting for such an extraordinary time, and under such extraordinary conditions as are existing to-day in California, and it will be a monument in history, that the people of California were only, in despair, forced to seek and obtain relief in this manner.

SEAWELL: Colonel, I think you made a very eloquent argument upon the present condition of matters affecting railroad legislation, and I think these things ought to be regulated by statutes. I think you are perfectly right in that and correct in your motives. But I think your argument is against putting that in the Constitution. I think the Railroad Commission has not done its duty—I agree with you upon that.

BARRY: Well, you want to have this in the interim.

EARL: But, Colonel, that interim—how long is that interim? That goes into the Constitution forever, until changed by constitutional amendment. How long is that interim?

BARRY: Well, Senator, it don't seem as long as fourteen years.

EARL: But this goes into the Constitution forever.

SEAWELL: Cannot it be based upon the Constitution in some other way so it can be applicable?

GESFORD: No, sir. Of course, if the Legislature, as it undoubtedly will, fixes a system of freights and fares at the next session of the Legislature; if it becomes incorporated, it will be so much dead timber in the belly of the Constitution, so to speak.

EARL: But this clause says: "The Legislature shall have no power to exceed these rates——"

GESFORD: I say, Mr. Chairman, that specific distance tariff would become inoperative, in all probability, because the Legislature would change it in many respects; it would be the maximum rate.

EARL: But how could they do it? They could not exceed them.

GESFORD: No; they could not exceed it, but they might make a less rate.

SEAWELL: In case it worked a hardship to the small roads, how could that be overcome? If you put it in the Constitution, you destroy the road.

BARRY: That assumes a state of facts that we do not see exists.

SEAWELL: You admit my premises. Am I not right?

BARRY: If it would destroy a road, your premises are correct.

SEAWELL: That would make the Constitution unyielding and unpliable upon the small roads.

BARRY: If it would destroy a road, your premises are correct. On the other hand, the Legislature meets every two years and could adjust it.

SEAWELL: Of course, in asking the question it didn't indicate anything at all. I am simply asking for information. I have not attended the meetings of the committee.

GESFORD: I want to state to the committee, when asked whether this matter should be embodied in the Constitution, I don't know—I understand—I want to say that, under the present condition of affairs in this State, why, that is the only time I would do it.

SEAWELL: In time of war, you say, and not peace, you mean.

GESFORD: Yes.

BARRY: Yes, in time of war—it is a war measure.

EARL: Take the Atchison road, against which there does not exist any prejudice. They have shown to the committee they are doing business to-day in this State at a loss, yet their annual income per mile exceeds this in gross; it is $6,000. They are doing business at an actual loss in this State. If that be true, would it be just or right to put a maximum in the Constitution, which is, I will say, according to their showing, a less sum per ton than they are now charging; would it be just and right to put it in the Constitution?

GESFORD: If they are doing business at a loss, Mr. Chairman, and honest in their endeavors to compete with the Southern Pacific Company, which I understand they are, it will be a very little while before they are doing business at a profit.

EARL: How can that be Senator? They are operating in the southern part of the State, over a large section of the country, in some places where there is not a house in miles, and they want to come north.

GESFORD: When they get ready to come, they are going to come.

EARL: It would cost a vast sum of money. And, if they are doing a losing business now down there, if this rate is less than they are now charging, they would be making still less instead of more money, as they have shown conclusively to the committee. They would not be likely, in view of that, to invest $20,000,000, which I suppose is not an excessive estimate of the expense of coming to San Francisco.

GESFORD: Well, Mr. President, in answer to that proposition, and it may be considered no answer at all, I had rather the Atchison, Topeka, and Santa Fe, or Southern Pacific, or any other railroad company, would operate at a loss than the producers should operate at a loss. That is the only answer I have to it.

EARL: Would it not discourage the entering of competing lines, which we all desire?

GESFORD: I don't think so. The Southern Pacific operated at a loss for awhile, until it got in and got a foothold and got the trade.

EARL: Have the committee any questions—anything to say?

BURKE: No questions.

EARL: Any questions, Senator?

SEAWELL: Nothing.

EARL: Any one that desires to make any statement to this committee? Is there any one present that wants to say anything to this committee?

[The Chairman here arose and looked around the room and again repeated his question aloud, but no one answering, he said:]

"If not, we will consider the matter of this amendment submitted."

[The committee were leaving the Senate chamber, when Mr. Barry addressed the Chairman, as follows:]

"Senator Earl, Mr. Sneath does not think he has been fairly treated, because the committee has not heard him."

EARL: I asked if any one was present who wished to address the committee, but no one answered.

MR. SNEATH: I sent my name up, and thought that sufficient.

EARL: That makes no difference. The gentleman should have come forward when he was asked for. If you want to make a statement now, I will call the committee together to hear what you say.

SNEATH: Well, I sent my name up; I came up from San Francisco and I think I should be heard.

EARL: But you did not answer that you wanted to be heard.

SNEATH: Well——

EARL: If you want to be heard, I will sit now and hear you.

SNEATH: I just want to make a statement of the facts.

[The Chairman then called the committee together for the purpose of hearing Mr. Sneath's statement.]

STATEMENT OF R. G. SNEATH.

CHAIRMAN EARL: Mr. Sneath, would you like to make a statement to the committee? Senators—Mr. Sneath came up here from San Francisco on this matter, and would like to be heard; he did not understand that it was taken under advisement.

MR. SNEATH: Mr. Chairman, and Gentlemen of the committee—I came here for the purpose of stating some facts that have come to my knowledge in relation to the matter of railroads in this State and elsewhere, and more particularly in reference to the Southern Pacific, for I have had more dealings with them. My own particular case: I handle considerable freight; and in relation to one portion of it—that is the ice business—I find by the figures which I have, and which were presented before the Railroad Commission, that they are charging me nine times as much per ton per mile as they do in the East for the same privilege. I furnished those facts before the Railroad Commission. The fact is not disputed; the facts are plain; and the rates in the East, and I only refer to combination rates, that is of the lines of railroads connecting with the lakes for the interior and to some two thousand different places. The Southern Pacific charge nine times the average charge there, which is about one half a cent per ton per mile, the charge here being 4½ cents per ton per mile in carload lots; that makes just nine times as much. In relation to the matter of grain: I also handle a great deal of grain.

BURKE: To what points do you ship? A. From San Francisco.

Q. Over what lines? Over what lines is it 4½ cents? A. I ship wherever I can from San Francisco.

Q. Do you ship very much, Mr. Sneath? A. I cannot ship very much.

EARL: I thought you stated that you shipped a large amount of ice, Mr. Sneath.

MR. SNEATH: I manufacture a large amount; I don't ship much, I ship around the bay of San Francisco near San Francisco; am not able to ship in the interior very much on account of high rates. I go round the bay of San Francisco and near San Francisco; we cannot compete with other parts simply because the rates are lower from other points, from the mountains.

In the matter of hay and grain, I receive most of my hay and grain from Hollister, that is about 100 miles from San Francisco. The rates from Hollister for instance on grain are $3 per ton; that is 3 cents per mile for 100 miles. Now the rates on grain from the Mississippi River East to Atlantic ports is about one half a cent per ton per mile; sometimes it is less, but that is considered really a good rate—one half a cent per ton per mile. From St. Louis to New Orleans, the rate is $2 20 per ton. You call that one thousand miles; that is .22 of a cent—less than a quarter of a cent per ton per mile. They find money in that business. If you will notice the financial reports in relation to the value of railroad stocks in the East, you will find the stocks depend very materially on the quantity of grain that is carried by the roads. If the grain crop is short in the West, and the freight is low, stocks go down.

It shows for itself, on the face of it, you know, that even one half a cent per ton per mile is considered good profit for railroads in the East. There is, of course, a large amount of freight taken for much less than that. They send it as low as 16 cents a hundred from Chicag › East—as low as 16 cents per hundred pounds; 22 cents a hundred, or about $4 40 per ton for about nine hundred miles. If 22 cents is considered a good high rate, which it is, and I have seen it quoted at 16 cents for this one thousand miles. To show that the railroad people really themselves think that that is a reasonable rate, they charge themselves that rate on all the freight they handle in their own accounts. They charge about one half a cent per ton per mile. On their Pacific division, for instance, the Southern Pacific road charges .53 of a cent, I believe, as shown in their last report; that is about one half a cent. Now, I tell you, they now charge me on grain from Hollister 3 cents per ton, or six times as much as they charge themselves. Then in the same way from San José, it is $1 75 per ton on grain to San Francisco—50 miles—or 3½ cents per ton per mile, or seven times as much as they charge themselves per mile. These are very high prices, but I have taken the rates for one hundred and twenty-one different places through California, and the average of those one hundred and twenty-one different places was 2.52 cents per ton per mile; well, that is just five times what is charged from the Mississippi River East—one half a cent a ton a mile. The question is, can our people stand any such charge as that; it seems strange to me.

MARTIN: Allow me to ask you a question. You made a complaint before the Board of Railroad Commissioners of this State concerning the charges on ice from San Francisco, some time ago? A. Yes, sir.

MARTIN: Did not the Railroad Commission reduce the rate at that time very materially? A. They reduced it from ten times as much—the original rates were ten times as much—to nine times as much. It does not affect the business, simply because it was reduced to points we did not reach.

MARTIN: Don't you know the rate from San Francisco to Fresno, a distance of two hundred and six miles, is less than two cents a ton a mile, now, to-day, and has been for some time? A. Well, that was a point we could not ship to if we wanted to; that is out of our district; we cannot reach that—that is going toward another company.

EARL: To what company? Los Angeles?

SNEATH: Well, the Truckee people get it for $3 a ton from the Truckee River, I believe, and we are charged $4 from San Francisco to Fresno, as a matter of course.

MARTIN: That is two cents a ton a mile, is it not?

SNEATH: Yes; but natural ice can be harvested and put up cheaper than manufactured ice can be made here. The Truckee company are charged about one cent, from .32 of a cent per ton per mile for ice from Truckee to San Francisco, while we are charged 4½ cents per ton per mile to go out of San Francisco.

MARTIN: Not to Fresno?

SNEATH: No, but you understand we do not ship to Fresno. We cannot reach there; that does not belong to us. That is the reason the railroad companies fix the rates, so we could not use them, so they could not do any good.

EARL: Mr. Sneath, how much more do you sell ice for here than they do in the East? Did you ever figure on that?

SNEATH: Well, the ice costs a great deal more here than in the East on account of the coal, and on account of other things. Coal is the principal thing in the manufacture of ice.

EARL: The coal also costs more to the railroads to move the ice, does it not? A. No, sir; it does not; the railroad company can get coal for $3 a ton, while it costs us here $6 and $7 a ton; there is the difference. The railroad company can get coal at Ogden, first-class coal for about $3 per ton.

Q. How about it here; how much do they pay for coal here? As to Ogden, you might say they could go back into Kansas and get it for 75 cents per ton? A. Well, their road reaches from here to Ogden.

Q. Well, it costs something to get that coal from Ogden here? A. Well, that furnishes that end of the road.

Q. How about this end of the road; is that the price of coal here; is it the same price here? A. Yes; but on the El Paso portion, on and along the line of that road, they probably get it fully as cheap as at Ogden; possibly cheaper; and it is likely the coal down there for $2 50 per ton, the——

Q. But the ice is cheaper there, is it not? A. No, sir; I think the ice is higher in that section.

Q. If it depends upon the price of coal, it would be? A. Well, they have smaller machines, and don't make it on so large a scale, that is the difference; they cannot afford to make it as cheap with a small machine as with a large machine; but this matter of fuel, I note the railroad company put in its coal for $5 85 this last year; as I told you, they can get all the coal they want at Ogden for about $3 per ton, and all they want south for less, and here in San Francisco for less than $5 85 per ton of 2,000 pounds. And wood they put in for $4 60 or $4 70 a cord. I know parties that have offered them wood at $1 a cord and they would not take it.

Q. Was that at Ogden, too? A. No, sir; not at Ogden. The wood, as I understand it, can be cut and be put alongside the track for about $1 25 a cord. And why should they enter it in their accounts as high as $4 and the odd cents a cord for wood?

MR. GAGE: You say one half a cent is the rate the company charge themselves. Add this to the cost of coal at Ogden, one half a cent per mile, what would it be worth in San Francisco? What is the distance? A. Well, I suppose it is 900 miles to San Francisco.

MR. CURTIS: At half a cent for nine hundred miles, that would be $4 50. Add $4 50 to $3; that is $7 50, isn't it?

MR. SNEATH: I imagine that class of coal is not used in San Francisco; it is probably used only as far as Sacramento. I understand the coal from the South is going up as far as Fresno, being supplied from Los Angeles. The Atlantic and Pacific road put down in their reports $1 50 per ton for coal, and wood at $1 per cord. I speak of these things to show that the operating expenses of the Southern Pacific Company are kept up by such charges. Notwithstanding these high charges, the Central Pacific, as I understand it from their report—their operating expenses last year were only 55 per cent out of the earnings. I do not know of another road in the United States where they are as low as on the Central Pacific. I can give you the net earnings. I can show you what those roads are capitalized at; what the earnings show. I can show you what the road is actually doing, and their purpose is—I had better speak of that, if you have the time.

SEAWELL: Do those figures agree with the statements of Colonel Barry; he gave us that.

EARL: If so, you had better file them with the clerk. A. I do not think Mr. Barry has said anything in relation to that.

MR. GAGE: I know something about the price of coal. For about fourteen years on the Central Pacific I bought every pound of it. I have paid for cargoes, and only regretted I could not get more of them, from $10 to $12 per ton by the cargo in San Francisco.

SNEATH: Oh, yes; coal has been very high; on three occasions, at least. You take the Southern Pacific of California, 1,403.5 miles ——

BURKE: Did you get those figures from Poor's Manual? A. No, sir; from the Southern Pacific's reports. I have it here. The Southern Pacific Railroad of California has a gross revenue of $6,611 54 per mile—that is what you call the Coast Road—with a net revenue of $2,744 09 that capitalizes at 15 per cent.

EARL: You differ $1,800 per mile there from Colonel Barry's figures. A. I took it from the Southern Pacific report; from their last report.

BARRY: Ours are from Poor's Manual, 1892.

SNEATH: $2,744 09, that is the net; that is the way it is given here.

BURKE: For the same mileage?

SNEATH: Capitalized at 5 per cent it would make a valuation for that road; it would make good security for $54,881 80; that shows what the net earnings would capitalize the road for at 5 per cent.

EARL: How much was that? A. That was $541,881 80. That is the load that road would carry in the shape of bonds. What you might call capitalizing it. This road, the Southern Pacific road of California, is nearly all level road, and I estimate that road could be built for $20,000 per mile. If that is the cost, the revenue they receive on that road would be equal to 14 per cent, a 14 per cent dividend on a valuation of $20,000 per mile. I made these figures to show what a promising property they have got, you know. The South Pacific Coast is one hundred and four miles in length. They report gross earnings, $10,651 66. Does that tally with your figures?

BURKE: Some figures.

EARL: Net earnings? A. The net earnings were $3,786 61.

BARRY: My net earnings were in bulk for the whole line of the road, Mr. Chairman. And Mr. Sneath's are for each individual road.

SNEATH: Yes, for each individual road. That road would capitalize for $75,732 20 from the net earnings of the road at $20,000 per mile, or about 19 per cent interest per annum on the net revenue that they report; that is a pretty good sized interest, 19 per cent. I think that South Pacific Coast road could certainly be built for $20,000 per mile. It is a narrow gauge road all the way.

Take the Northern Railway, 390.38 miles; its gross revenue was $7,465 65, and the net revenue $3,522 65, which would capitalize

$70,451 per mile. At a cost of $20,000 per mile—and that is a level road—it would pay about 20 per cent per annum dividends. That ought to be good property.

The Northern California Railway, 51.02 miles, has a gross revenue of $1,876 16, and a net revenue of $1,663 33—no, I mean $166 33—that would capitalize $3,266; that is all it will carry at 5 per cent; that pays seven eighths of one per cent per annum. That don't pay very well.

The Central Pacific Railroad Company, with a gross earnings of $12,224 76, and a net revenue of $5,452 80; that would capitalize at 5 per cent so as to carry $109,056 40 in bond, or at $20,000 per mile it would pay 27 per cent per annum profit. This Central Pacific road is 1,360 miles long; there is probably 50 to 100 miles of that that is mountainous, and some parts of it may cost over $20,000 per mile.

Burke: How long is that? A. That is the Central Pacific, 1,360.28 miles. That includes from Ogden clear through to San José, to Sacramento, and some other branches, all together 1,360.28 miles. They put them together in their reports as all belonging to the Central Pacific, although a portion of the property is non-aided, and I have put it in that shape simply because they have separated in this way.

Burke: I understand. A. Out of 1,360 miles, perhaps 100 miles is mountainous road, costing a great deal more than $20,000 per mile—probably $60,000 per mile, I imagine it can be built for; probably 100 miles of it for $40,000 per mile, and the balance for $20,000 per mile, but I will take $20,000 per mile, that would give interest at 27 per cent per annum, judging from net earnings.

Gage: Is that the Central Pacific? A. Yes, sir.

Gage: Do you remember what it is bonded for? A. No; I did not look at that, but it will capitalize with the net earnings as a basis. They made enough money to give them a clear 5 per cent; that would capitalize at $109,000 per mile, which is good interest.

Sneath: That is pretty good property, gentlemen.

Gage: I believe the Central Pacific bonds are all six per cent? A. Well, I assume—some of the bonds are five, they could be disposed of at five per cent without any trouble.

Martin: What you and Colonel Barry term the net profits is, as you understand, the amount left after deducting the operating expenses from the gross earnings—is it not? You don't mean that is the amount of money applicable to dividends? You mean after deducting the actual operating expenses from the gross earnings? A. I took it right from the books, the net earnings over and above operating expenses, as I understand it, fixed charges and taxes—or what are called fixed charges; interest that the investment is entitled to and taxes will go together, all the balance goes to operating acccount; that is the way I understand it.

Martin: You don't mean by the net earnings the amount applicable to dividends? A. Yes, sir; that is the dividends and taxes, and as you don't pay your taxes, they don't figure.

Earl: Would you not pay the fixed interest? A. As a general thing railroads—that is the majority—consider that as a part of the fixed charges. It goes with interest on the investment as the operating expense. That covers every charge of every kind and nature, against the railroad for operating—everything; and then the fixed charges are the taxes and the interest.

EARL: On bonded debt? A. Yes, sir.

BARRY: Bonded indebtedness—funded indebtedness.

SNEATH: Well, it may not be bonded; the interest on capital; what the capital gets, what is called fixed charges.

The Southern Pacific of Arizona—the first of those roads here—384.91 miles, has gross receipts of $3,788 61; the net earnings are $1,481 95; that would capitalize at 5 per cent, $296,338 80 per mile, at $20,000 per mile. I suppose to-day if it could be built for that, it would pay 7 per cent for those net earnings.

The Southern Pacific of New Mexico. The gross earnings are $3,486 20 per mile, the net earnings $2,647 67 per mile; that would capitalize at 5 per cent, $52,953 40 per mile, and pay 13 per cent on a cost of $20,000. I put in $20,000—I suppose somewhere between $15,000 and $20,000. The profits received there would be 13 per cent per annum on the business.

BURKE: What are the gross earnings? A. $3,486 20.

SNEATH: Now, take the California and Oregon road, 558.50 miles. It has a gross revenue of $3,821 57, and a net revenue of $680 55 per mile; that would capitalize at $13,611. Or it would pay 3½ per cent interest on $20,000 a mile; that would capitalize, at 5 per cent, at $13,611.

The Oregonian Railroad. That pays a loss of about 1 per cent on a valuation of $20,000.

The Portland and Willamette, 28.5 miles, has a gross income of $3,151 46, and a net income of $751 50; that would capitalize at about $15,000, or pay 3½ per cent on $20,000.

The California Pacific Railroad. That has an income of $13,242 79 on 115.44 miles of road. Its net earnings are $6,879 40. That would capitalize at about $131,000 per mile at 5 per cent. The net earnings of that road would pay a dividend on $131,000 per mile, in round numbers. Or at $20,000 per mile, this California Pacific Railroad, which is on a dead level almost (it runs from Sacramento to South Vallejo, and from there up to Calistoga, 115.44 miles); it is almost on a dead level—on $20,000 a mile, which would build that road, it pays 32½ per cent on a cost of $20,000 per mile.

EARL: You don't figure on any engine or cars?

A. Yes, sir; figure in this whole business. I calculate the $20,000 per mile would build the road and equip it; all of these figures are based on the building of the road and their equipment. These figures are all made in that way, account of construction and equipment. Now, there are a good many small roads running that are built for $8,000, $10,000, and $15,000 per mile, and we don't know as a matter of course whether it is absolutely correct, or water has got in it or not, but it is generally stated that you can build a road now with anything like decent economy at $15,000 per mile. I think the Great Northern was built for something like $24,000 a mile, and it is through a mountainous country. Isn't that true, Mr. Gray? Don't they report $24,000 a mile?

MR. GRAY: Yes, sir.

MR. SNEATH: That is a mountainous country. The idea of $24,000 a mile; it don't seem possible, hardly; but they are building roads very cheaply now. Now, the question is, Are the people to pay interest on what these roads cost twenty or thirty years ago? Everything else that has been built twenty or thirty years ago has been torn down or rebuilt. They have got their money out of it—they have made money out of it, and are putting up new edifices; they have thrown the old ones away. That is what I have been doing for the last twenty or twenty-five years, and I have certainly felt I have got my interest on investments made at that time; I believe we have a right to ask, as citizens of this State—we have a right to ask that they shall not charge us more than a fair rate of interest on the cash value of their property. I think we have a legal right to ask that. I certainly don't want them to lose anything on the property—I don't want them to work for me for nothing, still, at the same time, every one, of course, is trying to get in this world all they can, and the easiest way they can get it; and those that have to pay their money, they, of course, are holding back all they can. But there is, of course, a legal and moral position that we, of course, must occupy, and as far as a legal point is concerned, I suppose there is no doubt they can hold us to a reasonable compensation for the use of their capital. Now, the proposition is to fix what that capital ought to be—what this property should be worth, and then it is a very easy matter for the Legislature, or the gentlemen of the committee, or the Railroad Commission, or what not, that is authorized to fix the rates of fares, etc. Gentlemen, you can fix the rates and fares, provided you will allow them 6, or 7, or 8 per cent, if you please, interest on the capital invested on that property. Now, you can arrange your rates and fares to bring that. If they don't bring that, then you have no legal right to make it so low that they will not get their legal rate of interest. There is the point; there is the key to the whole thing. This property must pay a reasonable rate of interest on its value, on its cash value at the present time—not what it cost twenty-five years ago.

Mr. Gage: May I ask what you would do with the Central Pacific, that is bonded to the Government, say for $54,000 a mile—a Government contract. California is great for stickling to the Specific Contract Law, which was passed a few years ago. What would you do with that which was bonded to the General Government? A. I don't think the Government has the right to charge us any more than an individual charges us.

Mr. Gage: Then it is the fault of the Government. I want to find one thing that this railroad company is not chargeable for, that would be the fault of the Government? A. I don't think the Government has any more right than you have to charge us more than the service is worth. I believe the Government ought to be able to do it for what the service is worth, and she certainly ought to be able to make rates, and my idea is that they should be fixed without regard as to who owns the bonds; that there is railroad property worth so much, and they are entitled to 6 per cent interest on that property after paying all expenses. Now you fix your rates to bring that money, and be sure you do not get them too low, and see that they get their money. I am perfectly satisfied to see them all get full interest on their investment, but, good gracious, I don't want to see them pay 20 per cent to the Government or anybody else.

Mr. Gage: But those bonds are mortgaged to the Government at 6 per cent—those bonds are not due yet or payable. Would you be for breaking, forever violating it? We are great sticklers for specific contract laws here in California? A. Well, as I said before, I should fix the rates upon that road, or any other road, just the same as though there were no bonds on it at all. Of course I should be careful in estimating the value of that road—the bonds of that road—I should not get it any lower than they ought to get it. Because the road is bonded for twice what it is worth, that is no reason the people of this State should pay twice the charges that are necessary.

Mr. Earl: How would you enable the roads to pay their bonded indebtedness? A. Let them lose the bonds, the same as we all of us have to do when we make a bad trade or investment.

Mr. Earl: Suppose the road is foreclosed? A. It is simply a mistake in issuing so many bonds on that road. If that road is only worth so much money, let the Government foreclose it. And if the whole property is not worth $65,000 per mile, or any other sum the road may be owing, the road will sell for what it is worth, and whoever has the last mortgage on it is the one that makes the loss. Let the Government lose it. It shows they make bad mistakes all the time in matters of legislation, and there is no one to make it good to them. If we make a bad trade we have got to stand it, the same as all of us when we make a bad trade. But really, as far as the Central Pacific is concerned, I have shown you the receipts of that road—the net earnings of that road, to-day—is equal to $109,000 capitalization at 5 per cent. Now, that is good property. The indebtedness of that road is not any such sum as that. Now, suppose—I don't know exactly, I haven't figured what the bonded debt was—I suppose, with the interest and all, it may run up to $70,000 and $75,000 a mile.

Mr. Gage: You wouldn't pay that? A. Well, I don't know about that. That road, you see——

Mr. Gage: It is too much. You wouldn't pay that? A. I tell you the way this is divided up in your reports. This Central Pacific is not the same Central Pacific upon which the Government has issued her bonds; it is mixed up. In this case there is thirteen hundred and sixty miles. In the road that was subsidized there was seven hundred and thirty odd miles, and consequently this don't apply, only in a general way. I put it in here in this way because the railroad folks have seen fit to put it together in their report that way. But there is a large portion—there is five hundred or six hundred miles—that the Government has nothing to do with, and this five hundred or six hundred miles increases the value of that road very much; so really it is not fair. The Central Pacific does not earn of itself—that portion that has been subsidized—does not earn the relative proportion that appears in this report; it don't earn that. I didn't figure it out, and I couldn't do it, because the freight is not separated in the accounts. You don't know what business passes over the Central Pacific; that is, what proportionate amount that has been received per mile has really passed, has passed over the Central Pacific.

The books are not kept in that shape, because it is difficult, indeed, to do it, because they have to take into account freight at Sacramento, and as the road goes to San José by the Western Pacific—and, of course, the bulk of it going to San Francisco, back and forward—it is almost impossible to keep the books, to keep the accounts, so as to have the equivalent freight that passes over the subsidized road kept by itself. It is a very difficult matter to do it. I have an article here from the "Scientific American," taken from the "North American Car-Builder," I think it is called, in which they undertake to prove that in the winter season in the East, that a locomotive, if it will do a certain amount of work in the month of July, that she can only do half as much in January, and they give us an instance on a Western road where the coal account in the winter season amounts to some $24,000 or $25,000 more, I believe, than in the summer season, for the same amount of business—the same number of locomotives, I believe, exactly. It goes to show that our climate here is very favorable to this kind of business. The points in this article are these: You will all understand and appreciate the fact that, in the first place——

Mr. Burke: Have you the article? A. Yes, sir; I have the article.

Mr. Burke: Can't you file it with the clerk? A. It is a paper, you know. I can file it, and the committee could then examine it.

Mr. Burke: We are going to be pressed for time, and you can pass on to those other points—you have other points, have you not? A. I am very nearly through. This is the "Scientific American" Supplement. I can get another copy of it.

Mr. Burke: I will ask you to file it with the clerk, and then we can look it over.

Mr. Sneath: The feeding water is ice cold, and goes into the hot boilers—it requires more fuel in order to heat it up. Every moving part of the engine, where the lubricating oil is, is more or less stiff—it freezes up, it becomes tough, and it is almost impossible to move. All of those that are accustomed to seeing the old fashioned wagons which used tar on the wheels know the difficulty they had in the morning, of starting their wagons—it is all tight, you know; it would get tight as soon as it got cold, and on a frosty morning it was almost impossible to move the wagon.

This article states that lubricating material for car wheels, for instance, that it is necessary to use a heavy material, something that would not heat up and run off; if it was too light and oily, and the weather warm, it will all run away, and the axle will become hot. If it is too thick, and the weather gets very cold, it freezes up, and there is a friction there that requires an immense amount of force to move. And then again, the track being frozen, the car wheels slip. The track being rough, as a matter of course, it requires more force to move the train, and then again they can't take advantage of the down grades. When there is no snow or ice on the tracks, they can shut off steam and let their engines run along perhaps a quarter or half a mile until they come to their station. When there is ice and snow on the track, they have got to keep on steam until they get right to the station, using almost double the amount of steam all the way. That, together with a great many other items, makes——

Mr. Gage: Makes it very expensive.

Mr. Sneath: Yes, makes it very expensive in the winter season.

Mr. Gage: Certainly, and makes it very difficult to do business. I want to say a word, Mr. Sneath; we have felt that a great many years on the Central Pacific; more than one half of the Central Pacific labors under just exactly what disadvantages you are talking about, where the thermometer is frequently below forty degrees below zero. It runs for over four hundred and fifty-two miles of that road in the State of Nevada, where it labors under that disadvantage. About two thirds of the Central Pacific has been operated ever since it was built under just the contingency you are speaking of.

Mr. Sneath: This was all new to me until I saw this article in the

"Scientific American." I believe it is absolutely true for that reason. In California the bulk of the business is in the valley, where we have no snow and ice. It is only in the mountains. And on this line there is only a small percentage of the business.

MR. CURTIS: Allow me to ask a question; are there any grades on those roads with which comparisons are made?

MR. SNEATH: Oh, those Eastern roads have all sorts of grades, up and down, all over the country.

MR. CURTIS: Have they any very high mountains, such as in California?

MR. SNEATH: Well, yes; when it comes to the question of grades they are very expensive.

MR. CURTIS: Do you think it takes more or less coal to go up the mountain from Sacramento to the Summit, ascending an elevation of seven thousand feet in one hundred and five miles, than it does in the valley?

MR. SNEATH: Perhaps you have heard it stated that the cable cars of San Francisco are run more easily on the hills than they are in the valleys.

MR. CURTIS: There might be a reason for that—that these cars are counterbalanced.

MR. SNEATH: It is on the same principle. You go over a grade of seven thousand feet on one side for a hundred miles, and then down on the other side. Going up you require a great deal of steam, but going down you don't require any.

MR. CURTIS: There is another element—the use of air brakes on descending grades. There is a great deal of wear on descending grades.

MR. SNEATH: Well, there is wear there; I have not given any thought to that. I have read a good many authorities that you could operate a road in the mountains about as cheap as you can in the valleys—just like a cable on one side of the hill pulls a car up on the other side of the hill. I have read all the Interstate Commerce Commission reports, and there is some first-class information in them in reference to the cost of operation.

MR. CURTIS: Is it not a fact, Mr. Sneath, taking whatever may be said as true about the winter resistance of trains over East, the grades of California so offset that, as a matter of fact, the whole year round, to move a car one mile it takes more coal in California than in the East? A. I think it would take less, on account of the grades. The heavy work in California, as I understand it, is towards the sea; the grade, as I understand it, from Bakersfield, is not over four feet to the mile, and the average grade in the whole State is between one and four feet to the mile. I haven't had it surveyed, but that is about the average grade. I took the railroad time tables as a guide, you know.

MR. CURTIS: Have you made those computations, Mr. Sneath? A. Yes, sir; the grades of California I don't believe can be any more per mile than in the Eastern States—I honestly believe it. Now, these gentlemen of the Central Pacific, as well as the other railroads of California, have not got out of the way of buying two-bit cigars, and have an expensive way of doing things. They are running along and trying to be better than anybody else, and the result is there is no profit here at all, no progress to anybody, and we think that the railroads are getting more than their share by a good deal.

Mr. Gage: You didn't think so during the war, along about the time you were trading and getting your share of the business in San Francisco—you didn't think so then? You were getting your share then, too.

Mr. Sneath: Well, that was a war measure—at that time we had to put everything aside on that account. Whenever it comes to a crisis you have got to do the best you can and get there in some way or another.

Mr. Gage: Charge it to the Central Pacific; that is the modern way of doing things.

Mr. Sneath: I am in favor of the Central Pacific getting a good round interest on the investment; but do not believe it is entitled to twice as much as anybody else. I think the Southern Pacific Company should be satisfied with a reasonable rate of interest. There is another point, in relation to the matter of labor. I notice by the report of the Southern Pacific that they employ 324 men per 100 miles of road. The average employed by all the railroads of the United States is about 479 to the mile of road. The average employed by these railroads in the East that have about the same revenue as the Southern Pacific, they employ nearly twice as many employés as the Southern Pacific, nearly twice as many.

Mr. Lansing: Name one or two that have about the same earnings and employ twice as many employés.

Mr. Sneath: I think it is in the Interstate Commerce Commission reports. I think it is in the second or third group where they have a revenue of $15,000 per mile, and where they employ 1,176 men to the mile of road. I think it is the second or third group.

Mr. Lansing: They earn much more, very much more, don't they?

Mr. Sneath: They earn twice as much, and they employ nearly three or four times as many. You take the Michigan group, Michigan, Ohio, Indiana—I forget the number of that group, the fourth or fifth—and they employ about twice as many and have about the same revenue as the Southern Pacific revenue, about $8,000 a mile, and there are six or seven hundred men, five hundred and seventy-six I think it is. I have it in my pocket book, but it isn't——

Mr. Gage: Let me ask you a question. Is it not true that you belong to what is called the Traffic Association, and is it upon the figures that you are giving us here to-night you are going to build the next transcontinental road? It is based upon that kind of figuring, is it not? A. I don't know. Really, I don't know. I am not interested in the railroad. I havn't taken any stock in it, and I havn't made any figures on it, and I don't think the Traffic Association has made any figures on it. This railroad question is entirely outside of the Traffic Association, but I don't think the Traffic Association as a body are interested in it.

Mr. Burke: What has that got to do with the question? We would like to get through with the points. A. It is claimed by the Southern Pacific folks that they are paying a great deal higher wages than they pay East. They are paying $1 61 for nearly one third of all their people—$1 61 for twenty-five or twenty-six days' work. Now, it strikes me for a married man, boarding himself, it is not very good wages—it seems to me they get about as much as that in the East.

Mr. Curtis: Do they get as much as that in the East, as a matter of fact? A. As near as I can find out by inquiry in various quarters, wages here are not over 10 per cent higher at most. I was rather surprised they were only paying $1 61.

MR. BURKE: I understood they were paying a little over $2. A. I say that is for nearly one third of all their employés—that is the lowest class, you know. The engineers, they pay them $4 32 per day; that is very good I am paying that myself for engineers. I think from what I know of that business that that is not very far out of the way. I don't think they are paying for wages over 10 per cent more than the same help can be had for there; but I can't satisfy myself exactly how it is that they employ such a much smaller number, unless it is the fact that they make us shippers do all the loading and unloading. That is where the whole business comes in. The railroad folks do it on the other side, and, as I have said, I can't account for it in any other way. I don't see how they can handle that amount of material with so few men. But their argument in regard to the cost of fuel and labor is certainly not carried out by any figures I have seen yet.

There is nothing else, gentlemen, that I have to say.

MR. EARL: The matter stands submitted, then.

REPORT OF COMMITTEE.

SENATE CHAMBER, SACRAMENTO, February 23, 1893.

MR. PRESIDENT: Your Committee on Constitutional Amendments, to whom was referred Senate Constitutional Amendment No. 8, have had the same under extended consideration, and respectfully report as follows, to wit:

The proposed amendment strikes from the present Constitution those provisions establishing a Railroad Commission, and proposes as a substitute in lieu thereof the regulation of the railroad companies by the Legislature, as before the adoption of the new Constitution, save and except that a limitation is placed on the legislative control by a uniform maximum distance tariff for passenger and freight service, and also a freight classification known as the "Western Classification," comprising a quarto publication of some eighty pages. This uniform distance tariff and classification is made applicable to all the railroads in the State, some thirty in number, under independent ownership and control, regardless of the length of the road, or amount of business, or cost of construction or operation, or whether operated in mountains or valleys.

In the investigation of this amendment, your committee has had before it not only the advocates and proponents of the amendment, but also the representatives of a large number of the independent roads of the State, who were especially earnest in unanimous opposition to its adoption. Various amendments have been suggested by the proponents of the measure, which were designed to meet admitted objections to the original draft. The principal one of these amendments was designed so to classify the roads with reference to the amounts of their respective gross earnings, that nearly all of the so-called "little roads" should be exempted from the operation of the uniform maximum distance tariff in the measure, but otherwise leaving their rates subject to legislative control. Under the proposed amendment, if adopted, the duty of fixing passenger and freight rates upon all the roads of this State would be cast upon the Legislature, but as to roads whose gross annual earnings exceed four thousand dollars per mile, the legislative rates, no matter how small the net profits may be, could not exceed the constitutional schedule, but if the gross annual earnings per mile do not exceed four thousand dollars, the legislative rates, no matter how great the net profits may be, could be without maximum limit.

Your committee believes that it is not wise to confer upon the Legislature of this State the duty of fixing railroad rates. It would be a constant source of contention at every session, and with the constitutional limit of sixty days, the Legislature would have little time for the consideration of any other subject.

One of the main reasons for adopting the provision of the Constitution limiting the sessions of the Legislature to sixty days, was the removal from the Legislature of the vexed question of regulating the rates of transportation companies. The people have recently overwhelmingly voted down the proposed amendment to the Constitution extending the length of the session of the Legislature.

The adoption of the present Constitution was an expression of the majority of the people of this State, that the subject of fixing rates of freights and fares should be removed from the legislative halls, and this conclusion was based upon years of experience. The establishment of a permanent Railroad Commission was believed to be a remedy for many evils attending the election of members of the Legislature, and attending every session of the Legislature. If the remedy has not met the expectation, but has disappointed the hope of the people, it is not necessarily the fault of the constitutional provisions establishing the Commission, but rather of the people themselves in their selection of the members of the Commission. A large majority of the States of the Union have Railroad Commissions, and the tendency is so strongly in favor of their establishment that it is believed that in a short time no State will be without its Railroad Commission. The Congress of the United States, for the regulation of interstate commerce and interstate railroad rates, has established an Interstate Commerce Commission, to which the entire subject of interstate rates has been referred. There is no effort made nor intention expressed anywhere to abolish this Commission and to refer the matter to the necessary investigation and direct determination of the Congress. In fact, the Interstate Commerce Commission is growing in favor as the proper solution of a difficult problem. Able, and fair, and honorable men compose this Commission, and there is no reason why as able, and as fair, and as honorable men should not compose the Railroad Commission of the State of California.

The people of this State have the power to make their Railroad Commission all that could be desired if they will take the care necessary in the selection of the members of the Commission. It is easier for the people to select three fit men for the Commission than one hundred and twenty fit men for the Legislature. The evils of a former system of direct legislative regulations are not so far behind us as to be forgotten or to require enumeration, and in the opinion of your committee it would be going backward for California to return to the system that produced those evils. Your committee is also of the opinion that to adopt as a part of the Constitution of this State a maximum or other schedule of uniform distance rates for passenger and freight traffic, and an eighty-page book of commodity classification, would be not only a grotesque departure from the accepted American idea of what a State Constitution should be, but would place rigid fetters upon transportation companies in this State, which would bring disaster to some of the industries of California, which could only be remedied by a repeal of the proposed amendment.

Your committee does not believe that it is practical or right that a uniform maximum distance tariff should apply to all roads alike, or to all sections of the same road. All roads or all sections of the same road cannot be constructed or operated at a uniform cost. To do this would be to utterly disregard the cost to the carrier of its service—an important factor in making fair and equitable rates.

As it costs more to construct and operate a road over mountains, grades, and curves, and through tunnels and snowsheds, than over level plains, it does not appear to be unreasonable that greater rates should be charged where the cost to the carrier is great, and lesser rates where the cost to the carrier is small.

It is the opinion of your committee that if the amendment, as originally proposed, should pass, many of the short lines of railroads in California, which have been built by the communities through which they run and without help from others, would be destroyed in the hands of their present owners, and if their existence should continue they would pass into the ownership and control of other and larger roads, and would not confer the benefits their promoters rightfully expected. Above all, California needs additional railroad facilities. There are counties which for years have been working and hoping for railroad connections with the larger towns and cities of the State.

The proposed amendment, if adopted, would surely retard, if it did not permanently stop, railroad building, with all the advantages of competitive lines in California.

The principal objections to the proposed amendment have not been met by any changes suggested to your committee, and cannot be overcome by the earnest consideration and manifest good faith of its proponents and advocates.

Your committee therefore respectfully reports said amendment back to the Senate, with the recommendation that it be not adopted.

GUY C. EARL, Chairman.

We concur:

R. B. CARPENTER.
E. C. HART.

www.ingramcontent.com/pod-product-compliance
Lightning Source LLC
Chambersburg PA
CBHW032222230426
43666CB00033B/498
* 9 7 8 3 3 3 7 1 5 4 3 5 6 *